THE TAOIST CLASSICS

The Collected Translations of
Thomas Cleary

THE TAOIST CLASSICS

THE TAOIST CLASSICS

VOLUME FOUR

The Taoist I Ching
I Ching Mandalas

SHAMBHALA
Boston & London
2003

Sʜᴀᴍʙʜᴀʟᴀ Pᴜʙʟɪᴄᴀᴛɪᴏɴs, Iɴᴄ.
Horticultural Hall
300 Massachusetts Avenue
Boston, Massachusetts 02115
www.shambhala.com

Printed in the United States of America

⊛ This edition is printed on acid-free paper that meets
the American National Standards Institute z39.48 Standard.
♻ Shambhala Publications makes every effort to print on recycled paper.
For more information please visit www.shambhala.com.
Distributed in the United States by Random House, Inc.,
and in Canada by Random House of Canada Ltd

Lɪʙʀᴀʀʏ ᴏꜰ Cᴏɴɢʀᴇss Cᴀᴛᴀʟᴏɢɪɴɢ ɪɴ Pᴜʙʟɪᴄᴀᴛɪᴏɴ Dᴀᴛᴀ

The Taoist classics: the collected translations of Thomas Cleary.
p.   cm.
ɪsʙɴ 978-1-57062-485-8 (v.1).—ɪsʙɴ 978-1-57062-486-5 (v.2).—
ɪsʙɴ 978-1-57062-487-2 (v.3).—ɪsʙɴ 978-1-57062-488-9 (v.4).—
ɪsʙɴ 978-1-57062-905-1 (v.1 paperback).—ɪsʙɴ 978-1-57062-906-8
(v.2 paperback).—ɪsʙɴ 978-1-57062-907-5 (v.3 paperback).
—ɪsʙɴ 978-1-57062-908-2 (v.4 paperback).
1. Taoism.   I. Cleary, Thomas, 1949– .
BL1920.T33   1999   99-27951
299'.51482—dc21   CIP

CONTENTS

THE TAOIST I CHING

Foreword

This volume presents an explanation of the classic *I Ching* based on the teachings of the Complete Reality school of Taoism, in particular that stream of the Complete Reality school known as the Clear Serene branch.

Taoism, an ancient mystic teaching intimately associated with the development of proto-Chinese civilization, is believed to have inherited and transmitted the original body of knowledge from which derived the technological, medical, psychological, and mystical arts and sciences of Chinese culture.

In time there evolved numerous specializations within Taoism, and over the course of millennia there was a scattering of the original knowledge among dozens of schools with thousands of techniques. The Complete Reality school, which arose during the Sung Dynasty (tenth—thirteenth century c.e.), purported to restore the central teachings of Taoism relating to elevation of consciousness.

Complete Reality Taoism emphasized the harmonious development of the physical, social, and spiritual elements of human life. It was a rigorous school, known for its constructive involvement in the ordinary world as well as for its production of mystics of high attainment.

Both monastic and lay forms of Complete Reality Taoism arose during the Middle Ages, both playing an important role in Chinese society during times of severe crisis. Eventually the monastic forms absorbed alien elements, and naturally became subject to the political and economic pressures that affect any visible organization.

Complete Reality Taoism is alive in the present without religious associations. Its practitioners are largely members of ordinary society, from many walks of life, who combine their worldly duties with mystical practice. In addition, a number of its artifacts, such as the exercise system known as T'ai Chi Ch'uan and certain meditation techniques, have long since passed into the public domain as part of the general lore of body-mind health.

The present work was written in the year 1796 by a Taoist adept named Liu I-ming to show how the *I Ching*, that most ancient and revered classic, can be read as a guide to comprehensive self-realization while living an ordinary life in the world.

Liu I-ming was well versed in both Buddhism and Confucianism as well as Taoism. Eventually known as a Free Man with the epithet One

Who Has Realized the Fundamental, during the course of his life travels he consciously adopted various roles in the world, including those of a scholar, a merchant, a coolie, a recluse, a builder, and a teacher and writer.

In his works Liu employs the terminology of Buddhism, Confucianism, and Taoism, of psychology, sociology, and alchemy, of history, myth, and religion. He undertook to lift the veil of mystery from the esoteric language of Taoist alchemy and yoga, and this commentary on the *I Ching* is one of his major contributions to the elucidation of this ancient science.

Introduction

I Ching, the "Book of Change," is considered the oldest of the Chinese classics, and has throughout its history commanded unsurpassed prestige and popularity. Containing several layers of text and given numerous levels of interpretation, it has captured continuous attention for well over two thousand years. It has been considered a book of fundamental principles by philosophers, politicians, mystics, alchemists, yogins, diviners, sorcerers, and more recently, by scientists and mathematicians. It was given notice in the West nearly four hundred years ago when a Christian missionary in China wrote to the German philosopher-mathematician Gottfried Wilhelm Baron von Leibniz about the similarity between the system of binary arithmetic Leibniz was working on and the structure of the ancient Chinese classic.

Traditionally, the *I Ching* is attributed to four authors: Fu Hsi, a prehistoric chieftain of perhaps c. 3000 B.C.E.; King Wen, an eleventh-century B.C.E. leader; the Duke of Chou, son of King Wen; and Confucius, humanistic philosopher of the sixth to fifth centuries B.C. All of these names represent outstanding figures in the birth and development of Chinese civilization. Fu Hsi is a cultural prototype believed to have taught his people the arts of hunting, fishing, and animal husbandry; he is credited with the invention of the sixty-four signs on which the *I Ching* is based. King Wen and the Duke of Chou, founders of the great Chinese Chou Dynasty, are held up to history as models of enlightened rule; they are said to have collected or composed sayings attached to the sixty-four signs and to each of the six lines of which every sign is constructed. Confucius was an outstanding scholar and educator, known as an early transmitter of the Chinese classics and credited with commentaries that eventually became incorporated into the body of the *I Ching*. In recent times, however, these commentaries are commonly ascribed not to Confucius himself but to anonymous representatives of the school of thought he is said to have founded.

Precisely what lore, secret or open, was attached to the original signs of the *I Ching* in remote antiquity is a mystery and a matter of speculation. Fu Hsi lived before the development of writing as it is now known in China, and according to one belief he invented the *I Ching* signs as a system of notation, replacing a yet more ancient and cruder system. Ancient tradition also suggests connection with the understanding of general principles involved in the operation of the world. One of the commentaries later embedded in the *I Ching* has it that subsequent cultural innovators devised various implements and techniques based on the inspiration of the signs. Specialization of study and use of the signs in various contexts may have taken place already in the very distant past; in more historical times, in any case, it is a matter of verifiable record that the *I Ching* signs came to be used as a more or less esoteric notation system for describing elements, processes, and experiences in certain developmental practices involving special uses of body and mind.

Given the pregnancy of the signs as indicators of such fundamental and pervasive relationships as opposition and complementarity, plus the cryptic quality of the sayings attached to the signs and their component lines, it is no wonder that over the centuries a vast body of interpretive literature grew up around the *I Ching*. According to one estimate, commentaries on the *I Ching* number in the thousands; and new studies continue to appear, in both the East and the West. Furthermore, this continuing interest in the *I Ching* is enhanced by the fact that the book has never been universally regarded as the sole property of any particular religion, cult, or school of thought.

Considering overall the various trends of interpretation of the *I Ching* that developed in the course of history, it may be immediately noticed that there is no one method or approach that has gained universal recognition and acceptance. Even divination, thought by some scholars to be the original function of the *I Ching*, is deemphasized by certain influential thinkers as a degeneration or trivialization—and this in spite of the fact that one of the embedded commentaries recognizes divination as one of the uses of the *I Ching*. As early as the third century B.C., the noted author Hsun-tzu, one of the founders of Confucian pragmatism, wrote, "Those who make skillful use of the *I Ching* do not practice divination." Some fourteen centuries later, the Sung Dynasty scholar Kuo Ying went even further to suggest that Confucius himself wrote his commentaries as a corrective to the "degenerate" use of the *I Ching* for divination: "By the time of Confucius, the great Way was not being practiced any longer, and only divination was current in society; so it was that Confucius composed commentaries to elucidate the Way."

The "Way" Kuo Ying speaks of—called *Tao* in Chinese—is perhaps the most fundamental concept of Chinese thought, representing universal and specific order or principle. It was in this that Chinese thinkers sought ways of life, both individual and social, that would lead to realization of human nature and destiny. It was as an aid to this sort of study that many thinkers esteemed the *I Ching*. According to Ch'eng I, an eleventh-century A.D. scholar and teacher who became one of the major figures in the Sung Dynasty reformation of Confucianism,

> The word *I* of *I Ching* means change; that is, changing in
> accord with the time so as to follow the Tao. As a book,
> the *I Ching* is vast and comprehensive: by following the
> principles of essence and life, understanding the reasons of

the obscure and the obvious, and comprehending the conditions of things and beings, it shows the way to enlighten people and accomplish tasks.

In the context of Confucianism, the term "essence and life" refers to human nature and destiny; in the context of Taoism, which embraces Confucianism within a wider scope, the term means mind and body, or spirit and energy. In either case, for such thinkers the primary function of the *I Ching* was connected with sciences of human development. Ch'eng I goes on in the introduction to his own commentary to emphasize the importance of this aspect of the *I Ching*, and to note how it had become lost to the majority of scholars.

> The concern of the sages for people of later generations may be said to have been consummate indeed; though they lived long ago, the classics they left still exist. Nevertheless, as early Confucians lost the meaning and only handed on the words, later scholars memorized the words and forgot about experience. So on the whole there has been no real transmission since the time of the Ch'in Dynasty [third century B.C.]. Born over a thousand years later, I regretted that the *I Ching* had been lost in obscurity, and composed this commentary to get latter-day people to follow the stream and seek the source.

During the centuries when Ch'eng I says transmission of the meaning of the *I Ching* was lost, the prevailing trend of interpretation of this text had in fact been in terms of prognostication, according to a number of elaborate numerological schemes. After Ch'eng I, there was a resurgence of interest in the *I Ching* as a divination tool, due to the work of Chu Hsi, an industrious Confucian scholar of the twelfth century whose writings were made the standard basis of the Chinese civil service examination system by government fiat during the Yuan, Ming, and Ch'ing dynasties (thirteenth to twentieth centuries).

Divination was also used not simply as a mechanical prognostication device but as a framework for contemplative practices of self-analysis and analysis of situations; it also could be made to function as a medium of contact between people who might be in a position to give advice and people who might be in a position to accept advice, in a cultural context where divination was accepted as a valid practice. These functions, however, require active participation with concentrated attention, and the danger of trivialization was seen by some thinkers as a product of reliance on the *I Ching* as an oracle independent of the efforts of the individual. The nineteenth-century scholar Chu Shou expressed this sort of dereliction in these terms:

> If they only left things to divination, without daily contemplation of the *I Ching*, and just did what was supposed to be auspicious and avoided what was supposed to be inauspicious, how would people "strengthen themselves un-

ceasingly," how would they "support beings with richness
of character"? Students then would have no use for discerning what is regrettable and what is shameful, they
would not need to exercise conscience so as to become
impeccable—the lessons and admonitions of the sixty-four
signs [of the *I Ching*] would all be empty words.

In Taoist tradition as well, although divination is not unheard of, it is
explicitly abandoned by some leading thinkers. In the late eighteenth century, Liu I-ming, author of the commentary translated in this volume,
wrote that after he had met genuine teachers following years of fruitless
search, "all my doubts disappeared, so that for the first time I realized that
the Tao of spiritual alchemy is none other than the Tao of the *I Ching*, the
Tao of sages is none other than the Tao of immortals, and that the *I Ching* is
not a book of divination but rather is the study of investigation of principles, fulfillment of nature, and arrival at the meaning of life." It is also
worthy of note that here Liu identifies the inner component of Confucianism ("the Tao of sages") with that of Taoism ("the Tao of immortals");
hence the social development and spiritual development of humanity,
nominally associated respectively with Confucianism and Taoism, are regarded as interrelated.

What, then, is the "Tao of immortals," the Way of Taoism, and how
does the *I Ching* fit in? The ninth-century Taoist giant Lu Tung-pin, an
erstwhile Confucian scholar who later became a mystic of high rank in the
esoteric Taoist hierarchy, wrote of the *I Ching*, "Although the words are
very clear, yet they are also very vague. The shallow may take the *I Ching*
to be a book of divination, but the profound consider it the secret of the
celestial mechanism."

The "celestial mechanism," or "workings of Heaven," is a central concept in Taoist thought. Heaven commonly refers to the source of creation
and direction of the universe; the Way of Heaven, or Celestial Tao, is the
body of universal principle underlying all manifestations. Thus the Way of
Taoism was sometimes expressed in terms of following the Celestial Tao
and harmonizing with its design; this was supposed to be the way to experiential understanding of the essence and purpose of life. Lu elaborates
further on this in the preface to his own commentary on the *I Ching*.

Is there anything in the science of sages which is so lofty
and remote as to be inaccessible? It is only a matter of
understanding the Celestial Tao, the Way of Heaven, and
harmonizing with it in human life. For humans to harmonize with the celestial is only a matter of living in concert
with the time.

In the philosophy of the *I Ching* as it is applied to the practice of Taoism, time is characterized by change, and particular times are characterized by specific relations of opposing or complementary forces taking
place in the course of this flux. Linear time, such as is represented by the
succession of the four seasons, is used as a metaphor for the "time" of hu-

man development; but Taoist texts warn that this is only a metaphor, and that the "celestial time," the relation of the individual's present condition to higher potential, is not a linear progression on the same order as terrestrial time. For Taoists, to harmonize with the celestial in human life means to deal with each "time," each combination of relations and potentials, in such a way as to achieve an appropriate balance of relevant forces and their modes of manifestation. Lu goes on to describe something of this harmony and balance as envisioned by a Taoist:

> Before the appropriate time has arrived, there is preserva-
> tion of tranquility and silence; once the time has arrived,
> there is caution lest fullness overflow. Observing the wax-
> ing and waning of positive and negative forces to discern
> the subtle portents of good and ill outcomes, of regret and
> humiliation, the sages therefore appeared and disappeared
> deliberately, changing freely, advancing and withdrawing
> as appropriate. Looking at it in this way, is not living in
> concert with the time the science of sages?

Here, "the appropriate time" seems to suggest the time for doing or accomplishing whatever is to be done or accomplished, the time when something becomes possible or necessary due to a suitable configuration of conditions. Also suggested here is the appropriate timing of action and inaction—harmonization with the time by active or passive adaptation to the present situation in order to proceed along the optimum line of development. Lu states that the *I Ching* was composed as an aid to the discernment of the quality of each time and its implications for doing or nondoing.

> In the superficial studies of petty scholars, conformity with
> the celestial pattern and deviation from it are not clear:
> Time and again they appear in society when they should
> disappear, coming forward when they should withdraw;
> not knowing how to maintain tranquil silence, not know-
> ing how to watch out that fullness does not reach over-
> flowing, they sometimes go awry by impetuosity,
> sometimes go awry by conceit. Heedless of subtle indica-
> tions appearing, failing to carefully examine changes
> when they occur, day by day they proceed along the path
> to misfortune, regret, and humiliation, so that the path of
> humanity is lost. This is why the sages composed the *I
> Ching*, to explain the Celestial Tao in signs, making plain
> therein the changes of positive and negative, fullness and
> emptiness, advance and withdrawal, survival and destruc-
> tion. Those indications of what to aim for and what to
> avoid are excellent indeed.

From this point of view, the *I Ching* is seen as a tool assisting the observation and understanding of the anatomy of events. This observation and understanding is in turn supposed to form a basis for living in harmony with the pulse of existential time. According to the *Book of Balance and Harmony,* a famous compendium of Taoist lore compiled during the Yuan Dynasty (1279–1368 C.E.), in its role as such an aid to contemplation the *I Ching* is threefold:

> The *Changes* is threefold: There is the *Changes* of Heaven, the *Changes* of sages, and the *Changes* of mind. The *Changes* of Heaven consists of the principles of transformation. The *Changes* of sages consists of representations of transformation. The *Changes* of mind consists of the Tao of transformation.
>
> In contemplation of the *Changes* of sages, what is important is to understand the representations; when the representations are understood, one enters into the sagehood. In contemplation of the *Changes* of Heaven, what is important is to comprehend the principles; when the principles are comprehended, one knows Heaven. In contemplation of the *Changes* of mind, what is important is practice of the Tao; when the Tao is put into practice, it completes the mind.
>
> If one does not read the *Changes* of sages, one will not understand the *Changes* of Heaven; if one does not understand the *Changes* of Heaven, one will not know the *Changes* of mind; if one does not know the *Changes* of mind, one will not be sufficiently able to master change. So we know that the *Book of Changes* is a book on the mastery of change.

This passage places the *I Ching,* as a book, in the beginning of a three-part process. Through understanding the representations of transformation in the *I Ching,* it says one is to gain access to the principles of transformation, which are of "Heaven" in the sense of being inherent in the design of the universe. Understanding the universal principles of change then is to enable one to practice the Tao, which in this sense means the reflections of these principles in the possibilities of the mind, considered the inner ruler of the human being. By practice of the Tao the mind is completed by being transformed into an objective reflection of Heaven or universal law. This is translated into action on the analogy of Heaven ruling earth, the celestial design ordering terrestrial affairs, the mind ruling the body, reason guiding desire.

The *Book of Balance and Harmony* goes on to speak of the linkage of understanding and action, of the eternal and the temporal, by which it is held that humanity can find its place and function in the total scheme of things.

> Eternity is the substance of transformation, change is the function of transformation. That which never changes is the substance of transformation, that which changes along with time is the function of transformation. Freedom from

thought and freedom from contrivance are the substance
of transformation; sense and response are the function of
transformation. When you know the function you can
fathom the substance; when you comprehend the substance you can sharpen the function. Sages observe above
and examine below, search afar and grasp what is near,
thus apprehending that substance; superior people develop
their qualities, cultivate their work, perform their tasks,
and regulate their capacities, based on that function.

Here understanding manifest in action is described as direct perception of
eternal laws of change and their temporal concretizations without the interference of subjectivity, becoming effective as sensitive response without
arbitrary actions. Sense and response, flowing from an openness characterized as freedom from thought and contrivance, here represent practical
expressions of two complementary modes of existence, movement and
rest: In this practical sense, to "grasp what is near" is to become aware of
these modes in oneself, to "search afar" is to observe them in the world at
large; as the *Book of Balance and Harmony* explains,

The waning and waxing of energy and matter are the
movement and rest of things; rising and retiring by day
and night are the movement and rest of the body. Everything, including the advance and retreat of the person, the
arising and vanishing thoughts, the fortune and adversity
of the world, the success and failure of tasks, is a matter of
the alternating rise and fall of movement and rest.

If you observe their patterns of movement and rest,
you can see the myriad changes of myriad events and the
conditions of myriad beings. When you are mindful in
times of rest, you are observant in times of movement. If
you have self-mastery in times of rest, you can be decisive
in times of movement. If you have stability in times of rest,
actions will not lead to unfortunate results. Rest is the
foundation of movement, movement is the potential of
rest. When you do not lose the constant in movement and
rest, your path will be illumined.

That "rest is the foundation of movement, movement is the potential
of rest," is a perennial Taoist theme, according to which stillness and action, receptivity and creativity, are complementary and interdependent,
both necessary to the complete human being, just as they are essential aspects of the entire fabric of being as a whole.

According to one mode of Taoist practice, receptivity to reality, which
is what gives creativity its positive quality of sanity, is achieved through
emptying the mind of its conditioned subjectivity, stilling personal pre-
dispositions so that unbiased understanding and action may take place.
Thus the state often described by such terms as "freedom from thought
and contrivance," "rest," "emptiness and stillness," is regarded as a sort of

passageway to the awakening of the whole human potential. In everyday terms, this might be likened to refraining from speaking and remaining silent in order to listen; by understanding gained through accurate reception, it may then be possible to respond objectively rather than automatically.

The "rest" or stilling of automatic thought and behavior, intended to provide room for impartial awareness and deliberate action, is an aspect of Taoist practice that is highly emphasized. This emphasis is so pervasive in Taoist literature, in fact, that it has sometimes been assumed that quiet and inaction were a Taoist policy rather than a specific technique; the *Book of Balance and Harmony* is one of those texts that makes it quite explicit that this is not ideological but instrumental.

> To successfully comprehend and deal with changes, it is
> best to know the times; to know the times, it is best to
> understand principles; to understand principles, it is best
> to be open and tranquil. When one is open, the mind is
> clear; when one is tranquil, the mind is pure. When one is
> imbued with purity and clarity, the principles of Heaven
> become evident. The changes of Heaven can be seen by
> observation of transformation; the tide of the times in the
> world can be witnessed by observation of forms; the truth
> and falsehood of people can be discerned by observation of
> their concrete manifestations.

The embodiment of openness and tranquility, or emptiness and stillness, is sometimes likened to polishing a mirror so that it can reflect clearly. This is held to not only improve personal efficiency in the everyday world, but to also clear the way for enhanced consciousness and continued development. This is again emphasized in the *Book of Balance and Harmony.*

> Sages are sages simply because of the application of the
> principles of the *I Ching.* Application of the *I Ching* is ac-
> complished simply by openness and tranquility. When
> open, one takes in all; when tranquil, one perceives all.
> When open, one can accept things; when tranquil, one
> can respond to situations. If openness and tranquility
> are continued for a long time, one becomes spiritually
> illumined.

The principles of the *I Ching* are founded on the interaction of yin and yang, the two modes of the universe, of which all manner of rest and movement, receptivity and creativity, are viewed as reflections. Yin and yang are represented as Earth and Heaven, respectively, and the various proportions in which the corresponding energies or qualities combine are believed to produce the range of human types. One manner of formulation of the Taoist path, based on the *I Ching* and carrying various implications depending on the meanings assigned to Heaven and Earth, is as the balanced unification of Heaven and Earth within humanity. One dimension of this is presented in the *Book of Balance and Harmony* in the following terms:

> Openness is the form of Heaven, tranquility is the form
> of Earth. Unceasing self-strengthening is the openness of
> heaven, rich virtue supporting beings is the tranquility of
> Earth. Boundless spaciousness is the openness of Heaven,
> boundless breadth is the tranquility of Earth. The Tao
> of Heaven and Earth is openness and tranquility; when
> openness and tranquility are within oneself, this means
> Heaven and Earth are within oneself.

According to this presentation of Taoist teaching, openness and tranquility, freedom from preoccupation and agitation, are qualities that allow humanity to deal adaptively and effectively with change. While the *I Ching* is used to stimulate perception of the patterns of change and their implications, to begin to learn—from a book, a situation, a teacher—Taoism recommends a posture of calmness and openmindedness.

Thus concentration in stillness and active contemplation are regarded as complementary procedures. Certain exercises have traditionally been employed in Taoist practice to clarify, unify, and stabilize the mind so as to achieve the attunement represented as embodiment of Heaven and Earth. Since the teaching itself has been formulated because of existing conditions of mental fragmentation and instability, Taoism commonly bases restorative practices on composure. *Cloud Nest Annals*, a Taoist text purporting to record sayings of the immortal Lu Tung-pin, contains the following passage dealing with this sort of practice:

> To restore the mind to its unfragmented origin, sit quietly
> and meditate: First count the breaths, then tune the breath
> until it is imperceptible; be mindful of the body as like the
> undifferentiated absolute, and you won't hear anything.
> Those who can regain their composure after a mountain
> crumbles before them are second best; not even being
> startled is expertise.

The exercise of joining mind and breath appears in many Taoist manuals as an elementary practice used for clearing the mind; in Buddhism as well it is traditionally prescribed as an antidote to the tendency of the mind to become distracted and scattered. *Cloud Nest Annals* goes on to say:

> As long as there is any thought left unterminated, one's
> essence is not whole; as long as the breath is even slightly
> unsettled, one's life is not secure. It is necessary to reach
> the point where mind and breath rest on each other, and
> thoughts are forgotten even in the midst of thought.

This mind-breath practice is taken up in somewhat more detail in *Alchemy for Women*, a practical manual by a noted female adept of the late nineteenth century; here it is spoken of in connection with "self-refinement," a Taoist term referring to the elementary practice of overcoming the impulsive self to become, as it is said, "empty," and forget the self.

> In general, when first taking up this study, what is most
> essential, the first issue, is self-refinement alone. If you
> want to know how to refine the self, it is a matter of mind
> and breath resting on each other. This means that the mind
> rests on the breath, and the breath too rests on the mind.
> But what is most important therein is harmony. As it is
> said, harmony means following along; it is also said, "Each
> attains its harmony." This harmony is not apart from bal-
> ance, and balance is not apart from harmony.

This text also emphasizes that the state of so-called "emptiness" that this exercise can lead to is not an end but a means; refining away the self is supposed to have a definite climax, followed by an awakening of potential that had formerly been blocked by the condition of the self.

> In daily practice it is essential to embrace the breath with
> the mind, and embrace the mind with the breath. Having
> done this for a long time, once you reach even balance
> you naturally become greatly stabilized and concentrated,
> and plunge into a profound trance where there is no sky,
> no earth, and you forget things and forget about your
> own body. This stage is what is referred to by the saying,
> "Knowing the white, keep the black, and the illumination
> of the spirit will come of itself."

The expression "knowing the white, keep the black" comes from the Taoist classic *The Way and Its Power*, and is frequently used in the literature of Complete Reality Taoism to refer to meditation procedure. Here, the "white" is the everyday world and the rational faculty; the "black" is formless abstraction, the nondiscursive "dark side" of the mind. In Taoism, the rationality, however well and usefully it may operate in its own sphere and in its own terms, is only a part of the totality of the human being. It is not rejected—"know the white"—but neither is it allowed to preoccupy the whole attention—"keep the black." The climax of "keeping the black"—standing aside from the content of the everyday mind—is the openness of awareness that allows "the illumination of the spirit" to come "of itself."

The words "of itself" used here have an important meaning—that the "illumination of the spirit" is not something contrived. Generally speak-ing, Taoist practice enters nonstriving spontaneity by way of striving; even stillness, while recommended as a practice, is considered contrived as long as it involves effort. To the extent that it involves effort—which means that there is a split within the mind—even the practice of stillness is regarded as a barrier to realization. In another collection of sayings, *Directions for Blessings*, Lu Tung-pin warns against literal-minded fixation on stillness.

If you have your heart set on the universal Tao, you should certainly practice concentration in stillness. However, concentration in stillness is not a matter of intentionally keeping the mind on something while remaining quiet. If you intentionally seek stillness while quiet, once you move or act your mind will again be aroused. When stillness culminates, there is spontaneous movement—this is the force of potential. If you can seek stillness while active, your mind stays on truth, so you can act without error. Then there is no further concern when quiet.

Situations of ordinary commotion are even considered by some Taoists to be better for practice of inner tranquility than are situations of external quiet. In his *Annals of the Hall of Blissful Development,* the Yuan Dynasty adept Huang Yuan-ch'i says:

> People are happy when there is quiet and vexed when there is commotion. Don't they realize that since their energy has already been stirred by the clamor of people's voices and the involvements and disturbances of people and affairs, rather than use this power to be annoyed at the commotion, it is better to use this power to cultivate stability. An ancient said, "When people are in the midst of the disturbance, this is a good time to apply effort to keep independent." Stay comprehensively alert in the immediate present, and suddenly an awakening will open up an experience in the midst of it all that is millions of times better than that of quiet sitting. Whenever you encounter people making a commotion, whether it concerns you or not, use it to polish and strengthen yourself, like gold being refined over and over until it no longer changes color. If you gain power in this, it is much better than long drawn-out practice in quietude.

The importance of practice in the midst of activity as well as quietude was also emphasized by certain distinguished teachers of the Ch'an (Zen) school of Buddhism, with which Complete Reality Taoism had much in common. Other Taoist teachers also affirm that the real stillness and openness which they esteem as a method for breaking through the bounds of conditioned subjectivity and opening up objective awareness cannot necessarily be accomplished simply by arresting or inhibiting the movement of the mind, as this can leave intact the clutter of ingrained habits, only to reassert themselves again on arousal. The classical Ch'an master Pai-chang, speaking of the need for insight as well as calm, said, "That which is held by the power of concentration leaks out unawares, to arise in another context." Similarly, the Taoist *Record of the Religion of Pure Illumination* speaks of an active dimension of self-clarifying practice.

> Practitioners should spy out the mind's habits, biases, prejudices, fixations, obsessions, and indulgences, so that

eventually they can catch them and treat them accordingly. It will not do to be too easygoing; even slight faults should be eradicated, and even small virtues should be developed. In this way entanglements may be cut off, and one may become constantly aware of true eternity.

What is more, Taoists assert that even the practice of stillness itself may arouse subliminal vagaries of mind that can lead the practitioner astray if appropriate measures are not taken to deal with them. According to *Craggy Mountain Annals,*

> There are many kinds of visions practitioners may have in stillness. All of them are productions of the discriminating consciousness, which appear due to stillness in order to seduce the mind. As an ancient said, all appearances are illusions; even the desire to get rid of them means the discriminating consciousness is still there. It will then manifest hallucinations to disturb the mind. If the mind remains unmoved, and sees as if not seeing, being like open space, not dwelling on anything, these visions will naturally disappear.

In *Cloud Nest Annals,* Lu Tung-pin also gives a description of several stages experienced in the exercise of quiescence.

> As for the states experienced through the exercise of quiescence, first there is dullness, oblivion, and random thought; then there is lightness and freshness; later it is like being inside curtains of gold mesh; finally it is like returning to life from death, a clear breeze under the bright moon coming and going, the scenery unobstructed.

According to these descriptions of basic Taoist practice, with the attainment of mental transparency one comes in direct contact with reality, "the scenery unobstructed." In the terminology of the *I Ching,* this is one meaning of "the culmination of yin, followed by the arising of yang." Such descriptions of practice and experience are, of course, highly generalized and simplified; the complexity of the matter when individual situations and experiential "times" are taken into account, as Taoist teaching says they must be, is the reason for detailed maps like the *I Ching* and the institution of teachership through which individualized instruction takes place.

The aforementioned expression "the culmination of yin, followed by the arising of yang," is used in Taoism to refer to the initial awakening of the original primordial potential of consciousness, however it may be achieved. "Culmination of yin" has a dual meaning, illustrated in the foregoing quotations from Taoist literature: on the one hand, "yin" means conditioning, mundanity; on the other it means quiescence, emptiness. Therefore the culmination of yin means the overcoming of conditioned mundanity by detachment, to allow the "arising of yang," energy and awareness uninhibited by conditioning. Huang Yuan-ch'i explains in his *Annals of the Hall of Blissful Development* how this mechanism operates not only in formal quiet meditation but also in the course of activities in the world.

> The adepts have spoken in various ways about the way yang arises, but in each case it comes from absence of cogitation and rumination.
>
> For example, it is like when a chaste woman who is intensely righteous and strong chooses to lose her life honorably rather than submit to improper advances.
>
> It is also like when a powerful knight pursues justice alone in spite of adversity, willing to give up his life and die for the cause.
>
> These are examples of genuine arising of yang; otherwise, how could people be so indomitable?
>
> Considering the matter along these lines, in the course of ordinary activities in daily life—fulfilling social duties, taking care of the orphaned, the widowed, the poor—all good deeds and just actions, when done appropriately, are not without a feeling of joy; these are all times when yang arises.
>
> The only thing to watch out for is when you suddenly become aware of it and are immediately blocked up by the mood, or become excited and ebullient, not knowing how to collect yourself and look upon being as nothing, so that the yang is dragged in by mental habits and becomes scattered.

To collect oneself and be careful that the surge of conscious energy does not overflow into excitement, impetuosity, or conceit, is referred to as nurturing yang by yin, where yin means calm and detachment. This is to protect the "celestial" yang that has arisen from forgetting the self against damage by residual mundane propensities. This "storage" and "maturation" process then makes it possible to integrate the illumination with the world, so that yin and yang, Heaven and Earth, are united harmoniously. Huang goes on to note other ways in which yang can arise, and tells what to do when it does.

> It may also happen that while you are reading books or reciting poetry, personal desires suddenly vanish and a unified awareness is alone present—this too is one aspect of the arising of yang.
>
> Also, sometimes when friends gather and talk, they reach a communion of the inner mind, and suddenly yang energy soars up and the true potential bursts forth—this is also one way in which yang arises.
>
> Furthermore, even when playing music, playing games, writing, drawing, fishing, cutting wood, plowing

fields, reading books, if you can harmonize spontaneously
based on the natural essence, without seeking or desiring
anything, there will be a serenity and contentment, clearing the mind so that you forget about feelings—this is in
each case a form of arising of yang.

What is essential is to become immediately aware of
the movement of yang energy and to gather it in as soon as
you become aware of it, so that the spirit is not attracted by
externals.

The terminology of yin and yang is a primary element of the foundation of the language of the *I Ching* and Taoist spiritual alchemy. In the *I
Ching* proper, and in alchemical texts, the words yin and yang are not used
directly but are indicated symbolically by other terms. Taoist commentaries use the words yin and yang on the primary level of interpretation,
but these in turn are given a variety of meanings, such as the mundane
and the celestial, the acquired and the primal, the human mind and the
mind of Tao. These pairs are used to refer to a dichotomy in the human
being that can be bridged by practice. Chang San-feng, the great Taoist adept credited with the invention of T'ai Chi Ch'uan, the well-known exercise system based on the harmonization of yin and yang, emphasizes that
the duality between the conditioned conscious mind and the primal unconscious mind is unfixed, and that the "true" mind can be brought to
the fore.

The mind of man is twofold; in one way it is true, in one
way it is false. So to look for the true mind, don't give rise
to arbitrary thoughts—then there is the true mind.

The true mind is broad and luminous; where the true
mind abides is peace and freedom. When you manage
your affairs with the true mind, everything is integrated;
when you seek the Tao with the true mind, myriad differences are of the same root.

But if people want to use the true mind to deal with
affairs, they need to foster it so that it is strong, and to
keep it calm and uncluttered. Then it can work without
weariness, and be responsive even while tranquil.

The teaching of spiritual alchemy says that when the
mind runs off one should gather it in; having gathered it
in, then let go of it. After action, seek rest; finding rest,
one develops enlightenment. Who says one cannot find
tranquility in the midst of clamor and activity?

In common Taoist terminology, used frequently in the present commentary on the *I Ching*, what Chang San-feng here refers to as the true
mind is called the "mind of Tao." The mind of Tao is in this text associated
with "celestial" yang, in contrast to the "human mind," or human mentality, associated with "mundane" yin. The human mentality is regarded
as lacking stability and being subject to acquired conditioning; the mind of

Tao, on the other hand, is referred to as primordial real consciousness. The human mind is under the influence of thought and emotion related to objects; the mind of Tao is attuned to true reality. Since the mind of Tao is obscured by the human mentality, Taoists practice what they call "repelling yin" and "fostering yang," overcoming the human mind and promoting the mind of Tao. The *Book of Balance and Harmony* says:

> Of old it has been said, always extinguish the stirring
> mind, do not extinguish the shining mind. When the mind
> is unstirring it is shining, when the mind does not stop it
> is astray.
> The shining mind is the mind of Tao, the straying
> mind is the human mind. The mind of Tao is subtle and
> hard to see; the human mind is unstable and uneasy.
> Although there is the mind of Tao in the human
> mind, and there is the human mind in the mind of Tao, it
> is just a matter of persistence in the midst of action and
> stillness: If the shining mind is always maintained, the
> straying mind does not stir; the unstable is stabilized, and
> the subtle becomes apparent.

Since the human mind and the mind of Tao are not really disparate entities, but rather different levels of the total potential of consciousness, the expression *extinguish* is an exaggeration, used for didactic purposes. In his *Direct Explanation of Understanding Reality*, Liu I-ming explains what this means.

> If the human mind lacks the mind of Tao, it can defeat the
> Tao by using consciousness to product illusion. If you
> govern it by the mind of Tao, the conscious light is clear
> and can thereby help the Tao. So the mind of Tao is not to
> be diminished, and yet the human mind is not to be anni-
> hilated—just do not let the human mind misuse conscious-
> ness. When the ancients told people to kill the human
> mind, what they meant was to kill the false consciousness
> of the human mind, not to kill the true consciousness of
> the human mind.

Here the desirable relation of the human mind and the mind of Tao, the earthly and the celestial, yin and yang, is viewed as one of subordination of the former to the latter. The tendency to think of the conditioned consciousness as the real mind is referred to in Taoism as mistaking the servant for the master. Some habits, some conditioning, are held to be useful and necessary for everyday life; it is when habits take complete charge of the individual, depriving the person of autonomy and choice, that they are regarded by Taoists as undesirable, imprisoning the greater potential.

The countermeasure is also expressed in terms of another expression from the classic *The Way and Its Power:* "Empty the mind, fill the belly." Commonly understood as a statement of a political policy, this phrase is used in Complete Reality Taoism to allude to spiritual practice; it is to be met with repeatedly in the present *I Ching* commentary to indicate proper harmonization of yin and yang. In *Direct Explanation of Understanding Reality* Liu I-ming explains it in terms of the mind of Tao and the human mind.

> Spiritual alchemy involves two tasks: to empty the mind and fill the belly. Emptying the mind means to empty the human mind; this is the task of cultivating essence. To fill the belly means to fulfill the mind of Tao; this is the task of cultivating life.

An analogous meaning of "emptying the mind and filling the belly" is to put aside preconceptions and become open to guidance. This again may be represented as yin obeying yang, and refers both to the relationship between learner and teacher, and to the relationship between the learner and reality.

Yet another meaning of "emptying the mind and filling the belly" is to refrain from arbitrary thought and action in order to accumulate energy simply by not dissipating energy. This was also practiced in Ch'an Buddhism, where it was referred to as gaining power by saving power. In Taoism, not only was this regarded as an important practice for physical health, it was also considered essential to accumulate energy in order to make positive use of the impact of the teaching. So again yin and yang, emptiness and fullness, receptivity and creativity, are presented as complementary aspects of Taoist practice.

In the present commentary on the *I Ching*, there is one more association of yin and yang that is repeatedly used and deserves close attention: Yin stands for flexibility, yang stands for firmness. These, and analogous qualities such as gentility and strength, are held to be complementary and both necessary for a balanced human being. In his *Record of Understandings of Tao*, Liu I-ming explains the mutual necessity of firmness and flexibility in these terms.

> When people practice the Tao to develop character, dealing with events and people, if they are always hard they will be impetuous and aggressive, excessively impatient, so that their actions lack perseverance and their keenness will become blunted. On the other hand, if people are always soft, they will vacillate, fearful and ineffective, being too weak to succeed in their tasks. That softness is useless.
>
> If people can be firm in decision and flexible in gradual application, neither hurrying nor lagging, neither aggressive nor weak, then hardness and softness balance each other; achieving balance and harmony, they will benefit wherever they go. If they study the Tao in this way, eventually they will surely understand the Tao; if they practice the Tao in this way, eventually they will surely realize the Tao.

One of the meanings of firmness and flexibility commonly used in Taoist texts is the firmness of the real knowledge of the mind of Tao and the flexibility of the conscious knowledge of the human mind. The reason for the use of simple code words such as yin and yang, firmness and flexibility, however, is the very pervasiveness of these principles or qualities, which makes it impossible to conveniently enumerate their manifold reflections. Nevertheless, so important are the qualities of firmness and flexibility in Taoist practice that Liu I-ming attempts a general explanation in his *Eight Elements of the Spiritual House.*

> Firmness is strength, sturdiness, decisiveness, power, energy, keenness. Those who use firmness well cannot be corrupted by wealth and rank, cannot be moved by poverty and lowliness, cannot be suppressed by aggression. The ancient philosopher Mencius was like this: Skillfully nurturing abundant energy, by the age of forty his mind was imperturbable. People with unflinching loyalty, who do not buckle in the face of difficulty, are able to be this way due to the energy of firmness. Though death is equal to life in their eyes, it is because what can die is the ephemeral body—sanity does not die.

After noting characteristics that may be described as the quality of firmness in people, Liu goes on to touch upon ways of developing firmness.

> If practitioners of the Tao can look upon the life of essence as the one important thing, see through material objects and cut through attachments at one stroke, then all things will be empty to them and they will be free. Not obsessed with food and clothing, not in a turmoil over worldly affairs, letting all vexations and problems run their natural course, leaving life and death up to fate, acting with nobility, maintaining an iron will, with this firmness one can finish what one begins; growing stronger with time, one has direction and purpose.

Liu follows up these practical suggestions with a description of what happens to people when they lack firmness.

> Generally speaking, when firmness is not established, one is weak and hesitant and makes no progress; energy scatters, the senses are restless, morbidity runs riot, concentration is unsteady, and doubts go unresolved. Also one fears hunger and cold, and fears that if one practices the Tao unsuccessfully one will have wasted one's life. One also fears obstacles, suffering, and difficulty, and fears that one's spiritual affinity will not develop and practice of the Tao will stagnate. Indeed, if people lack perseverance and constancy, they cannot even become sorcerors or curers, let alone accomplish the great matter of essence and life.

> Therefore if practitioners of Tao want to build the spiritual
> house, let them first establish firmness.

Finally, Liu concludes with descriptions of firmness in terms of both practice and realization, being and action.

> To establish firmness, first get rid of covetousness. Once
> covetousness is gone, firmness is established, and the pil-
> lars of the spiritual house are firmly stationed. Once the
> basis is firm and stable, there is hope for the great Tao.
>   What is firmness? Cutting through sentiment and
> clearing the senses is firmness. Not fearing obstacles and
> difficulties is firmness. Putting the spirit in order and going
> boldly forward is firmness. Single-mindedness and sus-
> tained consistency is firmness. Being harmonious but not
> imitative, gregarious yet nonpartisan, is firmness. Not
> doing anything bad, doing whatever is good, is firmness.
> Being inwardly and outwardly unified, working without
> ceasing, is firmness.

Thus Liu considers firmness the foundation of the spiritual endeavor; he
goes on to speak of flexibility as the beginning of the course of work, following a similar pattern.

> Flexibility is docility, yielding, self-mastery, self-restraint,
> self-effacement, humility, selflessness, consideration of
> others, absence of arbitrariness, pure simplicity, genu-
> ineness. Those who use flexibility well appear to lack what
> they are in fact endowed with, appear to be empty when
> they are in fact fulfilled. They do not take revenge when
> offended. They seek spiritual riches and are aloof of mun-
> dane riches; they do not contend with people of the world.

The practice of flexibility is described by Liu in terms of letting go of egotism and fixations so as to become receptive to truth.

> If practitioners of the Tao can realize things of the world
> are all temporary, and the body too is insubstantial, they
> will not set their minds on the evanescent world but will
> remain mindful of the realm where there is no form.
> Humbling themselves, seeking people capable of giving
> guidance, sincerely seeking truth, they find what is funda-
> mental and shed the polluted energy of temperament.
> Generally speaking, flexibility means according with the
> Tao, according with the time, and according with the pat-
> tern of reality; working gradually, one can thus reach high
> attainment. This is what is called being first by putting
> oneself last.

Liu portrays flexibility in the form of humility and nonassertion as a means
of getting through obstacles and preserving the endowments needed for
the path.

> If one is incapable of flexible adaptivity, one will run into
> obstacles at every turn; the fire of ignorance will erupt un-
> controllably. Vitality, energy, and spirit will be damaged,
> and the whole being will be ruined. The timber of the
> spiritual house will be burned to nothing, ending up in
> total destruction. How then can one fulfill the great Tao?
> Lao-tzu said, "Concentrating the energy, making it supple,
> can you be like an infant?" If you can be as supple and
> flexible as an infant, then all objects are empty of abso-
> luteness; knowing the active, you keep the passive, know-
> ing the white, you keep the black.

Finally, he again concludes with a summary of the quality of flexibility in terms of practice and realization.

> What is flexibility? If someone strikes you, you endure it
> meekly; if someone reviles you, you greet it with a smile.
> Unconcerned by illness, not entering into judgments,
> being courteous and humble, getting rid of arrogance,
> gradually dispelling force of habit, noticing your own
> faults at all times, checking your own state in all situations,
> being careful about what you have not perceived, acting in
> accord with your basic state and not wishing for anything
> else, you are not concerned with human sentiments or
> worldly affairs, you sweep away all false thoughts and idle
> imaginations, leaving not a trace.

The *I Ching* begins with overall descriptions of the paths of firmness and flexibility, represented by the signs for Heaven and Earth, pure yang and pure yin. These are the two general modes of the practice of the Tao; each line in the signs then describes the use or misuse of firmness and flexibility according to the experiential time.

The next sixty-two signs of the *I Ching* illustrate particular "paths" or aspects of the Tao in practice, again with each line of each sign showing the place of yin or yang in a given "time" or phase of that particular path. According to the state or phase of the path, according to the existential state of the practitioner, yin and yang take on different associations. These associations and their implications are elucidated by Liu I-ming in his commentary.

In all, there are sixty-four signs in the *I Ching*, with three hundred eighty-four lines. Each sign consists of six lines, and so is called a hexa-gram; each line is either solid ("odd"), representing yang, or broken ("even"), representing yin. Each hexagram is also seen as consisting of two sets of three lines, or trigrams. Meanings are extracted from hexagrams in three main ways: from individual lines in specific places, the order of the places assigned from bottom to top; from individual lines in terms of their relations to other lines; and from the relations between the two trigrams in each hexagram, every trigram having specific associations.

Four of the hexagrams are considered timeless, while the other sixty have their own times. This means that what is represented by the timeless hexagrams is held to be inherent or necessary at all times, while what is represented by the other hexagrams is specific to the "time" of that experience or practice. The three hundred sixty lines of the sixty hexagrams with specific times are metaphorically associated with the three hundred sixty days of a lunar year, standing for a complete cycle of evolution. Thus the sixty-four signs of the *I Ching* are taken to stand for the substance and function of the Tao.

The four timeless hexagrams are *heaven, earth, mastering pitfalls,* and *fire.* These are held to obtain in some way at all stages of practice. *Heaven* and *earth* represent firmness and flexibility, fostering the mind of Tao and emptying the human mind; these concepts have already been dealt with in the foregoing pages. *Mastering pitfalls,* overcoming internal and external obstacles, dealing with difficulties and dangers in the mind and the environment, is considered the way in which human development is achieved. *Fire* stands for illumination, awareness, understanding, which are required all along the way to guide action.

These and the remaining sixty hexagrams represent the permutations of eight trigrams, each of which has specific associations. The eight trigrams are *heaven* ☰, *earth* ☷, *fire* ☲, *water* ☵, *thunder* ☳, *mountain* ☶, *lake* ☱, and *wind* ☴. In the core text of the *I Ching*—the sayings on the hexagrams and lines—these are held to represent fundamental elements of life through which human development can be fostered; hence in Taoist alchemy they are sometimes called the "cauldron of the eight trigrams," in which the refinement of consciousness is carried out.

In the interpretation of the core text, each trigram has two sets of associations, developmental and debilitating, which depend on the balance of the quality represented by the trigram. *Heaven* stands for strength, firmness, creativity; imbalanced, it becomes force, aggression, arbitrariness. *Earth* stands for submission, obedience, receptivity, flexibility; imbalanced, it becomes weakness, lack of autonomy, slavishness, dependency. *Fire* stands for illumination, clarity, understanding, knowledge; imbalanced, it becomes superficial intellectualism, uncontrolled attention, fixation on appearances. *Water* stands for danger, difficulty; this is considered to be developmental insofar as it is used as an impetus for personal growth, and considered to be debilitating when one allows oneself to be overcome by it. *Thunder* stands for activity; this is considered developmental when guided by understanding, arbitrary and prone to error without understanding. *Mountain* stands for stillness, stopping, such as in specific exercises of stillness and restraint, used to balance and nurture strength, activity, and illumination in order to prevent premature use; imbalanced, stillness becomes passivity or quietism, without developmental dynamic. *Lake* stands for joy, enjoyment; this is considered developmental or debilitating according to its orientation and balance with other factors. *Wind* stands for entering and following: In reference to the developmental process it represents entering into reality by following an initiatory path; in reference to debilitation it represents the entering of conditioning influences through following arbitrary personal inclinations and cravings.

The place of a specific line in a sign may be defined in terms of the trigram or the hexagram. Generally speaking, the first (bottom) line may be taken to represent the beginning of the path or state indicated by the sign, while the third (in relation to the lower or "inner" trigram) or sixth (top) lines may be taken to represent the end. When the trigrams are considered, the lower trigram is taken to refer to the inner state of the person, while the upper trigram is taken to represent the outer state of the person or the environmental situation.

When the place of a specific line is defined in terms of its relation to another or other lines, this is done in one of two ways. One way is that a line may be considered in its relationship to the neighboring line, above or below it. Another way is that the line may be considered in its relationship to the corresponding line in the other trigram; that is to say, lines one and four, two and five, three and six, are held to correspond: If corresponding lines are opposite, that is, if one is yin and the other yang, it is taken as a relation of balance. Lines two and five, being in the center of their respective trigrams, are in themselves considered positions of balance, indicating correct orientation of firmness or flexibility in the context of the path being described.

The present commentary on the *I Ching* consists of two parts. The first part is the text of the *I Ching* proper—the sixty-four signs plus sayings on the signs and their lines—with Liu I-ming's commentary. The second part is Liu I-ming's commentary on two sections added to the *I Ching* by earlier commentators, believed to be members of the original Confucian school; these two sections are known as the Overall Images and the Mixed Hexagrams.

In the presently known form of the *I Ching*, the Overall Images are included in the main text, following the sayings on the hexagrams. Liu I-ming has separated them, according to a Taoist tradition. Ch'en Chih-hsu, a distinguished Taoist author of the Yuan Dynasty, points out that the Overall Images and other additions to the *I Ching* are not part of the original text; since they present their own specific interpretive framework, he says, their inclusion in the midst of the original text has the effect of limiting or confusing the meaning. The value of the Overall Images is not denied, however; it is simply that Taoists found more meaning could be extracted more easily from the core text when it was separated from these early commentaries.

As a matter of course, the manner of translation of the text comes to differ when the core text and early commentaries are separated. The treatment of the trigrams and hexagrams in the Overall Images and Mixed Hexagrams differs from that of the core text presented in the first part; this difference has led at times to different renderings of even the names of the hexagrams. The separation of strata also naturally leads to translations of the core text that are at times quite different from translations that have been based on the interpretations afforded by the embedded Confucian commentaries such as the Overall Images.

The Overall Images and Mixed Hexagrams, being products of Confucians, tend to be presented in terms of humanity in society, the major concern of the followers of Confucius. These sayings are given further dimension by our present commentator, Liu I-ming, as he draws parallels with the path of higher psychological development. In this he follows the contention of many Taoists that there is a kind of continuity or analogy between the social and spiritual planes of activity, though the latter is more comprehensive.

In dealing with the original core text, then, Liu is not inhibited by those commentaries that had generally become regarded as part of the *I Ching* itself. Rather, in his commentary on the core text, Liu generally uses the vocabulary of Taoist alchemy. Alchemical terminology is one of the major frameworks of Taoist teaching, and its origin is attributed to one Wei Po-yang of the second century A.D., who composed the famous *Triplex Unity*, known as the ancestor of alchemical treatises, revealing the inner content of the *I Ching*. In his own introduction to his commentary, Liu I-ming explains this approach, and defines some of the most basic terms.

> The origin of alchemical classics comes from the adept Wei Po-yang of the Latter Han Dynasty (23–220 C.E.). After Wei had achieved the Tao, he pitied students of his time for being confused by sidetracks and false teachings, ignorant of the great Tao of sages, most of them wasting their whole lives, growing old without attainment. Finally he composed the *Triplex Unity*, following the Tao of the *I Ching*, so as to elucidate the source of essence and life, the reality and falsehood of yin and yang, the laws of cultivation and practice, the order of work.
>
> Using things as symbols, his metaphorical language is multifaceted. Essence and life, yin and yang, firmness and flexibility—these he called medicines. Cultivation and practice, the order of the work—these he called the firing process. Consistency in the work of cultivation and practice he called refinement. Vigorous exertion he called the martial fire; easygoing gradual penetration he called the cultural fire. Correct balance of firmness and flexibility of yin and yang he called crystallization of elixir; merging of yin and yang, with total sublimation of firmness and flexibility, he called maturation of the elixir. Imperceptible, unfathomable spiritual transformation he called releasing the elixir.
>
> The meanings contained therein are like the *I Ching*, symbolizing things by descriptive comparisons; thus began the term "gold elixir," the teaching of "alchemy," and the principle of cultivating and maintaining essence and life.

A number of other terms and expressions commonly found in Taoist alchemical literature also appear in Liu's explanations of the *I Ching*. On the whole, the alchemical language Liu uses is not nearly so complex or arcane as that found in most Taoist texts of this genre, and the general sense of the terms if often indicated by the context and juxtaposition with more explicit modes of expression. Nevertheless, for the convenience of the reader, these terms are defined in a glossary appended to this volume.

SUMMARY

A frequently cited comment in the *I Ching* says, "Yin and yang constitute the path." The *I Ching* is held by Taoists to map critical junctures of human development in terms of yin and yang, two modes of being and experience through which the spiritual dialectic of Taoist practice takes place.

Taoist spiritual alchemy, a system of mental cultivation that uses the *I Ching* as an instrumental text, defines the "path" of human progress in three general ways: repelling yin and fostering yang; blending yin and yang; and transcending yin and yang. Within these contexts, yin and yang take on a variety of associations.

To clarify these formulations, Taoist alchemy further defines yin and yang as being true or false, opposite or complementary, mutually exclusive or mutually inclusive. The process of repelling yin and fostering yang is taken to mean repelling false yin and fostering true yang. Blending yin and yang is defined as effecting a balanced combination of true yin and true yang. Transcending yin and yang is spoken of in the sense of transcending the created world and attaining autonomy, so that "one's destiny depends on oneself." The first two formulations refer to the process of the path, while the third, reminiscent of the Gnostic idea of escaping the authority of the Demiurge, is sometimes represented as the result of the path.

The main structural difference between "true" and "false" yin and yang is that true yin and yang complement, balance, and include one another, false yin and yang are isolated and opposed. In many cases yin and yang are used in the sense of an opposition of false yin and true yang. Often there is no specific definition, because the qualities are not fixed; yinlike and yanglike qualities can be rendered into true or false yin and yang by cultivation. Thus Taoism speaks of refining away the false from the true and refining out the true from the false.

General associations of yin and yang as applied in the present text may be summarized as follows, with the first term of each pair being yin and the second yang: body/mind; desire/reason; temporal/primordial; conditioning/autonomy; ignorance/enlightenment; human mentality/ mind of Tao; fragmentation/integration; learner/teacher. In these terms Taoist teaching recommends that yin be subordinated to yang, that yang govern yin and yin obey yang.

Specific associations of true yin and true yang used in this text are represented by a number of terms commonly used to describe Taoist theory and practice: stillness/action; receptivity/creativity; flexibility/firmness; yielding/strength; innate capacity/innate knowledge; essence/life; spirit/energy; open awareness/real knowledge; nondoing/doing; nonstriving/striving. In these terms the aim is to employ these modes as appropriate to the time and effect a balanced integration. A basic procedure is referred to as "using yin to beckon yang." An example of this is a would-be

learner using humility and openness to become receptive to the enlightenment of a teacher; on an analogous dimension, it refers to using inner silence to allow inputs beyond habitual thought or sense to register.

By contrast, false yin and yang are seen as imbalanced exaggerations
of yinlike or yanglike qualities. Relevant associations here include quiet-
ism/impetuosity; weakness/aggression; dependency/self-assertion; vacil-
lation/stubbornness. While these are on one level referred to as yin and
yang, such qualities may also be referred to as all yin in the sense of being
negative or counterproductive. Taoist practice attempts to overcome these
qualities, or transmute them into their positive counterparts.

Nuances of yin and yang qualities, their interactions, and their effects
on human life, are the subject matter of the *I Ching*. Overall, Taoism uses
the idea of balanced integration of yin and yang in the sense of fulfillment
of the complete or whole human potential, living in the world and fulfilling worldly tasks, yet maintaining inner contact with a greater dimension,
referred to as "celestial," which interpenetrates the worldly plane in some
way. Thus Liu I-ming speaks of using things of the world to practice the
principles of the Tao, using human affairs to cultivate celestial qualities.

Finally, a special use of yin and yang as opposite terms is found in the
expressions "pure yin" and "pure yang." Pure yin refers to the mortal,
earth-bound material dross, which must eventually obey the laws of matter. Pure yang refers to pure unbound consciousness; held to partake of
the nature of infinity, this is represented as spiritual immortality. Pure yang
may be used to allude to a peak experience, after which there is a re-
integration of this enlightenment into life in the world, again balancing
yang with yin. It may also be used to refer to the primordial state, and to
the final liberation of the adept on leaving the world. Having no actual
mundane equivalent, attainment of pure yang is often referred to in such
terms as "ascending to heaven in broad daylight," which passed into folk-
lore but are said to have originally been dramatic expressions for the realization of total freedom.

Concluding this introduction with a simple survey of the articulation
points of the hexagrams, we may also use this summary as an index to the
text. For convenience of notation, we may refer to the sequence beginning
with *heaven* as the odd sequence, and the one beginning with *earth* as
the even sequence, since *heaven* is all yang, and yang lines are odd (—),
while *earth* is all yin, and yin lines are even (— —).

■ *Odd Sequence*

1.   Heaven

One of the four "timeless" hexagrams; pure yang, it represents strength,
firmness, life, innate knowledge, primal unified energy.

3. *Difficulty*

Beginning of the process of fostering the strength of primal energy, the difficult process of breaking out of acquired temporal conditioning and bringing the primordial to the fore, the process known as "advancing the yang fire."

 5. *Waiting*

Waiting for the proper timing in gathering primal energy, gradually restoring the primordial in the midst of the temporal.

 7. *The Army*

Using the primordial to repel conditioning, using the real to get rid of the false.

 9. *Nurturance by the Small*

Nurturing inner strength by outward submissiveness, being firm but not impetuous, growing through humility.

 11. *Tranquility*

Harmony of strength and flexibility.

 13. *Sameness with People*

Mixing in with the ordinary world, concealing illumination, assimilating to others.

 15. *Humility*

Inwardly firm, outwardly flexible, having personal attainment but not dwelling on it.

17. Following

According with conditions, going along with human desire to gradually introduce guidance.

19. Overseeing

Keeping watch over the restoration and growth of primal energy and repulsion of acquired energy of conditioning.

21. Biting Through

Investigating things and finding out principles.

23. Stripping Away

Submission to desire, acquired mundanity dissolving away the celestial energy.

25. Fidelity (No Error)

Vigorous advancement of celestial energy, attention to reality.

27. Lower Jaw (Nourishment)

Discernment of good, becoming empty to seek fulfillment.

29. Mastering Pitfalls

One of the four timeless hexagrams; restoring the celestial within the mundane.

31. *Sensitivity*

Harmonization of the celestial and the earthly.

 33. *Withdrawal*

Storing positive energy, subduing energy, exercising strength with restraint, not using power arbitrarily.

 35. *Advance*

Clearminded sincerity advancing illumination.

 37. *People in the Home*

Governing the inner: refining the self, mastering the mind, turning the attention inward.

 39. *Halting (Trouble)*

Preserving the primordial in the midst of the temporal.

 41. *Reduction*

Removing acquired conditioning, stilling mundane attraction.

 43. *Parting*

Detachment from discriminating consciousness, repelling the energy of external influences.

45. Gathering

Unifying vitality, energy, and spirit.

47. Exhaustion

Refining body and mind.

49. Revolution

Refining personal desires to become unselfish.

51. Thunder

Practicing introspection in action.

53. Gradual Progress

Gradual practice following appropriate order.

55. Richness

Balance of understanding and action, preventing danger by awareness.

57. Wind

Progress by flexible obedience.

59. Dispersal

Confusion of yin and yang followed by reordering.

61. *Faithfulness in the Center*

Avoidance of both obsession and negligence, seeking fulfillment by becoming empty.

63. *Settled*

Mutual completion of yin and yang; forestalling danger to stabilize attainment.

■ *Even Sequence*

2. *Earth*

One of the four timeless hexagrams. Pure yin; represents receptivity, submission, humility, obedience, yielding, flexibility, stillness, essence, innate capacity.

4. *Darkness*

Starting yin-convergence, making unruly yin submit, integrating with the world yet preventing mundanity from taking over. Negatively, it represents obscurity, unknowing; positively, it represents innocence. Also represents stopping in danger.

6. *Contention*

Depending on strength because of danger, causing danger by depending on strength. Conflict due to imbalance.

8. *Accord*

Learning through association; obedience in danger, rectification of imbalance.

10. Treading

Progress; advance of the positive, prevention of danger by caution, empowerment by calmness and trust.

12. Obstruction

Submitting inwardly to personal desire, acting aggressive outwardly.

14. Great Possession

Mutual enhancement of strength and lucidity; continuous renewal, inward discipline.

16. Joy

Proper timing in action.

18. Degeneration

Correcting degeneration by abandoning the false and returning to the true.

20. Observation

Alertness, gradually progressing through receptivity to the requirements of the time, inner vigilance.

22. Adornment

Private cultivation, without ostentation, mutual complementarity of clarity and stillness.

24. *Return*

Return of consciousness of reality, activity obeying the mind.

26. *Nurturance of the Great*

Being able to be still when strong; practicing nondoing to nurture incipient enlightenment.

28. *Excess of the Great*

Following desires, delighting in externals, inability to control strength.

30. *Fire*

One of the four timeless hexagrams; illumination with inner openness.

32. *Constancy*

Singleminded application, perseverance in real practice.

34. *Great Power*

Promoting vigorous positive energy; ability to act or not act, at will; transcendence of ordinary capacities.

36. *Concealment of Illumination*

Withdrawing effort after illumination, not using illumination lightly; being enlightened yet conforming to the times.

38. Disharmony

Focus on externals; requires inner emptiness to restore harmony.

40. Liberation

Taking advantage of the appropriate time to liberate positive primordial energy from the influence of negative, conditioned energy.

42. Increase

Entering the Tao gradually, without either rushing or lagging, increasing the positive while decreasing the negative.

44. Meeting

Warding off negative influences, preserving the positive.

46. Rising

Climbing from lowliness to the heights; carefully watching over the development process.

48. The Well

Accumulation of effort to cultivate character; nurturance of others.

50. The Cauldron

Refining illumination.

52. Mountain

Nurturing energy by quietude.

 54. Making a Young Girl Marry

Seeing the real within the false.

 56. Travel

Stabilizing and nurturing illumination, transcending the world.

 58. Joy

Communion of the inward and the outward; joy in practicing the Tao.

 60. Discipline

Being able to be joyful even in trouble; practicing obedience in trying circumstances, adaptably keeping to the Tao.

 62. Predominance of the Small

Being fulfilled but acting empty; inwardly strong, outwardly yielding, inwardly firm, outwardly flexible.

 64. Unsettled

Refining the self, repelling mundanity, waiting for the time to restore the primordial celestial positivity.

Book I

The Text

1. Heaven

Heaven creates, develops, brings about fruition and consummation.

EXPLANATION

Heaven is sound, in the sense of being strong and indomitable. The lines making up the body of the hexagram are all odd; this represents pure yang, so it is called *heaven*. This hexagram represents the advance of yang, whereby the science of building life acts with strength and uses the path of firmness.

In strength, nothing is stronger than heaven; heaven as the Tao is a flow of unitary energy, circulating continuously, never ceasing. There is nothing it does not cover, nothing that can harm it. This is the ultimate of soundness and strength.

Therefore, producing things in spring is the creativity of strength. Creation means the beginning, the first arising of positive energy. When positive energy is born, all things sprout. Such is the strength of creativity.

Developing things in summer is the growth of strength. Development is extension, the expansion of positive energy. As positive energy expands, all things develop and flourish. Such is the strength of development.

Maturing things in autumn is the fruition of strength. Fruition is goodness, the proper benefit of positive energy. When positive energy achieves its proper benefit, all things come to fruition. Such is the strength of fruition.

Storing things in winter is the consummation of strength. Consummation is quiescence, the resting of positive energy. When positive energy rests quietly, all things return to their root. Such is the strength of consummation.

Creation, development, fruition, consummation, the successive movements of the four seasons, all are carried out by one strength; the one is the body, the four are the function. The body is that whereby the function is carried out, the function is that whereby the body is completed.

Body and function are as one; therefore the Tao of heaven acts with strength unceasing. As for human beings, they first take form sustained by the energy of heaven, so they have the quality of strength of heaven inherent in them, and hence have this creativity, development, fruition, and consummation, the functions of strength.

The quality of strength in people is original innate knowledge, the sane primal energy. This is called true yang, or the truly unified vitality, or the truly unified energy. Confucianism speaks of singleness of mind, Taoism speaks of embracing the one, Buddhism speaks of returning to the one—all of them simply teach people to cultivate this strong, sound, sane energy.

This energy is rooted in the primordial, concealed in the temporal. It is not more in sages, not less in ordinary people. At the time of birth, it is neither defiled nor pure, neither born nor extinct, neither material nor void. It is tranquil and unstirring, yet sensitive and effective. In the midst of myriad things, it is not restricted or constrained by myriad things. Fundamentally it creates, develops, and brings about fruition and consummation spontaneously, all this taking place in unminding action, not needing force. It comes spontaneously from nature, not forceful yet strong, strong yet not forceful.

Strength having no perceptible form or trace is referred to as the celestial human. Once it mixes with acquired temporal conditioning, temperament appears and is seduced by objects. The essential intimacy of heaven and humanity then becomes estranged by habit; people abandon the real and give recognition to the artificial, so innate knowledge is obscured.

At this point, creation is not creative, development is not developmental, fruition is not fruitful, and consummation is not consummate; the quality of strength is already lacking, so the functions of strength are not what they are anymore. The spirit is dim, the energy is polluted, essence is disturbed, life is shaken; though the body moves, positive energy dissipates, and death is inevitable. This is why the sages have the science of building life, to restore the primordial in the midst of the temporal, whereby it is possible to sustain the original qualities of the strength of *heaven*, never to decay.

The method of cultivation and practice is none other than this function of creation, development, fruition, and consummation. When people can see through everything, look deeply into themselves, and turn around to set their minds on essence and life, then in the midst of trance there will be a point of living potential that will subtly emerge—this is the creation of strength. If people can cultivate and nurture this singlemindedly, putting it into actual practice, persevering indefatigably, acting so as to achieve their aim, this is the development of strength. If people can cultivate their vital spirit and powerfully go forward, so that strong energy is stabilized, objects do not obstruct them, and life and death are as one—this is the fruition of strength. If people can investigate things and attain knowledge, distinguish what is so and what is not, what is wrong and what is right, staying in what is appropriate and not deviating from it, this is the consummation of strength.

Creation is whereby that strength is born; development is whereby that strength is expanded; fruition is whereby that strength is fulfilled;

consummation is whereby that strength is consolidated. Creation, development, fruition, and consummation are functions of one energy. Starting from effort, you end up in spontaneity, integrating completely with natural principle: Then this is the original face of innate knowledge, whereby you can share in the function of heaven, and share in the eternity of heaven.

However, in this science there are medicinal substances, there is a firing process, there is a course of work, there is intensification and relaxation, there is stopping at sufficiency; you can advance into its marvels only if you practice it according to its laws, and develop it with the appropriate timing. If you deviate in the slightest, you will fail altogether. If one of the four aspects—creation, development, fruition, or consummation—is lacking, then the quality of strength will not be complete, and life will not be your own. So it is necessary to know this firing process of advancing yang.

■ *First yang:*   **Hidden Dragon: Do not use it.**

EXPLANATION
In the beginning of strength, when the quality of strength is activated, it is like a hidden dragon. This is the time to nurture the sound energy; one should not yet rely or presume on this strength, so the text says "do not use it."

■ *2 yang:*   **Seeing the dragon in the field: It is beneficial to see a great person.**

EXPLANATION
When strength gains balance, and is not one-sided or partial, firmness and flexibility match each other. This is like seeing the dragon in the field; the living energy is always there, natural goodness is not obscured, the spiritual embryo takes on form. A great person is one who does not lose the innocent mind of an infant, and is therefore "beneficial to see."

■ *3 yang:*   **A superior person works diligently all day, is careful at night. Danger, but no error.**

EXPLANATION
The abundantly flowing energy is full to repletion, firm and strong yet correctly oriented; by day one works diligently, by night one examines one's faults. Working by day, careful by night, strong practice does not cease; one can therefore be without error even though there is danger.

■ *4 yang:*   **Sometimes leaping, or in the abyss: no error.**

EXPLANATION
The quality of strength has developed, the spiritual embryo is complete, awaiting the time to molt and transmute. This is like a dragon which may

leap up or remain in the abyss. One carefully examines the climate and takes precautions against danger so that one can be free from error.

■ *5 yang:* **The flying dragon is in the sky: It is beneficial to see a great person.**

EXPLANATION
Firm strength properly balanced, yin and yang merge and transmute: one has a body outside the body, and is physically and mentally sublimated. Uniting with reality in the Tao, one does not only perfect oneself, but others as well. This is like a flying dragon in the sky, appearing and disappearing unfathomably, aiding people whenever there is the opportunity. What is called a great person here is one who rectifies herself or himself and also rectifies others, and so is "beneficial to see."

■ *Top yang:* **A proud dragon has regrets.**

EXPLANATION
Promoting strength excessively, being only strong and not flexible, knowing how to go forward but not how to withdraw, is being like a dragon of drought: When the dragon gets to be proud, it cannot give life; when strength goes to excess, one will fail in one's tasks. When yang culminates, it must shift to yin. The celestial jewel gained is again lost. It is a logical matter of course. This is why the text says a proud dragon, one who goes too high, has regrets.

■ *Using yang:* **Having dragons appear without heads is good.**

EXPLANATION
In general, the way to act with strength and use firmness requires appropriate timing. Creation, development, fruition, and consummation can then be strong everywhere, and strength cannot be damaged anywhere. The sage, fearing that people would not know the way to use strength, specially wrote "in using yang, having dragons appear without heads is good." This statement is very clear. Using yang means using strength; the dragon, as the radiance of consciousness, changes unfathomably, able to ascend and able to descend, able to be large or small, able to hide or appear. When you face it, you do not see its head; when you follow it, you do not see its back. Cultivating the path of strength is like riding a dragon. Using strength while being able to accord with the time is like the transformation of dragons, disappearing when it is appropriate to disappear, appearing when it is appropriate to appear, being active when it is appropriate to be active, leaping when it is appropriate to leap, flying when it is appropriate to fly, being strong without going to excess, rising high without becoming proud, relaxing, hurrying, and resting in sufficiency, each according to the time. This is strength "without a head." When you employ this, you will always be fortunate.

However, the way of headless transformation requires real knowledge and clear insight. If you engage in guesswork without insight, even if the celestial treasure is in view you won't be able to use it. First you must see it, then use it. Then there is no function within function that has function, making effort within the effort that is effortless. Being and nonbeing do not stand, for and against do not bind; knowledge is everywhere, go where you may. The Tao is in everything; the source is encountered at every turn.

Only when you use strength and are not used by it can you develop the pure unadulterated vitality in which firm strength is properly balanced. Then your fate depends on you, not on heaven; you are a peer of heaven.

2. *Earth*

With earth, creativity and development are achieved in the faithfulness of the female horse. The superior person has somewhere to go. Taking the lead, one goes astray; following, one finds the master. It is beneficial to gain companionship in the southwest and lose companionship in the northeast. Stability in rectitude is good.

EXPLANATION

Earth is submissive; it means flexible, receptive humility. In the body of the hexagram, all six lines are even; this represents pure yin, so it is called *earth.* This hexagram represents convergence in yin, whereby the science of cultivating essence practices submission and receptivity and uses the path of flexibility.

Nothing is more submissive than earth. Earth is originally pure yin and cannot produce or develop things. The reason it does produce and develop myriad things is that it is receptive to the yang energy of heaven, producing and developing by progression and recession. This earth originally does not create or develop; its achievement of creativity and development lies in its capacity for faithfulness.

The receptivity of earth to heaven cannot be seen, but the receptivity of earth can be known by observing the submissiveness of a female horse. "Female" is a general term for the flexibility of yin; whatever is yin in something is classified as female. A "horse" is something that travels strongly: when a mare follows a stallion, the mare can go wherever the stallion goes; so though it is gentle, it is also strong. The benefit of the faithfulness of the receptivity of earth is like the benefit of the faithfulness of the female horse.

Human beings receive the yin energy of earth and take form thereby, so they have this quality of flexible receptivity. When people are born, this quality of flexible receptivity is their innate capacity: When this capacity mixes with temporal acquired conditioning, it is confined by temperament and stained by accumulated habits; so people do not obey what they should obey, and instead obey their desires, so innate capacity turns into artificial capacity.

When sages teach people to travel the path of submission, this starts from artificial submission and changes into true submission, returning to the pristine state of unconscious obedience to the laws of God. Therefore the text says, "The superior person has somewhere to go. Taking the lead, one goes astray; following, one finds the master." Firmness is the master of flexibility; firmness is able to govern flexibility, whereas flexibility cannot govern firmness—it just follows the firm obediently.

Yielding obedience to strength is not only a matter of the incapable following the capable: Reforming error and returning to rectitude, changing wrong and taking to right, maintaining truth and getting rid of falsehood, is all a matter of the human mind submitting to the mind of Tao. This is all represented in terms of the flexible obeying the firm. "Taking the lead, one goes astray" means that when you act through the human mentality, the mind of Tao is buried away; following human desires, you damage the real by falsehood, losing the master by going astray. "Following, one finds the master" means that when you act through the mind of Tao, the human mind is peaceful and quiet, obedient to natural principle, extinguishing falsehood by reality, finding the master and not straying. If people can develop understanding from confusion, make yin follow yang, use the human mind to return to the mind of Tao, use the mind of Tao to govern the human mind, finding the master after they had previously lost it, even if they are stupid they will become illumined, and even if they are weak they will become strong.

In the path of submission nothing is greater than earth; for a symbol of receptivity, nothing is more obvious than the moon. The moon is basically pure yin, with no yang; it meets the sun in the spacious heights, travels to the southwest, the position of *earth* ☷, and on the third day of the lunar month gives off a light like a wispy eyebrow, producing the yang spirit within the yin spirit—this is called "gaining companionship." On the fifteenth day, the moonlight waxes full; on the sixteenth, the sunlight begins to shift away gradually, and the moonlight henceforth begins to wane, producing the yin spirit within the yang spirit. When it reaches northeast, the position of *mountain* ☶, on the twenty-eighth day, the remaining light vanishes—this is called "losing companionship." The moonlight appears in the southwest, yin follows the advance of yang; the moonlight disappears in the northeast, yin follows the receding of yang. When yang advances, the moon brightens; when yang recedes, the moon darkens. The brightening and darkening of the moon also follows the advance and withdrawal of the sun. If superior people practicing the Tao are able to be like the moon following the sun when they travel the path of flexibility by means of submission, then they know what gain and loss are, and they are effective in advancing as well as in withdrawing.

What is efficacy? It is effectiveness in submission to what is right, most effective in abiding in faithfulness to rectitude. Only thus is it an auspicious path that is sound in the beginning and sound at the end. "Stability in rectitude" means resting in what is right; one is at peace because of rectitude, and rests in what is appropriate. One aims for the submission of unruliness, the rectification of error, cultivating oneself and controlling the mind, getting rid of all seeds of vicious circles, not letting any pollution remain in the mind; being utterly empty, serene and sincere, the human mentality does not arise and the mind of Tao comes into being. After rectitude comes creativity, and while flexible one is firm, and while receptive one can be strong: Whatever one creates grows, whatever grows bears fruit, and the fruits are all good. So the submission and receptivity of abiding in rectitude is no small matter.

■ *First yin:*   **Walking on frost: Hard ice arrives.**

EXPLANATION
In the beginning of submission, on the borderline of true and false, if there is any deviation, external influences will creep in, and one will come to the point where all negative forces gather when one negative force arises. So there is the image of "walking on frost: Hard ice arrives"—therefore submission and receptivity must begin with prudence and care.

■ *2 yin:*   **Straightforward, correct, great: Unfailing achievement without practice.**

EXPLANATION
Flexible receptivity is balanced correctly; by being balanced the mind is straightforward and capable of prudence and care; being correct, one's activities are orderly. Inwardly straightforward, outwardly correct, following rules and acting in accord with guidelines, one can naturally make good works great. Therefore the text says "unfailing achievement without practice."

■ *3 yin:*   **Hiding one's excellence, one can be correct: If one works in government, there is completion without fabrication.**

EXPLANATION
Nature flexible, will firm, hiding one's refinements, one obeys and maintains rectitude, not allowing external falsehood to damage internal reality. So when there are events where one cannot but obey externally, if one works in government, one will want to accord with others, yet will not lose oneself; therefore there can be "completion without fabrication."

■ *4 yin:*   Closing the bag, there is no blame, no praise.

EXPLANATION

Remaining flexible by giving way, thoughts do not come out from within, or come in from outside; one accords with the times, submitting to the decree of fate, not causing trouble yet not seeking good fortune. This is like tying up the opening of a bag, inside and out one emptiness; so there is no blame and no praise.

■ *5 yin:*   A yellow garment is very auspicious.

EXPLANATION

Flexible receptivity open and balanced, one's virtue is sufficient to make people obey; one is trusted without speaking, one educates without teaching. This is like a yellow garment on the body, representing the sun emerging in the darkness; the refinement and virtue within naturally show outwardly. Therefore it is the great auspicious manifestation of the path of submission.

■ *Top yin:*   Dragons battle in the field;
the blood is dark yellow.

EXPLANATION

Self-aggrandizement making softness hard, being unable to obey others but wanting others to obey oneself, is like dragons battling in the field. One turns away from harmony and loses balance; yin is off kilter, yang is amiss. Without yet having won others, one has already harmed oneself; therefore the blood is dark yellow.

■ *Using yin:*   It is beneficial to always be correct.

EXPLANATION

As I see submission and receptivity in the six lines, they are unequal in being right and wrong. They are each different in terms of error and correctness. When we look for the submissive receptivity that is beneficial to oneself, it is only in the yin in the second place; submissive receptivity that can influence others seems to be only in the fifth place. The path of submission and receptivity is not easy; the slightest slip and one is far off the track. If one is not careful in the beginning, one will surely fail in the end.

The sage specially wrote "in using yin, it is beneficial to always be correct," opening up a great road for people of later times, so that those who travel the path of submission and receptivity would be constant in rectitude, for only then can submission be receptive to truth, and only thus can it be beneficial. The way to use yin is to use the path of submission and receptivity. Using submission and receptivity is the way to seek fulfillment by means of emptiness, to seek truth by openness, to seek being by nonbeing.

Students past and present have presumed on their intelligence, relying on their own views alone, engaging in arbitrary guesswork and personalistic interpretation, unwilling to humbly seek the aid of others. For this reason they grow old without attainment. Then again, there are those who seek out teachers and colleagues, but are unable to distinguish the false from the true, and get off into tangents and twisted byroads, never understanding all their lives. Also there are those who can distinguish false and true, who investigate and understand the principles of essence and life, and who proceed along the path, and yet give up along the way. Those who are not constant in rectitude are not using yin correctly; they cannot attain the Tao.

If you want to attain the Tao, you need to know how to submit to it and be receptive to it, and you must follow it correctly. It is also necessary to follow it correctly forever. If you are able to follow it correctly forever, there will be firmness in flexibility, unconcealed, unobscured, never changing till death. Shedding the conditioned temperament, you expose the original face of primordial unconscious obedience to the laws of God; both essence and life are perfected. So the path of eternal rectitude and flexible receptivity is consummated.

3. *Difficulty*

In difficulty, creativity and development are effective if correct. Do not use. There is a place to go. It is beneficial to set up a ruler.

EXPLANATION

Difficulty means having trouble progressing. As for the qualities of the hexagram, above is the pitfall of *water* ☵, below the movement of *thunder* ☳. Acting in danger, action in danger cannot easily get out of danger; so it is called *difficulty*. This hexagram represents starting the advancement of yang; it follows on the hexagram *heaven*. *Heaven* is the quality of strength; advancement of yang is advancement of that strength. It is precisely because of not being strong that one promotes strength.

The quality of strength is primordial real yang, the original true energy. When this energy mixes with acquired conditioning, it is concealed. But even though it is not manifest, it never completely disappears; sometimes it does appear. But people are confused by things of the world, enveloped in wandering thoughts, so they miss it even when it is right there, unwilling to recognize reality.

When this primal energy appears, this is what is called the "living midnight" in our bodies. At this time we are merged in the qualities of heaven and earth, joined with the light of sun and moon, harmonized with the order of the four seasons. This is the gate of yin and yang, the door of life and death, the wellspring of essence and life, the root of strength and submission, the crucible for creating life, the alchemical furnace.

The original energy of primordial true yang is herein: Those who know it diligently cultivate it, restoring the primordial within the temporal. From vagueness, it becomes clear; from one yang it gradually grows, until it inevitably reaches the pure completeness of six yangs. This means that in difficulty too there is a path of creativity and development.

However, people are restricted by temperament, influenced by accumulated habit; the primal energy of true yang is deeply buried. Even though there be a time of restoration, the true sane energy is weak and aberrated energy is strong; as long as the true does not prevail over the false, it cannot immediately expand and rise. So it is a matter of carefully containing and securely storing it, preserving this living potential, not letting it be damaged by external influences, making it the basis of restoration. This is why the text says "effective if correct," and it also says "Do not use. There is a place to go."

Correctness is not vacant emptiness without action; "do not use" does not mean there is absolutely nothing to do. But when you have done things by the human mentality for a long time, the mind of Tao is not manifest. Restoring the positive within negativity is action in danger; if you proceed recklessly, desirous of rapid progress, you will increase the danger.

If you want to restore positivity, it is best to first correct the mind. When the text says "It is beneficial to set up a ruler," this symbolizes correcting the mind. The ruler is the leader of a country, the mind is the leader of the body. Set up a ruler, and the difficulties of the nation can gradually be overcome; rectify the mind, and the perils of the body can gradually be dissolved.

Once the mind is right, the root is firm, and the original energy does not dissipate: then one can "advance the fire" according to the time, gradually culling, gradually refining; then what has been lost can be regained, what has gone can be restored. Benefit lies in correctness while in action; this action is not random action, but properly timed action. Then whatever is begun develops, and whatever develops bears fruit.

■ *First yang:*   Not going anywhere, it is beneficial to abide in correctness. It is beneficial to set up a ruler.

EXPLANATION
Firm in the beginning of difficulty, the positive energy at the base, like the foundation of a house, it is beneficial to abide in correctness and make the basis firm. This is like the ruler of a nation; it is beneficial to set up the ruler and nurture the original energy.

■ *2 yin:*   Difficult to advance, hard to make progress. Mounted on a horse, not going forward. It is not a

matter of enmity, but marriage. The girl is chaste, not
engaged: After ten years she is engaged.

EXPLANATION
Right in the middle of difficulty, one therefore has difficulty making progress—hardship in advancing. With flexible receptivity correctly balanced,
one refines oneself and waits for the proper time to act, therefore is
"mounted on a horse, not going forward." Mounted on a horse, not going
forward, means that one wants to act but does not act. One does not injure
people by the newborn yang, as an enemy, but wants to wait until yin and
yang are balanced, to seek a match in marriage. The image of waiting for
the proper time for marriage is of a girl who is chaste and not engaged
becoming engaged after ten years. This means not seeking immediate solutions when in difficulty.

■ *3 yin:* Chasing deer without a guide, just going into
the forest. The superior person, knowing the dangers,
had better give up; to go would bring regret.

EXPLANATION
Petty people without knowledge act arbitrarily, in ignorance, wrongly
coveting the celestial treasure; they act dangerously on a dangerous basis.
This is like "chasing deer without a guide, just going into the forest." And
it is no surprise. As for superior people who understand the Tao, they
should know the dangers, and had better give up and wait for the proper
time. If you do not wait for the proper time and rush forward in hopes of
speedy accomplishment, you will certainly regret having beckoned danger. This is rushing to seek solutions when in difficulty.

■ *4 yin:* Mounted on a horse yet not going forward.
Seeking marriage, it is good to go, beneficial all
around.

EXPLANATION
Flexible yet correctly oriented, refining oneself and awaiting the proper
time, the real yang is in view: Precisely the time when one should blend
the elixir, one should not slip up on the threshold; therefore, "seeking
marriage, it is good to go, beneficial all around." This is seeking solutions
according to the time when in difficulty.

■ *5 yang:* Stalling the benefits. Rectitude in small
matters is good. Self righteousness in great matters
brings misfortune.

EXPLANATION
The firmness of yang centrally balanced, the spiritual embryo takes on
form; one has "filled the belly," and it is as though one has received bene-

fit. However, though the spiritual embryo has formed, negative energy has not yet withdrawn, and one is still in danger; this is like "stalling the benefits." At this point striving ends and nonstriving comes to the fore. Therefore propriety in small matters is good, while self-righteousness in great matters brings misfortune. This is being great but conscious of the small, waiting for the time to be able to get out of difficulty.

■ *Top yin:*   **Mounted on a horse, not going forward, weeping tears of blood.**

EXPLANATION
At the end of difficulty, this is now the time to get out of difficulty. Weak and helpless, one is astride a horse but does not go forward, and has no whip in one's hand. Though true yang is in view, one still cannot get it oneself, and weeps tears of blood—of what use is it in fact? This is being small and incapable of greatness, having difficulty even when there is no difficulty.

Generally speaking, in the course of operating the fire advancing yang, it is necessary to know the proper timing. By knowing the time to take the medicine, using the temporal to restore the primordial, one can get out of difficulty, one can resolve difficulty. If you do not know the proper timing, and go too far or not far enough, real yang will be trapped by negative energy and will not be able to get out. This is why the statement of the hexagram says that creativity and development are effective if correct; only when correct can they be effective. When effective, the creativity leads to development. Creativity and development that are effective by correctness mean waiting for the appropriate time to get out of difficulty.

4. *Darkness*

In darkness is development. It is not that I seek naive innocence; naive innocence seeks me. The first augury informs; the second and third defile. Defilement does not inform. It is beneficial to be correct.

EXPLANATION
Darkness means obscurity and unknowing. In the body of the hexagram, *mountain* ☶ is above, with two yin advancing under one yang; *water* ☵ is below, with one yang fallen between two yins. Both have forms of yin injuring yang; therefore it is called *darkness*. As for the qualities of the hexagram, danger is within stillness; there is danger, yet ability to stop—this includes the meaning of stopping darkness.
    This hexagram represents starting the operation of yin convergence.

The hexagram follows on the previous hexagram *earth*. *Earth* means going on the path of submission and receptivity; carrying out yin convergence means returning recalcitrant yin to submission.

After the primordial yang in people culminates, conditioned yin arises; the original spirit is obscured and discriminatory awareness does things. One drops the real and recognizes the false, using intellect mistakenly, producing all sorts of cleverness; though overtly there is light, inside is really dark. This is where darkness comes from.

Once you have entered darkness, essence is disturbed and life is destabilized; in a single day you are born a thousand times and die ten thousand times, not knowing how to stop. This is most perilous.

If you know there is danger and are able to stop it, silencing the intellect, being as though ignorant and dumb, though you be without knowledge outwardly, inwardly you really have knowledge. From false darkness you return to true darkness. Thus it is that in darkness there is paradoxically a way of development.

The best development of darkness is innocence. The darkness of innocence unconsciously follows the laws of God, tranquil and unstirring, yet sensitive and effective. All actions flow from the fundamental essence. This is the dignified status of a sage, the aspect of the celestial human.

Those who travel the path of darkness must go back to the darkness of innocence; only then is it the darkness that is returning to the origin. However, this darkness of return to the origin is not a matter of seeking naive innocence oneself—it is naive innocence that seeks oneself. Not seeking innocence oneself means that it does not come about by formal effort, and is not attached to forms. Innocence seeking oneself means that it comes naturally and does not fall into voidness.

Not clinging to forms, not falling into voidness, not material, not empty, since it is not a matter of seeking the real, one does not exclude the artificial either. Ever calm yet always responsive, always responsive yet ever calm, it is not darkness yet resembles darkness; it is darkness but actually not darkness. External things cannot enter; inside, thoughts cannot arise. One does not seek reality, but reality is here.

But this path that is neither form nor void has two methods, nurturing darkness and opening darkness, which should be known. When yin and yang are mixed, and natural reality has not yet been injured, and external influences have not yet entered, darkness belongs to reality. It is like a first augury, when the yarrow sticks are not yet divided, surely giving direction at first. One should be open, calm, sincere, and serious, thereby going on the path of noncontrivance. Once yin and yang have divided, there is a lack of natural reality; external influences creep in, and darkness winds up in falsehood. It is like when the yarrow sticks are messed up after two or three auguries; without awaiting their directions one may change arrangements, thus going on the path of striving.

The path of noncontrivance nurtures the darkness of reality; the path of striving transforms the darkness of falsehood. Nurturing reality, transforming falsehood, striving and nonstriving, are to be used according to the time and situation, as appropriate. One may proceed from striving and wind up nonstriving, or one may succeed in striving by way of nonstriving. In either case the ultimate accomplishment is to use the highest good, without evil, wholly integrated with natural principle, to go back to the origin, return to the fundamental, and revert to innocence. Those who travel the path of darkness must do so in the correct way.

■ *First yin:*   Opening up darkness, it is advantageous to
use punishments. If restrictions are removed, it will
lead to regret.

EXPLANATION
In the beginning of darkness, when the human mentality first arises, one should immediately conquer it and regulate it strictly. This is like the advantage in using punishments. If you are loose and indulgent, allowing your nature to go bad, this is like removing restrictions; as you go on you gradually get into an irremediable state of base ignorance, and nothing can save or stop you, so you will surely become conditioned by externals. This emphasizes guarding against negativity in the beginning of darkness.

■ *2 yang:*   Taking in darkness is good, taking a wife is
good; the heir ably takes over the family affairs.

EXPLANATION
Being firm yet capable of flexibility, using yin to nurture yang, is "taking in darkness." When darkness is taken in, outside is dark while inside is light; not only is yang energy not damaged, it even grows. This is like the good fortune of taking a wife, with the heir naturally taking over the family affairs. This is the time when one can nurture positive energy in darkness.

■ *3 yin:*   Don't take this woman in marriage; if she sees
a moneyed man, she'll lose herself. Nowhere
beneficial.

EXPLANATION
When the softness of yin is not balanced or correctly oriented, you indulge in feelings and desires. So "don't take this woman in marriage." What is cautioned against is doing things on the basis of the human mentality, greedy for material goods and sensual pleasures, like a loose woman who loses herself when she sees a moneyed man. Without having won others, you have already lost yourself—there is no benefit. You should know this is darkness increasing darkness.

■ *4 yin:*   Stuck in darkness, there is regret.

EXPLANATION
When you are basically ignorant and foolish yourself, and also keep company with petty people, not knowing enough to approach the high

minded and illumined so as to expand and master consciousness, you will after all be stuck in darkness and be unable to get out. You will suffer regret and worse. This is being in the dark without even knowing it is dark.

■ **5 yin:**   Innocence is auspicious.

EXPLANATION
In stopping, knowing when and where to stop, being incapable so following the capable, using firmness to balance flexibility, borrowing strength to compensate for weakness, though dark this is not darkness; this is the auspicious path of innocence unconsciously following the laws of God. This is darkness aware of its darkness.

■ *Top yang:*   Attacking darkness, what is not helpful is inimical, what is helpful prevents enmity.

EXPLANATION
Firmness at the culmination of darkness is ability to control anger and desire, and to powerfully repel external influences. This is like attacking darkness. On the path of withdrawing yin, the human mentality is not helpful, so it is inimical; it is the mind of Tao which is helpful, defending against what is inimical. If one removes the human mentality, activates the mind of Tao, negative energy recedes and positive energy becomes pure and complete. Then you again see what you were originally like. This is darkness ultimately being able to not be dark.

Looking over the six lines of *darkness,* there is a great difference between real and false. When the real is used and the false removed, nurturing the one and repelling the other, doing what is appropriate in each case, then the path of yin convergence is consummated.

5. *Waiting*

**In waiting there is sincerity and great development.
It is good to be correct. It is beneficial to cross a
great river.**

EXPLANATION
Waiting means there is awaiting. As to the qualities of the hexagram, above is *water* ☵, a pitfall, below is heaven ☰, which is sound and strong. Being sound and strong and able to manage in the midst of danger, it is therefore called *waiting.*

This hexagram represents nurturing strength, awaiting the proper time; it follows on the previous hexagram *difficulty. Difficulty* is movement and action in danger, restoring the primordial while in the midst of the temporal. Therefore one travels the path of strength and firmness and takes the true yang fallen in *water* ☵ out.* However, when the yang has been trapped in *water* for a long time, it is not possible to get out of danger immediately; one must lead it on gradually, waiting for the proper time to gather it. One cannot presume upon one's strength and set about the task impetuously—that would bring on danger.

People give rise to yin from the culmination of yang. The yang in the center of *heaven* ☰ runs into the palace of *earth* ☷, so that *earth* is filled in and becomes *water* ☵. The yin in the center of *earth* enters the palace of *heaven*, so that *heaven* is hollowed and becomes *fire* ☲. At this point, working with false yin and false yang, the strong becomes weak and the submissive becomes stubborn; the intent is not sincere, and the mind is not right. Being aggressive, one is not aware of danger, and is not receptive enough to notice obstacles; one acts dangerously, hoping for the remote chance of luck, knowing no limits.

Now if you want to get out of danger, it is necessary to know danger. Being able to recognize danger is being able to believe it is dangerous. Once you believe in the danger, you have inner control; being careful and wary, you refine yourself and wait for the proper time. Every act is confined to its proper place, and one is not damaged by external influences. Therefore in the path of *waiting* "there is sincerity and great development," gaining good fortune by being correct.

Having sincerity and great development means believing in danger and being able to cope with it; that correctness is good means that by maintaining correctness you can be free from danger. Once you believe in the danger, and keep to what is right, you fend off danger by strength and firmness, and use danger to nurture strength and firmness, awaiting the time to move forward, and "enter the lair looking for the tiger." Not only are you able to avoid being injured by negative energy, you can also take the true yang fallen into *water* and return it to the palace of *heaven*. This is the reason that "it is beneficial to cross a great river."

A great river is most dangerous; this is the image of *water*, which is something that fells and traps yang. That danger is most great: Believing in the danger, you cross it correctly; when the time is not yet ripe, you nurture strength, and when the time comes you advance strength. Advancing it and nourishing it at the proper times is how you can be in danger yet cope with it, and how you can get out of danger. That strength is beneficial wherever it goes.

■ *First yang:*   Waiting on the outskirts, it is beneficial to employ constancy; then there is no fault.

EXPLANATION
Being strong and firm yet humble, having strength but not using it, being in the world yet able to leave the world, unaffected by fame and profit, is

---

*I.e., one takes the primordial out of the conditioned.

like waiting in the outskirts. However, strong people with a lot of talent and ability usually don't like to be below others; it may happen that there is the fault of not being steadfast in waiting, so here "it is beneficial to employ constancy," for only then can one bring to a conclusion what one has started, and there is not the fault of changing halfway along. This is firm and steadfast waiting.

■ *2 yang:* **Waiting on the sand, there is some criticism, but it turns out well.**

EXPLANATION

As soon as you presume upon strength, there is danger. This is likened to waiting on the sand. The danger of waiting on the sand may not be very horrendous, but the going is apt to get bogged down, making it hard to avoid a bit of criticism and repentance. Once one is able to repent, the overbearing mind is transformed, and while firm one can be flexible. Then one does not go into danger, and danger does not come; it is possible to finish auspiciously. This is waiting which is firm and yet aware of danger.

■ *3 yang:* **Waiting in the mud, bringing on enemies.**

EXPLANATION

When adamant strength rushes ahead, unable to wait for the proper time, eager for achievement, though one originally wanted to go ahead, one suffers a fall behind. This is likened to "waiting in the mud." The strength waiting in mud calls danger on itself where there is no danger, "bringing on enemies." It should be resolved. This is waiting that is firm but unaware of danger.

■ *4 yin:* **Waiting in blood. Leaving the cave.**

EXPLANATION

Being weak and helpless, by nature in danger, is likened to waiting in blood. Also, when the quality of yielding is in a position of weakness, in a realm of darkness, and one is unable to get out on one's own, it is like being in a cave: lucky is the quality of yielding that keeps to what is right, following the virtuous because of having no virtue oneself, depending on others to save oneself; then it is possible to get out of the cave, and ultimately not be injured by negative energy. This is waiting that is yielding and follows firmness.

■ *5 yang:* **Waiting with food and wine, it is good to be correct.**

EXPLANATION

Positive firmness correctly balanced, one has inner control, and uses the artificial to cultivate the real. Though there is danger, it as as if there were no danger. This is like "waiting with food and wine." Food and wine are

things that soothe the mind and fill the belly. Enjoying the path, one forgets about age. Sometimes there is danger, but the path is not dangerous.
Outwardly there is danger, but inwardly it is not dangerous. By correctness everything turns out well. This is waiting that is firm and remains
correct.

■ *Top yin:*   **Entering a cave. Three people come, guests
not in haste: Respect them, and it will turn out well.**

EXPLANATION
At the end of waiting, one should get out of danger, yet one goes into danger; this is like entering a cave. One goes into a cave because of inability to
refine oneself. If you can refine yourself, when you have refined yourself to
the point of having no self, light appears in the emptiness, and spiritual
illumination comes of itself. First going into a cave, after all you come out
of the cave. Therefore "three people come, guests not in haste: Respect
them, and it will turn out well." The guests who are not in haste are the
three yangs of *heaven* ☰ . They are the original immortals who run
away to other houses after birth and become guests; awaiting the time to
bring them back, from one yang you gradually arrive at the pure completeness of the three yangs—then as before they belong to your home. Let
them be the hosts and yourself be the guest. They are to be respected and
not defied. If you respect and obey them, yin and yang merge, the golden
elixir crystallizes, life and health are preserved and completed—this is
great fortune. This is the waiting of cultivating oneself and crystallizing the
elixir.

So in the path of advancing the fire, sometimes you nurture strength,
sometimes you use strength, sometimes you leave strength be, sometimes
you balance strength; each has its time. If you wait for the proper time
to act, always in the appropriate way, strong, cognizant of danger, even
though you "cross a great river," it will be beneficial.

6. *Contention*

**Contention: There is blockage of truth. Caution and
moderation lead to good results, finality leads to
bad results. It is beneficial to see a great person, not
beneficial to cross a great river.**

EXPLANATION
Contention means contention to decide right and wrong. As for the qualities of the hexagram, inside is *water* ☵ , dangerous, and outside is
heaven ☰ , strong. Relying on strength because of danger, and causing

danger by force, both have the meaning of violation of harmony; therefore it is called *contention*.

This hexagram represents the downfall of truth and the contest for victory; it follows on the previous hexagram *darkness*. In *darkness* there is danger, yet one is able to stop, whereby to effect progress of the yin of the acquired temperament. People receive the energy of the temporally conditioned yin and yang and five elements, which forms their body; those who have received excessive yin energy are wily, while those who have received excessive yang energy are impetuous. Those whose yin and yang energies are mixed up are both wily and impetuous.

People are such because of their temperaments. Only great sages can change their temperaments, while lesser people are bound by their temperaments; when they are run afoul of, the poison in their negative side acts, and they get excited—they contest for victory, eager for power, they plot and scheme to deprive others and benefit themselves. All such things that deviate from harmony and lose balance—arguments, battles of wit, issues of right and wrong—are called contention.

People who practice the Tao need to know that the nature of the temperament is most harmful. To practice the principles of the Tao in the context of the events of the world, first erase wile and impetuosity at one stroke. Be inwardly strong but not outwardly aggressive; then there may be danger in the environment but there will be no danger in the heart. In this way one may gradually transmute the temperament, and not remain in the clamor of the realm of right and wrong.

However, as long as one is still in the world, there is still the possibility of being afflicted by troubles and difficulties. Even if you are not wily yourself, people can hurt you by their craft; even if you are not impetuous yourself, people can fool you by what they do. This hurts your self-confidence without reason, and even though you have nothing to be ashamed of, you suffer frustration because of it, and reach an impasse. When matters get to where vindication is necessary, rather than desire justification outwardly, it is better to contend with yourself inwardly. Therefore the text says, "Contention: There is blockage of truth. Caution and moderation lead to good results." If you can be cautious and moderate, wrong thoughts will stop and right thought will arise; the impasse can be penetrated, and wile can be changed, victory-seeking can be eliminated.

Otherwise, if you cannot be cautious and moderate, you will lose out in an important matter because of a little anger; impetuosity will appear outwardly while guile will arise inwardly. Without having won others, you will have already hurt yourself. If you are not careful in the beginning, the end will surely be bad.

However, there are also situations where caution, moderation, and self-struggle do not clear the matter up, and it is necessary to appeal to another, depending on someone to distinguish right and wrong. To distinguish right and wrong it is beneficial to see a great person. If you do not see a great person, you will not be helped. A great person is one who corrects both self and others, who is able to restrain people's excesses and encourage their virtues, able to solve people's doubts and develop their intelligence. It is most beneficial to see such a person: Otherwise, being unable to exercise caution and moderation so as to change your own temperament, and also unable to see a great person to expand your perception, relying on your own craft alone, contesting for victory, eager for power, overthrowing truth and following falsehood, contending over what should not be contended about, you will call disaster on yourself. Therefore, it is "not beneficial to cross a great river." By caution and moderation you can see a great person; not being cautious or moderate is "crossing a great river." Caution and moderation lead to good results; being incautious and immoderate lead to bad results. Should not those who practice the Tao contend with themselves to begin with?

■ *First yin:*   One does not persist forever in an affair.
There will be a little criticism, but it will turn out well.

EXPLANATION
Being flexible and deferential, having something to contend about but having no contentiousness in the mind, one therefore does not persist forever in one's affair. However, once involved in a matter of contention, it is necessary to clarify the issue; though there is a little criticism, ultimately it does not turn into a contest, and finally it is possible to conclude the matter well. This is being flexible and not contentious.

■ *2 yang:*   Not pressing one's contention, one returns
home to escape: If there are three hundred families in
one's domain, there will be no trouble.

EXPLANATION
When the adversary is on a par, one cannot win, so one does not contend, but returns home to escape. If there are three hundred families in your domain, you can thereby escape the barbs of opponents; though there is trouble, it cannot reach you. This is being strong but not contending.

■ *3 yin:*   Living on past virtues, rectitude in danger will
turn out well. If working in government, do not do
anything.

EXPLANATION
Being weak and not daring to contend to begin with, one therefore lives on past virtues. Living on past virtues, keeping to yourself in danger, being careful and prudent, not causing contention and having no contention yourself, ultimately you can finish well. However, once in the midst of contention, even if you don't contend, others will contend; then you should rely on the high-minded and wise to distinguish right and wrong. When the matter is clear, then stop. Therefore in this case if you are involved in government, you do not do anything on your own initiative. This is the weak being able to follow the strong and not producing contention.

■ *4 yang:*   Not pressing one's contention, one abides by the decree of fate: Changing to rest in rectitude leads to good fortune.

EXPLANATION

When the adamant meet the adamant, an argument is sure to start; but if you can deal with it flexibly, you do not press your suit and so do not contend. Changing the nature of your temperament to revert to the nature of celestial decree, from not resting in rectitude you change to resting in rectitude; then even though you do not seek good fortune, good fortune will follow you. This is being adamant yet reversing oneself and not pressing one's suit.

■ *5 yang:*   Contend; it will be very auspicious.

EXPLANATION

Firm strength balanced and correctly oriented, one can subdue others by virtue, and is able to change all who are wily and fond of power so that they ultimately do not contend. This is why it is very auspicious to contend in this case, where you correct yourself and others and are able to cause there to be no contention.

■ *Top yang:*   Even if one is given a badge of honor, it will be taken away thrice before the day is out.

EXPLANATION

Contesting for victory, eager for power, not knowing how to reverse yourself, when you reach the end of contention, even though you have gained victory outwardly, the inward reality is that you have lost in terms of worth of character. Even if you are given a token of honor, it will be taken away thrice before the day is out. To receive a gift once and be stripped of it thrice means that you have gained little from others and lost much from yourself. This is being selfish and inconsiderate of others, and so after all losing one's suit.

So not to contend is auspicious, while contention is inauspicious. If you are not cautious in the beginning, you will surely fail in the end. This is why there should be no contention.

7. *The Army*

For the leader of the army to be right, a mature person is good; then there is no error.

EXPLANATION

The army is a group. This has the meaning of one person leading a group. The qualities of the hexagram are *earth* ☷ ☷ above, submissive, and *water* ☵ below, dangerous: Following obediently in danger, it is therefore called *the army*. This hexagram represents using yang to drive back yin; it follows on the previous hexagram *waiting*. *Waiting* is advancing yang in accord with the time, and advancing yang is the way to drive yin back.

The method of repelling yin is to get rid of wrong by means of right, to destroy falsehood by truth, like righteousness in the leader of an army. The "leader of the army" is the way of punishment and execution; it requires both firmness and flexibility, both humanity and justice, command of authority and ability to change, in order to be effective. Otherwise, if one can be firm but not flexible, or if one is only humane and does not know how to apply justice, or if one is only dutiful and does not know how to act humanely, none of this is right, and without correctness good fortune cannot be attained—instead one will provoke censure.

Only mature and developed people understand good and bad, distinguish wrong from right, know what bodes well and what bodes ill, perceive when to hurry and when to relax, are not confined to either firmness or flexibility, apply both humanity and justice together, are able to obey in danger and by obedience neutralize danger, use the temporal to restore the primordial, use the primordial to transmute the temporal, not only do not let yin trap yang, but even get all yin to follow yang—this is the path of good fortune without error.

If people are immature, their perception of truth is not clear. They do not distinguish wrong from right, and so enter aberrated detours. They set out impulsively and not only are unable to make yin retreat, they even accentuate yin. They are sure to bring on error; how can they effect good results and achieve the Tao?

When people have not yet lost the primordial, this is pure natural reality. It is like when the nation is at peace—even if there are intelligent knights and good generals, there is no need for them. Then when people get mixed up in acquired conditioning, their senses trouble them and their emotions run wild. It is like when there is trouble in the land, with rebels causing disturbance; if there is no way of rooting them out by punishment and execution, it is impossible to restore peace in perilous times.

Therefore the method of striving in spiritual alchemy is to burn away all the pollution of acquired conditioning, and not let the slightest flaw remain in the heart, so that one may eventually reexperience original completeness. This is why the path of direction is valued.

■ *First yin:* The army is to go forth in an orderly manner: Otherwise, even good turns out bad.

EXPLANATION

In the beginning of direction, it is necessary to know the stages of the firing process, the rules of advance and withdrawal, to progress according to the proper order and act in accord with the appropriate method; if one is able to be careful in the beginning, one will naturally be victorious in the end. This is like an army going forth in an orderly manner. If one rushes to act without understanding the firing process, that is like an unruly army, which is disastrous regardless of whether its intentions are good or bad. In causing yin to retreat, it is important to understand the process.

■ *2 yang:* At the center of the army, good fortune, no error; the king gives orders thrice.

EXPLANATION

With flexibility in the midst of firmness, in command of both advance and withdrawal, changing effectively according to the time, one is not only not harmed by negative energy, but is also able to transmute all negativities and restore them to their proper place. This is like gaining good fortune at the center of the army, and being able to be free from error. This good fortune in the middle of the army relates to the effort of adjustment of the external furnace, and also requires the mind, as leader, to be sincere and single-minded, without fragmentation; only when inside and outside assist each other is it possible to be completely fortunate, without error. This is also like a king giving orders thrice; if the king trusts the ministers and the ministers respond to the king, all can accomplish their tasks. So causing yin to retreat requires mutual assistance of inside and outside.

■ *3 yin:* The army has casualties; bad luck.

EXPLANATION

If one acts ignorantly on one's own without knowing the method of advance and withdrawal of the firing process, courting danger on the chance of striking it lucky, though one seeks long life one instead hastens death. This is the calamity of casualties. This represents the adventurers who do not know how to make yin withdraw.

■ *4 yin:* If the army retreats and camps, there is no error.

EXPLANATION

Being flexible and yielding, knowing one does not have the science of building life, one does not dare to pretend or act arbitrarily, but keeps to one's place. This is like an army retreating and camping; though one cannot effect good, one can yet avoid error in this way. This represents those who cannot repel negativity and yet are able to keep to what is proper.

■ *5 yin:* There are animals in the fields—it is beneficial
to catch them; there will be no blame. A mature
person is to lead the army; if it is an immature person,
there will be casualties, for even if he is righteous the
outlook is bad.

EXPLANATION

Flexible receptivity in balance, one opens the mind and manages oneself,
responding appropriately to whatever comes, causing external influences
to dissolve of themselves. This is like when there are animals in the fields it
is beneficial to catch them. However, reason convinces superior people,
while law restrains petty people: It is necessary to have both firmness and
flexibility to manage affairs successfully. If one is only flexible, without
firmness, that can cause failure. A "mature person leading the army"
means flexibility balanced by firmness can accomplish affairs; "if it is an
immature person, there will be casualties" means being only flexible without firmness can ruin affairs. This means to cause yin to retreat requires
firmness and flexibility to balance and equalize each other.

■ *Top yin:* The great leader has orders, to establish states
and families; do not employ petty people.

EXPLANATION

At the end of direction of the army, acquired energy has all been sublimated; the basis stable, the country peaceful, the mental ruler at peace,
there is no more need for punishment and execution. Then when external
ills have been removed and the master sits peacefully in the center, it is
possible to discern subtleties, keeping even a single thought of good and
getting rid of even a single bad thought, rewarding those of meritorious
achievement and chastising those of no merit. This is also like a great
leader with orders to establish states and families, for which petty people
should not be employed. It is necessary to root out the seeds of ages of
vicious circles before one is done. This means making negativity withdraw
requires inward and outward purity and calm.

The six lines each have a path of repulsing yin, but they are not equal in
terms of boding good or ill. Only the yang in the second place has both
firmness and flexibility, masters authority yet is capable of change, and
thereby is able to transmute negativities and not be injured by negativities.
Great is the accomplishment of striving.

8. Accord

Accord is auspicious. Investigating and ascertaining, if the basis is always right, there is no error: Then the uneasy will come; but the dilatory are unfortunate.

EXPLANATION
Accord has the meaning of association with one another and learning from one another. In the body of the hexagram, one yang dwells in the place of honor, while the five yins above and below all follow it accordingly. Also, the quality of the hexagram is obedience by which to get through danger; therefore it is called *accord*.

This hexagram, representing yin following yang, follows on the previous hexagram *contention*. In *contention*, yin does not obey yang, but instead overthrows yang; yin and yang are at odds, the five elements injure each other, harming their reality, therefore ending in calamity. If you know this is wrong and cultivate the reverse, yin does not overthrow yang but submits to yang; yin and yang harmonize, the five elements are one energy, essence is stable and life is solid. This is the path of making the wrong accord with the right, making the artificial accord with the real.

What is auspicious about accord is that it is good to accord with what is right and what is real, and nothing is more important than to accord with the basis of true reality. The basis here is the primordial positive energy, trapped in the palace of *water* ☵. This energy is produced by heaven, and so is called the vitality of the true one, the water of the true one, and the energy of the true one. This is the basic energy that produces things.

In human beings, this energy is basic humanity, which is the reality in which yin and yang are united. But this basic energy, falling into yin, is covered up by acquired conditioning. It is easy to lose and hard to find; if you are not utterly empty and calmly attentive, with your mind steadfast and your will firm, you cannot recover it. That is why one can only be free from error if one investigates and ascertains the basis that is always right.

If one is always correct, under that correctness rises the basic energy, and once the basic energy is restored, yin energy submits to it; then this is the original flawless undamaged integral pattern of nature, which is impeccable, the complete original basis. The classic *The Way and Its Power* says, "Effecting utter emptiness, maintaining calm attention, as myriad things act in concert, I thereby watch the return." The *Spring Suffusing the Garden* says, "The seven-times restored elixir is in people—first you should refine the mind and await the time."

The way to be always correct is to become empty and keep quiet, to refine the mind. If you do not refine the mind thoroughly, the true yin within yourself will not become manifest; if you do not become thoroughly empty and quiet, the external true yang will not come.

If you want to conquer feeling, first conquer essence; "then the uneasy will come." This is whereby to refine the mind and wait for the time, to seek restoration. In the word *uneasy* are various processes, like adjustment according to the time, and warding off danger. This explains the meaning of "always right."

If I am uneasy and the other then comes, this is what is referred to by the saying "If you want to get, first you must give." First giving means following the other's wish, making oneself accord with the other, thereby to get the other's pleasure. Afterward getting means that sincerity can move people; others come and accord with oneself, whereby one can take their living energy.

When before and after are clear, and other people and oneself are all taken care of, then the restored elixir can be crystallized. Otherwise, if one cannot first give, and idly imagines others will come, what should be first is put after, and what should be after is put first, reversing the accord. This is called acquired conditioning. As it is said, if ordinary people want to seek heaven, when they seek it they need worldly goods; if they give little and withhold much, the spirits and immortals will not come, and they are sure to have bad luck. How can they effect good fortune and realize the Tao?

- *First yin:*   **When there is truthfulness, accord is impeccable. When there is truthfulness filling a plain vessel, ultimately there will come to be other blessings.**

EXPLANATION

Being humble, using flexibility to accord with the firm, is accord in which there is sincerity and truthfulness, so one can be without error. This is because when there is sincere truthfulness in accord, one can empty the mind, and if one can empty the mind one can fill the belly. Then not only is there truthfulness without error, but also there is truthfulness filling an unadorned vessel, ultimately bringing on other blessings; one will surely thereby accord with the ultimate good. This represents sincere and truthful accord turning out well.

- *2 yin:*   **Accord coming from within is correct and bodes well.**

EXPLANATION

Here flexible receptivity is central; before according outwardly, one first accords inwardly. This is accord coming from within. Accord from within is refining oneself and mastering the mind, gathering medicine (vital energy) according to the time, desiring to receive from the other, not losing oneself. This is internal accord being correct.

- *3 yin:*   **Accord with the wrong people.**

EXPLANATION

When one is oneself ignorant and foolish and also associates with ignorant and foolish people, this is accord with the wrong people. Accord with the wrong people has no benefit and is harmful. What is the value of accord then? This represents incorrectness of outer accord.

■ *4 yin:*   Accord with one outside is right
and bodes well.

EXPLANATION
Flexibly according with the firm, seeing the wise and wanting to be like them, even the ignorant will become illumined, even the weak will become strong. This is external accord being correct.

■ *5 yang:*   Manifesting accord. The king uses three
chasers and loses the game ahead. The citizens are
not admonished. Auspicious.

EXPLANATION
Firm strength in proper balance, positive energy is replete and negative energy spontaneously converts. This is manifest accord. It is not forced, but comes about naturally. It is like a king chasing game, leaving one of four sides open, using three chasers, losing the game ahead. Using three chasers means taking the real, taking in the receptive; losing the game ahead means abandoning the false, letting the rebellious go. Taking the real and abandoning the false, the real comes and the false vanishes. Taking in the receptive and letting the rebellious go, the receptive attain and the rebellious disappear. When the practice of Tao gets to where the real and false are both transmuted and opposition and submission both return to the basis, then the heart is profoundly calm, always tranquil, ultimately good with no evil. Confused thoughts do not arise; it is like the citizenry spontaneously being civilized without being admonished. This is the accord of inside and outside as one energy.

■ *Top yin:*   Accord without a leader bodes ill.

EXPLANATION
Being ignorant yet acting arbitrarily on one's own, one is incapable of inner accord and also incapable of outer accord. Relying on one's own yin alone, acting as one pleases, after all one will never get out. This is accord without leadership. Accord without leadership is a waste of one's life; one will grow old without accomplishment, bringing about one's own downfall. This is someone who from start to finish does not know how to accord with people.

The barriers of practice of reality involves accord with those imbued with the Tao on the part of those lacking in the Tao, accord with those imbued with virtue on the part of those lacking in virtue. It all requires the true aspiration of the real mind, applying effort with every step, so that the power of the Tao will eventually be correctly centered and balanced. When the power of Tao is correctly centered and balanced, the golden elixir enters the mouth and transforms all negativities. It is like a cat catching a mouse.

When gathering medicine, it is necessary to use the bellows; when refining oneself, true lead is needed. If you carry out the path of accord without knowing the fundamental, without knowing the basis which is always right, acting arbitrarily, even if you don't fall into accord with the wrong people you will wind up in accord without leadership, causing error and suffering misfortune—this is the way it will inevitably turn out. So students should indeed approach true teachers.

9.   *Nurturance by the Small*

Nurturance by the small is developmental. Dense clouds do not rain, proceeding from one's own western province.

EXPLANATION

Nurturance by the small is making the small one's nourishment. As for the qualities of the hexagram, above is *wind* ☴, submissive, below is *heaven* ☰, strong: Being strong, yet acting submissively, the submissiveness subdues the strength, and strength cannot act on its own. Therefore it is called *nurturance by the small,* which also means being held back by the small.

This hexagram represents nurturing the great by the small; it follows on the previous hexagram *army.* The path of the army is using yang to repel yin, for which it is important to first nourish the yang. When one is able to nourish the yang, then one keeps to oneself by the small, full but not overflowing, firm but not aggressive, having yet appearing not to have, full yet seeming empty. The heart grows daily humbler, while the virtue grows daily higher. One can thereby gradually get to the realm of sages. This is why nurturance by the small is developmental.

However, though nurturance by the small is developmental, if the smallness is excessive, this is doing things weakly, so that the path of firmness recedes from its proper place, the will is not robust, and one becomes feeble and ineffective: With the nurturance small, the development is small, so that the action is not far-reaching, and the great Tao is therefore hard to attain. This is like "dense clouds not raining, proceeding from one's own western province." Yin energy coalesces as clouds, yang energy arrives as rain: As long as clouds do not rain, the yin energy is prevalent while the yang energy is weak, and the living potential is on the verge of cessation; that which is near, in oneself, is not even taken care of, so how could one seek that which is afar, in the other? When one small empty voidness enters into quietism, how can one restore one's celestial original state? So one must know the process of nurturance by the small.

■ *First yang:*   Returning by the path—how could that be blameworthy? It bodes well.

EXPLANATION
Being strong yet remaining humble, concealing one's light and nurturing it in obscurity, embracing the Tao and keeping settled, not injuring inner reality by outward artificiality, is to be able to return by way of the path. Being able to return by the path, though the nurturance is small, one can gain its nourishment, and strong energy grows day by day; not only is it blameless, it brings good fortune. This is the nurturance of being great yet being humble and appearing small.

■ *2 yang:*   Leading back bodes well.

EXPLANATION
Strength acting with flexibility, being sharp yet fond of learning, unashamed to humble oneself to inquire, associating with superior people, benefiting each other, understanding what is good and returning to the origin, is "leading back." The nurturance of leading back is outwardly increasing in emptiness while inwardly increasing in fulfillment; small, yet gaining good results. This is the nurturance of being great yet knowing the small.

■ *3 yang:*   The wheels are detached from the cart; husband and wife look away from each other.

EXPLANATION
When strength acts on its own and one is self-centered and inconsiderate of others, this turns away from harmony and loses balance, sure to end in ruination of strength. This is like the wheels being detached from a cart, so the cart cannot move. It is also like husband and wife averting their eyes from each other, so the family cannot flourish. This is the nurturance of being great and not knowing the small.

■ *4 yin:*   If there is truthfulness, blood goes and fear leaves, and there is no fault.

EXPLANATION
If one has no ability and is in the midst of those with ability, one will surely err with the result of sustaining bloody injury. But to be weak and yet find what is right, having confidence in one's own pure yang alone, is most injurious. Still, if one can borrow others' positive energy, be cautious and diligent, refine oneself and control the mind, then one can escape the harm of what originally would be harmful, and can wind up without fault where originally there would be fault. This is the nurturance of being small yet knowing the great.

■ *5 yang:* There is truthfulness in companionship; prosperity is shared with the neighbor.

EXPLANATION

The strength of yang proceeds docilely into the center of balance; truth is in the center, yin and yang are merged, the gold elixir crystallizes. This is having truthfulness in companionship. With truthfulness in companionship, the basis is stable, the country is peaceful, the basis of life is firm; one should hasten to transmute the nature of the temperament to return it to the essence of real knowledge. This is like sharing prosperity with the neighbor. This is the nurturance of being small yet containing the great.

■ *Top yang:* It has rained and settled. Esteeming virtue, putting the wife on top, though she be chaste there is danger. The moon is almost full; it bodes ill for the superior person to go on an expedition.

EXPLANATION

Firmness is in the position of flexibility at the end of nurturance by the small. This is like when it has rained and settled. Rain is that whereby extreme dryness is ended; once it has rained, the yang energy is settled and does not rise too high. Once it is settled, the yang energy is harmonious and there is no need for rain. The reason cultivation of the Tao uses yin is just to control the vehemence of artificial yang. Once artificial yang has ceased, real yang should advance. The end of nurturance by the small is precisely the time for nurturance by the great; if one winds up small and cannot be great, yin then injures yang. This is like esteeming virtue and putting the wife on top, so the woman controls the authority. It is also like the moon nearing full, after which the light will gradually wane. If noble people who cultivate the Tao only know the small and do not know the great, they may thereby maintain quietude in solitary tranquility, without action or striving, but if they try to thereby fulfill their nature and reach their destiny, to travel the Path to its further reaches, they will only call misfortune upon themselves. This is the nurturance of ending up small and not knowing the great.

As we observe nurturance as represented in the six lines, though nurturance by the small basically is developmental, it is all a matter of how a person is small. If the smallness is appropriate, then one can nurture greatness by smallness and bring about good results. If the smallness is inappropriate, then one will damage greatness by smallness and bring on calamity. Students should first thoroughly investigate the process within smallness.

10. *Treading*

Even when they tread on a tiger's tail, it doesn't bite people. This is developmental.

EXPLANATION

Treading means forward progress. As for the qualities of the hexagram, above is *heaven* ☰, strong, and below is *lake* ☱, joyous. Yin is rejoicing in yang; with the advance of one yin, the hexagram will change into pure yang. Representing this, it is therefore called *treading*.

This hexagram symbolizes progression of yang and prevention of danger; it follows on the preceding hexagram *accord*. In *accord*, yin follows yang. But if you want yin to follow, it is necessary first to advance yang. When the progression of yang reaches proper balance, yin naturally follows it. This is the appropriate priority of the path of advancing yang.

The true yang in people is inherent and need not be sought from another. When it mixes with acquired conditioning, true feeling is obscured and arbitrary feelings arise; then true yang runs away outside. This is likened to a tiger running off and staying elsewhere as a member of another house; though it is in another house, originally the tiger is one's own. It is just that people are not willing to call it back.

The way of calling it back is not sought in *heaven*, or *earth*, or *fire*, or *water*, but only in *lake*. *Lake*, as the youngest daughter,* travels the path of receptive submission in place of mother *earth*, and is able to revert to yang by the culmination of yin. Its nature is harmonious and joyous. Being harmonious, it can relax; being joyous it can trust. Being relaxed, it can go gradually; trusting, it can endure long. Able to relax and trust, powerful practice unrelenting, it is thereby possible to advance to the stage of indestructible firmness and strength, to again see the original face of heaven, and not be injured by false yin and false yang. This is likened to treading on a tiger's tail without its biting people, and having a way of development and growth.

A tiger is something that bites people; it is most dangerous to tread on it. If one can tread with harmony and joyfulness, without excessive ferocity, it is like treading on a tiger's tail. If one is careful, as if treading on a tiger's tail, looking ahead and behind, striking a balance without obsession or indifference, proceeding gradually in an orderly manner, forestalling danger, aware of perils, carrying out the firing process without error, then the yin can be transmuted into yang, and the yang can be restored to purity. Not only is one not bitten by the tiger—one can even take over the living energy in its killing, and preserve life and being whole. This path of

---

*In the so-called temporal arrangement of the trigrams, the trigrams are associated with members of a family: *heaven* is father, *earth* is mother, *thunder* is eldest son, *wind* is eldest daughter, *water* is middle son, *fire* is middle daughter, *mountain* is youngest son, and *lake* is youngest daughter.

development and achievement without obstruction or hindrance through advancement of yang, treading strongly with harmony and joy, is of great benefit.

■ *First yang:*   **Treading plainly, going without fault.**

EXPLANATION
Those with strength of mind and robust energy, who are plain and sincere in treading the Path, are able to tread it with confidence in their steps. If they proceed in this way, they will surely progress to where there is no fault. This is treading with firmness of purpose.

■ *2 yang:*   **Treading the path evenly, the aloof person is upright and fortunate.**

EXPLANATION
With happiness in balance, there is naturally true joy, and one is not attracted to artificial enjoyment. No external things can move one, so one therefore treads the path evenly. Treading that is even is without greed, without craving; the mind is at peace, the spirit tranquil. Only the aloof person who consistently remains upright can tread the path happily, forgetful of the years.

■ *3 yin:*   **Able to see with a squint, able to walk with a limp. When they tread on the tiger's tail, it bites people. Inauspicious. A soldier becomes a ruler.**

EXPLANATION
If one goes on the Path impetuously, acting on one's own in ignorance, not knowing the medicinal substances, not understanding the firing process, thinking ignorance to be knowledge, thinking incapacity to be ability, that is like seeing with a squint, walking with a limp—treading on the tiger's tail, it will bite; one calls misfortune on oneself. This is also like a soldier becoming a ruler, bringing on disaster. This is treading the Path ignorantly on one's own.

■ *4 yang:*   **Treading on the tail of a tiger, with caution it will turn out well.**

EXPLANATION
Being firm but not impetuous, truthfully clear-minded, flexible in action, forestalling danger, aware of perils, is like treading on a tiger's tail with caution, wary and careful. Not only can the tiger not bite; one will eventually tread on the ground of pure yang and attain felicity. This is treading the Path with both firmness and flexibility.

■ *5 yang:* Treading decisively. Even if one is upright, there is danger.

EXPLANATION

With strength in proper balance, following one's heart's desire without exceeding what is appropriate, treading the Path decisively, without getting into difficulty—still when the treading of the Path reaches central balance and the gold elixir has formed, it is necessary to be upright and undivided, to master oneself in danger, so that one can avoid the problem of losing what has been gained. This is treading the Path in which there is no one but oneself.

■ *Top yang:* Observing the treading, considering what is felicitous, the return is auspicious.

EXPLANATION

Here yang is in the position of flexibility: Observing the firing process trodden, considering the balance of gravity and energy in the medicinal substances, proceeding in an orderly manner, completing the cycle from start to finish, completing the beginning by the end, one aims to reach the merging of yin and yang in complete original wholeness. This is treading the Path consummating the beginning and completing the end.

So the path of advancing yang requires flexibility within firmness and firmness within flexibility. It is important that firmness and flexibility balance each other, and one neither rushes nor lags, but is harmonious, joyous, equanimous, and serene.

11. *Tranquility*

The small goes, the great comes. This is auspicious and developmental.

EXPLANATION

Tranquility means going through in harmony. As for the qualities of the hexagram, above is *earth* ☷, submissive, and below is *heaven* ☰, strong: Yang is strong inside, yin is submissive outside. Strength and submission unified, yin and yang correspond; it therefore is called *tranquility*.

This hexagram represents the mixing of yin and yang; it follows on the previous hexagram *nurturance by the small.* In *nurturance by the small,* one yin nurtures five yangs; yin energy is in charge, and yang energy is not active. Being small in nurturance and unable to be great in nurturance, the activity cannot succeed; the way to successful activity requires that great and small be unharmed, that yin and yang balance each other, yin obeying yang, yang governing yin.

Only when yin and yang are harmoniously combined is it possible to accomplish things. Therefore the way of *tranquility* is that the small goes and the great comes; it is auspicious and developmental. The small is yin and the great is yang: "The small goes" means yin submits, "the great comes" means yang is strong. With yang strong on the inside and yin submissive on the outside, the primordial gradually returns and acquired conditioning gradually melts away; thereby it is possible to reach the realm of pure yang with no yin. It is a matter of course then to be fortunate in action, and for activity to develop.

However, in the path of bringing about tranquility, there is a firing process, there is a course of work. If advancing and withdrawing are done with the proper timing, and one is strong yet acts docilely, using docility to nurture strength, one can bring about tranquility and preserve it, understanding essence through understanding life, attaining nonstriving through striving, completing the great Way. Of this one can be sure.

■ *First yang:*   When pulling out a reed by the roots, other reeds come with it. It is auspicious to go forth.

EXPLANATION
When one yang subtly arises, all the yangs have motivation. This is like pulling out the connected root of a reed, bringing other reeds with it. One who is going to bring about tranquility sets about cultivation on the appearance of this first yang, gradually gathering and refining positive energy, from subtle to manifest, so there is no yang that is not strong and no yin that is not submissive. This is why it says it is auspicious to go forth. This is firmly taking advantage of the right time to bring about tranquility.

■ *2 yang:*   Accepting the uncultivated, actively crossing rivers, not missing the remote, partisanship disappears, and one accords with balanced action.

EXPLANATION
Firm strength correctly balanced, one is able to adapt to changes, and therefore accepts the uncultivated, actively crosses rivers, does not miss the remote, and ends partisanship. Accepting the uncultivated means being broadminded and tolerant, applying flexibility. Crossing rivers means being courageous, applying firmness. Not missing the remote means calmly observing, quietly examining, the consummation of flexibility. Ending partiality means stopping falsehood and sustaining truth, the consummation of firmness. Having flexibility within firmness, firmness within flexibility, applying both gentle and intense forms of cultivation as appropriate, one can gain accord with balanced action. This is firmness and flexibility balancing each other to bring about tranquility.

■ *3 yang:*   There is no levelness without incline, no going without returning. If one is upright in difficulty,

there will be no fault. One should not grieve over one's
sincerity; there will be prosperity in sustenance.

EXPLANATION
The three yangs full, as yang culminates it must shift to yin; when tranquility ends there must be misfortune. This is like there being no levelness
without incline, no going without return. At this time it is mandatory to
know when to advance and when to withdraw. If one remains upright in
difficulty, forestalling danger, wary of perils, only then can one be free
from the fault of losing what has been gained. Once free from that fault,
accomplishment is achieved in society, and one's fame resounds to the
heavens; also one is sustained by natural prosperity and enjoys life without end—what grief is there? This is preserving tranquility by remaining
upright at the culmination of strength.

- *4 yin:*   Unsettled, one is not rich, along with the
neighbors, being loyal without admonition.

EXPLANATION
When yang culminates and mixes with yin, one cannot forestall danger;
one yin subtly arises, and all the yins stir. This is like being unsettled, not
being rich, along with the neighbors, joining them loyally without needing to be admonished; the gold elixir, once gained, is again lost. This is
losing tranquility by softness injuring firmness.

- *5 yin:*   The emperor marries off his younger sister,
whereby there is good fortune; this is very auspicious.

EXPLANATION
When properly tranquil, one uses yin to nurture yang, so yang energy solidifies. This is likened to an emperor marrying off his younger sister, extending good fortune to his minister, who marries her. Yin loves yang and
yang loves yin; yin and yang share the same energy, so that there is spontaneously a natural true fire glowing forever in the furnace. Although
tranquility is already a fact, yet one does not lose the fortune of beginning
tranquility. This is completing tranquility by using flexibility to nurture
firmness.

- *Top yin:*   The castle walls crumble back into dry moats.
Don't use the army. Giving orders in one's own
domain, even if right, there will be regret.

EXPLANATION
At the end of tranquility, the culmination of submission, if you just know
the submission of tranquility and not the opposition of tranquility, by not
preventing it early on you will surely fail in the end. This is like castle walls
crumbling back into the dry moats. At this time good things are already

gone, and cannot be used for strength, so the text says "don't use the army"; misfortunes are at hand, and regret does no good, so it says "giving orders in one's own domain, even if right, there will be regret." This is being weak and not knowing to safeguard tranquility early on.

So there is a time to bring about tranquility, and a time to preserve tranquility; striving and nonstriving both have their methods. Acting according to the time, based on the proper method, being strong where appropriate, being docile where appropriate, by strength one effects tranquility and by docility one preserves tranquility. If one is able to effect and preserve tranquility, why worry that one will not be fortunate and not develop, and not accomplish the Path?

12. *Obstruction*

Obstruction's denial of humanity does not make the superior person's rectitude beneficial. The great goes and the small comes.

EXPLANATION
Obstruction means blockage. As for the qualities of the hexagram, inside is *earth* ☷, submissive, and outside is *heaven* ☰, strong: Submitting to one's desires, outwardly acting adamant, negative energy is in charge, while positive energy retreats; because strength and receptivity are separated, it is called *obstruction*.

This hexagram represents yin and yang not joining; it follows on the previous hexagram *treading*. *Treading* is promoting strength with harmony and joyfulness, causing yin and yang to join, so strength and receptivity are united. In general, when yin and yang do not combine, true yin changes into false yin and true yang changes into false yang; the primordial is lost and false energy enters; false energy enters and true energy recedes. That is why "obstruction's denial of humanity does not make the superior person's rectitude beneficial." "Denial of humanity" is false energy, the "superior person" is true energy. When the primordial has not been injured and true yang is within, the single mass of true energy is the "superior person." When the primordial has been lost, and the true yang is scattered externally, whatever the body has is false energy.

To follow that conditioned yin, indulging in emotions and giving free rein to desires, without any limit, is "denying humanity." That denying humanity is not beneficial to the superior person means that false energy is not beneficial to true energy. At this time the practitioner of the Tao should get rid of intellectualism and gather the energy and spirit within to preserve true yang. Particularly at this disadvantageous time, just when the great goes and the small comes, when negative energy does things, if one does not know how to forestall danger, one will increasingly produce obstruction, and it will be very disadvantageous.

■ *First yin:* **Pulling out the roots of a reed takes others with it. It is good and developmental to be correct.**

EXPLANATION

When one yin subtly arises, the root of obstruction is already established, and the potential of obstruction will surely emerge; this is likened to pulling out a reed by the roots, taking others with it. At this point, when yin energy has just arisen and yang energy is not yet injured, if one can immediately effect balance, it is possible to change a state of obstruction into one of tranquility. In general, when one forestalls obstruction by being correct, obstruction does not occur, and one attains a good state in reason and growth in action. This is forestalling yin before obstruction takes place.

■ *2 yin:* **Embracing servility, the petty person is lucky; for the great person, obstruction is developmental.**

EXPLANATION

When the yin energy gradually advances, the killing energy about to burst forth, and one is externally a superior person but inwardly a petty person, this is called embracing servility. Though the yin of embracing servility has not yet reached the point where it harms yang, it already has momentum toward harming yang. For a petty person, false energy acting obediently is good luck, while for a superior person, the inability of true energy to get through is obstruction. For practitioners of the Tao, if they are virtuous in danger and avoid difficulty, not being deluded by yin energy, they can find a way of development even in obstruction. This is guarding against yin just as obstruction takes place.

■ *3 yin:* **Hiding shame.**

EXPLANATION

When yin energy clusters, and one follows one's desires, taking the false for the real and considering that good strategy, really concealing shame and unaware of one's disgrace, this is following yin and not knowing there is obstruction.

■ *4 yang:* **If there is an order, there is no fault. The companions attain felicity.**

EXPLANATION

At the point where yin culminates and mixes with yang, within obstruction is concealed tranquility, and the living potential also appears. The original order is again in force. The quality of strength in people is the innate mind that is the natural order, the celestial command. This mind is inherently complete in everyone, no more in sages and no less in ordinary people. But when it is constrained by temperament and covered by human desires, one takes pain for pleasure and will not turn back. If people will turn back, natural goodness will appear; one good can dissolve a hundred evils, and one can immediately climb up on the shore of the Tao. Then those with fault can arrive at impeccability. Even if people are ordinary and mundane, if they know and practice this path, calamity turns into fortune, and companions attain felicity. This is ability to not obstruct yang when it arises.

■ *5 yang:* **Ending obstruction, great people are fortunate, but tie themselves to a tree trunk lest they go to ruin.**

EXPLANATION
When firm strength is properly balanced and one preserves the mind of Tao and gets rid of the human mentality, even without seeking the end of obstruction it ends of itself. That ending is because of ability to forestall obstruction in a time of tranquility. Abiding inside three yangs is the time of tranquility proper. Tying oneself to the trunk of a tree for fear of going to ruin means forestalling ruination before it happens, to think of unrest in times of tranquility. Then how can negative energy penetrate? This is warding off yin in the time of tranquility.

■ *Top yang:* **Overturning obstruction: First there is obstruction, afterward joy.**

EXPLANATION
At the end of obstruction, negative energy should recede and positive energy should advance; this is precisely the time to overthrow obstruction. Practitioners of Tao take advantage of this opportunity so that the celestial and the human are activated together, suppressing yin and supporting yang; first there is obstruction, afterward there is joy. It is as easy as turning over the palm of the hand. This is advancing yang at the end of obstruction.

So that which cannot bring about tranquility without obstruction is the repetitious path of conditioning; that which can effect tranquility in the midst of obstruction is the achievement of the primordial in reversing the flow of events. But it is necessary to recognize the medicinal substances and know the firing process clearly, advancing and withdrawing according to the time without rushing ahead or lagging behind.

13. Sameness with People

Sameness with people in the wilderness is developmental. It is beneficial to cross great rivers. It is beneficial for a superior person to be upright.

EXPLANATION

Sameness with people means other people and oneself are as one. As for the qualities of the hexagram, above is *heaven* ☰, strong, and below is *fire* ☲, luminous: Employing strength with illumination, making illumination effective by strength, being truthful within and adept without, developing oneself and others as well, it is therefore called *sameness with people.*

This hexagram represents mixing in with the ordinary world, concealing one's illumination, skillfully assimilating to others. It follows on the previous hexagram *tranquility.* In *tranquility,* yin and yang match each other, strength and receptivity are united. When practitioners of Tao reach the point where yin and yang are balanced, strength and receptivity are unified, and the spiritual embryo is formed, then they can merge with the ordinary world, hiding their illumination, to cultivate advanced practice.

But to mix with the ordinary world, concealing one's own light, requires great impartiality and impersonality. This is a matter of being selfless. If there is no self, there are no others. When there is no self or others, the sense of others and self leaves; when the sense of others and self leaves, then others are oneself and oneself is identified with others. This is like the sky's covering everything, like the sun's shining everywhere. One can thus return others and self to emptiness, being like others in the wilderness, as it were, this assimilation being unfailingly developmental. The wilderness is a vastness where there are no people: Being like people as though in a wilderness means there is no image of self, no image of others, no image of people.

If one cannot be the same as other people with a true heart, and can only be the same as them in favorable circumstances but not in adversity, only in times of ease but not in danger, then this sameness is not true and sure, and is ultimately not developmental. When the text says "It is beneficial to cross great rivers," it means that if one can go along through situations of danger and difficulty, then where there is no danger or difficulty, wherever one goes it will be beneficial.

Every ordinary person in the world assimilates to others; but most people do so for personal reasons, and do not do it correctly—they assimilate to those they should be the same as, but they also assimilate to those whom they shouldn't be like. This is not the meaning of sameness with people in the wilderness. Therefore the benefit of crossing great rivers is beneficial insofar as one is upright like a superior person. The superior person assimilates based on correctness, not on sentiment. What is correct is only a matter of what is right and true; sentiment changes, while truth has no change.

If one assimilates based on truth, then there is no sentiment; when there is no sentiment, the ideas of others and self both are transformed. Only truth is to be preserved; inwardly one can thereby develop oneself, and outwardly develop others. Seeing afar by means of illumination, acting directly by means of strength, strength and illumination both working, firmness and flexibility balancing each other, inwardly not losing oneself, outwardly not hurting others, round and bright, clean and bare, one stands in the midst of myriad things without being inhibited by myriad things; one is within yin and yang without being constrained by yin and yang.

■ *First yang:*   **Sameness with people at the gate is blameless.**

EXPLANATION

In the beginning of sameness with others, when one is strong and lucid, going to go out the gate to assimilate to others, before one is even out the gate, one already distinguishes right and wrong, whether it is suitable to be the same as people or not, and then after that one assimilates to those whom it is right to be like. Thus one can assimilate blamelessly. This is sameness with strength and prudence in the beginning.

■ *2 yin:*   **Sameness with people in the clan is regrettable.**

EXPLANATION

Dwelling in the inner body, in the same place with two yangs, this is being the same as people in the clan. If one can only be the same as relatives or friends and not strangers, this is the path of shame and regret in being the same as others. This is sameness which is weak and not far-reaching.

■ *3 yang:*   **Subduing fighters in the bush, climbing up a high hill, even in three years there will be no flourishing.**

EXPLANATION

When one is too strong and bright and honors and aggrandizes oneself, sometimes assimilation to others is forced and unnatural. This is likened to subduing fighters in the bush and climbing up a high hill. Sameness on a high hill is being able to be the same as those who accord with oneself but unable to be the same as those opposite to oneself. Such people cannot make the work of being the same as other people thrive even after a long period of three years. This is sameness with adamant forcefulness.

■ *4 yang:* **Mounting the wall, unable to attack.**
This is auspicious.

EXPLANATION
Mounting obstinacy with obstinacy, others powerful and oneself strong, others and oneself cannot be of the same mind. This is likened to mounting the wall yet being unable to attack. However, if one is firm and yet able to be flexible, and does not try to force the issue when unable to assimilate, this too is an auspicious way of sameness with others. This is sameness with firmness and ability to be flexible.

■ *5 yang:* **In sameness with people, first there is**
weeping, afterward laughter. A great general wins,
then meets others.

EXPLANATION
When firm strength is in proper balance and correct orientation, the path is completed and one is full of virtue; before there was no one who was the same, but afterward there will surely be those who will emulate. This is represented by first weeping and later laughing in sameness with others. To those whose way is lofty slander comes; toward those cultivated in virtue criticism arises—it is not to be wondered at if there are few who understand and appreciate. But after one has perfected oneself, if one would perfect other people one must be completely firm and impartial, assimilating correctly, like a great general winning over them, eventually able to move people by sincerity and truth—only then will they honor and submit and all emulate him. Why worry that sympathizers will not be met? This is sameness with great fairness and impartiality, beneficial for great undertakings.

■ *Top yang:* **Being the same as people in the**
countryside, there is no regret.

EXPLANATION
When strength is used with flexibility, one can be in the world yet out of it at the same time; though outwardly the same, inwardly one is not the same. This is likened to sameness with people in the countryside. Sameness in the countryside is having great knowledge yet appearing ignorant, having great skill yet appearing inept. Circumstances cannot move one; one does not cause regret, and does not have any regret oneself. This is sameness that is harmonization without being influenced.

So in the path of sameness with people, it is necessary to be able to adapt to changes, to assess the time and determine what is to be done; it is important that assimilation be correct. If assimilation is correct, being strong and lucid, one can assimilate wherever one goes, without any forced assimilation anywhere. Then the meaning of sameness with people in the wilderness is realized.

14. Great Possession

In great possession are creation and development.

EXPLANATION

Great possession means greatness of possession. As for the qualities of the hexagram, above is *fire* ☲, luminous, and below is *heaven* ☰, strong. Acting strongly with lucidity, producing understanding in the midst of strength, growing increasingly illumined as strength increases, growing increasingly strong as illumination increases, it is therefore called *great possession*.

This hexagram represents wealth with daily renewal, governing the inward with strictness; it follows on the previous hexagram *obstruction*. In *obstruction*, yin energy acts while yang energy retires; one accepts the false and loses the real, obstructing the openness of consciousness, becoming darker and darker daily until the original celestial virtues are completely gone. If you want to restore celestial qualities, producing something where there is nothing, it cannot be done but for the path of strength and illumination.

What is strength? It is the moment of pure truth, adamantly strong and unbending. What is illumination? It is illumining myriad things, with open consciousness undimmed. If one can be strong, the mind is firm and the will far-reaching, cultivating every appropriate path and establishing every virtue, having such wealth in abundance. If one can be lucid, one can discern principles clearly and thoroughly, seeing surely with real knowledge, taking to whatever is good, reforming every fault, being daily renewed.

Once one is strong and lucid, one has inner autonomy and cannot be moved by anything. This is real true practice. It is like the sun being in the sky, its light shining on everything, covering everything; nothing can deceive it. Yellow sprouts cover the earth, golden flowers bloom throughout the world; wherever one may walk, everywhere is the Tao. With the greatness of possession and the far range of action, nothing started fails to develop.

■ *First yang:* **If there is no association with what is harmful, one is not blameworthy. If you struggle, there will be no fault.**

EXPLANATION

In the beginning of great possession, what one has is not great; one should practice hidden inward cultivation, not injuring internal reality by outside things—therefore, not associating with what is harmful, one is not blameworthy. However, even if one doesn't get involved in external things, if there still are wrong thoughts arising within, these too are "things," and are harmful and blameworthy. One must struggle to deal with them, cultivating oneself and mastering the mind, so that the false leaves and the real comes, and one can have what one had not; only then is it possible to be faultless start to finish. This is the beginning of possession, which requires quiet nurturing within.

■ *2 yang:*   Using a great car for transport, when there is a place to go there is no fault.

EXPLANATION
When firm strength is balanced and one already has inner abundance, this is like using a large car for transport, able thereby to bear the weight. One can thus avoid injury by external things. But when virtue is mastered within, it should be evidenced outwardly. Only if there is a place to go, passing lightly through events and situations unperturbed, is it really great possession, impeccable inwardly and outwardly. This is already possessing, requiring external effectiveness.

■ *3 yang:*   The work of barons serves the son of heaven. Petty people are incapable of this.

EXPLANATION
When firmness is in its proper place, with greatness of possession and greatness of action one can complete celestial virtue. This is likened to the work of the barons serving the "son of heaven," the emperor. The service of the work of the barons to the son of heaven is the active ability of firm rectitude; the service of the practice of Tao to heaven is the active virtue of firm rectitude. Serving heaven by virtue, one's own mission is not ordinary; only thus can one be a partner of heaven, without any barrier to heaven. As for petty people who are adamant but not upright, who think they have what they haven't, and glorify themselves as sages, they are opposing heaven and are unable to serve heaven. This is great possession requiring care that firmness be correct.

■ *4 yang:*   Repudiate self-aggrandizement and there is no fault.

EXPLANATION
When one is imbued with both strength and illumination, having strength but not presuming on it, having brilliance but not using it aggressively, this is repudiating self-aggrandizement. Strength and illumination repudiating self-aggrandizement outwardly appear to be insufficient, yet inwardly are always superabundant. What one has grows ever more, what is great grows ever greater; the fault of losing what has been gained naturally does not occur. This is great possession valuing most firmness with the ability to be flexible.

- *5 yin:* **The trust is mutual. Power is auspicious.**

EXPLANATION
Being flexible, receptive, open-minded, inwardly believing in the nonexistence of oneself as an individual alone and knowing the existence of other people, using flexibility to seek strength, using strength to balance flexibility—thereby trust is mutual and power auspicious. Originally having no power oneself, by ability to associate with the strong one will become enlightened even though originally ignorant, and will become strong even though originally weak; while lacking, one will be able to have, and while small one will be able to be great. This is possession in the sense of those who as yet have not, needing to seek other people.

- *Top yang:* **Help from heaven is auspicious, unfailingly beneficial.**

EXPLANATION
In the end of great possession, firmness and flexibility match each other, strength and lucidity are as one; integrated with celestial principle, the gold elixir crystallized, one's fate depends on oneself and not on heaven. Therefore help from heaven is auspicious, unfailingly beneficial. That by which heaven commands people is the quality of strength; that by which people obey heaven is the quality of illumination. When one preserves strength by illumination, the order of heaven is always present; when the order of heaven is present, then heaven helps one. This is great possession requiring the completion of the celestial.

So in the real study of great possession, unless strength is used to refine inner illumination, so as to respond outwardly, one cannot carry it out. Once strong and lucid, those who have not can have, and those who have can expand it. When strength and illumination are both used, and one fills the belly and empties the mind, the path of abundant possession and daily renewal is consummated.

15. Humility

Humility is developmental. The superior person has a conclusion.

EXPLANATION
Humility means possession without dwelling on it. As for the qualities of the hexagram, above is *earth* ☷, submissive, and below is *mountain* ☶, still: Firmness still within, flexibility accords without; inwardly firm while outwardly flexible, it is therefore called *humility*.

This hexagram represents preservation of yang by yin; it follows on the previous hexagram *sameness with people.* Sameness with people means mixing in with the ordinary world inconspicuously, using strength with clarity, so that strength is not used arbitrarily. Unless one's development and maturity is quite deep and rich, one cannot do this. The work of deepening development is precisely the work of preserving yang by yin. Preserving yang by yin is that whereby openness is consummated and tranquility pure, staying in the appropriate place.

Mountain is where one kills the self, *earth* is where one enlivens the self. Those who have not yet died first learn to die; this is the stilling of yang. Nonbirth is eternal life; this is the submission of yin. The stilling of yang is stopping false yang and nurturing true yang; the submission of yin is using true yin to repel false yin. When false yang stops and true yang remains, this is called nurturing; when false yin retreats and true yin appears, this is called submission. When one is able to nurture and to submit, one governs oneself with strictness and responds to others with openness; the mind becomes increasingly humble, while the way becomes increasingly lofty—outwardly one is lacking, inwardly one has more than enough. Submitting to truth and according with people, one rests in the highest good and does not move. This is why the path of humility is beneficial.

However, if one can be humble in the beginning but not in the end, this is having a start but no conclusion. When stillness is not stable and submission is not appropriate, humility is false and not real, so it cannot be developmental. Only superior people who practice the Tao know where to stop, disregard what they have and appear to have nothing; they are single-minded on pure reality, they have a start and a conclusion, following the Tao in their acts, growing ever stronger the longer they go on. Therefore they attain the primordial emptiness, coming from within nothingness, congealing into the elixir.

Those who are not superior people think they have what they have not, think they are fulfilled when in fact they are empty. Self-satisfied, though they be reverent outwardly they are not respectful inwardly; diligent in the beginning, they end up lazy. They inevitably wind up stopping true yang and using false yang, obeying human desires and violating celestial principles. This is not only unfortunate, it is also not developmental. How could it be considered humility?

■ *First yin:*   **Humble about humility, the superior person thereby crosses great rivers. This is auspicious.**

EXPLANATION
When one's nature is flexible and receptive, and one is already naturally capable of humility, and one also abides in a humble position, not presuming to take precedence over others, this is called humility. A superior person who is humble about humility is certainly capable of humility in favorable circumstances, and is also capable of humility in adversity, using this to cross the perils of "great rivers," bringing about good effects in every case. This is the humility of having the flexibility to lower oneself.

■ *2 yin:* **Expressing humility is upright and good.**

EXPLANATION
When flexibility and receptivity are properly balanced, and one follows the capable because of having no ability oneself, this is called expressing humility. Being humble yet expressive, one shows one's own lack and honors the attainments of others. Emptying the mind, one can fill the belly, gaining fortune by being humble. This is the humility of flexibly following the strong.

■ *3 yang:* **Working with humility, the superior person has a conclusion. This bodes well.**

EXPLANATION
With one yang dwelling in the midst of a group of yins, it is possible to convert the yins by way of humility. This is called working with humility. Being humble and hardworking, one's virtue grows daily, while one's consciousness of it shrinks daily; being humble oneself, others spontaneously become humble. Only a superior person with a true heart and genuine mind can do this. This is the humility of being firm and bringing tasks to a conclusion.

■ *4 yin:* **Beneficial to all, extending humility.**

EXPLANATION
Being flexible yet maintaining rectitude, already capable of humility toward the worthy, also capable of humility toward the low—this is called extending humility. Extending humility to the utmost, in all situations, this is the humility of flexibility benefiting all.

■ *5 yin:* **Not enriching oneself, one shares with the neighbors. It is beneficial to make an invasion, which will profit all.**

EXPLANATION
Flexibility in balance, one is not only personally humble, one is also capable of inducing others to be humble. Therefore one does not enrich oneself, "one shares with the neighbors." The neighbors are people who are close. If it can influence those who are close but not those who are remote, it is not real humility. "It is beneficial to make an invasion" means to apply it to strangers and opponents; when humility reaches the point where it is not concerned with sympathy or opposition, and is extended to friend and stranger alike, then its action is beneficial wherever it goes. This is the humility of being noble and able to act with an open heart.

■ *Top yin:*   Trumpeting humility, it is profitable to use
the army to conquer one's land.

EXPLANATION
Elevating oneself, concerned with oneself but not with others, this is
called trumpeting humility. Humility trumpeted above, incapable of being
humble oneself, how can one influence others to be humble? This is why
"it is profitable to use the army to conquer one's land." "One's land" means
those who are close and sympathetic to oneself. Even then, if profit is
gained only after using the army to conquer them, how much the more so
for those who are remote from and opposed to oneself. This is the humility of one in a high position unable to lower himself.

Humility as a path is manifold—there is being firm and strong yet humble,
there is being humble through yielding and being flexible, there is yielding
and being flexible through humility, there is being humble to the strong.
All of these value emptying the mind and lowering oneself. If you empty
the mind you can fill the belly; if you lower yourself you can rise high.
Herein lies using yin to equalize yang.
    Indeed, humility receives benefit, satiety brings on resentment.
Though humility is a slight matter, its effect is most great. If students can
genuinely practice humility, with a start and a finish, then inwardly yin
and yang will be in harmony, while outwardly there will be communication between oneself and others. The conditioned temperament will
change, natural reality alone will be manifest, and the life-giving energy
will always be there—what worry is there that the gold elixir will not crystallize and the Tao will not be attained?

16. *Joy*

It is advantageous to set up a ruler and
mobilize the army.

EXPLANATION
Joy is happiness. As for the qualities of the hexagram, above is *thunder*
☳, active, and below is *earth* ☷, compliant: acting in accord with
the time, active yet also compliant, it is therefore called joy.
    This hexagram represents summoning yang by yin; it follows on the
previous hexagram *great possession*. In *great possession*, strength and understanding are employed together; it is the path of wealth and daily renewal.
For wealth to be daily renewed it is necessary to act in accord with the
time; only then can one succeed.
    If one can accord with the time, then the promotion of strength can
be correct, and the use of intelligence can be appropriate: The firing pro-

cess does not go wrong, the measure of the elements is regulated, haste and relaxation are in order, and advance and withdrawal accord with the appropriate time and measure; reaching effortlessness by way of effort, there is no problem of losing what one has gained.

What is the happiness of harmonious action like? As an image of harmonious action, nothing compares to setting up a ruler and mobilizing the army. The ruler is the leader of the nation, and the general is the leader of the army. When the leader is set up in accord with the timing of heaven, then the country is peaceful; when the mobilization of the army is in accord with people's hearts, then the troops are complete.

The mind is the leader of the body, like the ruler and the general. As it is beneficial to set up a ruler and mobilize the army for harmonious action, so is it beneficial to rectify the mind and train the body. If one acts in accord with the time, it is beneficial; if one's action is not in accord with the time, it is not beneficial. When it is beneficial, one attains happiness; when it is not beneficial, one is not happy. The path of producing happiness is the consummation of harmonious action.

■ *First yin:*   **Trumpeting joy is inauspicious.**

EXPLANATION
In the beginning of *joy*, also at the bottom of three yins, this represents being foolish and moreover associating with petty people, ruining oneself, taking misery for happiness. This is called trumpeting joy. Trumpeting joy means considering oneself happy when in fact one has no happiness, ultimately to enter the state of inflexible ignorance and not attain happiness. This is happiness that is not true and brings misfortune.

■ *2 yin:*   **Firm as a rock, not procrastinating,
rectitude is good.**

EXPLANATION
Having no greed, no ambition, happy with knowledge of celestial order, solid as a rock, steadfast, not letting external artificialities injure inner reality, when it comes to improper enjoyment one does not delay in getting rid of it; this is the happiness of preserving rectitude and thus gaining good fortune.

■ *3 yin:*   **Looking up to joy, if repentance is tardy,
there will be regret.**

EXPLANATION
Abandoning one's own happiness and looking up hopefully at the happiness of other people is called looking up to joy. When one comes to looking up to others for happiness, before one gets it from others one loses it in oneself. The way to repent is to do so quickly once it is realized that there is no benefit in looking to others; then one can be without regret. Other-

wise, one cannot repent quickly and repentance is late, so there is regret and one does not attain happiness.

■ *4 yang:* **Being the source of joy, there is great gain.**
Do not doubt. Companions gather.

EXPLANATION
With one yang dwelling in the midst of a group of yins, not confused by the yins, it can also convert the yins, so that all come and follow it. This is called being the source of joy, having great gain. The image of great gain is as of tousled hair being gathered back into one bunch; it means overcoming confusion by unity, stopping distraction by concentration. Then the yang energy is ever flourishing and the yin energy spontaneously transmutes. What happiness can compare with this? This is the happiness of gain through the use of firm strength.

■ *5 yin:* **There is a persistent illness, but one never dies.**

EXPLANATION
Being flexible and yielding without firmness, keeping to quietude in solitary silence, empty without fulfillment, is like having an illness and being incapable of enjoyment. However, if flexibility is properly balanced, even if one cannot bring about happiness one still does not get to the point of bringing on misfortune; though one has illness, one never dies. Not dying and not living, keeping to one principle alone, resting in a small vehicle, even if true yang is in view, one cannot have it oneself; this is sticking to indifferent emptiness, in which there is no joy.

■ *Top yin:* **Oblivious in joy. What comes about has**
change; there is no blame.

EXPLANATION
At the end of joy, only knowing how to go along with enjoyment, not knowing how to operate enjoyment in reverse, is called oblivion in joy. When joy reaches oblivion, and one clings obstinately to it and doesn't pass through it, submitting to the enjoyment of what one desires, although what one enjoys comes to be, it must undergo change; when happiness culminates, that gives rise to sadness. After all it is self-defeating; it is not the fault of other people. This is pursuing what one likes and losing happiness.

So happiness as a path is all a matter of compliance; the way to bring about happiness is to be able to act in accord with the time. When one acts in accord with the time, the yang energy is expansive, like thunder going out of the earth and rising forcefully into the sky, startling an area of a hundred miles with its rumble, so that all demons flee. The life-giving potential continues increasing, and the earth is always covered with yellow sprouts, the world blooms with golden flowers. Wherever one may walk, everywhere is the Tao. No happiness is more delightful than this.

17. Following

Following is greatly developmental: It is beneficial if correct; then there is no fault.

EXPLANATION

Following means going along. As for the qualities of the hexgram, above is *lake* ☱, joyous, and below is *thunder* ☳, active: it means self and others in accord, others rejoicing when one acts, acting to the delight of others—therefore it is called *following*.

This hexagram represents seeking feeling through essence; if follows on the previous hexagram of *humility*. Humble people make naught of what they have and reveal what they lack; thereby they use yin to make yang complete. However, this is after the return of yang; before yang has returned, true yang will not come unless there is a way to summon and absorb it. The way to summon and absorb it is the path of *following*.

In this hexagram, *thunder* ☳ and *lake* ☱ join: *Thunder*, associated with the east, represents the essence, the self; *lake*, associated with the west, represents feeling, the other. In the beginning of life, essence and feeling are one. The primordial true yang is originally in oneself, but when it mixes with acquired conditioning it is lost outside, is no longer one's own but belongs to other. If you want to get back to the origin and return to the fundamental, you have to steal it back from the other.

Following as a path is going along with what is desired, gradually introducing guidance. Going along with desire means the self follows the other and gets the other's favor, inducing the other to come follow the self. Other and self following each other, essence seeks feeling, feeling returns to essence, and that which had been lost is restored to oneself. This is great development by way of the path of *following*.

However, though the path of following can be greatly developmental, yet there are true and false medicinal substances, there is progression and order in the firing process, there are times for action and stillness, there are times for advance and withdrawal—a small slip produces a tremendous miss. Therefore, for the great development of the path of following, correctness is most beneficial. Correct means right—following rightly, the self sensing rightly, the other responding rightly; when self and other are both right, even artificial feeling transforms into true feeling, and even artificial essence changes into true essence. Essence loves receptivity and rectitude in feeling, feeling loves compassion and benevolence in essence; strength and flexibility one energy, essence and feeling joined, we return to pristine purity. Wholly integrated with natural principle, the golden elixir crystallizes, tranquil and unperturbed yet sensitive and effective, sensitive and effective yet tranquil and undisturbed. Those who are faulty at the outset wind up impeccable in the end. Try to understand when following is right or wrong, good or bad.

■ *First yang:* **Standards change; it is good to be correct.**
Going outside and mixing is effective.

EXPLANATION

In the beginning of following, is following right or wrong? Once the standard of following is the standard, it must undergo change. It is necessary to distinguish what is appropriate and what is not—only by correct following is it possible to attain good fortune. If, once one knows what is right, one then goes out and mixes with people, using things of the world to cultivate the practices of the Tao, one will not fail to accomplish one's work. This is following with care in the beginning.

■ *2 yin:* **Involved with the child, one loses the adult.**

EXPLANATION

Being weak and without knowledge, following yin that arises later, one loses the original yang; this is being "involved with a child, losing the adult." This is following that is weak and loses reality.

■ *3 yin:* **Involved with the adult, one loses the child.**
Following with an aim, one gains. It is beneficial to
abide in rectitude.

EXPLANATION

When one's nature is weak but one's will is firm, and one can follow the yang of the other and not follow the yin in the self, this is being involved with the adult and losing the child; following with an aim will attain it. However, many weak people are not earnest in their faith in the Tao, and they easily lose focus. It is essential to abide in right and not move, growing ever stronger; only thus can one get the yang of the other and return it to the self. This is following in which one is weak yet abides in what is right.

■ *4 yang:* **Following has gain. Even if right, it is**
inauspicious. Truthfully remaining on the path,
using understanding, what blame is there?

EXPLANATION

If one is strong and yet can follow, following strength will surely result in gain. However, strength following strength is excessive strength, and is inauspicious even if correct. Strength had better be used with flexibility and gentility, truthfully remaining on the path, understanding right and wrong, true and false, knowing when to advance and when to retreat, not bringing on blame and being blameless oneself. This is the following of strength trusting in the Tao.

■ *5 yang:*   **Truthfulness in good is auspicious.**

EXPLANATION
Happiness is herein: concealing the bad, extolling the good, following strength, following flexibility, mastering both and using balance, every act is right, every affair is proper; following the heart's desire, one does not step over the line. This is following trusting in goodness.

■ *Top yin:*   **Binding and tying up; the king sacrifices on west mountain.**

EXPLANATION
When one is foolish and ignorant and is compulsive and whimsical, unable to first go and follow others while wanting others to follow oneself, this is like binding and tying. Forced seeking and forced joining, an excess of false ideas, is like a king sacrificing on west mountain; though the celestial treasure is in view, after all it remains in the west (other) and does not return to the east (self)—in the end it is effort in vain. This is useless and insubstantial following.

So what makes the path of following developmental is effectively a matter of correctness. In following correctly, when one wants to get one must first give; if the self can follow the other, the other will follow the self. Then true yin and true yang join: Within rapture there is form, within ecstasy there is vitality—the primordial energy comes from within nothingness, congealing into a pearl, vague at first, then becoming clear. Creativity grows, growth bears fruit; where is there any fault in the path of following that bears fruit through rectitude? As it is faultless, the great Tao can be attained.

18. *Degeneration*

**Correcting degeneration is greatly developmental.
It is beneficial to cross great rivers. Three days
before the start, three days after the start.**

EXPLANATION
Degeneration means deterioration. As for the qualities of the hexagram, above is *mountain* ☶, stopping, and below is *wind* ☴, penetrating: it represents one yin entering and yang stopping it. Also, *wind* is inside stop-

ping, representing stopping the yin so that it does not advance upward; it includes the meaning of correcting degeneration.

This hexagram represents abandoning the false and returning to the true; it follows on the preceding hexagram *joy*. *Joy* is harmonious action, in accord with the time and in accord with truth, not acting in any way that would be improper, so as to prevent degeneracy of action. When people are first born they are utterly good, with no evil, integrated with natural principle. Originally there is nothing to cultivate, nothing to realize; since there is no defect, there is nothing to correct. But when they get to be sixteen years old, yang peaks, producing yin; by the development of habits they become estranged from what is near by nature. This is like the one yin of *wind* arising below two yangs; as negative energy advances, the original being degenerates.

However, before the celestial Tao has yin, it cannot be yang; before human affairs have degeneration they cannot be repaired. This is why the path of correction of degeneracy is valuable. The path of correction of degeneracy is like the one yang of *mountain* stopping on top of two yins, not injured by negative influences. Using this one yang to go back to the root and return to life is the study of working on the fundamental. When the fundamental is established, the path develops. Once you recover your potential, it is like it was always there; this is attaining great development in degeneracy.

Great development is not in degeneration but in correcting degeneration. The way to correct degeneracy is not in empty tranquility without action; it is necessary to work in the midst of great danger and difficulty, to act in the dragon's pool and the tiger's lair. Only then can one restore one's original being, cultivating it into something indestructible. This is why degeneration is developmental, and it is beneficial to cross great rivers. Great rivers are most dangerous and hard to cross; if great rivers are crossed beneficially without injury, then places of little or no danger cannot harm.

However, the benefit of crossing great rivers involves action and process, from which no deviation can be admitted. "Three days before the start, three days after the start" is the secret of the active process. The yin and yang in people is like the waning and waxing of the moon. In the first three nights of the moon's appearance, the yang light appears in the southwest. This is represented by the trigram *thunder* ☳. On the night of the fifteenth, the moon appears in the east. This is represented by the trigram *heaven* ☰. On the thirteenth, fourteenth, and fifteenth, the light becomes round; this is "three days before the start." On the sixteenth, seventeenth, and eighteenth, the light starts to wane; this is "three days after the start." When people's yang energy is pure, this is "three days before the start." Once their yin energy has arisen, this is "three days after the start."

"Before the start" is yang, "after the start" is yin. This is the boundary of primordial and temporal yin and yang. People who practice the Tao need to know clearly whether things are degenerate or not. It is all in this boundary of "before the start" and "after the start." When yang energy is about to become pure, ward off yin to preserve yang; after yin energy has arisen, repel yin to restore yang. If you ward off yin energy before it arises, and repel yin energy after it arises, then the yang energy that has not degenerated can be preserved, and that which has degenerated can be restored. This is the real science of working on the fundamental, getting rid of falsehood and returning to reality. Correctness is unfailingly developmental, development is unfailingly beneficial.

■ *First yin:*   Correcting the father's degeneracy; if there is a son, the deceased father is without blame. Danger, but in the end it turns out well.

EXPLANATION
In the beginning of degeneration, the fundamental is still complete; if you ward off yin before degeneration, this is like correcting the father's degeneracy. If he has a son to follow him, the deceased father, who should be censured, can be without blame. However, the way to correct degeneracy is not empty inaction; it requires caution in peril, preventing alien energies due to external influences from arising, and preventing the fundamental from being adversely affected. If one can be careful in the beginning, there will naturally be good luck in the end. This is warding off yin before degeneration.

■ *2 yang:*   Correcting the degeneracy of the mother, it is improper to be righteous.

EXPLANATION
When strength is used flexibly, flexibility is the root and firmness is the branch. Not being excessively firm, not damaging the flexibility, firmness and flexibility are united, and one is able to change adaptively according to circumstances. This is like correcting the degeneracy of the mother, in which it is not proper to be self-righteous. This is correcting degeneracy without being excessively adamant.

■ *3 yang:*   Correcting the degeneracy of the father, there is a little regret but not much blame.

EXPLANATION
Correcting the strong by strength, strength is excessive. It is like when the father is strong and the son is strong, correcting the father's degeneracy cannot avoid a little regret. But when degeneracy is corrected rightly, though there be a little regret, it is possible to have not much blame. This is correcting degeneracy too adamantly.

■ *4 yin:*   Forgiving the degeneration of the father; if one goes on, there will be shame.

EXPLANATION
Only being yielding, with no firmness, not immediately correcting degeneracy when it occurs, relaxing and letting deviousness grow, is like the fa-

ther being degenerate and the son forgiving it. If one goes on this way to cultivate the Tao, one will reap only regret. This is being too weak in correcting degeneracy.

- *5 yin:*   **Correcting the degeneracy of the father, using praise.**

EXPLANATION
Being flexible and receptive, emptying the heart, showing oneself as lacking while praising what others have, is like using praise in correcting the degeneracy of the father. Acting with praise, using the strength and clarity of others to break through one's own ignorance, when there is degeneration one can then restore the state of no degeneration. This is skillful use of flexibility in correcting degeneration.

- *Top yang:*   **Not serving kings and lords, one makes one's concerns loftier.**

EXPLANATION
When strength dwells in flexibility, without greed or ambition, there is no degeneration, and no detriment. Thereby one does not serve kings and lords, but makes one's concerns loftier. Not serving kings and lords means not aiming for fame or profit; making one's concerns higher means valuing spiritual virtues. When one values spiritual virtues and does not aim for fame or profit, one's abode is lofty and one's concern is great. Resting in the highest good without vacillating, one looks down on all—all things are empty. With the basis firm, even without cultivation there is naturally no degeneration. This is not correcting in the absence of degeneration.

So the path of correcting degeneration, working on the fundamental, is all a matter of staying in the highest good by combining yin and yang. If one has not arrived at the realm of ultimate good, even if there is no great degeneration, it is hard to avoid minor degeneration. So great development based on degeneration is made successful by crossing great rivers. When great rivers are crossed beneficially, one enters from striving into nonstriving: essence and life are both realized, and one is physically and mentally sublimated; merging with the Tao into reality, one becomes eternally indestructible, and the path of correcting degeneration is completed.

19. *Overseeing*

Overseeing is creative and developmental, beneficial if correct. In the eighth month there is misfortune.

EXPLANATION

Overseeing is watching over. As for the qualities of the hexagram, above is *earth* ☷, following, and below is *lake* ☱, joyful: joyfully following truth, acting in accord with that joy, it is therefore called *overseeing*.

This hexagram represents watching over the furnace, culling the elixir; it follows on the previous hexagram *following*. In *following, thunder* seeks *lake, lake* returns to *thunder;* this means that when feeling returns to essence, it can be called restored elixir. Once positive energy has been restored, it becomes increasingly manifest, gradually expanding; at this point you watch over the furnace and get to work, fostering the positive and repressing the negative. Then positive energy grows and negative energy wanes; this is why *overseeing* has creativity and development. Creativity is the first return of one yang; development is the increase and rise of the second yang. Watching over the furnace and getting to work, one culls these two yangs.

But even though the two yangs are growing, yin energy is still abundant and yang energy is still weak; it is necessary to be careful to ward off danger. Don't be negligent, but don't be eager either. Take harmony for substance and accord for function; acting in accord with the time, to take from the other without losing from the self, it is beneficial to be correct. Correct means right; overseeing correctly, before the proper time arrives one does not seek forcibly, and when the time has arrived one does not let it slip by. When process and measure are right, the original creative energy does not leak away, and the mechanism of life does not stop; that practice is creative and developmental, without obstruction.

Otherwise, if one does not know when the medicinal substances are too dense or too feeble, and does not understand when to intensify the work and when to relax it, but starts out impatiently, eager for quick success, then the medicinal substances will not be genuine and the firing process will not be correctly tuned; those who spurt ahead quickly will fall back rapidly. What will happen then is that once the two yangs have grown smoothly they will soon dissipate—the positive energy that has developed will disperse—and *overseeing* will turn into *observing* (next hexagram); "in the eighth month there is misfortune."

If one's effort is not correct, it will not bear fruit; if it doesn't bear fruit, what is begun will not develop—one loses what one has gained, and the great affair is gone. Therefore the path of overseeing requires harmonious accord with the time; it is important not to miss in the firing process.

- *First yang:*   Sensitive overseeing leads to good results
when correct.

EXPLANATION
In the beginning of watching over the furnace, when positive energy has just arisen, and one can handle it firmly, all at once the attention is purely on reality, and when there is any sensing one watches over it—one senses correctly and is not influenced by aberration; as long as it is correct, it is good. This is overseeing being careful in the beginning.

- *2 yang:*   Sensitive overseeing is good,
of unfailing benefit.

EXPLANATION
When the positive energy grows and strength and flexibility unite, one is tranquil and undisturbed yet sensitive and effective: yang and yin are attached to each other, great and small are not injured, and the mechanism of life goes on unceasing, vague at first then becoming clearly manifest, eventually to reach the state of pure wholeness of positive energy. This is overseeing in which strong energy is good and beneficial.

- *3 yin:*   Presumptuous overseeing is of no benefit.
If one is troubled over this, there is no blame.

EXPLANATION
Being weak and ignorant, saying the right things but not being right at heart, working on externals and losing the inner, is called presumptuous overseeing. When overseeing gets to be presumptuous, and one can talk but not act, there is no benefit at all. Since there is no benefit, presumption turns into bitterness, and there is sure to be grief. But once one is troubled by this, becomes humble, sets oneself at naught and seeks the guidance of others, the goal is not far off. One then turns away from presumption, and even one who was blameworthy can thereby become blameless. This is overseeing that rejects the false and returns to the true.

- *4 yin:*   Consummate overseeing is blameless.

EXPLANATION
Being weak yet preserving rectitude, refining oneself and mastering the mind, thereby awaiting the newborn positive energy, is called consummate overseeing. Watching over the quintessential, when the great medicine appears one naturally does not make the mistake of missing it. This is overseeing that takes advantage of the opportunity to cull the medicine.

■ *5 yin:*   Knowing overseeing is appropriate for a great
lord, and is auspicious.

EXPLANATION

Flexible receptivity in balance and correctly oriented, seeking being by
nonbeing, seeking fulfillment by emptiness, is called knowing the overseeing. When able to know its overseeing, the mind-lord is clear and peaceful; spiritual light shines within: When the other comes the self awaits it,
when yang comes yin receives it. Intensity, relaxation, and stopping at sufficiency are all as they should be, and the primordial energy congeals out
of nothingness. This is overseeing merging yin and yang.

■ *Top yin:*   Attentive overseeing is good and blameless.

EXPLANATION

At the end of overseeing, from striving entering into nonstriving, returning to pristine purity, totally good, without evil, unconsciously following
the laws of God, this is called attentive overseeing. When overseeing
reaches ultimate attention, it is at peace with suchness as is; neither being
nor nonbeing can be established, others and self are void of absoluteness,
and the "original face" becomes completely manifest. This is overseeing that completes the beginning and completes the end, auspicious and
impeccable.

Looking over the six lines, we find a way of overseeing in each of them;
only the third, presumptuous overseeing, is not beneficial. The other five,
when put into practice according to the proper timing, advancing and
withdrawing as appropriate, with urgency and relaxation as necessary, all
have marvelous functions. This is really a guide to the firing process as one
watches over the furnace; if students study and find out the facts in the
hexagram *overseeing,* then they can grasp most of the process of firing the
gold elixir.

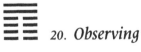

20. *Observing*

Observing, one has washed the hands but not made
the offering; there is sincerity, which is reverent.

EXPLANATION

Observing means alert observation, being careful. As for the qualities of the
hexagram, above is *wind* ☴, penetrating, and below is *earth* ☷, receptive; it has the meaning of gradually progressing in accord with proper
timing, advancing without impetuosity, with alert observation; therefore
it is called *observing.*

This hexagram represents alert observation with clarity of mind; it follows on the previous hexagram *degeneration*. In *degeneration, wind* is inside stopping, which stops yin energy from entering; this is how degeneration is corrected. The way of correcting degeneration is not possible without the achievement of attentive observation with clarity of mind.

The achievement of attentive observation is all a matter of restoring the primordial while in the midst of the temporal, reversing the ordinary flow while in its very midst. When the yin in people is strong and the yang is weak, it is like the present hexagram's four yins arising one after another while the two yangs gradually dissolve; the strength of yang energy is going to be erased by yin energy. Attentive observation with clarity of mind reverses this weak yang so that it is not injured by yin energy.

But people's temperaments are fixated, and accumulated habits are already deep-seated. The yin energy cannot be made submissive all at once, so it is necessary to use gradual cultivation, going along with its desires to gradually soften and guide them, causing it to naturally evaporate, naturally transform, naturally submit, naturally retreat.

This means that when the real comes the false naturally submits; if one can be truthful inwardly, then acquired influences will naturally disappear. Yang gradually advances upward, and yin submissively retreats downward. Yang governs yin and yin obeys yang; yin and yang in harmony, inside and outside are one. This is like when honoring a deity, when one has washed the hands but not yet made the offering, there is sincerity, which is reverent. Whenever you honor a deity, first you clean your hands and make your faith sincere within; after that you present offerings, reverent without. By the gradual effect of sincerity, you communicate with the spirit of the deity, not in a physical sense. This is the meaning of looking up to a deity.

The path of cultivation of reality is like honoring a deity: first you make the mind sincere and truthful, then you practice it in the body. Spiritual clarity works silently, swift without being hasty, entering by sincerity, functioning with flexibility, penetrating the barrier between yin and yang, producing light in the openness within. From observation of the spirit reaching observation of the great, a black pearl hangs in the great void, illumining the whole world as though it were in your palm. Then every step is in accord with the sublime Tao; all yin submits and all yang returns.

The understanding of the spirit is up to the person: It requires clear knowledge of the subtle meaning of this hexagram, being receptive yet advancing like the wind, the advance based on receptivity. If you know this, then with spiritual observation and great observation you preserve the real and eliminate the false, so there is eternal life. If you don't know it, then with small observation and shortsightedness you accept the false and reject the real, thus injuring life. It is simply a matter of the difference between truth and falsehood in observation.

- *First yin:*   **Ignorant observation is not blamed in inferior people, but is shameful in superior people.**

EXPLANATION
In the extreme of ignorance, people ruin and abandon themselves, willingly remaining in base folly without changing. Stubborn ignorance and opinions without knowledge are not worth blaming in inferior people whose only concerns are material comforts, but when it comes to superior people who practice the Tao, who should observe the great and not the small, if they willingly remain in a base state, this is simply shameful. This is the lowest observation.

- *2 yin:*   **Peeking observation is beneficial for a woman's chastity.**

EXPLANATION
When flexible yet balanced, even when in the midst of inferior people one is not influenced by them. But even if one is not influenced, when only cultivating one's own yin without seeking the yang of the other, one's vision is not far-reaching; it is like observing by peeking out from inside the door, not daring to go out the door. In women, it is beneficial for keeping their chastity, but when it comes to men doing work it is not advantageous. This is observation which is not far-reaching.

- *3 yin:*   **Observing personal growth, promoting and repelling.**

EXPLANATION
On the boundary of upper and lower observation, this is observing whether one's personal growth is good or bad, and promoting the good while repelling the bad. Observing one's own growth, if it is actually good, one promotes it, and also observes the good in others to increase one's own good where it is deficient. Observing something that is not good in one's growth, one withdraws from it and repels it, but does not immediately observe the good in others, first getting rid of what is not good in oneself. This is observation knowing when to advance and when to withdraw.

- *4 yin:*   **Observing the glory of the country, it is beneficial to be the guest of a king.**

EXPLANATION
Being flexible and finding what is right, associating with people imbued with the Tao, is called observing the glory of the country. When one is able to observe the glory of the country, borrowing the great vision of others to remedy one's own small vision, then the small can become great. Letting another be the host while one is the guest oneself, this is like the benefit of being the guest of a king. This is observation borrowing greatness through humility.

■ *5 yang:*   Observing personal growth, a superior person
is blameless.

EXPLANATION

When *wind* advances into the position of central balance, firmness and
flexibility match each other: Just as when the great medicine emerges and
crystallizes the jewel of life, observing personal growth is observing the
great medicine produced in the self and returning it to correct balance.
When the medicine returns to correct balance, the medicine itself is the
fire, the fire itself is the medicine—in one hour you watch the elixir form.
But the accomplishment of this one hour is hard to attain and easy to lose;
it is necessary to be a superior person of great vision with profound understanding of the firing process before one is free from stumbling in error.
This is great observation with striving.

■ *Top yang:*   Observing the growth, the superior person
is blameless.

EXPLANATION

At the end of observation, the spiritual embryo is already formed, and one
can dwell in flexibility with strength, from observation of the great again
observing the spirit, giving up striving and entering into nonstriving. Observing growth here means observing the surreptitious growth of yin energy so as to repel it. When yin energy is completely withdrawn and yang
energy is pure and whole, the real person emerges, not bound by creation.
Only then is one a superior person practicing the Tao. This is observation
completing beginning and end impeccably. This is nonstriving spiritual
observation.

So the path of alert observation, involving observing the spirit and also
extensive observation, should never be departed from by those who practice the Tao. It begins with striving, by extensive observation, and ends in
nonstriving through spiritual observation. When spiritual observation and
great observation are as one, the medicine is real, the firing process is in
order; how could the gold elixir not develop? The function of observation
is great indeed.

21. *Biting Through*

**Biting through is developmental. It is beneficial
to administer justice.**

EXPLANATION

Biting through has the meaning of the mouth closing when eating something. In the body of the hexagram, the yangs on the top and bottom sym-

bolize lips, the three yins symbolize teeth, and the yang in the middle represents something in the mouth. Also the qualities of the hexagram are *fire* ☲, luminous, above, and *thunder* ☳, active, below: Acting with unfailing clarity, acting only after clear understanding, it has the meaning of action that is not in vain; therefore it is called *biting through*.

This hexagram represents the study of investigating things and finding out principle; it follows on the previous hexagram of *overseeing*. In *overseeing*, two yangs oversee four yins, whereby to advance yang and gather medicine. However, the medicinal substances have different degrees of gravity and energy, the firing process has intervals of time; the slightest miss can produce a tremendous loss; so this work of finding out principle is indispensible.

Excellence or inferiority in learning to comprehend essence and life is all a matter of finding out principle. Understanding one part, you can practice one part; understanding ten parts, you can practice ten parts. If you know essence but not life, or know life but not essence, or know striving but not nonstriving, or know nonstriving but not striving, or know the medicinal substances but not the firing process, or know the start but not the finish, this is all incomplete investigation of principle, which will inevitably result in failure of practice.

If you want to act on something, you should first understand it; first understanding, then acting, all actions will be as you will. This is why *biting through*, using action within understanding, is developmental. Action with clarity is always based on understanding; its development and fruition may be symbolized by the administration of justice. Nothing in the world is harder to administer than justice; if the true conditions of justice are not clear, right is considered wrong and wrong is considered right—arbitrarily applying penalties, the calamity extends to the innocent, mistakenly injuring essence and life.

Practice of the Tao is like administering justice: Discerning true and false, right and wrong, is like the judge deciding good and bad; getting rid of falsehood and keeping truth, so as to preserve essence and life, is like the justice administration rewarding the good and punishing the bad, so as to alleviate the burden of injustice. When you investigate and find out true principle, it is clear in the mind and evident in practice; fully realizing essence and perfecting life, it is unfailingly developmental and beneficial.

■ *First yang:* **Wearing stocks stopping the feet, there is no blame.**

EXPLANATION

If one is strong but unenlightened and goes forward rashly, this forward movement will surely bring error. This is why stocks are put on to stop the feet, so as to regulate one's steps and prevent wrong moves. If one does not make any wrong moves in the beginning, one will not bring about error and blame in the end. This indicates that in traveling the path it is important to first thoroughly investigate its principles.

■ *2 yin:*   **Biting skin, cutting off the nose.**
There is no blame.

EXPLANATION
If one is weak and not firm, and one's perception of principle is not yet true, one gets only the surface skin and does not yet get the deep gristle. If one is in a hurry to practice principles that are not truly understood, this will not only fail to help one's inner state, it will also harm one externally. This is like biting skin and cutting off the nose. The nose is that by which fragrance and odor are distinguished. When the mouth eats something, the nose smells it first: As the mouth does not know the flavor, though the nose can discern it, it is still of no use. It is fortunate if when one is weak one is still balanced, and does not presume to practice as long as perception of principle is not yet true. Then one may be without blame. This is investigating principle without yet penetrating it.

■ *3 yin:*   **Biting on dried meat, running into poison.**
There is a little shame, but no blame.

EXPLANATION
On top of two, the conscious perception is a bit higher than those two, and is a stage further advanced than the two. This is like biting dried meat. Meat is inside skin: When meat is dried, it is necessary to tear into it to taste the flavor. In this third place, though one is advancing, one has not yet attained the real. It seems to be right, but isn't; if one acts in error, it will surely bring on trouble, like biting into dried meat and coming upon poison. So if the will is strong but the nature is weak, one will not be able to accomplish things, yet neither will one fail; though there is a little shame, after all one can be without blame. This is investigating principle and gradually penetrating.

■ *4 yang:*   **Biting bony dried meat, one gets the**
wherewithal to proceed. It is beneficial to work
hard and be upright: This leads to good results.

EXPLANATION
Dwelling in the body of light (*fire*), above three, investigation of principle has advanced a stage beyond those three. This is like biting bony dried meat. Bony dried meat is meat on the bone; it is sinewy and bony, and when it is dried it is not easy to strip off the meat. If one does not penetrate cuttingly and go in deeply, one cannot see reality; in terms of representation, this is getting the wherewithal to proceed, while in terms of principle this indicates the benefit of hard work in the correct manner. The benefit of hard work in the correct manner is that one can forcibly discern what one could not discern, attaining deep realization, penetrating every subtlety, so as to be able to strip away all falsehood, which only seems to be right, and thus find the reality with lucid clarity. When one clearly under-

stands action, one's actions are all bound to lead to good results. This is investigating principle and seeing truth.

■ *5 yin:*   Biting into dry meat and finding gold, if one is correct and cautious, then there is no error.

EXPLANATION

Above four, flexible, open, balanced, the investigation of principle is a stage more advanced than the four. This is like biting dry meat. When investigation of principle reaches the fourth stage, right and wrong and false and true are clearly distinguished. This is like dry meat that is flavorless when bitten into, and is not to be chewed on further. However, even though there is no flavor, one should still be familiar with the old and know the new, doing further work on the principles one has already understood; seeking further clarification of what is already clear, one can make sure there is not the slightest doubt or confusion, and then seriously put it into practice. This is represented as finding gold, and in terms of principle means being correct and cautious. Gold means understanding that is ultimately balanced; being correct and cautious means being right yet remaining alert and wary. Open and balanced, alert and wary, one will truly see that there is a primary principle; understanding it within and proving it without, all acts conform with the Tao and all affairs are auspicious. This is finding out principle with no doubt whatsoever.

■ *Top yang:*   Wearing a cangue, destroying the ears—misfortune.

EXPLANATION

If one is strong but unenlightened, not knowing how to distinguish truth, one misuses intelligence and gets sidetracked, wasting a whole life, eventually going to one's destruction. This is why wearing a cangue or pillory-like yoke, destroys the ears. If the eyes are bright and the ears sharp, but one cannot understand truth, one should shut the eyes—why go so far as to destroy the ears? In general, when deluded people do not understand the great Tao, it is because of wrong study and wrong inquiry, listening to blind teachers, not distinguishing reality from falsehood, either sticking to emptiness or clinging to appearances; when they therefore bring on misfortune and suffer harm, the root of the calamity is in the ears. What comes from you returns to you; if you are unclear in the beginning, you suffer injury in the end—this is certain. This is not knowing how to find out principle at all.

So the work of investigating principle requires you to strip off layer after layer, stripping away until you get to the bones and marrow of the Tao. When there is no doubt or confusion at all, only then is this true knowledge and clear vision. If you haven't gotten to the marrow of the Tao, there is still obstruction, and you cannot be said to have found reality; you should not act arbitrarily, for then you will bring disaster on yourself.

"Even if you know the cinnabar and lead, it is useless if you don't know the firing process. The whole thing depends on the power of cultivation; if you deviate in the slightest, you won't form the elixir." Indeed, the work of investigating principle is no small matter.

22. *Adornment*

Adornment is developmental. It is beneficial to go somewhere in a minimal way.

EXPLANATION

Adornment means beautification. As for the qualities of the hexagram, above is *mountain* ☶, still, and below is *fire* ☲, luminous: clear about where to rest, resting in what is clarified, one naturally clarifies illumination and rests in the highest good; therefore it is called *adornment.*

This hexagram represents hidden practice and secret cultivation; it follows on the previous hexagram *observing. Observing* is the path of spiritual clarity and alert observation, gradually progressing along with time; alert and observant, one turns the awareness around to look within. Wise yet appearing ignorant, adept yet appearing inept, one stabilizes clarity, so that clarity develops, and understands stopping and stilling, so as to rest in the appropriate place. Clarity and stillness adorn each other; thus clarity is not misused, and stillness does not degenerate into quietism. Clarity is the body of stillness, stillness is the function of clarity; thus clarity is not damaged and stillness is correct, so clarity and stillness are developmental.

Although clarity and stillness adorn each other, one should value still clarity. Still clarity is not empty inaction that does not use illumination at all. But while one is illumined within, one does not show it outside. One rests in clarity and does not rest where it is unclear. Clarity is within stillness; one does not lightly use the clarity of illumination. This is the meaning of self-minimization.

Minimizing oneself, one is prudent and cautious, getting rid of intellectualism, inwardly preserving clarity of spirit; with open awareness that is unclouded, one cannot be moved by anything. There is much benefit in this, but minimization that is too extreme is stillness without illumination; it is not the form of union of clarity and stillness that this hexagram represents—how could it be developmental or beneficial?

Stillness means resting in the highest good, being tranquil and imperturbable. Clarity means clarifying the quality of illumination, being sensitive and effective. Uncontrived when quiet, creative when active, clear in stillness, tranquilly employing illumination, attaining it in the mind and proving it in affairs, only then is it called true stillness and true clarity. When the text here says "it is beneficial to go somewhere," this simply means that this is the way to test and prove this stillness and clarity. When ordinary people have no concerns their minds are clear, and they know where to rest, but when they have matters to attend to they get muddled and confused, and don't know where to rest.

If one can be still by virtue of clarity, thereby to nurture illumination, and can be clear by virtue of stillness, thereby to master illumination, clarity and stillness will not be restricted, and can be used according to the time, planting lotuses in fire, hauling a boat through mud and water, the ineffable being of one spirit pervading the universe, clear in stillness and resting in the place to rest.

■ *First yang:*   Adorning the feet, leaving
the car and walking.

EXPLANATION
Being firm and clear-minded, voluntarily humble and self-effacing, living embracing the Tao, is like adorning the feet. The firmness of adorning the feet does not let external artifice injure internal reality; therefore one leaves the car and is content to walk. This is the adornment of firmly preserving rectitude.

■ *2 yin:*   Adornment is seeking.

EXPLANATION
Dwelling in between two yangs, emptying oneself and seeking others, knowing one's personal understanding has a limit while the understanding of many people is endless, one must seek before knowledge and vision can expand. This is the adornment of weakness borrowing strength.

■ *3 yang:*   Adorned and luxuriant,
perpetual rectitude is auspicious.

EXPLANATION
When firm clarity is excessive, and one only knows how to use understanding and does not know how to open understanding, the clarity of understanding will surely not reach far. Thereby one is "adorned and luxriant," but it is best if one's firmness is correct, never changing in constancy. Then even if one cannot adorn the exterior, still one can adorn the interior, also a way to bring good fortune. This is the adornment of being firm and acting with clarity.

■ *4 yin:*   Adorned or plain? A white horse runs swiftly.
It is not an enemy but a mate.

EXPLANATION
Dwelling in the upper body, weak and unclear, there is correspondence with the first yang, and one is not ashamed to lower oneself to inquire. Therefore "Adorned or plain? A white horse runs swiftly," hurriedly seeking clarity because of unclarity. However, because one above seeks below, there is the danger of self-importance, which makes most people insin-

cere. It is best if one finds what is right when one is weak; the true heart and genuine intention come forth spontaneously, not forced—when there is no enmity or injury, then it is desirable to seek partnership. This is the adornment of the weak seeking clarity.

■ *5 yin:* **Adornment in the hills and groves, the roll of silk is small; there is shame, but it turns out well.**

EXPLANATION

Being flexible but not firm, holding to the mean without power, alone and silent, keeping to quietude, thus "adornment in the hills and groves, the roll of silk is small." "Hills and groves" are the wide open spaces where there are no people, and no social concerns. A small amount of silk, yet rolled up, means there are no formalities to be concerned about. No society and no manners is excessively austere, not close to human sensibilities; so it is something practitioners of Tao are ashamed of. However, if flexibility is balanced, even if one does not illumine the great Tao, still one does not slip into quietism, and after all will be able to complete the path auspiciously. This is the adornment of flexibility and self-sufficiency.

■ *Top yang:* **Adornment by simplicity is impeccable.**

EXPLANATION

When firmness and flexibility match each other one naturally clarifies illumination and rests in the highest good, adorned without adornment. When adornment reaches colorlessness, this is called adornment by simplicity. When adornment is utterly plain, clarity and stillness are unified, energy and substance both transmute, integrating with celestial principle, without the slightest fault of human desire. This is the adornment of merging of firmness and flexibility.

So in terms of adornment as a path, the mutual necessity of clarity and stillness is what must be considered important. Understanding stillness and resting in the appropriate place, stabilizing illumination so that its clarity is not clouded, using clarity and stillness according to the time— herein lies the work of hidden cultivation and secret practice.

23. *Stripping Away*

Stripping away does not make it beneficial to go anywhere.

EXPLANATION

Stripping away is dissolving. As to the qualities of the hexagram, above is *mountain* ☶, stopping, below is *earth* ☷, following: Yin grows as it goes along and yang stops; furthermore, in the body of the hexagram, there are five yins, which have dissolved it down to one yang—the yang energy is about to be exhausted and the yin energy is about to become pure; therefore it is called *stripping away.*

This hexagram represents acquired yin dissolving yang; it follows on the previous hexagram *biting through.* In *biting through*, action requires understanding, so we first investigate principle. Investigating principle means investigating the principle of waning and waxing of yin and yang.

People are born with five elementary combinations of yin and yang from heaven and earth; once they have life, they have essence—essence and life reside in one body. When people are first born, essence and life are one, the primordial and the temporal are merged into one, yin and yang are as yet undivided, wrong and right are as yet not distinguished; they are the image of wholeness. Then as they grow up and their energy becomes full, the primordial yang culminates and mixes with acquired conditioning—one yin surreptitiously arises. Then as the days and years go by, yin energy gradually grows, and yang energy gradually weakens. Until it wanes completely, yang energy does not stop; this is like the body of this hexagram, which five yins have stripped down to one yang.

At this point, yang cannot overcome yin; what remains is very slight yang. If people do not know this and still take the false for the real, and go somewhere to do something relying on their strength, they will surely come to the complete exhaustion of yang energy, which is very detrimental.

Here developed people have a way to suppress yin and enhance yang, which does not let yin energy dissolve yang completely away. That is where this one point of yang energy is not yet exhausted; they accord with it and stabilize it, getting rid of intellectualism, shutting out conditioning influences, and returning to the fundamental, original foundation.

What does not allow yang to avoid turning to yin is the circulating energy mechanism of heaven and earth; yet what is able to preserve yang in the midst of yin is the power of the practice of reverse operation of sages. Since sages have a path that is before time and yet not violated by nature, they can use it to usurp creation and turn life and death around. As for ordinary people, they go along with the course of creation, which strips away yang by yin; when yang energy has waned away and become pure yin, how can they not die? At the one hexagram *stripping away*, the sage has simply said that it is not beneficial to go anywhere—any who value essence and life would do well to understand this right away.

■ *First yin:* **Stripping a bed of the legs, destroying rectitude brings misfortune.**

EXPLANATION

Yin surreptitiously arising, dissolving yang from the bottom, is like stripping a bed of its legs. The stripping away of the legs of the bed may be slight in terms of energy, but the harm is very great; the misfortune of destroying correctness begins here. This is stripping away in which yin energy has just begun its advance.

■ *2 yin:* **Stripping a bed of its frame, destroying rectitude brings misfortune.**

EXPLANATION

The yin energy creeps up as it grows, like stripping a bed of its frame. Below the frame are the legs, above the frame is the bed; as the yin energy gradually climbs, about to rise onto the bed, it struggles with yang for power—the misfortune of destroying correctness arrives inexorably. This is stripping away in which the yin energy gradually grows strong.

■ *3 yin:* **Stripping away without fault.**

EXPLANATION

At the top of the body of submission (*earth* ☷), not submitting to yin but submitting to yang, corresponding with yang (top line), this is the yin of peace and quiet, even when in stripping away it is possible to be without fault. This is stripping away in which yin energy submits to stopping.

■ *4 yin:* **Stripping away even the skin on the bed, misfortune.**

EXPLANATION

Yin energy has aggregated and climbed up, the six yangs have already been stripped away to the fourth yang, the yin is strong and the yang is weak, and the action takes place on top of the bed—the disaster drawing near is like stripping away even the skin of the person on the bed; misfortune has arrived. This is stripping away in which one does things with yin energy.

■ *5 yin:* **Leading fish, gaining favor through court ladies: beneficial in every respect.**

EXPLANATION

In the middle of the body of stillness (*mountain* ☶), close to yang, the true yin that appears within energy is admitted. The phenomenon of true yin not only does not harm yang, it also can govern the group of yins, leading them to obey the yang. This is like one fish in the lead, with a school of fishes following behind as one; in human terms, it is like a queen advancing to the favor of the king with a group of court ladies. Those who know this use true yin to preserve true yang; thus when one is true all are true, and stripping away cannot strip this away. This is good and beneficial in every respect. For those in whom this is actualized, this is yin energy obeying yang, with no stripping away.

■ *Top yang:*   A hard fruit is not eaten. The superior
person gets a vehicle. The inferior person is stripped
of a house.

EXPLANATION
At the end of stripping away, the yangs have been stripped away, still leaving one yang that has not yet been stripped away. Those who know this
accord with it and stabilize it, so that it is not damaged by the mass of yin,
like a hard fruit that is not eaten. In the fruit is a pit; if you keep the pit,
you live, if you lose the pit you die. Life or death is only a matter of gaining
or losing this one pit. Ordinary people lose this pit, while superior people
keep it. This is because superior people know this pit is the basis of continual renewal of life and continual evolution, and so they preserve it and
protect it. Then not only are they invulnerable to yin energy, they can
even use yin to complete yang. This is like obtaining a vehicle and riding in
it safely. As for inferior people, who follow their desires, they can only
press forward and cannot step back; when they have used up yang, they
will in the end return to the great flux. This is like being stripped of one's
home, losing one's shelter.

Among the six lines of *stripping away,* those in which yin damages yang are
inauspicious, while those where yin obeys yang are auspicious. Practitioners should accord with these latter and stop there, so as to preserve the
yang. Accordingly stopping there, in the moment of reversal *stripping away*
turns into *return.* If people can know that *return* is latent in *stripping away,*
and set to work where this one yang is not yet exhausted, then they will
find the way to restore the primordial while in the midst of the temporal.
How many people can know this celestial device?

24. *Return*

Return is developmental. Exiting and entering, there
is no ill. When a companion comes, there is no fault.
Reversing the path, returning in seven days, it is
beneficial to have a place to go.

EXPLANATION
Return means coming back. As for the qualities of the hexagram, above is
earth ☷, obedient, below is *thunder* ☳, active; when activity obeys
the mind, the heavens turn in their course while human affairs proceed
successfully. Also, in the body of the hexagram one yang moves below a
group of yins; this is the first return of yang energy. In both senses equally
is the path of return, so it is called *return.*
　　This hexagram represents the return of yang within primordial yin; it

follows on the previous hexagram *adornment*. *Adornment* is being clear-minded and resting in the proper place, thereby to nurture clarity and operate the "fire" to gather primordial true yang. Gathering true yang is the path of returning yang in the midst of yin, reordering personal affairs, by which one can appropriate the creativity of nature and comprehend life and death, so that return is unfailingly developmental.

Though the path of return is developmental, nevertheless people accept the false and neglect the real; most do not know the return of the real. If you know it, it is near at hand—the mind of Tao appears, the human mentality retreats, and you can exit and enter the midst of yin and yang without being adversely affected by yin and yang. It is necessary to know the timing of return; it is not to be forcibly sought before the proper time, and should not be missed once the time has come. Only then can one find the real.

When people are first born, they are all good, with no evil; then when they get mixed up in acquired conditioning, yin injures their yang, and there is loss of original natural reality. But even though it is lost, it is never totally nonexistent; there still is a breath of living potential within. This may appear at times, but people do not recognize it even when it does, because they are deceived by personal desires and confused by worldly affairs.

To return it, restore it, it is necessary to take advantage of times when this living potential appears and set about quickly gathering it—only then can it be one's own. If the living potential has not yet appeared, and you keep to quietude in empty silence, how can it return? Thus it returns "when a companion comes," and only then can one be without fault. The character for "companion" is written as a conjunction of two moons; one is yang, and one is yin. When yin culminates, yang is born; there is yang within yin—this is called "a companion comes." If yin does not culminate, yang is not born, and the companion does not come; if the companion does not come, yin and yang do not interact—then where would creative energy come from?

Therefore it is necessary that a companion come for the living potential to appear; the living potential appears with the interaction of yin and yang—gather it and put it in the furnace of creation, and in a moment calamity turns into blessing, punishment turns into reward. Before there was fault because of loss of true yang; now that true yang is restored, one can be without fault.

But though one can be impeccable by restoring this, the way to do it involves work in an orderly fashion, restoring it gradually; one cannot restore it immediately, or even if one does restore it immediately it cannot be stabilized. It is necessary to first refine oneself and master the mind, waiting for the time to act. Therefore, "reversing the path," reality returns "in seven days." "Reversing" means turning around and operating in reverse, away from progressive conditioning back to the original integrity of the real mind; "seven days" is the number of the yang fire. The energy of harmony of essence and feeling in people is the yang fire; this is the real. The restlessness of acquired energy in people is the yin fire; this is the false.

The real completes life, the false injures life. "Reversing the path" means first reversing this false fire so as to return to the real fire. In seven days the yang fire arises and the yin fire dies out: Utterly empty and silent, within black there is white; the primordial energy becomes manifest from within nothingness. Gradually gathering and refining it, one can crystallize the restored elixir.

This path is not difficult to know, but it is difficult to practice; when you know it, it is most important to practice it. If you know it but do not practice it, that is tantamount to not knowing. "Having a place to go" and promptly setting about cultivating it, it will surely return gradually, from a single yang, until six yangs are pure and complete. What can compare to the growth and fruition of that return?

■ *First yang:*   **Returning not far; no regret. Very auspicious.**

EXPLANATION

In the beginning of return, true yang has not been lost; as soon as some external influence creeps in, it is immediately repelled, most serenely and easily. This is return which is not far. Returning not far, the human mentality does not arise, the mind of Tao is always present, and there is naturally no regret. If you can be careful in the beginning, it naturally turns out well. This is return in which the original yang has not been lost.

■ *2 yin:*   **Good return; auspicious.**

EXPLANATION

When knowledge is limited and one cannot understand how to return to the beginning, but nevertheless one is flexible and receptive in the right way, aspires to equal the wise, sees and associates with superior people imbued with the Tao, borrowing their clear knowledge to break up one's own ignorance, then even one who does not know return will know return, and even one who cannot return will be able to return. This is called good return. This is return in which the weak borrow strength, the flexible borrow firmness.

■ *3 yin:*   **Repeated return; danger, no fault.**

EXPLANATION

When return to good is not stable, and you return again and again and lose it again and again, this is called repeated return. Yet if your nature is flexible and your will is firm, and you are singlemindedly intent on return, and you handle yourself in danger, if you can do it once you can do it a hundred times, and if you can do it a hundred times you can do it a thousand times. Even though you may be ignorant, you will surely gain understanding, and even though you may be weak you will surely become strong; even though faulty at first, you can thereby come to be without fault. This is return in which one studies when at a loss and strives diligently to carry it out.

■ *4 yin:*   **Traveling in the center, returning alone.**

EXPLANATION
Being flexible but finding what is right and not being influenced by petty people even while in their midst, using the things of the world to cultivate the principles of the Tao, able to be clear-minded by oneself and skillfully returning to the beginning, is return in which one knows by learning and carries it out keenly.

■ *5 yin:*   **Attentive return; no regret.**

EXPLANATION
Flexible receptivity in proper balance, following appropriate guidelines, proceeding in an orderly manner, acting on the basis of what is fundamentally inherent and not wishing for what is outside of it, this is called being attentive in returning. Returning to attentiveness, one attains without thought, hits the mark without striving. This comes from natural realization, and since there is no loss, there is also nothing to restore. Not bringing on regret, one is spontaneously free from regret. This is return in which one knows by birth and practices it easily.

■ *Top yin:*   **Straying from return is bad; there is trouble.**
A military expedition will end in a great defeat, which
is disastrous even for the ruler of the nation; even in
ten years there is no victory.

EXPLANATION
At the end of return, following acquired conditioned yin, not knowing primordial yang, doing things by the human mentality, with the mind of Tao totally obscured, this is straying from return and after all not knowing how to turn back; it is inevitable that this momentum will call on misfortune and bring about disaster. People like this are deluded and do not understand: outwardly they contend for victory and crave power, while inwardly their mental spirit is maimed. This is like carrying out a military operation ending in major defeat, which is disastrous even for the ruler of the nation. Even if there should be victory over the long run of ten years, still there will inevitably be only ruin. This is never knowing there is return, from start to finish.

There is the *return* of natural time and the *return* of human affairs. The *return* of natural time is the manifestation of true yang, which comes about spontaneously. The *return* of human affairs is the stabilization of true yang, which comes about through effort. Only when natural time and human affairs are united can there be completion. Leaving aside the top line of the six, "straying from return," the other five lines all indicate a path of return, whether carried out intensely or calmly or with concerted effort; in all of them the ultimate accomplishment is returning to the original self.

25. Fidelity (No Error)

Fidelity is creative and developmental. It is beneficial to be correct; if it is not correct, there will be disaster, and it will not be beneficial to go anywhere.

EXPLANATION
Fidelity means wholehearted sincerity without duplicity. As for the qualities of the hexagram, above is *heaven* ☰, strong, and below is *thunder* ☳, active. Being active, firm and strong, wherever one's determination lies, one carries it out; therefore it is called *fidelity.*

This hexagram represents vigorous advancement of yang; it follows on the previous hexagram *stripping away. Stripping away* means that when one submits to one's desires, yin strips away yang. The stripping away of yang is all because of not knowing how to advance yang, and having it stripped away by yin. If you know how to advance yang, and with total attention purely on reality, twenty-four hours a day, without interruption, consider essence and life the one matter of importance, then external things cannot thwart you, and you can gradually reach true fidelity, the state of integration with celestial principle; this is fidelity with the path of creation and development.

In the hexagram, the action is in the inside; this is setting the will on the Tao. Once the heart is set on the Tao and the living potential is activated, the original creative energy returns. In the hexagram the strength is on the outside; this is earnestness in practice. When earnest in practice, celestial qualities can be cultivated and the original creative energy can grow. It is through this restoration and growth that fidelity is creative and developmental.

However, though one be capable of creativity and development, it is of course inevitable that it is only beneficial if the action is correct and the strength is correct. When action is correct, the original creative energy is not damaged; when strength is correct, the original creative energy increases. By correct fidelity, the mind of Tao is always present, the human mentality becomes extinct, and one sees again the original self as it really is, at peace, unmoved by myriad things.

If fidelity is not right, then when one acts it is not at the right time, and exertion of strength is inappropriate; though one originally wanted fidelity, without error, on the contrary one produces falsehood and error—this is called disaster, in which case it is not beneficial to go anywhere. The advancement of yang is aimed at fidelity to truth, because there is vanity and falsehood; fidelity that is not right does things on the basis of the human mind, acting in pursuit of personal desires. Then the medicinal substances are not genuine, the firing process is amiss—how can one complete the great Path? Therefore the path of fidelity, in which creation and development are inherent, is most beneficial when correctly oriented; only then is it genuine fidelity, without error.

■ *First yang:* **Fidelity, without error; it is auspicious to go.**

EXPLANATION

In the beginning of fidelity, when one is firm and has found what is right, one does not dare to have any vanity; the fortunes of human affairs all are in the beginning of arousing thought. If thought is correct, then action is correct; if thought is wrong, action is wrong. If one can be without error within, then one will naturally be without error outwardly; if one goes on thereby to practice the Tao, one will not fail to attain good fortune. This is fidelity in which one is able to be careful in the beginning.

■ *2 yin:* **Not plowing or harvesting, not making new fields, then it is beneficial to go somewhere.**

EXPLANATION

When one is flexible but not firm, it is appropriate to be still, not to be active; this is like not plowing or harvesting, not making new fields. To plow and harvest, to open new fields, requires that one have strength and seed to do this. When one is yielding, without firmness, one has no strength, no seed—how can one presume to act arbitrarily? However, if flexibility is properly balanced, and one keeps oneself open minded, one can borrow another's yang to balance one's own yin. Emptying the mind, one can fill the belly; using flexibility in this way, it is beneficial to go somewhere. One with error can thus be freed from error. This is fidelity flexibly following the firm.

■ *3 yin:* **The misfortune of fidelity; a tethered ox is a gain for a traveler, misfortune for the townspeople.**

EXPLANATION

If one's wisdom is small yet one has great schemes, wrongly seeking the treasure of heaven, not only will there be no gain, it will even harm one. This is the misfortune of fidelity. Causing misfortune by fidelity is following the contrivances of the mind, clinging tightly, without giving way. This is like a tethered ox, a gain for a traveler, misfortune for the townspeople. Before one gets anything from others, one first loses oneself. Even if true yang is in view, it is not one's own. This is fidelity following desires.

■ *4 yang:*   One should be correct; then there is no error.

EXPLANATION
Promoting strength by action, when one is compounding the elixir, if
there is the slightest carelessness the medicine and fire fly off, so that there
is error in spite of fidelity. However, using strength with flexibility, one can
be correct and preserve correctness, guarding against danger, quietly
awaiting action, using yin to nurture yang, thus naturally free from the
fault of losing what one has gained. This is fidelity in which one is firm yet
can be flexible.

■ *5 yang:*   For sickness without error don't use
medicine; there will be joy.

EXPLANATION
When firmness and strength are balanced correctly, and one follows one's
heart's desire without stepping over the line, the spiritual embryo has
formed, striving is completed, and effortlessness comes to the fore. This is
like sickness without error, which need not be treated with medicine for
there to be the joy of health. This is because the spiritual embryo has solidified and the primordial has already been restored; there is fundamentally no sickness, and what sickness there is is no more than the residual
acquired yin that has not yet been transmuted—but the basis is firm, the
homeland is at peace; ultimate sincerity will naturally return to freedom
from error. This is fidelity in which firmness and flexibility are mixed
together.

■ *Top yang:*   If fidelity in action has faults,
there is no benefit.

EXPLANATION
At the end of fidelity, one is already strong and yet still applies strength,
knowing how to advance but not how to withdraw, continuing to go at full
blast. If one wants to comprehend essence and life by fidelity to strength
alone, this will surely cause the firing process to go awry, losing what has
been gained; therefore if fidelity in action has faults, there is no benefit.
This is fidelity not knowing when enough is enough.

So the benefit of the path of fidelity is all a matter of gaining balance and
correct orientation. Without balance and correctness, action and strength
are not properly regulated, and cannot produce good fortune, but instead
bring on misfortune.
   The "moon reaching fullness" is in oral transmission of the secret;
the subtlety of "the hour reaching midnight" is communicated mentally. If
one does not get the instruction of a teacher, one is vainly indulging in
guesswork. When the one yang of *thunder* ☳ arises under the yins, the
hour has reached midnight; when the three yangs of *heaven* ☰ return

to pure wholeness, the moon has reached fullness. At midnight, advance yang; when the moon is full, activate yin: Advancing yang has its time, activating yin has its day. If you know yang but not yin, know how to advance but not how to withdraw, any time you get your hands on the gold elixir you will surely lose it after getting it, and the misfortune of fidelity is a matter of course then. So practitioners of the Tao should make haste to seek the personal instruction of enlightened teachers.

26. *Nurturance of the Great*

In nurturance of the great it is beneficial to be chaste. It is good not to eat at home; it is beneficial to cross great rivers.

EXPLANATION

Nurturance of the great means taking care of the great. As for the qualities of the hexagram, above is *mountain* ☶, still, and below is *heaven* ☰, strong; having strength yet being able to be still, it is therefore called *nurturance of the great.*

This hexagram represents incubation nurturing the spiritual embryo; it follows on the previous hexagram *return. Return* means restoration of the primordial energy. When the primordial energy comes back within, slight and vague to begin with, then becoming clearly evident, it restores the original self; the foundation of life is stabilized, the spiritual embryo is formed, and one enters from striving into nonstriving. Then one should carefully seal it and store it securely, forestalling danger, incubating and bathing, aiming for the great transformation, the unfathomable state of spiritual sublimation, making it indestructible and incorruptible.

On this path, it is beneficial to still strength, not to use strength. Therefore the text says "it is beneficial to be chaste." Chastity here means quietude. Stilling strength is nurturing strength. The work of nurturing strength is the work of keeping centered, embracing unity; to keep centered and embrace unity, it is good to be still, not active—if one is still, this preserves strength; if one is active, this damages strength.

Stilling is not leaving the world, quietude is not empty inaction: Therein there is a way of adjustment, addition and substraction; therefore one should not "eat at home." Only thus is one capable of great nurturance, producing good fortune. Not eating at home means externally adjusting the furnace while internally operating the true fire, still within and also still without, continuing subtly, not forgetting, not forcing. Then when one encounters great danger and difficulty one is unmoved, unshaken—only then is it real nurturing, only then is it greatness of nurturance. Therefore it is also "beneficial to cross great rivers."

The crossing of great rivers is that whereby inner nurturance and outer effectiveness is accomplished. This is the work referred to as "nine years facing a wall." "Facing a wall" is the state of being like a wall of immense height, detached from all kinds of biases and extremes, stopping in unknowing, breaking through space. When you break through space, the spiritual potential is freed, both body and mind are sublimated, merging with the Tao in reality. With greatness of nurturance comes greatness of development, and one becomes a companion of heaven.

■ *First yang:* There is danger; it is beneficial to stop.

EXPLANATION
In the beginning of nurturance of the great, if you promote strength there will be misfortune, if you still strength there will be good fortune; there is danger—it is beneficial to stop. Just at the point of giving up striving and entering into nonstriving, this is nurturing strength in the beginning.

■ *2 yang:* A cart is divested of its axles.

EXPLANATION
When strength is used flexibly, protecting the spiritual potential, awaiting the time for its release, it is like a cart divested of axles, so the cart doesn't move. In practice of the Tao, when firmness and strength are in balance, and the spiritual embryo has congealed, one should quickly stop the firing, stop the wheel, and not advance strength any further, lest it damage the basic energy. This is nurturance of strength gaining balance.

■ *3 yang:* A good horse gives chase. It is beneficial to struggle for right. Daily practicing charioteering and defense, it is beneficial to go somewhere.

EXPLANATION
When nurturance of strength has been fully accomplished, the energy is full, the spirit complete; truthfulness within is about to reach outside, like a good horse about to give chase. However, though the spiritual embryo is complete, as long as there is negative energy in one's person that hasn't been thoroughly transmuted, it is all-important to struggle to stay right, being single-minded without distraction, like daily practicing charioteering and defense, at all times guarding against stumbling and slipping; in ten months, when the work is complete, there is a spontaneous liberation and transmutation—so "it is beneficial to go somewhere." This is nurturing strength and stabilizing the basic energy.

■ *4 yin:* The horns of a young ox are very auspicious.

EXPLANATION
In correspondence with the first yang, the quality of strength begins to grow, and one then nurtures it; this is like the horns of a young ox. The ox

is docile by nature; its strength is in its horns. When the ox is young, its horns begin to grow. If one can nurture it when it begins to grow, the basic energy does not scatter; gradually nurturing it as it grows, eventually one will nurture it to the point of pure wholeness. The good fortune is already in the nurturing of the incipient strength. This is nurturing strength and stabilizing the basic energy.

■ *5 yin:*   **The tusks of a gelded boar are auspicious.**

EXPLANATION
At the time of nurturance of the great, when one uses yin to nurture yang, this is like a gelded boar. When a boar is gelded, its energy and temperament both change; to empty the mind and completely fill the belly is like the tusks of a gelded boar—the boar is soft, but the tusks are hard. Using flexibility and yielding to nurture firmness and strength, when firmness receives the nurturance of flexibility there is no injury. This is nurturing strength and merging yin and yang.

■ *Top yang:*   **Carrying the crossroads of heaven; development.**

EXPLANATION
At the end of nurturance of the great, the achievement complete, the practice fulfilled, with a peal of thunder the real person emerges, startling the ignorant, amazing the mundane. Beginning with striving, which no one sees, when one arrives at nonstriving, for the first time one is known to others—who does not extol carrying the crossroads of heaven? When practitioners of the Tao reach liberation and attain reality, there is a body outside the body, beyond heaven and earth. One does not only complete oneself but others as well. From greatness of nurturance comes greatness of manifestation. What can compare to that development? This is nourishing strength culminating in spiritual transformation.

So the path of incubating the spiritual embryo requires clear knowledge of nurturance of the great, strength held in check. Once one is strong and also still, in the beginning there is striving but in the end there is nonstriving. One is strong and healthy and rests in ultimate good without evil, integrated with the absolute. A single energy circulates, indefinable as being or nonbeing; self and others will return to emptiness, and the path of twin cultivation of essence and life is consummated.

27. *Lower Jaw (Nourishment)*

In nourishment, it is good to be correct. Observe
nourishment, and seek fulfillment for the mouth
by yourself.

EXPLANATION
The lower jaw moves whenever the mouth eats something; from that it has
the meaning of nourishing people. As for the qualities of the hexagram,
above is *mountain* ☶, still, and below is *thunder* ☳, active: action
does not depart from stillness, stillness nurtures action; action is not random, stillness is not vain—action and stillness unified, it is therefore called
nourishment.

This hexagram represents choosing good and holding fast to it, becoming empty to seek fulfillment. It follows on the previous hexagram *fidelity. Fidelity* involves strong action; without the work of care and nurturance, action and strength cannot be appropriate, and fidelity thus errs.
This is why the path of nourishment is important; nourishment means
nourishing what is right and getting rid of what is not right.

What is right is beneficial to body and mind; what is not right is
harmful to body and mind—therefore the path of nourishment requires
correctness to be good. So if you want nourishment to be correct, first you
must observe whether the way of nourishment is true or false. Observing
does not mean looking with the eyes; it means distinguishing in the mind
what is so and what is not so, in order to find out truth. When truth is
clear, then with real knowledge and lucid perception, in action one cultivates what is right, and in stillness one nourishes what is right. When one
attains what is properly nurtured in both action and stillness, one can
thereby seek fulfillment by oneself.

It does not say "seek food for the mouth," it says "seek fulfillment for
the mouth." It does not merely say "seek fulfillment for the mouth," it
says, "seek fulfillment for the mouth by yourself." This means what is
sought is what is right, and what is fulfilled is what is important. It is not a
matter of rich food, it is a matter of benevolence, justice, and enlightened
qualities. But the way to fill oneself with benevolence and justice and taste
enlightened qualities is all in seeking by oneself, not relying on others.
One day when you conquer yourself and return to true order, the whole
world will revert to humanity.

If you seek fulfillment, you find fulfillment; if you seek food, you find
food—it is simply a matter of what you seek for yourself. The "mouth" is
something empty inside; "fulfillment" means satisfying, filling. Emptying
the mind, filling the belly, emptiness and fullness correspond: When the
time calls for action you act, actively furthering yang; when the time calls
for stillness you remain still, quietly using yin. Cultivating the external by

action, nurturing the internal by stillness, unconstrained by action or stillness, inwardly and outwardly merging with the Tao, stillness as ever nurturing, action also nurturing, action and stillness consistently correct, ultimately one can perfectly attain the great Tao, auspiciously completing it.

Those who consider the harm of hunger and thirst to be harmful to the mind all nurture the small and lose the great. This could be called seeking food by oneself, but it could hardly be called seeking fulfillment by oneself. Once one has lost true fulfillment, how could it be called nourishment?

■ *First yang:* Abandoning your spiritual tortoise, you watch my moving jaw—this is unfortunate.

EXPLANATION

Being strong but acting in error, not nourishing the inward but seeking nourishment outside, abandoning the real and accepting the false, is like abandoning your sacred tortoise and watching my moving jaw. This is nourishment that is nourishing the mouth and losing real fulfillment, not being careful in the beginning.

■ *2 yin:* Perverting nourishment goes against the constant. Feeding on high ground—to go brings misfortune.

EXPLANATION

To wish to nurture virtue without having any virtue, elevating and aggrandizing oneself, presuming to have what one in fact lacks, being empty yet considering oneself replete, is perverting nourishment; it goes against the constant norm of using the strong to nurture the weak, and persists in feeding on high ground. This is the nourishment of the ignorant who act arbitrarily, not knowing how to seek truth.

■ *3 yin:* Going against nourishment, even with rectitude this is inauspicious. Don't act on this for ten years; there is no benefit.

EXPLANATION

Dwelling at the extreme of action, following one's desires, concerned only with food and clothing and not with essence and life, nourishing the little body and being a petty person, is going against the nourishment of nurturing truth. Even if the food is gained rightly, it is still an inauspicious path. People like this may spend their entire lives unaware that there are qualities that should be cultivated—it is not merely ten years that this should not be acted on, there being no benefit. This is nourishment in folly and ignorance, ending up without true fulfillment.

■ *4 yin:*   Reverse nourishment is auspicious; the tiger
watches intently, about to give chase. No fault.

EXPLANATION
Having correspondence with yang (bottom line), restraining the base
by the noble, not being ashamed to ask those below, borrowing others'
strength and understanding in order to break up one's own weakness and
ignorance, is called reverse nourishment. However, in restraining the base
by the noble, there may be the defect of pride while inquiring, the heart
not being sincere. It is fortunate if one is flexible and finds what is right,
like a tiger watching intently, about to give chase, eyes focused and mind
truly earnest, proceeding naturally, without forcing the issue. Before
taking from others, seeking from oneself, if one seeks truth one finds
truth. Then one at first faulty can end up faultless. This is the nourishment
of the unfulfilled seeking true fulfillment, seeking below from above.

■ *5 yin:*   Going against the constant. It is good to abide
in rectitude. It will not do to cross great rivers.

EXPLANATION
Emptying the mind, with self-control, only knowing how to nurture the
inner and not knowing how to nurture the outer, is going against the constant norm of nourishing true fulfillment. Yet even though one cannot
nurture fulfillment, as one can nurture emptiness and openness and remain true to it unwaveringly, this too is a path which will bring good results. However, it will not do to cross great rivers to accomplish the work of
striving for the golden elixir. This is nourishment of emptiness unfilled,
maintaining quietude in solitary tranquility.

■ *Top yang:*   The source of nourishment; dangerous, but
auspicious. It is beneficial to cross great rivers.

EXPLANATION
Firmness abiding in flexibility, resting in its proper place, action and stillness unified, one is able to nourish the inner and the outer as well, able to
nourish oneself and also nourish others; great is that nourishment. This is
the source of the path of nourishment, whereby it is possible to complete
the beginning and complete the end. Able to nourish in adverse circumstances, one is then able to nourish in favorable circumstances, of one's
own accord, without waiting for anything to be said. When nourishment
reaches the point where it is unconstrained by adversity or favor, unobstructed by difficulty or ease, then energy and constitution both transmute, yin and yang merge, and one rests in the highest good, unwavering;
the spiritual embryo solidifies, and the great Way is completed. This is
nourishment that includes both emptiness and fullness together, that has a
beginning and an end.

In each of the six lines there is that which is nourished, but there are differences of right and wrong. If we look for firmness and flexibility to match each other, freedom from constraint by either adverse or favorable circumstances, both striving and nonstriving, completion from beginning to end, it seems we can only find this in the top yang. Practitioners of the Tao should calmly observe and closely examine, seek fullness by means of emptiness, nurture what is right and return to the state of highest good where there is no evil.

28. *Excess of the Great*

When the great is excessive, the ridgepole bends. It is good to go somewhere; that is developmental.

EXPLANATION

Excess of the great means there is an excess of yang energy. As for the qualities of the hexagram, above is *lake* ☱, joyous, and below is *wind* ☴, entering. Going along with what is inside, delighting in externals, following what one desires, when happiness culminates it produces grief. In the body of the hexagram, inside are four yangs and outside are two yins; yang exceeds yin, and yin does not come up to yang—therefore it is called excess of the great.

This hexagram represents harmonious blending of the medicinal substances, in which fullness requires use of emptiness. It follows on the previous hexagram *nurturance of the great*. In *nurturance of the great*, one is strong yet can stop and be still; stilling strength, not letting yang energy get too excessive, is properly the means to nurture strength.

In spiritual alchemy, the path of the gold elixir, we take two times eight ounces of the polar energies and congeal them into an embryo; it requires that the great and small be undamaged, and both realms be complete. If yang energy is too strong and yin energy too weak, then yin and yang are not in harmony, and you lose the path of continual renewal; when yin culminates there will be decay, and when yang culminates there will be deterioration—going on in this way, the trouble of "the ridgepole bending" and breaking is inevitable. When the ridgepole snaps, the whole house falls down. In the same way, practitioners of the Tao who promote yang too much, who do not know when enough is enough, who can be great but cannot be small, suffer damage to their spiritual house.

If you can proceed breezily without becoming too intense, being harmonious and easygoing without clinging, mastering the ability to adapt to changes, preventing danger and being aware of perils, then firmness and flexibility will correspond, yin and yang will balance each other: Though great, you can avoid excess, so that it is beneficial to go somewhere—consummating essence and perfecting life, you develop without hindrance.

■ *First yin:*   **Spreading white reeds; no fault.**

EXPLANATION
When one is by nature weak and also dwells in an inferior position, weakness is excessive; the extreme of prudence is like spreading a mat of white reeds to place an offering, not presuming to go ahead of others. Presumptuousness vanishes, and there is naturally no fault of excessive greatness. This is being small but nonetheless excessive.

■ *2 yang:*   **A withered willow produces sprouts; an old man gets a girl for a wife. Altogether beneficial.**

EXPLANATION
Firm, yet able to be flexible, using yin to balance yang when it is excessive, not letting excess go too far—this is like a withered willow producing sprouts, an old man getting a girl for a wife. Yin and yang match, so the living potential is always present; firm and strong but not injurious, this is naturally altogether beneficial. This is using flexibility so firmness does not go too far.

■ *3 yang:*   **The ridgepole bends; misfortune.**

EXPLANATION
Employing strength strongly, only knowing how to go forward and not how to withdraw, losing the gold elixir after it has been attained, the misfortune of the ridgepole bending is inevitable. This is excessive use of strength.

■ *4 yang:*   **The ridgepole is raised; good fortune. There is another shame.**

EXPLANATION
Great yet able to be small, the mind equanimous, the energy harmonious—this is like the ridgepole being raised and not crumbling; action meets with good fortune. When practice of Tao reaches the point of greatness capable of smallness, this is already the joining of yin and yang: One should not be too yielding any more, because if yielding is excessive it will damage firmness, and the great path will be impossible to complete—one will become a laughingstock, and only reap shame. This is firmness using flexibility appropriately and not excessively.

■ *5 yang:*   **A withered willow produces flowers, an old woman gets a young man for a husband: no blame, no praise.**

EXPLANATION
Being strong in joy but unable to yield in joy is like a withered willow bearing flowers, an old woman getting a young man for a husband: Being

too luxurious and self-satisfied, when yang culminates it gives rise to yin, and the real is injured by the false, as a matter of course. It is fortunate when strength is balanced, and one has inner autonomy and is not deluded by external influences; thereby one can be blameless. But, having filled the belly, if one cannot empty the mind and rest in the center, then there is no praise either. This is excess of the great in the sense of being strong and continuing to apply full strength.

- *Top yin:* **Excess reaching the peak of destruction is unfortunate; there is no blame on other people.**

EXPLANATION
At the end of excess of the great, being ignorant and acting arbitrarily, not knowing the medicinal substances or the firing process, doing whatever comes to mind, going astray and not returning, the damage is worse the higher one goes; excess reaches the peak of destruction. One calls misfortune upon oneself—it is no fault of others. This is excess of the great in the sense of being weak and entertaining illusions.

Looking over the six lines, excess of the great is inauspicious, not going too far is auspicious. Within excess of the great there is still a way of not going too far; it lies in people skillfully combining yin and yang so that they end up in proper balance—it is important not to be one-sided or partial.

29. Mastering Pitfalls (Double Pitfall)

In mastering pitfalls there is truthfulness; thus the mind develops. There is excellence in practice.

EXPLANATION
Pitfalls means danger, as of a precipice or pitfall; mastering pitfalls means getting through danger. As for the qualities of the hexagram, above is *water* ☵, dangerous, and below is also *water* ☵, dangerous; going from one danger to another, yet able to get through successfully in spite of danger, it is therefore called *mastering pitfalls*.

This hexagram represents the presence of white within black, restoring yang within yin; it follows on the previous hexagram *nourishment*. Nourishment means seeking fulfillment by emptiness, seeking the true yang that has fallen in a pit. In human beings, after heaven and earth interact, the one point of original yang runs to the palace of *earth* ☷; *earth* is filled in and becomes *water* ☵, and *heaven* ☰ changes into *fire* ☲. At this point yin traps the yang; the celestial root is obscured and the mind gets involved with things. Though near to reality by nature, people become estranged from it by habit—descending lower and lower by daily repetition of habit, they fall into a state of ignorant obstinacy and do not know how to stop.

However, if one practices evil one becomes evil; if one practices good one becomes good—it is simply a matter of how people habitually act. Practice of evil is a way into danger, practice of good is a way out of danger. Getting out of danger requires that one believe it is dangerous—belief rules the mind. If one can believe in the danger, then one will not be seduced by external things. Practicing good, one can then be good; as it is said, once you reform, it is the same as if you were originally thus. Therefore "in mastering pitfalls there is truthfulness; thus the mind develops."

If there is truthfulness, then the mind develops; without truthfulness, the mind does not develop. The mind with truthfulness is the mind of Tao; when the mind of Tao becomes manifest, the human mentality does not arise—sane energy grows, aberrant energy recedes, and one can thus go in and out of yin and yang without being constrained by yin and yang.

But believing there is danger requires one to practice so as to get out of danger; believing but not practicing is like not believing. Once one can believe and can practice, without hypocrisy or deception, practicing truly, one improves daily with daily practice, rising from lowliness to loftiness, gradually learning a state of exalted illumination, developing one's nature to the fullest extent and realizing one's purpose in life, returning to the fundamental, without difficulty. Therefore the text says, "There is excellence in practice." If one practices this one can rise; without practice one does not rise. Knowing this is only valuable when one puts it into practice.

■ *First yin:* **Repeating pitfalls, one goes into a hole in a pit: bad results.**

EXPLANATION
If one is originally foolish and also repeats folly, one degenerates daily by daily repetition; this is called repeating pitfalls. Repetition of base habits is like being in a pit and digging a hole still deeper, entering into debasement and not knowing where to stop, not being unlucky but bringing bad results on oneself. This is being foolish and habitually repeating folly.

■ *2 yang:* **There is danger in a pitfall. One finds a small gain.**

EXPLANATION
Dwelling in the middle of two yins, daily in the company of petty people and not knowing to approach people imbued with Tao, one will ultimately fall and become a fool, just as there is danger in a pitfall. Fortunately, if one is strong and balanced, and has not fallen far, though one may not be able to get out of danger one has inner autonomy and is not influenced by base people. But it is undesirable that one believe in the danger yet not learn how to get out of danger; there is only a small gain, and one cannot clarify the good and return to the primary, which would be a great gain. This is being strong but not knowing how to cultivate good.

■ *3 yin:* Coming and going, pitfall upon pitfall,
dangerous and obstructed, going into a hole:
Don't act this way.

EXPLANATION

If one is insecure by nature and is also foolish and arbitrary so that one
acts dangerously, resulting in danger upon danger, this is "coming and
going, pitfall upon pitfall." Also, edging upward is dangerous, going ahead
is dangerous, and retreating backward is dangerous; this is "dangerous and
obstructed." People like this do not believe there is danger, and get into
increasing danger as they repeat their habits. Long habituation results in a
profound decadence, like going into a pit. Ending up in a dangerous situation, such people are enslaved by things all their lives. This is being weak
and only knowing how to repeat what is bad.

■ *4 yin:* One jug of wine, two vessels. Use simplicity,
sincerity, and openness, and in the end there will be
no fault.

EXPLANATION

On the border of strength above and weakness below, being a middling
sort of person, if one practices good one can be good, and if one practices
evil one becomes evil. One can be good or bad—it is like there is one jug
of wine, but two vessels are used to serve it. However, this fourth line
dwells with the fifth; those who have faith in good believe in goodness and
defer to the wise with open minds, borrowing the lucid knowledge of
others to break up their own ignorance, using simplicity, sincerity, and
openness to let in light. In this way can those incapable of good become
capable of good, and the faulty can become impeccable. This is being flexible and able to practice good.

■ *5 yang:* The pit is not full, it has only reached level;
there is no blame.

EXPLANATION

In between two negatives, positive strength is properly balanced and in
command; able not to be full to overflowing, one does not see evil in common people, but also being able to be unmoved and unaffected, one is
vastly different from ordinary people. This is likened to a pit not being full,
only reaching level. Not self-satisfied inwardly, yet not pursuing externals
either, one fills the belly yet can empty the mind. This comes from natural
attainment, and therefore there is no blame. This is stability of superior
wisdom, being spontaneously good without training.

■ *Top yin:*   Bound with rope, put in a briar patch, for
three years one cannot find the way out; misfortune.

EXPLANATION
Even petty people are essentially not bad; it is just that in spite of essential
goodness they do not know how to practice and develop goodness—they
bind and restrict themselves and get tied up in what is not good, abandoning and ruining themselves, living in peril. This is like being bound with
rope and put in a briar patch. Ultimately they will inevitably perish. It is
not only for three years that they will not find a way out of danger. This is
base, foolish obstinacy, never cultivating oneself and ending up bad.

So those who practice the Tao should wake up and follow true teachers,
seeking a way out, in order to comprehend their essence and life. Don't
ruin and abandon yourself and become useless to the world just because
you may have little in the way of blessings. Everyone has a part in the study
of body and mind, essence and life. The goal is near at hand; one may
mount the foundation of sagehood directly. It is just a matter of people
being able to believe and practice. If one can actually believe in this and
practice it, one will improve with daily practice, and will eventually cultivate the state of perfect good without evil, integrated with celestial principle. What happiness do people find in not practicing good?

30. *Fire*

Fire is beneficial for correctness and development.
Raising a cow brings good fortune.

EXPLANATION
Fire is clinging, and it is illuminating. In the body of the hexagram, one yin
is stuck between two yangs; this represents illumination with inner openness. As for the qualities of the hexagram, above is *fire* ☲, luminous,
and below is also *fire* ☲, luminous; by inner illumination reaching
outer illumination, by outer illumination perfecting inner illumination, illumining inside and illumining outside, inwardly illumined and outwardly
illumined—a thousand illuminations, myriad illuminations, are all two
illuminations, inward illumination and outward illumination, which in totality are one illumination; therefore it is called *fire*.
This *fire* embraces the female within it; the hexagram symbolizes the
presence of yin within yang, and follows on the preceding hexagram *excess
of the great.* In *excess of the great,* there is too much yang strength, exercising
creativity at will, misusing its light. Illumination is the energy of open
awareness in the palace of *fire* (the heart); it is the spirit of humans, the
master of mind. When the mind is open it is aware; the original spirit is in

charge of affairs, and illumination is managed properly. One can thereby balance yang. When the mind is unruly, it wanders; the discriminatory consciousness handles affairs, and illumination is not properly directed. This is sufficient to damage yang. Therefore *fire* is beneficial to correctness and development.

However, although *fire* is beneficial to correctness and development, if you only know how to use illumination and do not know how to nurture illumination, you will not attain development. Using illumination means outer illumination; nurturing illumination means inner illumination. Outer illumination has to be based on inner illumination; using illumination requires that one first nurture illumination: Therefore "raising a cow brings good fortune." Raising means nurturing; the cow is a symbol of receptivity. The cow does not use its strength; its nature is most docile. If people can nurture illumination with flexible receptivity, turning the light of consciousness around to shine inward, shutting out deviation and preserving truthfulness, first illumining inside, then illumining outside, then inside and outside will both be illumined, open awareness will be clear; nothing can deceive it, nothing can influence it—naturally illumining the qualities of enlightenment and resting in the highest good, what can compare to that fortune?

But the path of illumination and production of good fortune has a process, a course of work; if there is the slightest carelessness, illumination will not develop. Therefore illumination must reach inside and outside, so that both are illumined and both are correct; only this is the benefit of illumination, the development of illumination, the good fortune of illumination.

■ *First yang:*   The steps are awry. If you are heedful of this, there will be no fault.

EXPLANATION
In the beginning of illumination, if you immediately exercise illumination without knowing how to nurture illumination, your steps will surely go awry; not only will you be unable to advance illumination, you will also do something that damages illumination. Only if you are heedful of this, study it extensively, inquire into it thoroughly, reflect on it carefully, discern it clearly, comprehend it completely from start to finish, and then put it into practice seriously, can you avoid the fault of going awry. This means to employ illumination it is necessary to first seek illumination.

■ *2 yin:*   Yellow fire is very auspicious.

EXPLANATION
When you know you are not illumined, and can open your mind and defer to the wise, seeking the illumination of others, this is called yellow fire. Yellow is the color associated with the center: When illumination returns to the center, and you show your own lack and respect what others have,

even if you are ignorant you will gain understanding, and even if you are weak you will become strong, without losing your basic flexibility and receptivity. What is auspicious and leads to good results is the ability to empty and open the mind. This is being unillumined and seeking the illumination of others.

■ *3 yang:* **The afternoon light; unless you drum on a jug and sing, there will be the lament of old age, which is unfortunate.**

EXPLANATION
If you are only strong and not flexible, and only know to employ illumination and do not know to nurture illumination, then strong illumination is excessive. This is like the light of the afternoon sun: Having reached the peak of its height, it inevitably goes down; having reached the peak of illumination, it inevitably grows dark. So if one cannot drum on a jug and sing, there will be the lament of old age; unbalanced, one will only reap misfortune. This is using illumination and ruining illumination oneself.

■ *4 yang:* **The coming forth is abrupt, burning, dying, abandoned.**

EXPLANATION
If strength is not right, and one is eager to understand outside without being able to understand inside, this is coming forth abruptly. The illumination which comes abruptly seeks in leaps, without due process; it is impulsive and onesided in action, its arbitrary doings bring on misfortune, "burning, dying, abandoned." Though one wants to seek eternal life this way, instead one will suffer the consequences. This is considering oneself illumined when one is not illumined.

■ *5 yin:* **Weeping and lamenting. Good fortune.**

EXPLANATION
Dwelling in outer illumination, those who illumine the external when they should illumine the internal are weak and incapable; it may be that their perception of principle is not true, or that their strength is insufficient—therefore they weep and lament. And yet, weeping and lamenting, not daring to act arbitrarily, keeping to one's place, is also a way of bringing good fortune. This is clearly knowing one is not illumined.

■ *Top yang:* **The king hereby goes on an expedition; there is good luck, and he crushes the leader. As the captive is not the common followers, there is no blame.**

EXPLANATION
Dwelling on top of double illumination, strong and purposefully active, able to illumine the inward and also able to illumine the outward, able to

understand accord and also able to understand reversal, is symbolized as a king thereby going on an expedition, having good luck and crushing the leader of the enemy, the captured not being the common followers. The true mind is like the radiance of the king; the quality of illumination is like going on an expedition. Illumining virtue, virtue is then illumined; this is like having auspicious achievement. Getting rid of the human mentality is like crushing the leader of the enemy. Not forcibly restraining random thoughts is like not taking the common followers captive. Using illumination to the point of illumination crushing the leader, then all acquired conditioning dissolves of itself without being repulsed. Then one is tranquil and imperturbable, yet sensitive and effective, illumined inwardly and outwardly, without a trace of fault of sense. This is illumination that is ultimately good, without anything wrong.

So the path of using illumination requires that one know the active but keep receptivity, having flexibility within firmness. It is important that illumination be right. If you are adamant without flexibility, then you will either fall into abruptness or end up like the setting sun; not only will you be unable to increase illumination, you will on the contrary damage it. Practitioners of the Tao, if they want to use its illumination, must first nurture that illumination.

31. Sensitivity

Sensitivity is developmental. It is beneficial to be correct. Marriage brings good fortune.

EXPLANATION

Sensitivity means feeling and influence. As for the qualities of the hexagram, above is *lake* ☱, joyous, and below is *mountain* ☶, still: Firmness rests within, flexibility rests without; stillness is the substance of joyfulness, joyfulness is the function of stillness. This hexagram has the meaning of yin and yang responding to each other, so it is called *sensitivity*.

This hexagram represents harmonization of yin and yang; it follows on the previous hexagram *pitfalls*. In *pitfalls*, yin traps yang—yang is not strong and yin is not docile; yin and yang do not combine. So this work of harmonization is indispensible. But harmonization of yin and yang calls for spontaneity, not force. Spontaneity is nonconscious sensitivity, while force is conscious sensitivity. With nonconscious sensitivity, yin and yang harmonize with each other, without any insensitivity. With conscious sensitivity, yin and yang are individually separate, and sensitivity has limits.

Therefore in sensitivity there is a path of development. But though the path of sensitivity is developmental, there is right and wrong nonconsciousness, and there is right and wrong consciousness. You cannot say that the nonconsciousness of a dead tree or cold ashes is the developmen-

tal path of sensitivity; dead trees and cold ashes are purely negative, with
no positivity—how could that be called sensitivity? "Sensitivity" means
the subtle communion of yin and yang, as in the image of the hexagram,
wherein a boy and girl are together, each unminding, till the yin and yang
energies are full, and their feelings stir and they naturally become sensitive
to each other.

This is unaffected sensitivity—how can you take ignorant mindlessness to be sensitivity? Nonconsciousness, or mindlessness, in the
proper sense of the term, means there is no human mentality; when there
is no human mentality, there is the mind of Tao. The mind of Tao is a mind
that is not minding. Minding means having the human mentality; when
one has the human mentality, one lacks the mind of Tao. The mind of the
human mentality is not the real mind.

The mind of Tao is real, the human mentality is artificial. When you
use the artificial mind, sensing is inaccurate; yin and yang dichotomize.
When you use the real mind, sensing is true; yin and yang commune.
Whether yin senses and yang responds, or yang senses and yin responds,
they are equally ruled by the mind of Tao, and sense correctly. When sensitivity is true, not sensing by mentality, what is there that cannot be
sensed, what sensing is not potentially beneficial?

In terms of correct sensitivity, no one in the world compares to a
chaste woman. The virtues of a woman are based on chastity and calm;
not easily losing herself to others, she will wait for a good partner to have
feeling. This is feeling not by the heart but by truth.

In the qualities of the hexagram, first there is stillness, after that joy;
joy comes from stillness. When practitioners of the Tao harmonize yin and
yang, causing yin and yang to communicate sensitively, if they can take the
virtue of a chaste woman as their sensitivity, then whatever they sense will
be right; tranquil and imperturbable yet sensitive and effective, sensitive
and effective yet tranquil and imperturbable, they rest in the proper place.
Whether they go along with things or reverse them, all is as they will, and
they attain that good fortune.

■ *First yin:* **Sensing in the big toe is inauspicious.**

EXPLANATION
When one is foolish and low-minded, unable to refine the self and discipline the mind, to arbitrarily imagine great things is like sensing in the big
toe. The big toe can move but not walk; to feel something one cannot carry
out is not right sensing. This is sensitivity that stirs the human mentality.

■ *2 yin:* **Sensing in the calf is inauspicious.**
 Biding is auspicious.

EXPLANATION
Being weak without firmness, inwardly lacking the mind of Tao, being affected by the human mentality, is like sensing in the calf. The calf is something that should be still and not move; if one acts arbitrarily when it is

not appropriate to act, the action will inevitably bring on misfortune. However, if flexible receptivity is balanced, even if one has the human mind, stirred by feeling, if one can abide in rectitude and not be deluded by the human mentality, this too is a way to bring about good fortune in the midst of misfortune. This is sensitivity without the mind of Tao.

■ *3 yang:*   Sensing in the thighs; when persistence turns
to indulgence, to go on is shameful.

EXPLANATION
Positive firmness should keep the mind of Tao and not be moved by external things. In the human mentality, positivity is not balanced; seeing scenes, it gives rise to feelings. This is likened to sensing in the thighs. Sensing in the thighs, one cannot stop in the proper place; giving rise to confusion according to influences, persistence in keeping the mind of Tao is not single-minded, and where there was the mind of Tao one again gives rise to the human mentality. To go on to practice the Tao in this way would inevitably bring one humiliation before the wise. This is sensitivity losing the mind of Tao.

■ *4 yang:*   Rectitude brings good fortune, and regret
disappears. Coming and going with an unsettled
mind: companions follow your thoughts.

EXPLANATION
Positive strength originally has the mind of Tao; this resembles being upright and gaining good fortune. Also, being strong yet able to be flexible, without influence but also without harm, is like having regret disappear— so there is correspondence with the first yin; being pulled by personal desires, mixing the human mind in with the mind of Tao, there is no influence outside but there is influence inside—therefore "coming and going with an unsettled mind: companions follow your thoughts." Thoughts that "come along with companions" obscure the mind of Tao by the human mentality. The essence disturbed, feelings confused, the whole being is affected by the human mentality. This is sensitivity that arouses the human mentality and again obscures the mind of Tao.

■ *5 yang:*   Sensing in the flesh of the back,
there is no regret.

EXPLANATION
At the border of yin above and yang below, controlling both, using them in a balanced way, the mind of Tao is always present, the human mentality does not arise; dealing with things as they are, all takes place without minding. This is likened to sensing in the flesh of the back. The flesh of the back is above the heart; it is near the heart yet apart from the heart. What separates the mind of Tao from the human mind is but a hairbreadth; sensing it in the flesh of the back means it is near the heart (mind) but really

not the heart (mind)—the mind that is not mind is called the true mind. The true mind is immaterial, yet not void; it has no location, it is open awareness unobscured—this is called no-mind. Sensing mind with no-mind, though there be mind it too returns to no-mind. No mind, no regret; integrated with celestial principle, one rests in the highest good without vacillation. This is sensitivity preserving the mind of Tao without the human mentality.

■ *Top yin:* **Sensing in the jaws and tongue.**

EXPLANATION
At the end of sensitivity, and also at the culmination of joy, following one's desires, working on the external and losing the internal, using clever words and a commanding appearance—all is artificial; this is called sensing in the jaws and tongue. These move whenever the mouth talks or laughs—and when the mouth moves, the mind moves. This is sensitivity using the human mentality, utterly lacking the mind of Tao.

The six lines each have a path of sensitivity: one may sense with the human mind, or one may sense with the mind of Tao; one may have the mind of Tao and also sense with the human mind, or one may turn away from the human mind and only sense with the mind of Tao. These are not equal in terms of right and wrong. Only when one rests in the highest good and senses it is the mind of Tao always present, while the human mentality vanishes forever; true yin and true yang subtly commune, crossing the gap, like magnet attracting iron, and then the gold elixir spontaneously forms out of nothingness.

32. Constancy

Constancy is developmental. Impeccable. It is beneficial to be correct. It is beneficial to have a place to go.

EXPLANATION
Constancy means long persistence. As for the qualities of the hexagram, above is *thunder* ☳, active, and below is *wind* ☴, penetrating: Acting gently as the breeze, active yet serene, neither identifying nor detaching, the mind steadfast and the will far-reaching, it is therefore called *constancy*.
　　This hexagram represents genuine application in real practice; it follows on the previous hexagram *fire*. *Fire* means illumining the inward as well as the outward, aiming at profound attainment of personal realization, so that illumination is all-pervasive. But the path of pervasive illumination is not possible without a constant mind. Constancy means single-mindedly applying the will, the longer the stronger, not becoming lazy and slacking off. Thereby one can comprehend essence and life; so there is

a path of development in constancy, and it is also possible to be impeccable thereby.

However, though constancy can lead to development and impeccability, it is only beneficial if constancy is correct. If it is not correct, abandoning the real and entering into the false, then it is not developmental, and is faulty. The blind practitioners in the world who go into deviant paths, taking what is wrong to be right, aggrandizing themselves, boasting of their practices and cultivating vain reputations, striving all their lives without ever awakening, most assuredly are capable of constancy, but they are constant in aberrated paths, not constant in the right path. If you want to seek eternal life in this way, you will on the contrary hasten death; when your time is up, you will have no way out, and cannot escape the blame—how could you gain good fortune? Therefore constancy in the developmental, impeccable way is only brought to fruition by correctness.

Even so, the benefit of correctness of constancy is preeminently the benefit in correctness of constant practice; so the text says "it is beneficial to have a place to go." The benefit lies only in constant practice of what is correct. What is correct is true principle, which is the Tao of body and mind, essence and life. This path appropriates yin and yang, takes over creation, sheds birth and death, escapes compulsive routine. This is a great work involving constancy and persistence; it cannot be accomplished in a day and a night. It requires flexible, gentle, gradual advance, ascending from low to high, going from shallow to deep, step by step treading in the realm of reality; only then can one be effective.

Generally speaking, a great affair which endures long unchanging requires great work that endures long unceasing before it can be achieved. The constancy that is beneficial if correct is the constancy that is beneficial if it is going somewhere. But if you want to practice what is right, first you must know what is right, investigating truth, reaching the basis of essence, thereby arriving at the universal order. The work of comprehending essence and arriving at the universal order of life is all a matter of thoroughly penetrating truth.

- *First yin:*   **Deep constancy; fidelity brings misfortune. No benefit.**

EXPLANATION
In the beginning of constancy, if one does not distinguish right and wrong and enters deeply into false ideas so that they persist extensively, this is "deep constancy." If one plunges in deeply without clearly understanding true principle, even if one wants to seek what is right, on the contrary one will bring on misfortune. This is constancy that brings no profit.

- *2 yang:*   **Regret disappears.**

EXPLANATION
When strength is balanced and one deeply understands the firing process, masters the ability to adjust effectively to changes, is constant in timing

rather than by minding, constant in the Path rather than in things, constancy being without form or trace, this is constancy in which regret disappears.

■ *3 yang:* **If one is not constant in virtue, one may be shamed; even if right, one is humiliated.**

EXPLANATION
As long as one is strong and remains correct, one is still determined in practice of the Tao. But if strength is not balanced, and one is in a hurry to achieve attainment, advancing keenly yet regressing rapidly, this is not being constant in virtue and so being shamed. What is the shame about? It is the shame of setting the heart on virtue but not being able to be constant in virtue, setting the will on what is right yet being unable to constantly practice what is right. Following the path in practice yet giving up along the way, even though one be correctly oriented one is humiliated. This is constancy with a beginning but no end.

■ *4 yang:* **Fields, no game.**

EXPLANATION
When strength is in the body of action, the time is for doing—this is like having fields to plow. If one then dwells in a position of weakness, the will inactive, constantly embracing the Tao but unable to put it into practice, that is like empty fields with no game to watch for. This is constancy without any action.

■ *5 yin:* **Constancy in virtue; this righteousness is good for a woman, bad for a man.**

EXPLANATION
When one is flexible and balanced, keeping to one's lot calmly and constantly, without thought or effort, sincere and single-minded, this can be called constancy in this one virtue. However, fidelity to this single-mindedness is suitable for cultivating quietude apart from society, but it is difficult to thereby comprehend essence and reach the destiny of life. Therefore it is good for a woman but bad for a man. This is constancy in solitary cultivation of tranquility.

■ *Top yin:* **Constancy of excitement is bad.**

EXPLANATION
Thinking one has what one lacks, that one is fulfilled when one is really empty, elevating and aggrandizing oneself, concerned with oneself and ignoring others, is called constancy of excitement. With constant excitement, the culmination of aggrandizement is inevitably followed by ruin, the culmination of elevation is inevitably followed by a fall. Ultimately one

winds up being destroyed. This is constancy fooling oneself and bringing on misfortune.

So practitioners of the Tao should be constant in the right way, especially in practice of the right path. Only then can they get somewhere beneficially, comprehend essence and arrive at the meaning of life, and perform the great work in the world that is eternally unchanging. But it is necessary to know the medicinal substances, the firing process, and when to advance or retreat quickly or slowly, not losing the proper way.

33. *Withdrawal*

Withdrawal is developmental. The small is beneficial and correct.

EXPLANATION

Withdrawal means retracting. As for the qualities of the hexagram, above is *heaven* ☰, strong, and below is *mountain* ☶, still: Strength is based on stillness; using strength with restraint, one has strength yet does not lightly use it arbitrarily. Therefore it is called *withdrawal*.

This hexagram represents storing yang and subduing energy; it follows on the previous hexagram *sensitivity*. *Sensitivity* is the path of producing joy by stillness, harmonizing yin and yang; to harmonize yin and yang, the most important thing is to first subdue energy. Subduing energy means to still strength and not presume upon it.

The quality of strength in people is connected to the primordial true energy; after one yin comes and mates with it, yin energy gradually grows, and yang energy of course recedes. The developed person at this point knows the yin energy is active as a natural process, and can hardly be fought, and so does not set about repelling yin but first aims to preserve yang. Preserving yang means gathering in the vital spirit and stabilizing it in its place, whereby to subdue the primal energy. If you can subdue that energy, the yang energy is not injured, and the yin energy spontaneously sublimates. Thus there is a path of development within withdrawal.

But withdrawal as a path does not mean avoiding yin, nor does it mean sitting there watching the way things turn out; it means using yin to complete yang. In using yin to complete yang, it is most important for withdrawal to be prompt; if prompt, the yang energy is strong and the yin energy is weak, so withdrawal is easy. If tardy, the yang energy is weak and the yin energy is strong, so withdrawal is difficult.

In this hexagram there are two yins and four yangs: The yin energy is still submitting to the yang energy. Withdrawing at this point, withdrawal is preemptive; thus the developmental path of withdrawal exists when the small (yin) is beneficial and correct. The small being beneficial and correct is when the yin energy has not gotten to the point of injuring the yang energy. When the third yin arises, yin energy is not beneficial and not correct; it gets out of control and beyond withdrawal. Therefore the developmental path of stilling strength and subduing energy must take place just when the second yin has come forth. Then neither yin nor yang is injured, and yin follows the withdrawal of yang; the benefit and correctness of the small is also the benefit and correctness of the great.

■ *First yin:*   Withdrawing the tail is dangerous; don't go anywhere with this.

EXPLANATION
Dwelling in lowliness is like withdrawal of the tail. In withdrawal of the tail, external influences cannot cause injury, so withdrawal is most beneficial. However, because yin is weak and helpless, if one abides in it, one will not avoid instability of withdrawal, being affected by things, bringing danger on oneself. If one does not use it to go anywhere, withdrawal is secure, and there is no danger. This means withdrawal calls for care in the beginning.

■ *2 yin:*   Use the hide of a yellow ox to fasten this; no one can loosen it.

EXPLANATION
When flexible receptivity is properly balanced and rests in its proper place, external influences cannot penetrate; this is like fastening with yellow ox hide, which no one can loosen. Fastening with oxhide means effecting emptiness and keeping quiet, so external objects do not enter and internal thoughts do not come forth. Withdrawal without withdrawing, this is withdrawal not losing control.

■ *3 yang:*   Entangled withdrawal has affliction, but it is lucky in terms of feeding servants and concubines.

EXPLANATION
Yang in the third place is near two yins; strength is pulled by weakness and does not know to withdraw promptly. This is withdrawal that has personal entanglement; that affliction is very dangerous. The true energy in people is like the master, acquired energy is like the servant; getting entangled in yin and thus damaging the real with the artificial is feeding the servant and losing the master—so it is "lucky in terms of feeding servants and concubines." This is withdrawal having personal entanglements.

■ *4 yang:*   A superior person who withdraws well is fortunate, an inferior person is not.

EXPLANATION
When strength is used flexibly, and one can store away the yang energy when yin energy has just arisen, this is being good at withdrawal, without

personal entanglements: Being as careful of life as of a jewel, not letting any yin energy subtly spring up in the heart, it is therefore good fortune for superior people. If inferior people are adamant in strength and act arbitrarily, not knowing how to subdue energy, accepting the false and damaging the true, this is unfortunate. This means withdrawal should be rid of personal entanglements.

■ *5 yang:* **Excellent withdrawal; correctness is auspicious.**

EXPLANATION
Firm strength correctly balanced, the positive is associated with, the negative is kept at a distance; choosing the good and holding firmly to it is called excellent withdrawal. Excellence of withdrawal does not let the artificial or false damage the real and true; it is correct and auspicious in every respect. This is withdrawal that is ultimately correctly balanced.

■ *Top yang:* **Rich withdrawal is wholly beneficial.**

EXPLANATION
At the top of withdrawal, strength and flexibility merge; myriad things cannot move you, creation cannot bind you—you are free and independent. This is called rich withdrawal. When withdrawal attains richness, inwardly there is no damage, outwardly no loss. Without subduing energy, energy is of itself subdued. This is withdrawal that is wholly beneficial.

Of the six lines, only in the top line is the body of the real undamaged, so there is no effort to preserve strength needed. In the others, yin and yang are mixed, and the body of the real is already defective—so it is necessary to first subdue the energy, and after that not be invaded by external influences. Practitioners of the Tao should practice the path of nondoing when the body of the real has not been damaged, so as to nurture yang; but once the body of the real has become even a little defective, it is necessary to practice the work of subduing energy so as to guard against yin. The bodies are not the same, so the functions are also different; it is important to know this precisely, for it is an individual matter.

34. Great Power

Great power is beneficial when correct.

EXPLANATION
Great power means yang energy is strong and vigorous. As for the qualities of the hexagram, above is *thunder* ☳, active, and below is *heaven* ☰, strong: Strong within, effective in action, strong action does not cease—therefore it is called *great power.*

This hexagram represents advancement of the vigorous energy of yang; it follows on the previous hexagram *constancy*. *Constancy* is the achievement of perseverance in the path. Perseverance in the path means strong practice in the body, with the mind firm and stable and the will far-reaching, never turning back for even a moment, reaching deeply into self-realization; this is possible only for people of great power.

People of great power have extraordinary direction in life; they observe all things with detachment, and may let them go or take them up. Having powerful will, they can carry out powerful affairs, do what others cannot do, be what others cannot be. Transcending the ordinary and entering into sagehood, they do what is rare in the world. Like a movement of thunder rising from earth to the sky, they startle the ignorant and amaze the worldly, shaking up all.

However, the path of great power calls for power to be correct; if it is not correct, power is not great and its application is not beneficial. The people in the world who follow deviated paths, whether they cling to voidness or stick to forms, taking the artificial to be real, and do not fear danger and trouble, sometimes never changing all their lives, are indeed powerful, but their power is not correct—not only is their vigor unable to be great, but they even harm life by power. Then what is the value of power?

So the path of great power is only beneficial when it is correct. Correct means correctly oriented, reasonably ordered. Orderly power means one has inner autonomy and self-control, and the will is upright and correctly oriented, while outwardly one does not act arbitrarily and so one's conduct is upright. When the will is correct one is firm and strong and irrepressible; unmoved by myriad things one is inwardly vigorous and powerful. When action is correct, it is effective and decisive; able to accomplish tasks, one is outwardly vigorous and powerful. Will makes action firm, action makes will complete. Cultivating the inner and the outer at once, even those without power can become powerful, and the powerful can become great. There is no limit to the benefits of power applied correctly.

■ *First yang:*   **With power in the feet, it is inauspicious to go forth on an expedition—there is truth in this.**

EXPLANATION

In the beginning of great power, one should empty oneself and seek people to learn from, thoroughly clarify the principles of essence and life and only after that act. When the powerful rest on their strength and go forth impetuously, imagining that they will climb to the heights, in a hurry for accomplishment, this is "power in the feet." The power of powerful feet advances rapidly but also regresses quickly—to go far would definitely be unfortunate. We can believe in this as a matter of principle. This is power without prudence in the beginning.

■ *2 yang:* **Rectitude is auspicious.**

EXPLANATION
Governing the inward with firmness, responding to the external with flexibility, outwardly lacking yet inwardly having more than enough, being powerful without being rambunctious, power is in balance; when it is balanced it is right, when it is right it leads to good results. This is power with strict self-mastery.

■ *3 yang:* **For inferior people the use is powerful, but for superior people the use is nil. It is dangerous to persist in this. A ram butting a fence gets its horns stuck.**

EXPLANATION
Advancing impetuously, without a care, not inwardly strong but outwardly vigorous—inferior people may hope for fame and gain in this way, but if superior people who practice the Tao persist in using outward power when it is appropriate to realize all is empty, that power is useless. It is not just that the power is not correct—even if it were, it would injure oneself before getting anything from another. This too is a dangerous path. It is like a ram butting a fence—it will surely get its horns stuck. This is power that adamantly strives for externals.

■ *4 yang:* **Correctness is good; regret vanishes. The fence opened up, one does not get stuck; power is in the axle of a large vehicle.**

EXPLANATION
When one is strong and firm yet able to be flexible, yin and yang merge, and the gold elixir crystallizes. This is the time when one should correct others, after having corrected oneself. Therefore correctness is good, and regret vanishes. "Correctness is good" refers to the goodness of correcting oneself; "regret vanishes" refers to the vanishing of regret in correcting others. Also, being close to associates who defer to the wise with open minds, represented by yin in the fifth place, one not only does not ruin one's own power, one can also expand the power of others; this is like the fence being opened up so that one does not get stuck, and putting power in the axle of a large vehicle. This is power correcting oneself and correcting others.

■ *5 yin:* **Losing the goat in ease, let there be no regret.**

EXPLANATION
When dwelling in the body of motion in a condition of weakness without firm strength, people cannot be vigorous even though the time calls for vigor; this is like losing a goat in a state of ease. But even if people can't be

vigorous, it would be fortunate if they opened their minds with flexible receptivity and borrowed the knowledge of others to break through their own obstructions. If they can empty their minds, they can fill their bellies, then those who are not powerful can become powerful, and those who are powerful can become great. This is borrowing the power of others when one is not powerful oneself.

■ *Top yin:*   The ram running into a fence cannot retreat, cannot go ahead; there is no benefit. Struggle will produce good results.

EXPLANATION
If one is ignorant and acts arbitrarily, indulges in guesswork and goes off on tangents, a lifetime of studies will after all be useless. This is like a ram having run into a fence, unable to retreat or go ahead. At the culmination of action, disaster has already developed, so it is impossible to pull out of it; at the end of an affair, it is too late for regret—how can one go on to success? Unable to withdraw, unsuccessful in going ahead, one's whole life is wasted—what benefit is there? So for people who are weak and lack capability, rather than apply power by themselves and get hurt in the process, it is better to quickly empty the mind and seek a teacher. Studying when stumped, exerting effort to practice what is learned, working intensely while struggling through difficulty, not worrying about not reaching the realm of great power—this is originally not being powerful yet becoming powerful through resort to what is right.

In each of the six lines there is a path of power, but they are not the same in terms of good and bad effects. Power within, able to correct the self, is only represented by yang in the second place. Power outwardly, able to correct others, is only represented by yang in the fourth place. So practitioners of the Tao, when they have not yet comprehended the Tao, should first rectify themselves; once they have comprehended the Tao, they should rectify others as well. Correcting oneself is practice of the Tao; correcting others is establishment of virtue. Practicing the Tao, establishing virtue—only this is correctness of power, greatness of power. The benefit in correctness of great power requires perfection of virtue by the Tao as its ultimate achievement.

35. *Advance*

Advancing, a securely established lord presents many horses, and grants audience three times in a day.

EXPLANATION
Advance is progress. As for the qualities of the hexagram, above is *fire* ☲, luminous, and below is *earth* ☷, receptive: Producing understanding

by receptivity,`using understanding to practice receptivity, according with the time and according with truth, illumination grows day by day; therefore it is called *advance.*

This hexagram represents being sincere and clear-minded, advancing the firing; it follows on the previous hexagram *withdrawal. Withdrawal* means stilling strength and not using it lightly. If one does not use strength lightly, then the mind is empty and open: When the mind is empty, it is observant and careful, not being fooled by desire for things; within black there is white—spiritual illumination comes of itself.

The original nature of innate knowledge and capacity in people is bright and lucid; its quality is fundamentally illumined. By mixing with acquired conditioning, however, the discriminatory consciousness takes over, and the human mentality arises, so the mind of Tao is concealed. Thus the strength of innate knowledge changes into delinquent assertiveness, and the receptivity of innate capacity changes into delinquent pliability.

When the mind gets mixed up in things, this shuts down the openness of awareness, and the spiritual luminosity is obscured. When sages teach people to "advance the fire," this is just a matter of promoting restoration of illumination from nonillumination. The work of fostering illumination cannot be done without obedience, which means according with the time and according with truth. When always maintaining the mind of Tao and not producing the human mentality, knowledge and capacity are good.

What heaven bestows on humans is good, and people who submit to heaven, obey heaven, and accord with heaven are good too. When heaven and humanity act in concert, there is spontaneous truthfulness and illumination; that illumination grows daily, from subtle to evident, gradually advancing to a realm of lofty understanding and far-reaching vision. This is represented by a securely established lord presenting many horses and granting audience three times in a day. A securely established lord is a ruler in a state of security, tranquility, and peace.

The hour of the horse is noon, which is in the province of the image of the light of *fire;* multitude is what is produced by the earth, so it is in the province of the image of receptivity of *earth.* "A day" is the light of day; illumination is above. Granting audience three times is the receptivity of earth; receptivity is below. People's real mind with innate knowledge and capacity is the master of the body, like a secure ruler. The real mind not turning away from innate good, using both illumination and receptivity, is like a secure ruler giving many horses as presents. Producing understanding by receptivity, using understanding to practice receptivity, is like granting audience three times a day.

Three audiences means repeated reception, so that the unreceptive will eventually become receptive. Therein is the work of eliminating falsehood and maintaining truth. When one eliminates falsehood and maintains truth, the human mind becomes submissive and receptive, and the mind of Tao becomes manifest. Truthfulness leads to illumination, illumination leads to truthfulness. When truthfulness and illumination are simultaneously included, one clarifies the quality of illumination and rests in the highest good; then the work of advancing the fire is completed.

■ *First yin:*   Advancing impeded, rectitude is good.
Lacking confidence, become fulfilled, and there will be
no fault.

EXPLANATION
In the beginning of illumination, when the universal principles are not yet clear, one should be still and not act; therefore in advancing one is impeded, so it is good to maintain rectitude. The good of maintaining rectitude is that one first investigates principle because of lack of self-confidence; with inner fulfillment, the operation of the firing will naturally not have the fault of deviation. This is first seeking illumination when illumination is not advanced.

■ *2 yin:*   Advancing, grieving, rectitude is good; this
great blessing is received from the grandmother.

EXPLANATION
In the middle of the darkness of three yins, one not only is unable to increase illumination, one even obscures it in some way; therefore in advancing one is aggrieved. However, if one preserves rectitude in spite of weakness, and is not deluded by false yin, one will not be aggrieved even if one does not progress. Therefore one is fortunate through rectitude. This is because if one can be correctly pure, one can effect emptiness and maintain calm, so the true yin appears and the false yin vanishes. This is like receiving "this great blessing" from one's grandmother. This is not rushing to promote illumination when in the midst of darkness.

■ *3 yin:*   The group concurs, regret vanishes.

EXPLANATION
Unable to humble oneself and obey, instead raising oneself to obey, seems to be incorrect and productive of regret; but when one's nature is flexible while one's will is firm, one does not follow yin but follows yang, borrowing the other's illumination to cure one's own ignorance. You go along with the other, and the other goes along with you. Therefore the group concurs in advancing, so where there was regret it can vanish. This is following the illumination of another when one is not illumined oneself.

■ *4 yang:*   Advancing like a squirrel, even if correct
it is dangerous.

EXPLANATION
In the body of light, one has made progress in illumination, but being inside two yins, the light is concealed within darkness, and it also is in correspondence with the first yin; there is illumination, yet it is in some way not

impersonal—false and true are not clearly separated, right and wrong are mixed. If one goes forward in this way, it is like a squirrel, active at night— the vision is not great, the action not far-reaching. Even if illumination is applied properly, after all there is danger. This is illumination that is strong but not entirely impersonal.

■ *5 yin:* **Regret vanishes. Loss or gain, don't worry.**
It is good to go: Everything will benefit.

EXPLANATION
In the middle of two yangs, having understood one's own nonillumination, and also understood the illumination of others, one borrows strength to cure weakness. Thus where there was originally regret, regret can vanish. Regret comes from the mind not being open. If one knows how to empty and open the mind, one can thus seek from others, and so be able to fill the belly. Once one has filled the belly, fortune, misfortune, and stopping at sufficiency are all in the palm of one's hand. One can thereby be free from worry about loss or gain, and go straight ahead without doubt, going ahead in advancing the fire and working, with good results beneficial in every way. This is the illumination of becoming empty to bring on fulfillment.

■ *Top yang:* **Advancing the horns; this requires**
conquering one's domain. There is danger, but it
bodes well, so there will be no blame. But even
though correct it is humiliating.

EXPLANATION
Adamant strength overcoming oneself, only knowing how to advance illu- mination but not how to empty illumination, this therefore calls for con- quering one's own domain. One's domain means one's personal domain; conquering one's own domain means the work of overcoming oneself. The work of overcoming oneself is emptying the human mind. If one does not empty the mind and relies on adamant strength alone, strength must over- come strength—there is bound to be danger before gaining good results and becoming blameless. Using illumination in this way, even though one conquers oneself and attains correctness, it is still in the province of striving and does not come about spontaneously, so one does not avoid humiliation before the wise. This is illumination in which one is strong but too proud.

So in the path of advancing illumination and operating the firing, before illumination one must first seek illumination; once illumined, then one should empty that illumination, making it open. With emptiness and fulfillment working together, firmness and flexibility balance each other: Spontaneously sincere and clear minded, with illumination based on truthfulness, the illumination progresses daily, grows daily more lofty, so it can be used without end, taken without exhaustion; the earth is ever cov- ered with yellow sprouts, the world is filled with golden blossoms. There is nowhere one cannot use illumination, nowhere that can damage that illumination.

Concealment of Illumination
36. *(Injury of Illumination)*

In concealment of illumination, it is beneficial to be upright in difficulty.

EXPLANATION

The name of this hexagram has two meanings: The word for "concealment" also means "injury." In the qualities of the hexagram, above is *earth* ☷, receptive, and below is *fire* ☲, luminous; illumination within receptivity, being illumined yet conforming to the times, using accord to nurture illumination, it is therefore called *concealment of illumination*. Also, light being within darkness, there is illumination but it is injured, so it is also called injury of illumination.

This hexagram represents being personally illumined and truthful, withdrawing the firing. It follows on the previous hexagram *power of the great. Power of the great* means strength in action. Being strong in action requires knowledge of when to advance and when to withdraw; if there is advance but not withdrawal, power is excessive and will surely injure the illumination. When illumination is injured, power is ruined. This is why the work of withdrawing the firing is important.

Withdrawing the firing means concealing illumination in the most recondite, secret place, and not using it lightly. In practice of the Tao, the reason for advancing the fire and using illumination is simply to advance to illumination because of not being illumined. Once one has advanced to illumination, and inside and out are lucid and clear, then one can conceal one's illumination and nurture it unbeknownst to others, eventually to reach the realm of consummate good without evil, causing illumination to be free of any defect. Only then can it be said the fire returns to the origin, a mass of harmonious energy, which has energy but no substance, the original spirit of innate knowledge and capacity unobscured, neither material nor void, yet both material and void, not constrained by matter or voidness. Inside and out, all is illumined.

Illumination that is not revealed is better than illumination that is openly employed; this illumination has no form or trace that can be espied. Only when there is no form or trace to be seen is it withdrawal of the firing so that the fire returns to the origin.

But this withdrawal of the firing, the path returning to the origin, is also a reverse path. What is reversed? The illumination that is produced is reversed back inward, so there is illumination but one doesn't use it oneself. Having illumination but not exercising it does not mean vacant inaction can accomplish the task; therein is the work of preventing danger and the path of constant recollection.

The essential point is in returning when in difficulty, where one cannot be free. If one returns in favorable situations but cannot return in adverse circumstances, then the fire will not return to the origin, and the light will not penetrate reality; eventually there is sure to be injury. Therefore in concealment of illumination it is beneficial to be upright in difficulty. Maintaining correctness in difficulty, withdrawing in accord with the time, illumination does not suffer injury, and the basis of the elixir does not leak away. This is referred to by the classic *Understanding Reality* in the lines, "Even if you know the cinnabar and lead, if you don't know the firing process it is of no use. It all depends on the power of practical application; if you deviate even slightly you won't crystallize the elixir."

The rule of spiritual alchemy is in the firing: Too little firing and the elixir doesn't form, too much firing and the elixir is damaged. When the elixir has been completed, you should quickly halt the firing, rest, and gently nurture it, keeping to the center and embracing the one, deeply concealing the illumination in imperceptibility, not allowing so much as a spark of fire.

■ *First yang:* Concealing illumination in flight, letting the wings hang down; a superior man on a journey not eating for three days has a place to go. The master is criticized.

EXPLANATION
In the beginning of concealment of illumination, though there is no manifest form of injury, there is already the imminence of injury; one should quickly withdraw the fire so as to avoid its harm. This may be represented as like "concealing illumination in flight, letting the wings hang down"; or in terms of a person, "a superior man on a journey not eating for three days has a place to go." Flying with the wings down, traveling without eating, understanding when to withdraw and hastening to do so, nevertheless "the master is criticized," because withdrawing the fire is something that is done after the solidification of the spiritual embryo; there is naturally real fire, and one doesn't use artificial fire, and so one appears to be ignorant and inarticulate, which people dislike, so there is unavoidable criticism. However, though there be slander and criticism, one may be hurt outwardly but one is not hurt inwardly. This is withdrawing the fire before injury.

■ *2 yin:* Concealment of illumination. Getting hurt in the left leg calls for rescue; if the horse is strong, it bodes well.

EXPLANATION
If withdrawal of the fire is a bit slow, and therefore damage is suffered, it is like illumination getting hurt in the left leg. However, if one is flexible,

receptive, and open minded, upon suffering injury one knows to use a strong horse to speed to rescue oneself from the fault of inability to withdraw early. It is possible thereby to avoid getting to the point of great damage to the illumination, so this too is a way that bodes well for good results. This is withdrawing the fire when damage is suffered.

■ *3 yang:*   Illumination concealed, going south hunting, catching the big chief; hasty correction won't do.

EXPLANATION
Equipped with both strength and illumination, operating the natural true fire, one burns away the human mentality, the chief villain. Once the human mentality is gone, aberrant fire naturally vanishes. This is like "illumination concealed, going south hunting, catching the big chief." However, the human mentality has discriminatory consciousness dwelling in it, which is the seed of routine existence throughout time; it is not easy to get rid of this, and if one is too fierce about getting rid of it, that will conversely stimulate deviant action of aberrant fire, and the true fire will suffer damage. So "hasty correction won't do." Gradually dissolving it, the human mentality will eventually vanish. This is operating the true fire so that illumination is not damaged.

■ *4 yin:*   Entering the left belly, finding the mind in which illumination is concealed, one leaves the house.

EXPLANATION
Nurturing illumination in profound secrecy is likened to "entering the left belly." The illumination in the left belly cannot be seen, is not perceived or cognized. Thus can one find "the mind in which illumination is concealed," and leave the house, leaving minding and entering into unminding—then how can any aberrant fire flare up? This is withdrawing artificial fire so that illumination is not damaged.

■ *5 yin:*   Concealment of illumination in a basket is beneficial if correct.

EXPLANATION
Keeping to the center, embracing unity, not using illumination at all, while illumination is always there, is what is referred to by the expression "within is the natural true fire; in the furnace, the glowing river." This is like illumination concealed in a basket; it is beneficial when correct. Concealment of illumination that is beneficially correct is outward insufficiency with inward abundance. This is nurturing the true fire so illumination is not damaged.

■ *Top yin:* **The darkness of nonunderstanding; first
ascending to heaven, then descending into the earth.**

EXPLANATION

If one does not understand the firing process and only knows how to go
along using illumination and does not know how to reverse and withdraw
illumination, this is reverting to darkness by not understanding. Reverting
to darkness by not understanding is without benefit, and in fact harmful;
one brings misfortune on oneself. This is like first ascending to heaven,
advancing illumination, then descending into earth, damaging illumination. The gold elixir is gained and then lost, and all the effort that has gone
before is wasted. This is not knowing to withdraw the fire, so that illumination winds up damaged.

Nurturing the fire is nurturing illumination; withdrawing the fire is concealing illumination. When illumination is concealed and stored within,
fire returns to its reality, open awareness without obscurity, eventually to
become sublimated, returning to formlessness. But it is necessary to know
the firing process of withdrawing the fire to nurture illumination. If you do
not know the process, not only will you be unable to nurture illumination,
you will also obscure illumination. This too is "injury of illumination"—
how can this accomplish anything?

37. *People in the Home*

**For people in the home it is beneficial that
the women be chaste.**

EXPLANATION

People in the home means there are people in the home; this is the path
of governing the inner. As for the qualities of the hexagram, above is *wind*
☴, entering, and below is *fire* ☲, luminous: When illumined one
can follow the Tao, and by following it one can gradually develop the illumination. Receptivity and understanding are necessary to each other, like
wind blowing fire so that fire grows with the wind. Here is a way to govern
the home, so it is called *people in the home.*

This hexagram represents refining the self, mastering the mind, turning the attention around to gaze inward. It follows on the previous hexagram *advance.* In *advance,* illumination grows from receptivity; it is the
work of advancing the fire and employing illumination. To advance the fire
and employ illumination, it is necessary to first illumine the inner; illumination of the inner is refining the self. Refining the self simply means refining the yin within oneself. What yin is this? It is the human mentality.

In the human body, the vitality, spirit, soul, psyche, and intent all belong to yin and all take orders from the human mentality. When the human mind is calm, they all are calm, and when the human mind is agitated, they all are agitated. Refining the self simply means refining away this human mind. When you refine away the human mind, the mind of Tao spontaneously becomes manifest. When the mind of Tao becomes manifest, the mind is illumined; then the vitality, spirit, soul, psyche, and intent all transform into guardian spirits of truth.

The human body is like a home; the human vitality, spirit, soul, psyche, and intent are like the people in a home. When you refine the human mind and produce the mind of Tao, the vitality, spirit, soul, psyche, and intent each rests in its own position and each discharges its own affairs; joy, anger, sadness and happiness are all harmonious and balanced, like a family being orderly. This is represented as the benefit in women being chaste.

Women consider preservation of chastity valuable. Refining the self is like a woman preserving her chastity and not getting engaged. Then the true yin within oneself will become manifest; when the true yin is manifest, the open awareness of the mind is unobscured, and outside things cannot get in. Thereby one can gradually progress in an orderly manner, to seek the yang of the other, to the benefit of all.

In the body of the hexagram, the second line is empty, below, while the fifth is solid, above: When one empties the mind one can thereby fill the belly. The benefit for female chastity is precisely that whereby one effects emptiness and preserves calm, as a strategy to establish the home and business. Therefore practitioners of the Tao are cautious and wary, and do not let any yin energy reside in the heart, even subconsciously.

- *First yang:*   **Guarding the home, regret vanishes.**

EXPLANATION
In the beginning of people in the home, being firm in refining the self is like guarding the home. Self-possessed, one can guard the self, conquering the heart so that it is empty and clear, thoughts not arising within and externals not entering from without. Whatever regret there may have originally been can thus vanish. This is refining the self in the beginning of self-possession.

- *2 yin:*   **Not concentrating on anything, being chaste in the kitchen is auspicious.**

EXPLANATION
Being gentle but balanced, turning the gaze around to inward examination, the heart pure and the mind quiet, not concentrating on externals but carefully watching over one's inner state, controlling movement by stillness, preventing fragmentation by unity, not taking in external things, impervious to outside influences, is like a wife in the kitchen, remaining chaste, invariably gaining good fortune. This is refining the self and using the path of gentility.

■ *3 yang:*   People in the home are strict. Conscientious
sternness bodes well. If the women and children are
too frivolous, it will end in humiliation.

EXPLANATION
When the work of self-refinement is diligent, and random thoughts do not
arise, this is like the people in the home being strict, conscientious and
stern, careful and wary, not daring to do wrong, thus naturally gaining
good fortune. Otherwise, there are thoughts that do not leave, and one
becomes lazy and tricky, indulging in feelings and desires, like women and
children being too frivolous, without any order in the home. How can one
then reach selflessness? Those who practice in this way never attain the
Tao; they only get humiliation. This indicates the need for firmness in refining the self.

■ *4 yin:*   A rich home is very fortunate.

EXPLANATION
With flexibility seeking firmness, using firmness to balance flexibility, neither clinging nor rejecting, gradually introducing guidance, by emptying
the mind one can fill the belly; wealth is renewed daily, and one accumulates spiritual riches and celestial treasure—that great fortune does not
stop at selflessness. This is flexibility using firmness in refining the self.

■ *5 yang:*   The king comes to have a home; no worry—it
is fortunate.

EXPLANATION
Positive strength being balanced, the mind is correct and the body disciplined. This is like a king coming to have a home and executing government, so that the land naturally becomes peaceful. That fortune comes
naturally, it is not forced—what worry is there? This is unification of
firmness and flexibility in refining the self.

■ *Top yang:*   There is trustworthiness, dignified; it turns
out well.

EXPLANATION
Being firm yet dwelling at the top of the body of gentleness (*wind*), it can
be trusted that the self-refinement has dignity. Refining the self with dignity, being strict in the beginning, one can naturally be fortunate in the
end. This is refining the self conclusively.

The writings of the masters say that if refinement of the self is immature,
the restorative elixir will not crystallize. The first step of spiritual alchemy
is to refine the self. When self-refinement reaches selflessness, "light appears in the empty room"—the primal energy comes from nothingness
and solidifies into a tiny pearl, whose light pervades heaven and earth.

How can any bewilderment or befuddlement befall you then? Certainly refinement of the self is no small matter.

38. *Disharmony*

Disharmony: A small matter will turn out all right.

EXPLANATION

Disharmony means mutual opposition. As for the qualities of the hexagram, above is *fire* ☲, luminous, below is *lake* ☱, joyous. Joy arises inside, illumination is used outside; rejoicing in what is not to be rejoiced in, bringing to light what is not to be brought to light, joy and light are not appropriate, so it is called *disharmony.*

This hexagram represents conciliation and adjustment when yin and yang are separated; it follows on the previous hexagram of *concealment of illumination. Concealment of illumination* has a meaning of true illumination being obscured; then artificial understanding emerges, discriminating consciousness takes charge of affairs, following what it desires, shedding light on the external without illumining the inward. One's essence is thus disturbed, life is shaken, and one is separated from the Tao. This is where disharmony comes from.

However, though disharmony is disharmony, there is still a way to bring about union. Even though the light of consciousness is focused on externals, if one can empty the mind one can thereby restore light within. Even though desires arise inwardly, if one can fill the belly, one can thereby sweep desires outside. When illumination is restored and desires swept out, the spirit is settled and feelings are forgotten; then the barrier separating yin and yang is penetrated, and disharmony can be reconciled. Therefore "a small matter will turn out all right."

"A small matter" refers to yin. When the human mentality has been doing things for a long time and the mind of Tao has been buried away, the great matter is already gone. Now if you want to achieve unification, it is necessary first to dismiss the human mentality; after that the mind of Tao will arise. Only after the mind of Tao has been restored will a great matter be auspicious. When right in the midst of disharmony, it is sufficient to seek to avoid the human mentality ruining things—how can one dare hope great matters turn out well? This is spoken of in tems of a small matter turning out all right.

■ *First yang:* **Regret disappears: When you lose the horse, don't chase it—it will return on its own. Seeing an evil person, there is no blame.**

EXPLANATION

In the beginning of disharmony, when the mind of Tao has just gone and the human mind has just come, if one can firmly maintain rectitude and not be deluded by the human mentality, the mind of Tao will return of itself; those with regret can thus be freed from regret. This is like "when you lose the horse, don't chase it—it will return on its own." However, one will surely "see an evil person, without blame." The "evil person" is the human mentality; the human mentality has five thieves (joy, anger, happiness, sadness, lust) that can ruin the path. If one does not see the human mentality, one will not know the calamities caused by the five thieves: Seeing the human mind and going along with its desires to gradually introduce guidance, then the five thieves cannot extend their wildness—this is how to avoid injury. This is settling disharmony when it has just arisen.

■ *2 yang:*   **Meeting the master in an alley, there is no blame.**

EXPLANATION
When yin and yang have gotten out of harmony, aberrant energy is strong and true sane energy is weak—the mind of Tao is not easy to meet. However, if firmness is applied with flexibility, advancing by way of a small path, using the human mind to produce the mind of Tao, this is like "meeting the master in an alley." The formerly blameworthy can then be blameless. This is setting disharmony right when it is in full force.

■ *3 yin:*   **One sees the vehicle dragged back, the ox halted; the person's hair and nose are cut off. There is no beginning, but there is an end.**

EXPLANATION
When one is foolish and acts arbitrarily, following desires, that is like a vehicle being dragged back, the ox being halted; not enjoying the inward but enjoying the outward, before getting anything from others one loses from oneself—this is like having the nose and hair cut off. People like this damage the inward in their striving for the outward, lose the real by accepting the false. After all when they are at the end of their rope and have nowhere to turn, for the first time they will regret their error; therefore they have no beginning but have an end. But if one cannot regret in the beginning and regrets at the end, that regret will be useless. This is causing disharmony by oneself where there had been no disharmony.

■ *4 yang:*   **Disharmony in solitude; meeting good people, associate sincerely, and though it be trying, there will be no fault.**

EXPLANATION
Yang being inside yin represents the mind of Tao trapped by the human mentality. The human mind is perilous, the mind of Tao faint; the solitary yang has no resort—this is called "disharmony in solitude." However, though the mind of Tao be faint, if one can study keenly, not be ashamed to lower oneself to ask questions, and associate sincerely with superior

people who embrace the Tao, this will be mutually beneficial; the human mentality will depart day by day, and the mind of Tao will grow day by day. After a long time of this, the human mind will vanish and the mind of Tao will remain. Yin and yang will merge, and the solitary can thereby not be solitary, the faulty can thereby become faultless. This is the higher associating with the lower, thereby able to solve their disharmony.

■ *5 yin:*   **Regret vanishes; the ally bites through skin. What fault is there in joy?**

EXPLANATION
Flexible and receptive, emptying the mind, in between two yangs, one has already clarified the pure yin in oneself, and also understands there is yang in another. Emptying the human mind to seek the Tao, the formerly regretful can be freed from regret. The mind of Tao is the ally of the human mind, which can reform the artificiality of the human mind as easily as biting through skin. If one goes on to tread the path in this way, what fault of disharmony will there be? This is using emptiness to seek fulfillment, thus able to solve disharmony.

■ *Top yang:*   **Disharmony results in isolation; see a pig covered with mire, a wagon carrying devils. First you draw the bow, later you put the bow down. It is not an enemy but a partner. Going on, it is fortunate if you encounter rain.**

EXPLANATION
At the extreme of disharmony, the mind of Tao has been long buried away, and people don't pay attention to it; this is disharmony resulting in isolation. With the mind of Tao buried away and the human mentality taking charge of affairs, the influence of habit becomes one's nature, and doubts and ruminations come forth by the hundreds; this is being like a pig covered with mire, a wagon full of devils.

   If you want to restore the mind of Tao, it is necessary to first understand the human mind. But to understand it, it is important to see it: Seeing it as a pig, as devilish, is truly seeing the human mentality and how injurious it is. Once you can see and understand it clearly, your former use of the human mind without understanding is like first drawing a bow, while your later ability to understand and restore the mind of Tao is like afterward putting the bow down.

   Without the human mind, you don't see the mind of Tao; without the mind of Tao, you cannot know the human mind. Using the human mind temporarily to restore the mind of Tao, even though the human mind is the chief of villains, it is also the chief in merit; it is not an enemy, but really a partner. Once the human mind is seen and the mind of Tao is restored, at this point if you empty the human mind and activate the mind of Tao, and go on to solve disharmony, then yin and yang combine harmoniously. It is like encountering rain, which washes away the filth of all the pollution of the past, so one is restored to original wholeness and soundness. What can compare to that fortune? This is taking advantage of the time to solve disharmony, inasmuch as disharmony must ultimately be reconciled.

In each of the six lines there is disharmony, and the path of reconciliation is only capable of escaping disharmony between yin and yang, not of balancing yin and yang. Therefore it says a small affair will turn out all right. But if a small affair can turn out well, then a great affair can turn out well. When disharmony is finally reconciled, and yin and yang commune, if you seek from here, a great affair will surely bring good fortune. So practitioners of the Tao should first seek good results in the small affair.

39. *Halting (Trouble)*

When halted, the southwest is beneficial, not the northeast. It is profitable to see a great person; innocence is auspicious.

EXPLANATION

Halting means forward progress is difficult. As for the qualities of the hexagram, above is *water* ☵, dangerous, and below is *mountain* ☶, stopping: Stopping in the midst of danger, it is therefore called *halting*.

This hexagram represents preserving the primordial in the midst of the temporal; it follows on the previous hexagram *people in the home*. In *people in the home*, illumination is not used outwardly; it is the work of refining the self. Refining the self is only refining the acquired yin. From the time people lose the primordial and temporal conditioning takes charge, the human mind is perilous, like the two yins being outside one yang in *water* ☵; the mind of Tao is faint, like the one yang fallen between two yins in *water*. With yang fallen into yin, the mind of Tao is burdened by the human mentality and cannot manifest actively—it is all the human mind that does things; this is the extreme of danger.

But as long as there is danger, it is necessary to be able to stop in danger. If one can stop in danger, then the human mentality gradually evaporates, and the mind of Tao gradually grows; it is possible thereby to deal with danger, and to leave danger, without being injured by the negative energy of acquired conditioning.

The statement "when halted, the southwest is beneficial, not the northeast" is precisely the secret of dealing with danger and leaving danger. The "southwest" is the province of *earth* ☷, the homeland of utter emptiness and complete stillness. Utter emptiness beckons fulfillment; when stillness is complete, then action goes into motion. The primordial energy comes from within empty nothingness; as the mind of Tao appears, the human mind naturally recedes. This is the place that gives life to the self, so it is called beneficial.

The "northeast" is the direction of *mountain* ☶, where yin energy has nearly stripped yang completely away. Yin energy stripping away yang, following its desires the human mind takes charge of affairs and the mind of Tao is on the verge of disappearance. This is the place that kills the self, so it is called not beneficial.

It is beneficial to enliven the mind of Tao and withdraw the human mind; it is not beneficial to arouse the human mind and damage the mind of Tao. If you enliven the mind of Tao, then you can deal with danger; if you can withdraw the human mind, then you can get out of danger.

So the fact that it is surely "profitable to see a great person" and "innocence is auspicious" is because a "great person" is one who has not lost the mind of an infant. The mind of an infant does not discriminate or cognize, has no greed or ambition—this is the mind of Tao. When one has the mind of Tao one is a great person; without the mind of Tao one is a petty person. Getting rid of the human mentality is not possible without seeing the mind of Tao; only when seeing the mind of Tao can one get rid of the human mind. So "it is profitable to see a great person" simply means it is beneficial to see the mind of Tao.

Once one has seen the mind of Tao, false and true are distinguished; at peace, in accord, essence is stabilized and feelings forgotten. No longer seduced by the human mentality, by stillness one can control danger, and by action one can solve danger. Stillness and action are both functions of the mind of Tao. Meeting danger with rectitude, maintaining rectitude in the midst of danger, eventually one will surely get out of danger, resolve danger, and fulfill the great path, completing it auspiciously.

■ *First yin:*   **Going results in trouble, coming in praise.**

EXPLANATION
In the beginning of halting, before getting mixed up in things, when the human mentality has not yet arisen, if you go and get mixed up in things then you will arouse the human mind and there will be trouble. Coming without going, the human mentality not arising and the mind of Tao always present, there is praiseworthy virtue herein. This is being careful before halting when one is weak.

■ *2 yin:*   **King and vassal both faithful in spite of difficulty, not for their own comfort.**

EXPLANATION
This second line is in correspondence with the fifth line. The fifth line is the true yang within *water* ☵, like a king; the second is the true yin within *mountain* ☶, like a vassal or minister. When there is danger for true yang, then there is danger for true yin: It is like a king and vassal being faithful in spite of difficulty; when there is trouble, if they can stay in their

proper places, empty the human mind and seek the mind of Tao, not letting difficulty and hardship alter their determination; this is what is called not for personal comfort. This is being able to deal with trouble in spite of weakness.

■ *3 yang:* Going leads to trouble. Come back.

EXPLANATION

When there is too much adamant hardness on the brink of danger, to go on would lead to trouble. It is lucky if firmness is correct and one can stop upon seeing danger, and come back rather than go on, sweep away the human mind and hold onto the mind of Tao, having no trouble even in difficulty. This is being firm and not getting into trouble.

■ *4 yin:* Going leads to trouble; come form associations.

EXPLANATION

When weak and alone, without strength, one is basically in danger; to try to force one's way out of danger would lead to trouble. It is lucky if one can restrain oneself and seek the guidance of others, not being ashamed to ask questions, coming to form associations with people imbued with the Tao, to broaden one's knowledge and vision. Then the mind of Tao will gradually grow, the human mentality will gradually leave, and one will eventually get out of danger and have no trouble. This is being weak but borrowing strength to solve trouble.

■ *5 yang:* Great trouble; a companion comes.

EXPLANATION

Yang is fallen into yin, the mind of Tao is covered by the human mind—this is called great trouble. However, if strength is balanced correctly, when one uses the human mind temporarily to cultivate the mind of Tao, once the mind of Tao comes, the human mind is transformed: Strength and flexibility combine, and the primordial energy congeals from nothingness to form the elixir. So in great trouble, one is capable of a great solution. This is strength and flexibility being one energy, with no trouble.

■ *Top yin:* Going is trouble, coming is great. For good results, it is beneficial to see a great person.

EXPLANATION

At the end of trouble, just when the human mind is calm and the mind of Tao appears, if one does not understand the process and tries to forcibly control the human mind, that will on the contrary obscure the mind of Tao—to go on thus would mean trouble. If one comes back to nurture the mind of Tao, without trying to control the human mind, there is great merit in this. However, it is surely beneficial to see a great person, who is someone that has understood the Tao, attained reality, and gotten out of danger, who thoroughly understands the remedy and process every step of the way out of danger. The end of trouble is precisely the gate of life, the door of death, the point where both fortune and misfortune are possible. It is necessary to have the verbal instruction and mental transmission of a true teacher before one can seek to live in the midst of killing, get out of trouble, resolve trouble, and not be confined by yin and yang. This is seeking a teacher's verbal instruction to solve trouble.

So the way to get out of trouble and solve it requires the instruction of a genuine teacher to break through the gate of life and the door of death; only then can the task be done. If you do not know the gate of life and the door of death, not only do you not know the mind of Tao, you do not even know the human mind. If you do not know the mind of Tao, how can you bring it to life? If you do not know the human mind, how can you get rid of it? If the mind of Tao is not brought to life and the human mind is not dismissed, only fooling around in deviated methods, you will bring on trouble where there was none. This is of no benefit to essence and life, and is in fact harmful. How can we not beware?

40. Liberation (Solution)

For liberation, the southwest is beneficial. When going nowhere, the return brings good fortune; when going somewhere, promptness brings good fortune.

EXPLANATION

Liberation means freeing. As for the qualities of the hexagram, above is *thunder* ☲☲, active, and below is *water* ☵☵, dangerous. When positive energy moves out of danger, action beyond danger moves according to the will; so it is called liberation.

This hexagram represents taking advantage of the right time to gather the medicine. It follows on the previous hexagram *disharmony*. *Disharmony* means yin and yang are not in harmony, delight and attention are not appropriate, negative energy is in charge of affairs, while positive energy is trapped. So this work of liberating the positive energy is essential.

Liberating the positive energy is "gathering the medicine." In gathering the medicine it is important to know the right time; otherwise you will fumble, and negative energy will remain while positive energy will again slip away—then even though the medicine be nearby, you cannot avail yourself of it.

Understanding Reality says, "When lead meets winter, hasten to gather it; after the full moon, metal is worthless." When the first yang is born on the ground of *earth* ☷☷ (thereby producing *thunder* ☲☲), the primordial energy comes from within nothingness, and the heart of heaven and earth turns. This is what is called "finding companionship in the southwest." Just when "lead meets winter" and the great medicine appears, when the mind of Tao becomes active and the human mind is still, this spontaneous liberation is the portent of good fortune. Therefore, "for liberation, the southwest is beneficial; when going nowhere, the return brings good fortune." Returning without going anywhere does not come about by human effort; it appears spontaneously at a given time, and comes from nature.

But once nature's time has arrived, human exertion is necessary; one should hasten to set about fostering positive energy and suppressing negative energy. When the celestial and the human act together, one uses the return of this one bit of positive energy to go back, back to where there is pure positivity without negativity, so the mind of Tao is always present and the human mentality is forever extinguished. Only then is one liberated from danger and difficulty, and able to act freely in any way, just as one wills.

This is why "when going somewhere, promptness brings good fortune." If one is prompt, when the medicinal energy has just arisen it belongs to the primordial; if one is tardy, once the medicinal energy has passed it belongs to the temporal. If you promptly gather the medicinal energy when it has just arisen, then the primordial is stable and you gain good fortune. If you gather it only when the medicinal energy has passed, then temporal conditioning will reassert itself and you will be unfortunate. There is profound meaning in the words "promptness brings good fortune." There is that which requires promptness; that is to say, when you reach the point where the first yang has just become active, you should advance the fire without delay.

■ *First yin:* **No blame.**

EXPLANATION
In extreme danger, weak and helpless, unable to get out by oneself, still if one knows to associate with people imbued with the Tao, borrowing the knowledge and wisdom of others to solve one's own ignorance, one who is blameworthy can still become blameless. This is borrowing strength when weak to be released from danger.

■ *2 yang:* **Catching three foxes on a hunt, having golden arrows, correctness brings good fortune.**

EXPLANATION
With one yang between two yins, one is firm yet can be flexible. Precise and singleminded, keeping to the center, one doesn't let the human mind do evil, like catching foxes in the fields and not letting the foxes run wild; yet neither does one seek forced extinction of the human mind, like having golden arrows and not hurting the foxes. Not indulging, not injuring, going along with its desires to gradually guide it, one causes it to naturally dissolve, so one is liberated without trying to be liberated. This is the

most fortunate liberation. This is being strong and using flexibility to be released from danger.

■ *3 yin:*   **Riding bearing a burden causes enemies to arrive. Even being righteous one is humiliated.**

EXPLANATION
Being ignorant and acting arbitrarily, with vain imaginings about the celestial treasure, trying to coerce the human mind without having the mind of Tao, using the mind to rule the mind, one is not only unable to get rid of the human mentality, one in fact invites the human mentality. This is like trying to get on a cart while carrying something, bringing injury on oneself. Even though one's resolution be correct, still if one relies on one's personal yin and does not seek yang from another, this brings humiliation on a practitioner of the Tao. This is trying to force release from danger when one is weak.

■ *4 yang:*   **Releasing your big toe, when the companion comes, then trust.**

EXPLANATION
When adamant but incorrect, and also in correspondence with initial negativity, the human mentality is mixed in with the mind of Tao, so one is not effectively liberated from negativity; this is like "releasing your big toe." Dispelling the human mentality is the way to activating the mind of Tao: The human mind is dispelled when the mind of Tao arrives—trusting the latter, you release the former. In the big toe, there is the ability to move but not to walk; you can see the human mind is perilous here and the mind of Tao here is faint. This is strength being dragged by weakness, so not being liberated from danger.

■ *5 yin:*   **In this the superior person has liberation, which is fortunate; there is earnestness in regard to the inferior person.**

EXPLANATION
Emptying the human mind to seek the mind of Tao is wherein lies the liberation of the superior person. The mind of Tao is the mind of the superior person, the human mind is the mind of the inferior person. Whether the mind of Tao has become liberated or not can be checked in the human mind. Only when the human mind has been thoroughly sublimated is the mind of Tao released from difficulty. If there is even a bit of the human mentality, the mind of Tao has not yet been released from difficulty. Therefore, those who practice the Tao should make the utmost effort to strike a balance between looseness and tightness, and not let there be the slightest pollution. This is liberation sublimating the aggregate of yin.

■ *Top yin:*   **The prince shoots at a hawk on a high wall
and gets it, to the benefit of all.**

EXPLANATION

At the end of liberation, when all acquired energies have been dissolved,
but there still remains the human mentality, which hasn't died yet, this bit
of human mind, greedy and ambitious beyond compare, is the greatest of
villains, like a hawk on a high wall, and should be promptly dispatched.
Luckily, at the end of liberation, sane energy is strong and aberrant energy
is weak; using the mind of Tao, one dismisses the human mentality, directly obliterating it, to the benefit of all. This is great impartiality clearing
away danger.

So on the path of liberation from difficulty and escape from danger it is
important to know the proper timing, and it is most important that
firmness and flexibility balance each other. Not getting ahead, not falling
behind, not tense, not lax, taking advantage of the right time to get to
work, anyone will obtain benefit. But the way to obtain benefit requires
knowledge of the southwest, the position of *earth* ☷ ☷. "The medicine
comes from the southwest—this is the position of *earth*. If you want to
look for the position of *earth*, is it apart from the human being? I clearly
explain; you should remember. I'm only afraid when you encounter it
your recognition won't be true." Do you suppose the southwest position of
earth is easy to know?

41. *Reduction*

**Reduction with sincerity is very auspicious,
impeccable. It should be correct. It is beneficial to go
somewhere. What is the use of the two bowls? They
can be used to receive.**

EXPLANATION

Reduction means diminishing excess. As for the qualities of the hexagram,
above is *mountain* ☶, still, and below is *lake* ☱, joyous: Having
something to rejoice over, yet immediately stilling it, by stilling the joy
there is no errant thought. In the body of the hexagram, in the second and
fifth lines strength and flexibility are balanced, emptiness and fullness are
in accord; strength does not become rambunctious, flexibility does not become weakness. Diminishing what is excessive, adding to what is insufficient—thus it is called *reduction*.

This hexagram represents the existence of increase within reduction;
it follows on the previous hexagram *halting*. In *halting*, one can stop
where there is danger, preserving the primordial Tao in the midst of the

temporal. But if you want to preserve the primordial, it is necessary to re-move acquired conditioning; and to remove acquired conditioning means to travel the path of *reduction*.

However, reduction as a path means not following desires but stop-ping desires; many people cannot be sincere in it. If one cannot be sincere, one may start but will not finish; then not only will one fail to gain good fortune, one will also bring on blame. If one can be sincere, every thought is true; sincerity in the mind naturally shows in action. Then good fortune comes even though one does not try to bring it about; as one does not bring about fault, fault is naturally nonexistent.

But even though sincerity in reduction is certainly auspicious and surely impeccable, it is most important that sincerity be correct, that re-duction be correct. People in the world who contemplate voidness, stick to quietude, forget about people, forget about their own bodies, and go on like this all their lives without change, are certainly sincere about reduc-tion, but they are faithful to what they should not be faithful to, and re-duce what they should not reduce—thus there is decrease with increase, which is still faulty.

So if one can be correct in sincerity, discern whether it is right or wrong, distinguish whether it is false or true, understand it in the mind and prove it in actual events, "there is somewhere to go," to the benefit of all. But while the benefit of going somewhere is beneficial insofar as sin-cerity is correct and reduction is correct, actual practice in real life is most important, to finish what has been started. As long as one has not yet reached the serene, equanimous realm of the middle way, work cannot be stopped; one must daily reduce for the sake of the Tao, daily increasing one's accomplishment. Reducing and reducing again, increasing and in-creasing again, until there is no more to be reduced and no more to be increased, so strength and softness correspond, inside and outside merge with the Tao, in perfect goodness without evil, wholly integrated with the design of nature—only then is the work of reduction and increase no longer needed.

Therefore the text says, "What is the use of the two bowls? They can be used to receive." A bowl is something hollow and round; the "two bowls" are the balance of strength and flexibility represented by the sec-ond and fifth lines in correspondence. When strength and flexibility are balanced, there is flexibility in strength and strength in flexibility; strength and flexibility are as one. The vitalities of the second and fifth lines subtly join and congeal, returning to the basis, going back to the origin; the spiri-tual embryo takes on form, and from this one receives the bliss of freedom and nonstriving. One's fate now depends on oneself, not on heaven. Be sincere in reduction, and within reduction there is increase. This is no small matter.

■ *First yang:* Ending affairs, going quickly, there is no
fault; but assess before reducing something.

EXPLANATION
When one is strong and decisive, bold and powerful, as soon as reduction
is mentioned one wants to carry out that reduction; therefore, "Ending
affairs, going quickly," reduction can surely be without fault. But reduction in the beginning has the possibility of excessive forcefulness, erring by
incorrect reduction. It is necessary to assess whether it is right or wrong,
appropriate or otherwise, before reducing anything. Only then can there
be increase within reduction, and reduction without any fault. This means
reduction requires care in the beginning.

■ *2 yang:* It is beneficial to be correct. An expedition is
inauspicious. No reduction or increase of this.

EXPLANATION
Strong yet balanced, the mind of Tao ever present, the human mentality
not arising, yin and yang harmoniously combined, the gold elixir takes on
form: Just when you should carefully stabilize it and store it securely, if
you do not know when enough is enough and go on reducing and increasing, you will reactivate the human mentality and thus obscure the
mind of Tao. This is not beneficial, and even brings misfortune. It is because the strong energy is balanced, not biased or lopsided, that there is no
more reduction or increasing to be done. This is not reducing and not increasing either.

■ *3 yin:* Three people traveling are reduced by one
person; one person traveling finds a companion.

EXPLANATION
When one is foolish and ignorant, gives rise to feelings in regard to experiences, cannot reduce the human mentality but uses the human mentality
instead, seeks increase but instead gets decrease, this is like three people
traveling being reduced by one person. If one knows there is loss within
gain, and can reduce the dualistic mind of the human mentality, and increase the united consciousness of the mind of Tao, then yin and yang
match each other, and there is gain within loss; this is like one person
traveling finding a companion. This means when seeking increase one
must use reduction.

■ *4 yin:* Reducing sickness, causing there to be joy
quickly, there is no fault.

EXPLANATION
In pure negativity without positivity, the sickness is already grave; it is
lucky if one is flexible yet upright, with yin obeying yang, sincerely seek-

ing the method of immortality of the other to reduce the illness of the self—then even those unable to reduce will be able to do so, and those unable to reduce quickly will be able to do so. Finding gain within loss, not only is there joy, but also there is no fault. This is reducing weakness and seeking increase of strength.

- *5 yin:*   **One is given a profit of ten sets of tortoise shells; none can oppose. Very auspicious.**

EXPLANATION
Flexible yet balanced, staying in the appropriate place, by emptying the mind one can fill the belly: Emptiness and fulfillment correspond, firmness and flexibility balance each other; the vitalities of the second and fifth places subtly combine and congeal, giving one a profit of ten pairs of tortoises. [Tortoise shells were anciently used for money.] "One is given a profit" means gaining without seeking gain; the gain comes about spontaneously, naturally, and does not involve forced effort. This is the auspicious path of return to the fundamental, reversion to the origin. Herein lies what is called "Drumming on bamboo, calling the tortoise (symbol of longevity), eating jade mushrooms, plucking the lute, summoning the phoenix (symbol of immortality), drinking from the alchemical crucible." This is the spontaneous increase of strength when weakness is reduced.

- *Top yang:*   **Not reducing or increasing this is faultless. Correctness brings good fortune. It is beneficial to go somewhere. Getting a servant, there is no house.**

EXPLANATION
At the end of reduction, this is reduction to the point where there is nothing to be reduced, increase to the point where there is nothing to be increased; by clarifying the qualities of illumination, one rests in the highest good, and there is no reducing or increasing this. Now there is no act at fault, nothing incorrect; completing what has been started, one gains its good fortune. When practice of the Tao reaches the point of resting in the highest good, the mind of Tao is always present, and the gold elixir crystallizes; going on thereby to transmute the human mind, there is all-around benefit. The mind of Tao is the master, the human mind is the servant. When the mind of Tao is in charge of things, every step, every undertaking, is celestial design; personal desires do not arise, and even the human mind transforms into the mind of Tao: "getting a servant, there is no house"—all pollution vanishes, aggregated mundanity is stripped away, and the elixir is perfected. Leaping out of the cage of the ordinary, one's life span is myriad years. This is returning to ultimate good by reduction.

The function of reduction is extremely fine and subtle. It is not a matter of fixed rules, but changes according to the time so as to be effective. In general, the ultimate accomplishment is the unification of strength and flexibility resting in supreme good without evil. Those who practice the path of reduction should be sincere in reduction, so that they can perfect the beginning and complete the end.

42. *Increase*

**For increase, it is beneficial to go somewhere;
it is beneficial to cross great rivers.**

EXPLANATION

Increase is adding what is lacking. As for the qualities of the hexagram, above is *wind* ☴, entering, and below is *thunder* ☳, active. Acting so as to enter gradually, entering without either rushing or lagging, it is therefore called *increase.*

This hexagram represents using reduction in the midst of increase; it follows on the previous hexagram *liberation.* In *liberation*, the yang energy is active and gets out of danger, gradually growing and maturing, adding good that is lacking. However, to increase good is not possible without reducing what is not good. Increasing good and decreasing what is not good, increasing and increasing again, reducing and reducing again, until there is no more increase or decrease possible, finally reaching the state of utter good without evil, one is then done. Therefore "it is beneficial to go somewhere."

Since beginningless time people have accumulated faults and defects, the seeds of habitual compulsion growing deeper as time goes on; now if they want to do something of benefit to essence and life, they cannot accomplish this unless they first extract the seeds of these compulsive habits. But the seeds of habitual compulsions cannot be removed all at once; there are processes, procedures. This does not admit falsehood—it requires orderly progress, putting forth effort at every step, increasing the mind of Tao, decreasing the human mentality, increasing sane energy, decreasing aberrated energy. Only when there is such reduction within increase is it possible to succeed, to make it "beneficial to go somewhere." The benefit is simply in one's practice producing beneficial phenomena.

But to practice what is beneficial, it is important to have a beginning and a conclusion. If there is a beginning but no conclusion, one's acts are still of no benefit—there is no gain, but loss. Therefore the way of gain and beneficial action lies in concentrated will, making thoroughly dedicated effort, made from within difficulty and hardship. Only when one has dissolved the seeds of compulsive habit of time immemorial will one be able to restore one's original being. Therefore it is also "beneficial to cross great rivers."

"Great rivers" are extremely dangerous; there one's life hangs in the balance. If one can go through extremely dangerous places, then wherever there is no danger one is at an advantage. According to the qualities of the hexagram, acting so as to progress harmoniously, gradually applying effort, without rushing or lagging, this is the path of increasing and decreasing according to the time.

■ *First yang:*   It is beneficial to act so as to do great
work; this is very auspicious, and blameless.

EXPLANATION
In the beginning of increase, one can go straight ahead with vigorous power into great works and great acts. This is so because once the initial thought is true one can gain increase in the beginning, naturally able to be blameless in the end. This is determining increase by use of firm strength.

■ *2 yin:*   One gains ten sets of tortoise shells, and none
can oppose. Perpetual correctness is auspicious. It is
good for the king to serve the lord.

EXPLANATION
Flexible receptivity balanced correctly, knowing when to hasten and when to relax, cognizant of good and bad, refining the self and controlling the mind, reducing and reducing again, till the primal energy comes forth from within nothingness, yin and yang merge: This is like gaining ten sets of tortoise shells. The gain of ten sets of tortoise shells means the vitalities of two and five (yin in the second line and yang in the fifth line, which correspond) subtly join and congeal, like a tortoise hiding; the spirit stores the energy, and the spiritual embryo takes on form. At this time it is appropriate to maintain undivided correctness, serenely incubating the spiritual embryo until the ten months' work is done, and the spiritual potential leaves the "womb" and becomes a reality. Building up accomplishment, accumulating practice, preserving the country and aiding the people, one is enfeoffed as a king, and serves the lord. When celestial nobility is cultivated to perfection, human nobility follows. What can compare to that good fortune? This is natural increase through the application of flexibility.

■ *3 yin:*   Using unfortunate events to gain increase is
blameless. Acting in a moderate, balanced way with
sincerity and truthfulness, public announcement uses
the imperial seal.

EXPLANATION
When one is unbalanced and off kilter, faults are very many; it will not do to gain increase by way of fortunate events—one should use unfortunate events to polish oneself, being careful and wary and cultivating introspection, being sincere and truthful in acting with balance and moderation. When one is truthful, the heart is sincere; when conduct is balanced and moderate, action is careful. When the heart is sincere and action is careful, one is impartial and not selfish, and there is nothing that cannot be told to

others. This is like using the imperial seal to send a message. Within reduction there is increase, and unfortunate events can turn into fortunate events. Whereas one was faulty in the beginning, one can be blameless in the end. This is using flexibility and gaining increase by effort.

- **4 *yin*: When balanced action is openly expressed, the public follows. It is beneficial to use a support to move the nation.**

EXPLANATION

In the body of *wind* ☴ above, after having profited oneself the time comes to profit others; therefore balance in action, whether pointed out in someone, or introduced through events, announces an impartial affair that is profitable for everyone, causing learners to rejoice, accept it sincerely, and gladly follow it. However, slander comes to those whose way is lofty, and criticism arises against those whose virtues are developed; it is necessary to rely on someone with great power before it is possible to appear in the world and teach, causing people to move to goodness and reform their faults. Therefore "it is beneficial to use a support to move the nation." The benefit of moving the nation is the large-scale practice of the Tao. An example of this is the Taoist master Ch'ang-ch'un being supported by Genghis Khan. This means that those with no status need to borrow the power of others in order to aid and benefit people.

- **5 *yang*: When there is truthfulness and a benevolent heart, there is no need to ask—it is very auspicious. Truthfulness and benevolence are charismatic qualities in oneself.**

EXPLANATION

When positive strength is correctly balanced, the great Way is completed, and one is integrated with the celestial design, it can be trusted that the benevolent heart is therein, and there is the auspicious good fortune of fundamental goodness. The benevolent heart is the innately good heart. When the innately good heart is always present, one looks upon myriad things as one body, and sees others and self as one family. Then each word, each action, is beneficial to the world. The mind of a person of the Tao also can be trusted to have the charismatic quality of benevolence. Once one has a benevolent heart, one also has the charismatic power of benevolence. It is like the wind blowing on things—all fly up. This represents those with status aiding and benefiting people without borrowing the power of others.

- ***Top yang*: Don't increase here, or you may be attacked. If determination is inconstant, that brings misfortune.**

EXPLANATION

Strength that is misused not only cannot benefit oneself; if you insist on trying to benefit others, not only will you be of no benefit to them, you will even be attacked and censured by them. The way to profit others requires first that one be able to reduce one's own faults. Eliminating one's own faults, one then increases goodness. Only after one is good oneself can one make others good. This is a consistent, constant determination that progresses gradually in an orderly fashion. If the determination is inconstant, and one wants to help others before having developed oneself, there is no gain, but loss, and one brings on misfortune. This represents those who are fond of strength and try to help others before having developed themselves.

So taking increase as a path requires that one first develop oneself as long as the path is not yet completed; once the path is realized, then one goes on to help others grow. Self-development and development of others each has its own time. One cannot help others grow until after one's own growth. But self-development and development of others both require that one first be able to eliminate one's own faults. If one can eliminate one's own faults and become impeccable, then one can help oneself and others as well, bringing benefit wherever one goes.

43. *Parting*

Parting is lauded in the royal court. The call of truth involves danger. Addressing one's own domain, it is not beneficial to go right to war, but it is beneficial to go somewhere.

EXPLANATION
Parting is separating and leaving. In the body of the hexagram, one yin is on top of five yangs—yang is about to become pure, while yin is about to disappear. The qualities of the hexagram are strength and harmony: Harmoniously acting with strength, strong but not violent, it equally has the meaning of using yang to get rid of yin, so it is called *parting*.

This hexagram represents repelling yin by yang; it follows on the previous hexagram *reduction*. In *reduction*, one stills rejoicing and does not rejoice arbitrarily, so as to foster yang and repel yin, using inherent sane energy to repel the energy of external influences. The energy of external influences is invited by the discriminatory consciousness; so if you want to repel external influences, nothing is better than to first part with the discriminatory consciousness.

After people get mixed up in temporal conditioning, the discriminatory consciousness takes charge of affairs; wine and sex distract them from reality, the lure of wealth deranges their nature, emotions and desires well forth at once, thoughts and ruminations arise in a tangle, and the mind-ruler is lost in confusion. Because habituation becomes second nature over a long period of time, it cannot be abruptly removed. It is necessary to work on the matter in a serene and equanimous way, according to the time: Eventually discrimination will cease, and the original spirit will return; the human mind will sublimate and the mind of Tao will be complete—again you will see the original self.

But this discriminating consciousness is loved by the human mind: If you want to part from it, it is best first to clarify the mind. Once the mind is clarified, the mind of Tao appears, and the discriminatory consciousness is easily dismissed. Therefore "parting is lauded in the royal court." The royal court is the abode of the mind-ruler, where true and false are distinguished. When the mind clearly understands true and false, then the mind is not deluded by the discriminatory consciousness, and easily parts from it.

But since the discriminatory consciousness has been in charge of things for so long, its roots are deep and its authority is tremendous; one cannot attack it impetuously, but must find the right way between intensity and laxity before it is possible to settle anything.

When the text says "the call of truth," it means the true mind and genuine intent, as the means to amass sane energy; when it says "involves danger," it means caution and wariness is the way to ward off aberrant energy. "Addressing one's own domain" means refining the self. "It is not beneficial to go right to war" means to wait for the proper time.

Once one has been able to amass the right kind of energy and ward off the wrong kind of energy, and also has refined oneself, awaiting the proper time to act, myriad objects are all empty, and there is just the discriminating consciousness alone—take advantage of the right time to detach from this, and there will be unfailing benefit.

The qualities of the hexagram are strength and harmony: serene, without pressure, awaiting the right time to act—this seems to be the secret of parting from yin.

■ *First yang:* **Vigor in the advancing feet, going but not prevailing, this is faulty.**

EXPLANATION
At the beginning of parting from yin, merely adamant and lacking flexibility, impetuously pushing forward, is "vigor in the advancing feet." Vigor in the advancing feet not only is incapable of parting from yin, on the contrary it even fosters yin. So the celestial does not prevail over the earthly, and where there was no fault one brings about fault by oneself. This is being strong but not careful in parting from yin.

■ *2 yang:* **If one is cautious and alert, though there be armed troublemakers in the night, one need not worry.**

EXPLANATION
If one is strong yet able to yield, is cautious and alert, taking strict measures of precaution, even if there are armed troublemakers in the night,

one has already spied them out before they act, so there is nothing to worry about. This is being firm yet gentle in parting from yin.

■ *3 yang:*   **Vigor in the face has bad luck. A superior person leaves what is to be left; going alone, encountering rain and so getting wet, there is irritation, but no fault.**

EXPLANATION
When one is excessively forceful, in a hurry to achieve, the vigor shows this in the face, and bad luck normally ensues. It is lucky if one uses truth to get rid of falsehood, as the decisiveness of a superior person leaving what should be left. The only trouble is that one is firm alone without flexibility; when one runs into rain, gets wet, and cannot immediately achieve the objective, there is irritation. However, once one has gotten wet, though at first one was unable to effect a firm resolution, in the end one will surely resolve it gently, and can avoid the fault of aggressiveness. This is adamantly rushing to part from yin.

■ *4 yang:*   **No flesh on the buttocks, not making progress. Leading a sheep, regret disappears. Hearing the words but not believing.**

EXPLANATION
When strength is not correctly oriented, the mind of Tao is burdened by the human mentality; this is like having no flesh on the buttocks, so being unable to sit at ease, and also not making progress in action, not successfully parting from yin. It is lucky if the mind of Tao has not yet disappeared, and one can therefore lead in positive energy to increase it; then the regret that was there can vanish. But the problem is that one does not believe words about parting from yin earthliness, still having the human mentality mixed in with the mind of Tao. This is strength being damaged by weakness, not knowing how to part with yin.

■ *5 yang:*   **Wild burdock root; cut through resolutely. Balanced action is impeccable.**

EXPLANATION
Close on the yin line above, while the earthly is in the upper position the celestial is in the lower position—the mind of Tao is fooled by the human mentality, and clings fondly to the discriminatory consciousness, now separating from it, now not separating. It is like wild burdock root, which must be cut through resolutely—the roots cannot be cut through all at once. However, the contest between the mind of Tao and the human mentality is a matter of a hairbreadth—on this side, the mind of Tao, on that side, the human mentality: If one succeeds in parting from earthliness, this is the

mind of Tao; if one does not succeed in parting from earthliness, this is the human mentality. The mind is the abode of the consciousness; the discriminatory consciousness is connected with the human mentality, so whether they can be split apart definitively is uncertain. Luckily when the celestial yang is about to become pure and the earthly yin is about to disappear, reason ultimately prevails over desire, and even if one cannot part from it spontaneously, one will be able to do so with effort. Therefore by balance in action one can be impeccable. This is parting from negativity by effort when strength is being dragged by weakness.

■ *Top yin:* **No call; in the end there is misfortune.**

EXPLANATION
At the end of *parting*, the aggregate of mundanity has receded, leaving only the single mundanity of the discriminatory consciousness as yet undissolved. At that time it should be parted with, and its force then must pass away. When the celestial energy makes one more advance, the mundane energy will then dissolve; therefore there is "no call; in the end there is misfortune." "No call" of mundane energy is none other than the "call of truth" of celestial energy. The "final misfortune" of mundane energy is the ultimate fortune of celestial energy. This is parting in which the celestial energy becomes pure and complete, while mundane energy vanishes entirely.

So in the path of parting from mundanity, it will not do to be too adamant or too yielding; one must have flexibility within firmness, and firmness within flexibility, parting gradually, advancing a portion of celestial energy, repelling a portion of mundanity, so that celestial energy advances to wholeness and mundanity spontaneously sublimates. If you don't know how to operate the process with appropriate intensity and relaxation, and wish to accomplish it rapidly, that will on the contrary foster mundane energy and damage celestial energy, so that after all you will be unable to repel mundanity. So the path of repelling mundanity requires deep understanding of process.

44. Meeting

Meeting, the woman is strong. Don't get married.

EXPLANATION
Meeting means encounter, unexpected encounter. In the body of the hexagram, there is one yin, which enters under five yangs; five yangs meet one yin, so it is called *meeting*.

This hexagram represents warding off mundanity and preserving celestial energy; it follows on the previous hexagram *increase. Increase* means augmenting insufficient celestial energy; to augment what is insufficient means adding from one yang until there are six yangs, so that finally positive celestial yang is pure and complete. However, when yang culminates, yin is inevitable; one yin surreptitiously arises, and the yang energy is damaged. This is why the text says "meeting, the woman is strong."

However, the inevitability of yin when yang culminates is the path of the temporal, going along with creation; if one can borrow the earthly to complete the celestial, the sages' science of reverse operation to get back to the primordial, and, as in the second and fifth lines of this hexagram, have strength in balance, attaining the power to adapt to changes, having flexibility within firmness and firmness within flexibility, one can thereby go in and out of yin and yang without being constrained by yin and yang.

Using yin without being used by yin is like meeting a woman but not marrying her. Though earthly yin energy be strong, after all it will obey celestial yang energy. Not only will the yang energy not be damaged, the yin energy will gradually sublimate. This is why the work of warding off mundanity is valued.

- *First yin:*   A metal brake is applied. It is good to be correct. If you go anywhere, you will see misfortune. An emaciated pig leaps in earnest.

EXPLANATION
When one yin surreptitiously arises, its strength is sufficient to oppose five yangs, just as a metal brake can stop a car so that it doesn't move. For practitioners of the Tao, it is good to preserve correctness without losing it, preventing trouble early. If there is arbitrary action, one will bring negativity on oneself, which brings misfortune. This is especially so since when one yin advances all yins go into motion, just as a single emaciated pig can leap ahead, bringing along a group of pigs; though the incipient impulse is very subtle, the harm it does is very great. This is the first arising of mundane yin energy.

- *2 yang:*   When the fish is in the bag, there's no fault. It is not advantageous to the visitor.

EXPLANATION
Strength applied with flexibility, cautious and wary, able to ward off the first arising mundanity, is like a fish being in a bag, unable to cause harm. The advantage is with the host, not the visitor, because the host (the celestial) has already espied the visitor (the mundane) early on. This is preventing mundanity before it acts up.

■ *3 yang:*   No flesh on the buttocks, having trouble
walking. If one is diligent in danger, there is no great
fault.

EXPLANATION
Strong and complacent, unable to guard against carelessness early on—
once mundane energy acts up it is very hard to subdue. Then the human
mentality is mixed in the mind of Tao; like having no flesh on the buttocks
and having trouble walking, the inner autonomy is unsettled. It is fortunate if one is strong yet can maintain rectitude, working by day and careful
by night, mastering oneself in danger; then one can avoid the fault of
damaging the celestial by the mundane.

■ *4 yang:*   No fish in the bag causes trouble.

EXPLANATION
Being strong yet losing mindfulness, unable to prevent mundanity and
even indulging mundanity, sitting by and watching the outcome—the
mind of Tao is obscured and the human mentality springs up wildly, so
trouble arises, creating obstructions, like a fish getting out of a bag, going
anywhere it wants. This is suffering damage through not knowing how to
prevent negative mundanity.

■ *5 yang:*   Wrapping a melon in river willow. Hiding
embellishments, being detached, one realizes the
celestial self.

EXPLANATION
When firm strength is balanced correctly, heaven and humanity merge;
one controls the human mentality by the mind of Tao, like wrapping up
the yin of a melon with the yang of river willow. Expelling intellectualism,
concealing illumination within, mundanity cannot get near: Dealing with
meeting in this way, one can return to heaven by human power; celestial
energy is not damaged, and earthly energy spontaneously sublimates.
This is preventing negative mundanity by positive celestial energy and suffering no damage.

■ *Top yang:*   Meeting the horn is humiliating. No blame.

EXPLANATION
When strong but arrogant, one is unable to prevent mundanity early on.
When yang reaches the extreme it must turn to yin; when strength reaches
the extreme, it will be defeated. The gold elixir, once attained, is again lost,
and it is one's own fault. But there is no blame on the yin. This is suffering
damage in the end by tardiness in preventing mundanity.

In the six lines, there is knowledge of preventing negative mundanity, lack
of knowledge of preventing it, preventing it early on, preventing it too late.

If we look for where negative mundanity is prevented early on so that it cannot arise, we find it only in the yang in the second place, where yang controls yin, causing it to sublimate spontaneously. As for the attainment of proper balance, we find it only in the yang in the fifth place. Preventing negative mundanity with proper balance, using yin without being used by yin, borrowing yin to preserve yang, seems to lie in this.

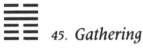

45. Gathering

Gathering is developmental. The king comes to have a shrine. It is beneficial to see a great person; this is developmental. It is beneficial to be correct. It is good to make a great sacrifice. It is beneficial to go somewhere.

EXPLANATION

Gathering means assembly. As for the qualities of the hexagram, above is *lake* ☱, joyful, and below is *earth* ☷, amenable: When one accords with others, they are joyful; so it is called *gathering*.

This hexagram represents gathering the medicines together; it follows on the previous hexagram *parting*. In *parting*, one parts from mundanity by celestial energy. The path of parting from mundanity is a task to be done after obtaining the elixir. Before the elixir is obtained, if not for the work of gathering together the medicines, the elixir will not form.

After people are born, habit estranges them from what is essentially near; they forget the original reality and pursue external artificiality. So their mind and spirit are unstable, their vitality and energy are dissipated. It is not possible to immediately recover and concentrate the dissipated vitality and energy; it is important to be obedient and act harmoniously, progressing gradually in an orderly manner, not deviating from the process, applying the will single-mindedly, the longer the stronger, so that what was lost may be naturally recovered, what has gone may be restored.

This is like a king coming to have a shrine for spirits. Ancestors are people's roots; if they forget their roots, people are disrespectful and inhuman. When the king comes to have a shrine for spirits, this is how to let people know there is a basis to be grateful to. People's original natural reality is like their ancestral roots: When people abandon reality and accept falsehood, that is like forgetting ancestral roots. If people can gather in their spirit and energy, cultivate essence and life, and restore the original natural reality, that is like not forgetting ancestral roots.

When the king does not forget ancestral roots, he can unite the hearts of the people in the land; when practitioners of the Tao do not forget the fundamental, they can gather the great medicines of essence and life. But this matter of not forgetting the fundamental requires a great person to carry it out; it cannot be done by lesser people who do not know essence and life. Therefore "it is beneficial to see a great person; this is developmental."

A great person is one who corrects self and corrects others. Correcting oneself, there is no ego; spirit and energy do not dissipate, and rectitude becomes the self. Correcting others, there are no personalities; character and constitution are sublimated, and rectitude becomes people. Correcting self and correcting others, inwardly thoughts do not arise, and externals do not enter: Inside and out are one single rectitude—benevolence, justice, courtesy, and knowledge are all based on truthfulness. When the primordial is gathered together, essence is stabilized and life is solidified.

Indeed, the benefit of development by gathering what is right is no small matter. What heaven enjoins on humanity is rectitude alone, and it is only by rectitude that humanity can answer heaven. Responding to heaven with rectitude, not forgetting the fundamental, is like making a great sacrifice to offer to heaven; it will not fail to bring about good fortune.

But the way to make a great sacrifice and bring about good fortune cannot be accomplished simply by a moment of emptiness; it is necessary to tread the ground of reality step after step before one can achieve it. If you know but do not act on it, it is the same as not knowing—how can you then attain good fortune? So "it is beneficial to go somewhere." The value of knowledge is only in its application.

■ *First yin:* Having sincerity that is not conclusive, there is disorder and mobbing. If you cry, in a moment it'll turn to laughter; don't grieve. To go is blameless.

EXPLANATION

When negative, weak, indecisive, not distinguishing right from wrong, sometimes believing one thing, sometimes another, people become disorderly and form mobs, believing what they shouldn't, rallying around what they shouldn't. Luckily there is correspondence with the positive yang in the fourth place; if you know disorderly mobbing is of no benefit, "cry" in regret, and approach true teachers, once you are guided by them and given direction in the darkness, you will understand that the Tao is not far from people, but what people do for the Tao estranges people. First you cry, then you laugh. Directly attaining understanding, you need not grieve; going right ahead to assemble the five elements and combine the four signs, why worry that you will not reach the state of impeccability? This is gathering in the sense of reforming error and returning to correctness.

■ *2 yin:* Drawing in brings good fortune; no blame. If one is sincere, it is beneficial to perform the spring ceremony.

EXPLANATION

In the midst of three yins, all darkness, the whole body is pure mundanity: Yet if one can go along with its desires to gradually draw it into guidance in the Tao, transmute its nature as materialized energy and gather its nature of true being-as-is, the benefit is like performing the spring ceremony to honor the spirits, communing by sincerity. One at first blameworthy can thus become blameless. This is gathering in the sense of preserving rectitude even when weak.

■ *3 yin:*   Gathering, lamenting; no benefit. If one goes, there is no fault, but a little shame.

EXPLANATION
When one is ignorant yet acts on one's own, clinging to one's own mundane ignorance alone and idly imagining attainment of the Tao, in vain, without reality, this kind of gathering must end in lament; obviously there will be no benefit. Luckily there are wise people in view; if one goes and associates with them, borrowing strength to overcome weakness, one can still avoid lamentable faults. However, because one could not join upright people early on, but only joined them after suffering from one's faults, it is hard to avoid a little shame. This is gathering in which the weak borrow strength.

■ *4 yang:*   Great fortune, no fault.

EXPLANATION
When one is strong yet able to be flexible, with yin and yang in balance, the restored elixir congeals, and the great elixir is within one's purview: Not only can one gather it at will and gain great fortune; one will surely gather it in an utterly impeccable state. This is gathering in the sense of solidifying the restored elixir.

■ *5 yang:*   Gathering, there is a state without fault.
Not taking oneself seriously, if one is basically always correct, regret will disappear.

EXPLANATION
When strength is correctly balanced and higher knowledge unwavering, one stablizes life in the true state; without cultivation or verification, not needing effort, the five elements are one energy. Fundamentally one is inherently without fault. However, though one is without fault, it is undesirable to dwell on joy, becoming complacent and self-satisfied, trusting what is untrustworthy—regret is sure to come. But if one knows how to fill the belly and also empty the mind, practices nondoing and incubates the spiritual embryo, ever correct and undivided, using the natural true fire to melt away the residual mundanity of acquired conditioning, such a one is called a true human without taint—how could regret not vanish? This is gathering in the sense of incubating the spiritual embryo.

■ *Top yin:*   **Sighing and weeping. No blame.**

EXPLANATION

Being foolish and ignorant, mistakenly entering into aberrant practices, taking the false for the real, even if the celestial treasure is in sight one cannot gather it oneself. Wasting one's whole life, when facing death one will finally regret it, sighing and weeping. One has done this damage to oneself—there is no blame on others. This is gathering that is careless in the beginning and ends in misfortune.

Each of the six lines indicates something being gathered, but they are different in respect to right and wrong, aberration and correctness. When we look for balance of yin and yang and unity of strength and flexibility, we find it only in the yang in the fourth place. As for using emptiness to nurture fulfillment, comprehending life and essence, it seems to be only in yang in the fifth place. It is those who accurately recognize the real who are the adepts.

46. *Rising*

Rising is greatly developmental; it calls for seeing a great person, so there will be no grief. An expedition south brings good fortune.

EXPLANATION

Rising means climbing from lowliness to the heights. As for the qualities of the hexagram, above is *earth* ☷, following, and below is *wind* ☴, entering. Progressing at an easy pace, going in accord with the time, neither clinging nor departing, one gradually enters true eternity; therefore it is called *rising*.

This hexagram represents carefully watching the firing process; it follows on the previous hexagram *meeting*. In *meeting*, docility enters into strength; when yang culminates, yin arises, so aberrant energy increases daily while sound energy decreases daily—the influence of habit becomes second nature, and one gradually enters an unchanging state of folly. What is the reason? Simply because the yang has lost its strength, the yin is no longer obedient. In spiritual alchemy, before restoring yang, it is necessary to make yin docile. Once yin becomes submissive, human desires do not arise and correct awareness is always present. Gradually progressing in an orderly manner, it is then possible to reach being from nonbeing, to arrive at fulfillment from emptiness. Learning below and arriving above, one comes to understand how to skillfully restore the primal without difficulty; therefore rising has a path of great development.

But this highly developmental rising, which is a matter of appropriating yin and yang and taking over creative evolution, transcending the ordinary and entering the holy, involves a subtle firing process and a long course of work—it cannot be carried out by any of the dilettantes and private experimenters who practice blindly. It requires the verbal instruction and mental transmission of a genuine teacher, true knowledge and certain insight, before it is possible to go straight ahead without obstacles and obstructions. Therefore taking the path of *rising* "calls for seeing a great person."

A "great person" is a sage who has completed the great path. Great people develop themselves and develop others; everything they say has a reason. Like the wind getting into everything, they can open up people's knowledge and wisdom; like the earth nurturing everything, they can save people from calamities. When you use them after seeing a great person, the medicines are real, the firing process is orderly—thus one can be without grief. Journeying far toward the light, each step has a step's benefit, each day has a day's accomplishment. Rising from lowliness to the heights, going from the shallow to the depths, eventually one will advance to the realm of the sages; what can compare to that fortune?

- *First yin:*   **Truly rising is very auspicious.**

EXPLANATION
When one is flexible yet has a strong will, and one opens one's mind and humbles oneself, approaching those who are imbued with the Tao and are highly illumined, one cannot fail to truly rise and receive truth. This is rising by being flexible and following the strong.

- *2 yang:*   **When sincere it is beneficial to perform the spring ceremony. No blame.**

EXPLANATION
Being strong and having attained balance, deeply understanding the medicines and the firing process, entering with sincerity, acting with flexibility, accomplishing the work gradually—it is like honoring the spirits with the ceremony of spring, using sincerity to feel the sense of communion; one will surely ascend to the state of impeccability. This is rising by being strong and applying flexibility.

- *3 yang:*   **Rising in an empty domain.**

EXPLANATION
If one considers oneself wise and does not know to seek out teachers and companions, indulges in guesswork and speculation and rushes impulsively ahead, in desiring to go forward one will instead fall back; this is like ascending into an empty domain—how can one progress into the realm of high illumination? This is rising without knowledge to seek a teacher.

■ *4 yin:*   **The king makes an offering on the mountain; this is auspicious and blameless.**

EXPLANATION
When one is flexible but keeps to what is right, advancing in accord with the time, refining oneself and controlling the mind, one ascends from lowliness to the heights, gradually entering a realm of beauty. This is like a king making an offering on a mountain, ascending to the heights. This is rising that is auspicious and blameless.

■ *5 yin:*   **Rectitude brings good fortune. Climbing stairs.**

EXPLANATION
Emptying the human mind and seeking the mind of Tao, when one empties the mind one can fill the belly. This is what is referred to by the saying that at the moment of restoration of potential it is like you always had it. The increase of virtue is as easy as climbing stairs. This is rising by flexibly opening the mind.

■ *Top yin:*   **Rising in the dark. Benefit lies in unceasing rectitude.**

EXPLANATION
When one is ignorant and acts arbitrarily, clinging to one's own mundanity while vainly imagining one will grow and rise in the qualities of the Tao and comprehend life and essence, the more one rises the more one is in the dark—how will it be possible to get out of darkness and advance to lofty illumination? If you want to rise without darkness, you must seek a teacher's instruction. The benefit is in ceaseless rectitude, eliminating anger and covetousness, stopping falsehood and maintaining truthfulness, getting stronger as time goes on; then you can still rise to the stage of clarifying the good and restoring the original. This is the rising of one who is weak but returns to rectitude.

Rising as a path is a matter of using firmness and acting flexibly. According to the quality of the hexagram, it involves docile conduct, being outwardly flexible but inwardly firm, progressing gradually in an orderly manner, not hurrying yet not lagging. Profoundly arriving at self-realization, one will rise into the inner sanctum of the sages. However, the secret of the process requires the verbal instruction and mental transmission of a genuine teacher. As it says in the text, "It calls for seeing a great person, so there will be no grief. An expedition south brings good fortune."

47. *Exhaustion*

Exhaustion develops the righteous. Great people are fortunate and blameless. If one complains, one will not be trusted.

EXPLANATION

Exhaustion means reaching an impasse. In the body of the hexagram, below is *water* ☵, in which one yang is fallen in between two yins; above is *lake* ☱, in which one yin is on top of two yangs. Both picture mundanity making inroads on the celestial, so that celestial energy does not come through. Therefore it is called *exhaustion*. As for the qualities of the hexagram, from the midst of danger (*water*) it produces joy (*lake*); joy comes out of danger—so it also has the sense of resolving exhaustion, resolving an impasse.

This hexagram represents polishing and refining body and mind; it follows on the previous hexagram *gathering. Gathering* involves attaining joy by accord, whereby one gathers together the medicines, goes back to the fundamental, and returns to the original. But if one can only gather in ease and cannot gather in difficulty, this is still inability to accord, inability to rejoice. People who try to practice the Tao can all keep steadfast when they are in easy circumstances, but many of them waver in determination when they are in difficult or perilous situations. They may change their minds because of the pressures of making a living, or they may slack in determination due to illness; their spirits may flag because of old age, or they may stop work because of obstruction by some obsession. All these are cases in which people do not exert the mind of Tao and are hindered by exhaustion, so they ultimately do not attain the Tao.

If the mind is not exhausted even though the body be exhausted, the path is not at an impasse even though the situation presents an impasse, and one can be joyful even when in difficulty, then there is a developmental aspect within exhaustion. But even though being able to rejoice even in difficulty is something people cannot fully attain, and there will inevitably be a point of exhaustion, nevertheless if they become exhausted where they should not, they will not attain development. This is beause the developmental aspect of exhaustion lies in being correct.

Dealing with exhaustion correctly, growing correctly, while exhausted one goes along in harmony with the time. Going along in harmony with the time is possible only for great people imbued with the quality of correct balance. Great people, while being very wise, appear to be ignorant; while being very skillful, they appear inept. Random thoughts do not occur to them, and they cannot be influenced by circumstances. Their conduct is unaffected, and they are not concerned with externals. Not only do they find good fortune wherever they are, they also accord with the order of life and are blameless.

As for those whose main concern is food and clothing, they are untrustworthy in an impasse. They will take trouble in hopes of fortune, but as soon as things don't go their way they show it in their words and expressions, complaining against heaven and blaming people. So blame goes along with them—how can this bring about good fortune? Those who deal with exhaustion and impasse rightly, who are able to be joyful even in difficulty, are great people. Those who are untrustworthy in an impasse, who take trouble only to please themselves, are petty people. It may be the same trouble and the same joy, but the distinction lies in how great people and petty people relate to the trouble and the joy. So those who practice the Tao should by all means maintain rectitude when exhausted and at an impasse.

■ *First yin:*   **Sitting exhausted on a tree stump, gone into a dark ravine, not to be seen for three years.**

EXPLANATION
In the beginning of exhaustion, the exhaustion is not great. Also, being near two yangs, one should not submit to exhaustion. This is weakness and self-destruction, resigning oneself to remain below others, like "sitting exhausted on a tree stump, gone into a dark ravine." People like this, who are exhausted when they should not be exhausted, will not get out of danger even in a long time, here represented by "three years." This is making much exhaustion of little exhaustion.

■ *2 yang:*   **Hard up for wine and food; then comes the regal robe. It is beneficial to make ceremonial offerings. To go on an expedition brings misfortune. No blame.**

EXPLANATION
With yang fallen in the midst of yin, this is when sustenance is insufficient, like being "hard up for wine and food." Luckily firmness here is balanced; forgetting oneself for the Tao, though the body be exhausted the mind is not exhausted. One day bitterness will end and sweetness will arise; the great Tao completed, one then wears celestial clothing and eats celestial food. Cultivating celestial nobility, human nobility will follow. First there are hard times, then there is success. We can be sure of this principle. The image of success after hardship likens the benefit to making ceremonial offerings to reach heaven with sincerity, seeing the effect after a long time. If, when one is in hard times, one wants to get out of hardship right away, that will instead bring on misfortune, and one cannot blame anyone if one comes to an impasse and doesn't get through. This line refers to success after hardship, growth after exhaustion.

■ *3 yin:* **Stymied by rocks, resting on thorns, going into the house without seeing the wife—inauspicious.**

EXPLANATION

When one is ignorant and acts arbitrarily, not knowing enough to honor teachers and respect companions, one will be despised by upright people; this is like being stymied by rocks, resting on thorns, getting into an impasse by one's own doing. People like this have no real learning, but they pretend to have attained the Tao. They strive for externals and lose what is within. This is also like going into the house but not seeing the wife. After all they will perish. These are people who exhaust themselves unnecessarily, creating an impasse where there really is none.

■ *4 yang:* **Coming gradually, exhausted in a golden cart; shame has an end.**

EXPLANATION

Leaving the state of danger (*water* ☵) for the body of joy (*lake* ☱), this is when exhaustion is to be overcome, but as firmness rests on weakness (☱) one cannot overcome it quickly. It is almost as if weakness is injuring firmness. One comes gradually, as it were, "exhausted in a gold cart," and there is shame. However, while one cannot proceed directly on the path, having long been in a state of exhaustion and impasse, if one comes gradually, one will eventually achieve one's aim. This is being exhausted, at an impasse, yet gradually overcoming it.

■ *5 yang:* **Nose and feet cut off, at an impasse in minister's garb, gradually there will be joy; it is beneficial to make ceremonial offerings.**

EXPLANATION

When positive strength is balanced correctly, but one does not meet an enlightened ruler who will employ one, one has great ability but not the opportunity to use it; it is difficult to carry out both spiritual and temporal work, and one cannot do as one wishes, like having one's nose and feet cut off, at an impasse in minister's garb. This is the great impasse of those who embrace Tao. Once in an impasse, they cannot forcibly seek a way out; they should dress themselves in humility and hide their treasure, suffer alone and work alone. Then gradually there will be joy. The benefit of gradual joy is like making ceremonial offerings, entering with sincerity. After a long time of deepening one's attainment, a time will naturally come when the great Tao is fulfilled. This is fidelity in an impasse, gradually getting out of the impasse.

■ *Top yin:*   Exhausted at an impasse, in distress, is called
regret over action; there is regret. It is auspicious to go
on an expedition.

EXPLANATION
Ignorant, lacking knowledge, yet pretending to be brilliant, indulging in
arbitrary guesswork and private speculation—this is like having stopped at
an impasse; trying to figure out the path of sages, believing oneself to have
attained reality, one flutters about, suffering damage as time goes on, unable to advance yet unable to withdraw, trapped in distress. This is called
regret over action; there is regret along with the action. It is better to repent and seek out teachers and helpers, to act only after understanding.
Then though one may have gotten sidetracked at first, and thus reached
an impasse and regretted it, after all one will hear about the great Path,
and go on it to attain happiness. This is experiencing regret and ultimately
getting out of an impasse.

Among the various kinds of exhaustion and impasses represented by the
six lines, there is the exhaustion, or impasse, of great people, and the exhaustion, or impasse, of petty people. That of great people involves being
joyful even in trouble, being faithful when exhausted and ultimately being
impeccable. That of petty people is courting danger for their own happiness, not being faithful in hardship and winding up with regret. The way
to succeed after hardship is to be able to rejoice even in trouble, to wait for
the proper time and preserve rectitude.

48. *The Well*

The well: Changing the village, not changing the well;
no loss, no gain. Those who come and go use the well
as a well. If the rope does not reach all the way into
the well, or if the bucket breaks, that is unfortunate.

EXPLANATION
A well is water with a source, which nourishes people inexhaustibly; it
has the meaning of nurturance, development. As for the qualities of the
hexagram, above is *water* ☵, dangerous, and below is *wind* ☴, penetrating: gradually progressing so as to get through danger, though there is
danger one can get out of it, as wood plunged in water emerges from the
water. Therefore this hexagram is called *the well*.
    This hexagram represents accumulation of effort to cultivate virtue; it
follows on the previous hexagram *rising*. *Rising* means harmonious progress in practice, a way to increase spiritual virtue. When spiritual virtue
increases, and one has accordingly advanced to the state where there is no

difficulty or danger, the basis is firm and stable; free from danger oneself, one can then resolve others' problems. With this one accumulates achievement and cultivates virtue, using what one has developed oneself to nurture others' development. Genuine within, this genuineness reaches out, so there is benefit to others and no harm to self. This is like a well: Changing the village doesn't change the well; no loss, no gain, passersby use the well as a well.

When the self-development of practitioners of Tao is sufficient, this is like a well having water in it. To develop others after having developed oneself is like "changing the village." To develop others by one's own development is like "not changing the well." Development of others must be based on self-development: As is self-development, so is development of others; this is like a well having "no loss, no gain." Developing others by self-development, others and self are both nurtured; this is like those who come and go using the well as a well.

If one insists on trying to teach people before one has attained the Tao oneself, this is called lacking the basis. Development without the basis lacks inward mastery; arbitrarily used, it creates confusion, and without having helped anyone else one first loses oneself. This is like trying to get water from a well, but the rope does not reach all the way, or the well water breaks the bucket; one brings misfortune on oneself. This is because the business of guiding others comes after the completion of the great path. When the path is completed, mind and body are autonomous; based on previous realization to enlighten others, one can thus benefit others and not harm oneself. Therefore the main theme in each of the six lines is self-development.

■ *First yin:* **Mud in a well is not to be consumed.**
There are no animals at an abandoned well.

EXPLANATION
If one is stupid and foolish and does not know to seek teachers for self-development, yet presumes to have what one has not, and wishes to develop others in imitation of lofty illuminates, this is like an abandoned well with mud in it and not water; with an accumulation of all sorts of pollutants in it, even animals ignore it. How can such a one develop others? This is one with no knowledge at all of self-development.

■ *2 yang:* **The depths of the well water a frog.**
The jar leaks.

EXPLANATION
While in the midst of self-development, if one wants to develop others before one's own development is sufficient, one will be of no benefit to others, and will harm oneself first. This is like the depths of a well producing water sufficient only for a frog, or a jar leaking water. There is a limit to the moisture; with little to help others, there is much loss to oneself. This is one whose self-development is insufficient.

■ *3 yang:* The well is cleared, but not drunk from; this
is the concern of one's heart. It is worth drawing from.
When the ruler is enlightened, all receive the blessing.

EXPLANATION
Having progressed to the top of the lower position, this is when one's own development is accomplished and one can thus develop others. However, there is difficulty at hand; if one does not meet people who can understand, this poses a limitation and makes development impossible. This is like when a well is clear but people do not drink from it. However, even though there is no one to drink from it, nevertheless when spiritual virtues are highly developed, people who observe them are subtly influenced. This is why it is "the concern of one's heart." Why is it a concern? Because it is worth drawing from. It is to be hoped that there are rulers or powerful people with clear eyes who will trust and employ the enlightened; then everyone will have a spiritual model, and will receive blessings without end. This line refers to one whose self-development is fulfilled.

■ *4 yin:* The well is tiled, without fault.

EXPLANATION
In the state of danger (*water* ☵), though one lack the power to develop others, it is fortunate if one remains upright even in weakness, and knows how to develop oneself. This is like a well being tiled to prevent danger, without damage inside or loss outside, so no one can fall in. This refers to one capable of self-development.

■ *5 yang:* The well is pure, the cold spring is used for
drinking.

EXPLANATION
Yang inside yin, outwardly empty while inwardly full, emptiness and fullness as one, firmness and flexibility combined, the great path is completed. This is called water with a source; it is like a well being pure, a cold spring—its nourishment is deep and rich, and it can be used without exhaustion. This refers to completion of self-development and ability to develop others.

■ *Top yin:* The well is being drawn from; don't cover it.
Great fortune.

EXPLANATION
When self-development is attained, that is like work on a well being completed—thus the mouth of the well is not to be covered. Guiding according to the person, one is able to benefit others and not harm oneself. The good fortune is already in the beginning of self-development. This means that development of others must be based on self-development.

So the work of developing others is to be done after attainment of the Tao. One cannot develop others as long as one has not oneself attained the Tao. If one insists on trying to develop others prematurely, one will suffer the misfortune of a "broken bucket." Those who would take care of others must first know how to take care of themselves.

49. Revolution

In revolution, the sun of the self is truth: This is creative, developmental, fruitful, and perfect. Regret vanishes.

EXPLANATION

Revolution means riddance. The reason for riddance is obsolescence. As for the qualities of the hexagram, above is *lake* ☱ , joyous, and below is *fire* ☲ , luminous; joy is based on illumination, while illumination controls joy. In joy, there should be no delusion; in illumination, there should be no obscurity. Producing joy from within illumination, having illumination within joy, therefore it is called *revolution*.

In the image of the hexagram, *lake* is *metal*, associated with the west; *fire* is the *fire* associated with the south. Refining metal by fire, when metal meets fire it produces brightness and is melted down; when fire meets metal it goes into storage and returns to the root. This too is the meaning of revolution.

This hexagram represents refining yin energy; it follows on the previous hexagram *exhaustion*. In *exhaustion*, joy is produced from the midst of danger; this is how to take the true yang in *water* ☵ , to get out of danger. However, even if you can take the true yang in *water*, if you cannot restore the true yin in *fire* ☲ , the gold elixir will not crystallize, and you will not attain joy. So this path of producing joy from within illumination is indispensible. Producing joy from within illumination is the working of refining yin energy. Refining yin energy means refining one's own personal desires to become unselfish.

Humans are the most conscious of beings, born with the true energy of the patterns of yin and yang of heaven and earth. When they are first born, they unconsciously follow the laws of the lord; completely good, with no evil, the true essence is bright and clear, the open awareness unobscured. Emotions do not stick in their hearts, wealth and poverty do not disturb their minds. Wild beasts cannot harm them, weapons cannot get at them, water and fire cannot overcome them, life and death cannot burden them. When hungry, they simply eat; when cold, they just put on clothes, without thought or reflection; their capacity is originally clear.

Then when people reach the age of sixteen, yang culminates, producing yin; as they deal with things based on acquired conditioning, they develop characteristic temperaments and intellectual knowledge. At this point, only sages of superior wisdom granted by nature, when they are not opposing nature in the primal state and when they serve nature in the temporal state, are able to preserve primal reality and not be damaged by acquired conditioning. Among mediocre and lesser people, rare are they who are not ruled and manipulated by acquired conditioning; after this, a hundred anxieties confuse their minds, myriad affairs belabor their bodies, they take the artificial to be real, abandon the true and enter the false. As the days and years go by, they become estranged by habit from what is close by nature, and the quality of clarity is damaged. The new piles up and becomes old, the pure becomes defiled. This is where the pollution of obsolescence and defilement comes from.

If we look into the source of the pollution of obsolescence, stagnation, and defilement, we see it all comes from having a self. Once one has a self, an ego, the mind of Tao is obscured and the human mentality arises. Conscious of what one should not be conscious of, enjoying what one should not enjoy, one goes to any lengths following personal desires.

So *revolution* simply means overthrowing the ignorance of the self to restore illumination. But if one wants to overthrow the ignorance of the self, it is necessary that the self first be understood. Once the self is understood, one can be sincere in revolution, and the ignorance of the self can be overthrown. Therefore, in the path of revolution "the sun of the self is truth." The sun is an image of illumination, understanding; truth means sincerity. If one does not understand, one cannot be sincere; if one can understand, one will be sincere. With understanding and sincerity, as the first thought is truthful, one will be able to overthrow and revolutionize the self. Therefore revolution contains a path of creativity and development.

However, though revolution is creative and developmental, it is necessary that revolution be correct. If right and wrong are not differentiated and true and false are not distinguished, but all are overthrown together, and one enters into nihilistic quietism, this is not correct and so is not fruitful; and not being fruitful it is not creative or developmental.

Only by correct revolution, conquering the ego and returning to propriety, getting rid of falsehood and maintaining truthfulness, burning away all the pollution of conditioning and bringing to light the true essence of the primal unified awareness, reaching this state, returning to the fundamental, integrating with natural principle, pure and clean without flaw, can the regret of having a self vanish.

This path is not hard to know; what is hard is to carry it out. It is simply a matter of people being able to be sincere in revolution.

■ *First yang:* **Wrapped up in yellow ox-hide.**

EXPLANATION
If one is strong but not illumined, one cannot oppose and change what is within oneself, so one follows along with change outside. This is like being wrapped up in yellow ox-hide, the ox being a symbol of submissiveness,

yellow symbolizing the heart; concerned with the outward, losing the inward, holding fast without flexibility, this is revolution that abandons the root and pursues the branches.

- *2 yin:*   The sun of the self is the good fortune of expedition in revolution; no blame.

EXPLANATION
Emptying the mind and governing oneself, one understands revolution and can first get rid of personal desires. If one can get rid of personal desires, then there is no ego. When there is no ego, then you realize the existence of other people, and can thus seek people to teach you. Then you can fill the belly. When the belly is filled, the self is increasingly illumined; this is why expedition brings good fortune, and there is no blame. This is the revolution of emptying the mind to seek illumination.

- *3 yang:*   It is not auspicious to go on an expedition; even if correct, there is danger. Revolutionizing words formulated thrice, there is certainty.

EXPLANATION
When one is strong and too extreme, excessively adamant, only knowing to reform others but not knowing to reform oneself, even if the reformation is correct it still has misfortune along with it. This is because if you want to reform others without being able to reform yourself, not only will others refuse to accept your reformation, they will also have something to say to reform you yourself, so that you cannot but change; therefore "revolutionizing words" are "formulated thrice." When the revolution or reform is formulated three times, you can be sure one is after all unable to reform oneself. This is the revolution of self-aggrandizement.

- *4 yang:*   Regret vanishes. With sincerity one changes destiny for the better.

EXPLANATION
Having strength but not asserting, one can thereby do away with regret. Regret comes from insincerity in reforming the self; if one is sincere in reforming oneself, while strong one can be yielding, and can transmute the temperament and not be constrained by yin and yang. Not only can the regret of having a self vanish, there can also be good fortune as a result of changing destiny for the better. This is the revolution of employing strength with flexibility.

■ *5 yang:*   A great person changes like a tiger. There is certainty without divination.

EXPLANATION

Yang strength correctly balanced, inwardly autonomous, fostering yang and suppressing yin, opening the gate of life and shutting the door of death, all acquired influences evaporate of themselves; this is like the majesty of a tiger being always there, changing without changing. There is no need for divination to be certain that a revolution has taken place. This is the forceful, purposeful revolution of a great person.

■ *Top yin:*   Superior people transform, inferior people change on the surface. To go on an expedition is unlucky, to remain correct is auspicious.

EXPLANATION

At the end of revolution, flexible yet correct, diligent in self-refinement, utterly empty and thoroughly serene, truthfulness within reaching without, temperament and constitution both transformed, defilements of the senses dissolved, clean and naked, bare and untrammeled, body and mind both sublimated, merged in reality with the Tao, this is the gentle, nonstriving revolution of the superior person. Gentle nonstriving revolution is only possible to superior people with faith. Inferior people without faith cannot accomplish it. Inferior people change their appearance, their surface, but they do not change their hearts; their wills are not firm, and they do not finish what they have started, eventually to fall into ruin, bringing on misfortune. Superior people always remain correct; their will becomes stronger with time, so that they ultimately attain the Tao and achieve good fortune. This is revolution in which false and true bear their fruits.

There is a path of revolution in each of the six lines, but they are not the same in terms of right and wrong. Overall, the point is to have no selfishness; if there is any selfishness, no revolution can put an end to mundanity and purify celestial energy. In old texts when it says that the alchemical elixir is in people, but first they have to refine the self and wait for the proper time, this means to make a radical purge of all the pollution of past influences and not let any flaws remain in the heart.

50. *The Cauldron*

The cauldron is basically good; it is developmental.

EXPLANATION

The cauldron is a vessel for refining by heat, whereby something new is obtained. As for the qualities of the hexagram, above is *fire* ☲ , luminous, below is *wind* ☴, penetrating: Producing illumination through following an initiatory process, the mind becomes daily more humble, while illuminaton increases daily. In the body of the hexagram, in the second line (yang) and the fifth line (yin), emptiness and fullness correspond—within illumination is the ability to be empty and open, within obedience is the capacity for fulfillment. When empty and illumined, that enlightenment illumines all, and the mind cannot be moved by the vagaries of wealth and status. When fulfilled yet docile, all virtues are developed, and neither fortune nor calamity can disturb one's nature. Producing illumination by following an initiatory process, following the process by opening awareness, emptiness and fullness balance each other. It is like the light of fire increasing when it gets wood, like the unrefined energy of wood being all transformed when it meets fire. Because it has the meaning of refining heating, it is called *the cauldron.*

This hexagram represents refining the great medicine; it follows on the previous hexagram *the well. The well* indicates following a process and passing through danger; having gotten through danger, the true yang trapped by conditioning is released, and the great medicine is born—then one can accordingly further illumination and operate the "fire" for refinement. The work of refinement is the means by which to sublimate earthly energy and stabilize celestial energy, causing the raw to ripen and the old to be renewed, whereby it is possible to illumine the mind and to solidify life. Therefore the cauldron is basically good and it has a developmental path. The basis is the potential of everlasting life of goodness; the cooking of the great medicine in the cauldron is the firing of this living potential to make it incorruptible and permanent. But in this path there is process and procedure; even the slightest deviation and the gold elixir will not form. Therefore people must first thoroughly investigate the true principle.

■ *First yin:*   **When the cauldron overturns on its base, it is beneficial to eject what is wrong. Getting a concubine, because of her child she is not faulted.**

EXPLANATION
At the bottom of the cauldron, if people have inferior qualities and are ignorant and foolish, their bases often overturn and are not upright. If you want to set up the cauldron, it is not useful to take the new, but rather it is useful to get rid of the old. If you can get rid of the old, then what is wrong is expelled and the base won't overturn; even and upright, it stays in its place and doesn't shift. This is like a concubine, whose status is originally low but becomes high when she bears a child; she can also thereby not be faulted for her earlier errors. This represents the matter of refining the self, the beginning work of setting up the cauldron.

■ *2 yang:*   The cauldron is filled. One's enemy is jealous,
but cannot get at one; this is lucky.

EXPLANATION
Strong and balanced, true yang has returned and filled the belly. Once the
belly is filled, the Tao mind is ever-present and the human mentality does
not arise. This is like one's enemy being jealous, but unable to get at one.
This represents nurturing the mind of Tao and naturally being free of the
human mentality.

■ *3 yang:*   The lifting hooks of the cauldron are removed;
the activity is impeded. Rich meat is not eaten. When
it rains, lack is regretted. It turns out well.

EXPLANATION
When only firm, without flexibility, not knowing to empty the mind after
having filled the belly, this is removing the lifting hooks of the cauldron;
though one comprehends life, one does not yet comprehend essence, and
the activity is blocked—one is unable to pass through the preliminaries
and arrive at the end, so that one's life be the same as that of the universe.
Remaining a single ignorant individual, missing the ultimate attainment, is
like not eating rich meat. It is lucky when one remains upright when
strong; when it rains, one's travel is impeded, when one has a lack or flaw
one repents. If one repents, one can empty the mind, and once one can
empty the mind one's activity will be unimpeded. From comprehending
life one also comprehends essence, and ultimately can complete them
with good results. This represents having the mind of Tao and also emptying the human mind.

■ *4 yang:*   The cauldron's legs are broken, spilling the
food received for service. The physical being is
enriched, but there is misfortune.

EXPLANATION
On entering illumination by following the initiatory process, the gold
elixir takes shape; this is when one should guard against danger, foreseeing peril, and use the spontaneous fire of reality to burn away acquired
mundanity. If at this point strength is dragged by weakness, the legs of the
cauldron will break; rousing the human mentality injures the mind of Tao.
This is like spilling the food received for service; the jewel of life is again
lost, after having been gained. Even though the physical being remains,
the spirit is lost—that misfortune is unspeakable. This represents arousing
the human mind and obscuring the mind of Tao.

■ *5 yin:*   The cauldron has yellow hooks with a gold handle. It is beneficial to be single-minded.

EXPLANATION
When flexible receptivity is correctly balanced, emptying the human mind and using the mind of Tao, this is like the cauldron having yellow hooks and a gold handle. Yellow symbolizes the center, and "yellow hooks" means the centers of the hooks are hollow. "Gold handle" means the handle of the cauldron is solid. The handle of the cauldron is passed through the hooks—strength and flexibility balance each other, emptiness and fullness correspond; the fire is the medicine, the medicine is the fire. At this point it is beneficial to be singleminded, with undivided attention, forestalling problems, not necessitating excessive augmentation or diminution. This represents emptying the human mind and nurturing the mind of Tao.

■ *Top yang:*   The cauldron has a jade handle. This is very auspicious, entirely beneficial.

EXPLANATION
In the end of use of the cauldron, when the work of renewal in the cauldron is finished, neither being nor nonbeing remains; things and self revert to emptiness. In stillness one is uncontrived, in action one is spontaneous. Strength is flexible, flexibility is strong. Without applying strength, strength is complete; without applying awareness, awareness is penetrating. One has reached the stage of complete sincerity, in which foreknowledge is possible. This is like a jade handle on a cauldron. It is a handle, yet is pure jade: Firmness and softness are as one. The temperament and constitution are transformed, body and mind are both refined. Merging in reality with the Tao, this is the ultimate achievement of practice of the Tao, the complete ability of sages. Transcending yin and yang, one is not constrained by yin and yang. Therefore it is very auspicious, entirely beneficial. This is the complete integration and assimilation of the mind of Tao and the human mind.

In working on the cauldron, there is firmness and softness, advancing and withdrawing, adding and subtracting. Unless you reach the stage where being and nonbeing do not stand, and spiritual creativity is incalculable, you cannot be said to have reached the ultimate achievement. If you do not know the methods of firmness and softness, advancing and withdrawing, adding and subtracting, then you will either fall into the removal of the cauldron's hooks of line three, or the spilling of the food of line four. The slightest deviation produces a tremendous loss. Therefore practitioners of the Tao should promote illumination slowly, according to the initiatory process, carefully watching over the firing.

51. *Thunder*

**Thunder is developmental. When thunder comes, there
is alarm, then laughter. Thunder startles for a hundred
miles, but one does not lose spoon and wine.**

EXPLANATION

Thunder is movement, action, represented as thunder. In the body of the
hexagram, one yang is born below two yins, symbolizing the presence
of movement within stillness. Here two thunders combine: From this action you arrive at that action, from that action you produce this action—a
thousand actions, myriad acts, are all this one action; therefore it is called
thunder.

This hexagram represents acting so as to proceed on the Path, warily
practicing introspection; it follows on the previous hexagram *revolution*.
Revolution involves gaining joy through illumination, refining metal by fire,
removing old impurities. Removing old impurities does not mean forgetting things, forgetting the body, extinguishing the mind, and stopping
thoughts; it is necessary to remove impurities in the midst of action in
order to accomplish the task. This is because the Tao is alive, in movement;
it is neither material nor void. We use worldly realities to practice the reality of the Tao, and use human affairs to cultivate celestial virtues; both
striving and nonstriving, comprehending essence and comprehending life,
the endless work all must be done in the midst of activity. Therefore there
is a path of development in *thunder*.

However, there is inner activity and outer activity. Inner activity
means the movement of inward thoughts, outer activity means the activity
of affairs that come up. Inner activity is in the realm of self, outer activity
is in the realm of other. If inner activity is genuine, outward activity will
also be genuine; if inner activity is artificial, outward activity will also be
artificial. Superior people are careful about what they do not see, wary
about what they do not hear; this means being careful and wary about
inner activity. If there is no random activity within, there will naturally be
genuine activity. The movement of genuine activity may go on all the time
without causing any disturbance; using this to deal with external activity,
one responds without minding. Therefore "when thunder comes, there is
alarm, then laughter."

The coming of thunder means that within stillness there is suddenly
movement; alarm followed by laughter means initial carefulness and subsequent ease. One moment of goodness in people's minds, and the mind of
Tao appears; this is heaven. One moment of evil in the mind, and the human mentality acts; this is hell. Hell and heaven do exist in the world—
they are both created in people's minds. It is the good and evil, falsehood
and truth of thoughts, which distinguish them.

When you have thoughts, if you can practice introspection, gradually eliminating bad thoughts and gradually producing good thoughts, after a long time of consistency thought after thought all return to correct orientation, so that the mind of Tao is ever-present, and the human mentality does not arise: Filled with living energy, the real self sits peacefully in the center, tranquil and unperturbed, yet sensitive and effective. Whatever comes up, you are cheerful and calm, responding with good humor, not minding at all—even if "thunder startles for a hundred miles," still you "don't lose spoon and wine."

A spoon is for eating; wine represents fine drink. When thunder peals over a hundred miles, it is very loud, and can easily startle people. If you don't lose your marbles when this happens, this means the vicissitudes of circumstance aren't able to disturb your balance. Because superior people are wary of inner activity, they do not fear outward activity.

Being wary of inner activity means nurturing the energy; not fearing outward activity means not agitating the energy. If one can inwardly nurture energy and outwardly not agitate energy, acting when the time is for action, not acting when the time is for inaction, accompanying the "thunder," going along with the time, myriad actions are all genuine activity— there is no impediment in action. Herein lies the developmental quality of *thunder*.

■ *First yang:* **When thunder comes, alarm; afterward, laughter. Auspicious.**

EXPLANATION
In the beginning of movement and action, if one can be careful and wary about what is as yet unperceived, this is how it is that there is alarm when thunder comes, laughter afterward. First being alarmed means distinguishing right and wrong, being careful in the beginning. Laughter afterward means mental attainment comes out in action, becoming complete in the end. First wary, afterward joyful; this is most auspicious for action. This represents action in which strength and firmness are correctly applied.

■ *2 yin:* **Thunder comes: dangerous thoughts. Losing valuables, you climb nine hills: Don't chase it—you'll get it in seven days.**

EXPLANATION
Mounting strength with weakness, arbitrary imagination gets too high, and one tries to do what one cannot do. This is losing basic sense and acting on dangerous thoughts, like "losing valuables" and climbing "nine hills." It is fortunate if you maintain rectitude when you are weak, not daring to act arbitrarily, even though you may have the thoughts. This is itself basic sense; without needing to seek basic sense any more, danger can be eliminated. Therefore the text says "Don't chase it—you'll get it in seven days." This represents wariness of inner movement when weak.

■ *3 yin:* Frightened by thunder; wary action is free
from trouble.

EXPLANATION

When there is weakness where there should be strength, fearing one's own
inability one also fears that action will lead into trouble; trembling in fear
inside and out, body and mind are incapable of self-mastery. However, if
the will is strong in spite of weakness of constitution, one can approach
people imbued with Tao and borrow their strength to overcome one's own
weakness. Then one will be able to do what one couldn't do before. Therefore by wary action one can eliminate trouble. This represents being wary
of one's own weakness and seeking the aid of others.

■ *4 yang:* Thunder gets bogged down.

EXPLANATION

When strength is not correctly oriented, and is also in the midst of negative or worldly influence, in daily association with petty people one lacks
the will to practice the Tao even if one has the strength to do so. This is
action that gets bogged down and cannot progress. This represents being
strong but incautious.

■ *5 yin:* Actively mulling over dangerous plans. No loss;
there is concern.

EXPLANATION

If one is only yielding and has no firmness, when it comes time to act one
lacks the qualities to do so; when one mulls over plans, those plans do not
come to fruition. What can be accomplished by fearful and perilous
thoughts? It is fortunate if one's flexibility is properly balanced, so that
one will not dare to act arbitrarily: Then there will be no external action
that will cause loss, and there will be wary concern for the inner state; also
one will not lose one's basic nature of flexibility. This represents being
wary and careful about the outside world when one is weak.

■ *Top yin:* Movement uneasy, gaze unsteady—an
expedition will bring misfortune. The action is not in
oneself but in the neighbors; there is no blame.
Association involves criticism.

EXPLANATION

At the top of double *thunder,* inside and out is fear alone and no real action. Therefore one's movement is uneasy and gaze unsteady. Uneasiness
and unsteadiness mean weakness and incapacity; if one ends up only fearing, one cannot get far—there will be misfortune even where there was
none to begin with. However, at the culmination of external action, the

action is not in oneself but in the neighbors, so even if one was blame-worthy, one can be blameless. One becomes blameless because the fear of people is bad; because it is bad, wise people will surely lead one to good-ness. Therefore "association involves criticism." This represents being weak and fearing others.

In all six lines there is a kind of fear—it may be inner fear or outer fear, it may cause misfortune or it may cause blamelessness; but none of them are the path of introspection by which good fortune is gained. Looking for fear for the inward without fear of the outward, being able to be careful about the beginning and complete the end, we find it only in the first yang line. So in practicing introspection it is important to fear for the inward and not fear the outward. Fear for the inward means being careful about one's inner state; not fearing the outward means manifesting it in action. If one is first wary, and then cultivates practice, one cannot be disturbed by external things. Thereby one can realize essence and make life complete, unaffected by ups and downs.

52. *Mountain*

**Stopping at the back, one does not have a body;
walking in the garden, one does not see a person.
No fault.**

EXPLANATION

Mountain represents stopping, stillness. In the body of the hexagram, one yang rests on top of two yins: The yang is above, the yin is below; yang governs yin and yin obeys yang, so the celestial is not damaged by the mundane. Inwardly still and outwardly still, one stops inside and also stops outside. Because one stillness pervades inside and outside, it is called *mountain*.

This hexagram represents nurturing energy by quietude, discerning the good and holding fast to it. It follows on the previous hexagram *the cauldron*. In *the cauldron*, one follows an initiatory process to produce illu-mination. Illumination comes from following the procedure; illumination, reaching everywhere without becoming defective anywhere, refines the great elixir. But if you want to refine the great elixir, you cannot do so un-less you discern the good and hold fast to it, staying in the proper place.

Staying in the proper place does not mean empty inaction; the path has both action and stillness, and both action and stillness must stay in the proper place. In the qualities of the hexagram, the inner stopping means stillness staying in the proper place, and the outer stopping means action staying in the proper place. By stillness you develop the abode of rest; by action you test the abode of rest. By the former stopping you reach the latter stopping, by the latter stopping you master the former stopping; action and stillness both end up in a single stillness.

Stillness upon stillness, it is like the one stopping on the back of the other. Therefore the text says "stopping at the back." Stopping on the back of stopping is acting from stillness, testing stillness with action, so action and stillness are one continuum. Then stillness does not become empty quietism, and action does not become unbridled indulgence. Action is none other than stillness, stillness none other than action. Stillness is of course still; action too is still. Inside and outside are one stillness, staying in the proper place without shifting, therefore "one does not have a body; walking in the garden, one does not see a person."

Not having a body means there is no self; walking in the garden, not seeing a person means there are no others. Ordinary people discriminate between self and others, inside and outside, because they have consciousness. When there is consciousness, there is self; when there is self, there are others. When there are self and others, one doesn't know where to stop. If one can stop at the back, then the consciousness of self and others sublimates. When there is no consciousness of self and others, then the human mentality leaves and the mind of Tao arrives.

There is only one truth; act and rest according to truth. In repose you preserve correctness: Stillness is accomplished by realizing truth, not by the body; resting in the proper place, inwardly you are unaware of having a body. In action, you act correctly, acting on the truth, not in obedience to other people; stopping in the proper place, outwardly you do not mind other people. With no self or others, having been able to stop inside, you can also stop outside. Active or still according to the time, inwardly and outwardly in communion with the Tao—both action and stillness come forth from mindlessness. Through this one principle all faults can be eliminated.

If learners can apply their efforts to this double stilling, stopping in the proper place without wavering, then they will finish all tasks by this one attainment. Why worry that the gold elixir won't form or the great Tao will not be realized?

■ *First yin:*   **Stopping at the feet, there is no fault.**
It is beneficial to be always upright.

EXPLANATION
Being humble and not daring to act arbitrarily is like stopping the feet. Stopping the feet, not proceeding in any improper way, since the first thought is genuine, one can then be without fault. However, those who are yielding often lack autonomy, and may lack firmness in stopping. So it is beneficial to be always upright, persisting in the Path; only then can one be faultless from start to finish. This is the stopping in which one maintains correctness always.

■ *2 yin:* Stopping at the calves doesn't help out the
following. The heart is unhappy.

EXPLANATION
Yielding, infirm, with stopping unstable, things get a bit further; this is like
stopping at the calves. The calves do not move by themselves; they follow
the feet—when you stop things at the calves, it is because there is no one
with firm understanding to help out. Therefore the heart is unhappy; one
cannot but stop. This is the stopping of the weak making forced effort.

■ *3 yang:* Stopping at the waist breaks the backbone;
danger inflames the heart.

EXPLANATION
Being strong without flexibility, impulsive and unrestrained, is like the
backbone at the waist; if you only know how to go forward and not how to
withdraw, that will surely destroy your strength—stopping only when
there is a limit is like breaking the backbone. Above a broken backbone,
the danger lies in inflaming the heart to crave victory and desire quick success. This is the stopping of the strong making forced effort.

■ *4 yin:* Stopping at the body, there is no blame.

EXPLANATION
Remaining upright in spite of weakness, not changing one's direction in
activity, is like stopping at the body. If one can stop at the body, take care of
oneself and not foist responsibility off on others, then one will be remote
from enmity, and therefore be without blame. This is the stopping of governing oneself in weakness.

■ *5 yin:* Stopping at the jaws, one's words are orderly.
Regret vanishes.

EXPLANATION
Weak yet balanced, stopping inside and also stopping outside, is like stopping at the jaws. The jaws move when the mouth opens: Stopping at the
jaws, the mouth does not open at random, so speech does not come forth
at random; if one speaks, one's words are orderly. One may speak so as to
benefit the human mind in worldly affairs, or one may speak concerning
the essence and life of body and mind; even if one cannot carry it out oneself, inducing people to goodness is also something that builds up virtue.
Even if there was regret before, the regret can disappear. This is the stopping in which one helps people in spite of weakness.

■ *Top yang:* **Careful stopping brings good fortune.**

EXPLANATION

At the top of double stopping, able to stop inside, one can also stop outside; inside and outside one stillness, this is called careful stopping. When stopping is most thorough, strength and weakness are entirely sublimated, one's essence is stabilized and feelings forgotten; resting in the realm of ultimate good and not moving from there, without birth or death, one is like a lofty mountain, everlasting as sky and earth. This is stopping in which one completes the beginning and consummates the end.

So the path of stopping in the proper place requires that doing and non-doing, action and stillness, be as one, and yin and yang merge and sublimate. The final achievement comes only when you rest in the realm of ultimate good without evil. If you do not reach the realm of ultimate good without evil, this cannot be called complete fortune. So those who practice the Tao should know where to stop.

53. *Gradual Progress*

Gradual progress is good when a woman marries.
It is beneficial to be correct.

EXPLANATION

Gradual progress means going slowly, not rushing. As for the qualities of the hexagram, above is *wind* ☴, entering, and below is *mountain* ☶, still: Staying in the proper place and slowly entering, therefore it is called *gradual progress.*

This hexagram represents gradual practice following the appropriate order; it follows on the previous hexagram *thunder. Thunder* involves practicing introspection in action, not acting arbitrarily. Not acting arbitrarily, one is cautious and wary; strong energy resides within, the mind is firm and the will far-reaching—one can thereby practice the path of striving for the gold elixir.

The path of striving is the path of restoring the primordial while in the temporal; therefore it is returning the nonexistent to existence, so that what is gone comes back. To return the nonexistent to existence, so that what is gone comes back, is not something that can be done in one day; the process involved is subtle, the course of work is long—it is necessary to progress gradually, following the appropriate order, before one can reach deep attainment of self-realization.

The firmness of the hexagram stays still within, the flexibility follows without: Using flexibility with firmness, nurturing firmness by flexibility, solidity is used with openness, openness is practiced by solidity; firmness and flexibility match, openness and solidity combine. This is like the yin and yang in the second and fifth lines corresponding; true yin and true yang naturally form a couple—this is not like trying to force the joining of false yin and false yang.

This path is like the way a woman marries. Usually when a woman marries a man, the man first seeks the woman, using an intermediary to communicate; if both families have no objection, then the woman marries into the man's family. Mutually attracted, the man and woman produce children, who produce grandchildren, and husband and wife grow old together. So what is good for a woman in marriage is good for the man. If the man does not seek the woman, and the woman seeks the man first, privately communicating without an intermediary, hastily seeking consummation, not only will the woman not be happy, neither will the man. Both the man and the woman will be unhappy, having merely attained a moment's pleasure, surely failing in the long run.

Therefore practitioners of Tao work gradually, not seeking quick success. Firmness used with flexibility is like the man seeking the woman. Not rushing yet not lagging, proceeding in an orderly fashion, more strongly as time goes by, is like communicating properly through an intermediary. When the work is done, it returns from effort to spontaneity; yin and yang join, firmness and flexibility merge, and a bead of spiritual elixir congeals from nothingness into form. This is like the woman marrying the man; man and woman espoused, they naturally give birth and rear offspring. Therefore the path of gradual cultivation is good when it is like a woman marrying.

However, though the gradual path is good, it is only beneficial if the gradual progress is correct. If it is not correct, it is not good. Among those in the world who practice material or sexual alchemy, those who cling to emptiness or stick to forms, there are those who do their practices all their lives without stopping—they are certainly proceeding gradually, but their gradual progress is not correct. So they waste their lives, growing old without achievement. What is the good of that? So it is necessary to proceed gradually in the correct manner, thoroughly investigating truth, completely realizing essence, to arrive at the meaning of life. From striving entering into nonstriving, from effort arriving at spontaneity, everyone can attain the great Tao.

■ *First yin:*   Geese gradually proceed on the shoreline. The small ones are in danger; there is criticism, no fault.

EXPLANATION
The very bottom of gradual progress is like geese gradually proceeding on the shoreline. Gradually proceeding on the shoreline, they lose the order they had in flight; carelessness in the beginning leads to misfortune in the end. When those who have gone wrong blame their errors on the alchemical classics, this is the small being in danger and there being criti-

cism. The danger of criticism is something they bring on themselves—it is no fault of others. This represents gradual progress that is weak and incorrect.

■ *2 yin:*   Geese gradually proceed on boulders; they eat
and drink happily. Good fortune.

EXPLANATION
Being still and balanced is like geese gradually proceeding on boulders. Boulders are stable. But boulders are not the place for geese to stay: Gradually proceeding on a boulder, one refines the self until the proper time, emptying the mind so as to fill the belly; therefore one "eats and drinks happily." There is enjoyment therein; it is obviously good fortune. This is gradual progress that is balanced in spite of weakness.

■ *3 yang:*   Geese gradually proceed on a plateau. The
husband who goes on an expedition does not return;
the wife who gets pregnant does not raise the child.
Misfortune. It is beneficial to defend against brigands.

EXPLANATION
Strong without balance, progress going too high, is like geese proceeding on a plateau. A plateau is a mountain with a flat top: Proceeding on a plateau means losing the order of climbing from low to high. In a hurry to succeed, yin and yang are not in harmony; getting involved in artificiality, one damages the real. This is like the husband going on an expedition and not returning, falling in love with another woman, while the wife gets pregnant but does not raise the child, having a secret affair with a lover. This can lead only to misfortune. The misfortune comes about because in the use of strength it is important to stop in the proper place and defend against brigands, not to act arbitrarily and become a brigand oneself. This is gradual progress in which one is strong but loses control.

■ *4 yin:*   Geese gradually proceed in the trees, and may
reach a level roost. No fault.

EXPLANATION
Remaining flexible by yielding is like geese gradually proceeding in the trees, possibly finding a level roost. Trees are not the place for geese to stay, but gradually getting to a level roost, they may rest there for a while. Similarly, becoming thoroughly empty and quiet, one thereby awaits the return of yang: Then naturally one does not commit the fault of missing it when it appears. This is gradual progress in which one is yielding and at the same time preserves correct orientation.

■ *5 yang:* Geese gradually proceed onto a mountain top.
The wife does not conceive for three years, but in the
end nothing defeats her. Good fortune.

EXPLANATION
Positive strength correctly balanced is like geese proceeding onto a mountaintop. The mountaintop is high and is centered; as strength gradually
proceeds to central balance, heat dissipates, and true yin and yang, essence
and feeling, join together, no longer blocked by false yin and yang. This is
like a wife not conceiving for three years but ultimately not being defeated. When the real returns and the false dissipates, the polar energies of
true yin and yang join to form the elixir; then conception takes place
where it hadn't before—that is to say, a bead of gold elixir is ingested into
the belly. Then for the first time one knows one's destiny doesn't depend on
heaven. What can compare to that fortune? This is gradual progress in
which strength and flexibility merge.

■ *Top yang:* Geese gradually proceed to level ground;
their feathers can be used for ceremonies.
Good fortune.

EXPLANATION
At the end of gradual progress, strength and flexibility are completely di-
gested; having climbed from low to high, and gradually progressed to
where no further progression is possible, the spiritual embryo is completely developed. This is like geese proceeding to level ground, resting in
an even and safe place. Having progressed to peace and security, it is time
to rest and stop work, to cultivate practices by which to contact and guide
people who come to learn. This is why "the feathers can be used for ceremonies. Good fortune." This is gradual progress culminating in complete
fulfillment of the whole process from start to finish.

Each of the six lines involves the path of gradual progress, but the first one
is too weak, and the third is too strong, so they are not favorable paths of
progress. The other four all indicate achievements of gradual progress in
appropriate order; sometimes yielding, sometimes firm, each carried out
according to the time, the whole body and great function of gradual progress is finally revealed.

54. *Making a Young Girl Marry*

Making a young girl marry: To go on will lead to misfortune; no profit is gained.

EXPLANATION

Making a young girl marry means intercourse is not proper. In the qualities of the hexagram, above is *thunder* ☳, movement, and below is *lake* ☱ joy: Inwardly delighted and outwardly moved, actively seeking enjoyment, behavior obeying emotion—this is like using a girl to seek a son; yin is first, yang comes after—the intercourse is not proper, so it is called *making a young girl marry.*

This is the hexagram of seeking the real within the false; it follows on the previous hexagram *mountain. Mountain* means stopping in the proper place, getting rid of incorrect enjoyment and improper action. Before the primordial in people is spoiled and mixes with acquired conditioning, yin and yang are united: Yang controls yin, yin follows yang, one energy flows, the living potential persists, wholly integrated with the design of heaven— they merge naturally, without depending on human effort. Then when acquired conditioning takes over one's actions, the primal true yang is lost outside, discriminatory awareness uses consciousness to produce illusions, yin and yang go awry, the elemental energies get mixed up, desires stir and emotions arise, the mind gets mixed up with things—delighting in externals from within, inwardly moved by externals, one's inherent true yang is evaporated by other.

Self is represented by the east, in the province of *thunder* ☳; other is represented by the west, in the province of *lake* ☱. The east is the host, essence; the west is the guest, feeling. *Lake* seeking *thunder* is disturbing essence by emotion, external energy injuring inner energy.

Furthermore, *lake* is associated with metal, governing punishment and killing; *thunder* is associated with wood, governing life and merit. When punishment and killing overcome life and merit, positive energy dissipates day by day, and negative energy grows day by day. When this dissipation and growth reaches the point where there is pure negativity and no positivity, even if you want to avoid dying you cannot. Therefore if a young girl is made to marry, "to go on will lead to misfortune; no profit is gained."

So making a young girl marry means using *lake* to seek *thunder*, or using emotion to seek essence—even if they interact, it is not right. Sages have a way to restore the primal while in the temporal: If one seeks *lake* with *thunder*, using essence to seek feeling, not only will one not be overcome by emotion, one will also be able to snatch the true yang within feeling and restore it to essence. When feeling returns to essence, punishment turns into merit; essence loves the righteousness of feeling, feeling loves the goodness of essence. Essence and feeling united, there is a return to correctness: Reverting to the original, going back to the fundamental, the spiritual embryo solidifies, and even when meeting misfortune it turns to fortune. Then there will be unfailing benefit where before there was none. This is an attempt to explain correctness in the midst of incorrectness.

■ *First yang:*   Marrying off a young girl as a junior wife.
The lame can walk. It is good to go on.

EXPLANATION
Being strong yet being in a low position is like a young girl marrying as a junior wife. A junior wife is a second wife. The young girl humbles herself as a junior wife: The time is not right but her virtue is right, and she does not do anything improper. This is like the lame being able to walk. External objects cannot impose any defilement. To go on and practice the Tao on this basis, enjoying what is properly enjoyed, will always bring good fortune. This represents the ability to maintain rectitude when the time is not right.

■ *2 yang:*   The one-eyed can see. The chastity of a hermit
is beneficial here.

EXPLANATION
Strength employed with flexibility, outwardly dark yet inwardly bright, is like the one-eyed being able to see. Embracing the Tao and dwelling in seclusion, remaining chaste and single-minded, considering essence and life the one important matter, there will naturally be true pleasure, and one will not care for artificial pleasure. One is upright at all times, effective in all matters. This represents preserving correctness and not getting into what is not right.

■ *3 yin:*   Making a young girl marry with expectation:
She turns back and marries as a junior wife.

EXPLANATION
Being weak and improperly oriented, striving for externals and losing what is within, accepting the false and injuring the real, degrading oneself, is like making a young girl marry with expectation. If she can turn back, regret error and wake up, thus seeking marriage as a junior wife, associating with the wise, even if she cannot enter the great path of sages she can still avoid the error of wrong orientation. This represents turning back from error to adopt correct orientation.

■ *4 yang:*   When it is the wrong time for the girl to
marry, she delays marriage until the proper time.

EXPLANATION
When one is strong but yielding, refining oneself, awaiting proper timing, this is like a girl delaying marriage until the proper time if it is the wrong

time for marriage. "When it is the wrong time" means not acting when it is not the time to do so, getting rid of the human mentality. Delaying marriage means that action must have proper timing, being the restoration of the mind of Tao. Getting rid of the human mentality and restoring the mind of Tao is wherein lies the meaning of the saying "Attaining utter emptiness, maintaining single-minded stillness, as myriad things act in concert, I thereby observe the return." This represents returning to right from wrong by awaiting the proper time.

■ *5 yin:* **The emperor marries off his younger sister; the attire of the empress is not as good as the attire of the young wife. The moon is nearly full. Good fortune.**

EXPLANATION
Being flexible and receptive, with an open mind, humble and deferential to the noble and wise, being wrong so seeking right, is like the emperor marrying off his younger sister and the attire of the empress not being as good as the attire of the young wife. Balancing oneself with the help of another, even the ignorant will be enlightened, the weak will be strong. This is also like the moon interacting with the sun, able thereby to shine, and approaching fullness: The light is immeasurably auspicious. This represents one who is originally incorrect ending up correct with the help of another.

■ *Top yin:* **The woman receives a chest but there is nothing in it; the man sacrifices a goat but there is no blood. No benefit is gained.**

EXPLANATION
Being ignorant and mistakenly getting into deviant practices, making a living on conditioned yin and yang, seeking and joining them by force, hoping for eternal life in the wrong way, thus on the contrary hastening death, is like the bride receiving a dowry chest with nothing in it, the groom sacrificing a ceremonial goat with no blood. With selfish, improper union, one day the endeavor will fail, and there will be injury to essence and life. Obviously no benefit will be derived from this. This is ending up wrong and not knowing how to return to what is right.

So those who follow conditioned yin and yang end up in annihilation, while those who go back to primordial yin and yang end up with true salvation. Following, one becomes an ordinary mortal; going in reverse, one becomes an immortal. But the path of turning around and operating in reverse therein is not easy to know.

55. *Richness*

Richness is developmental. Freedom from worry when the king is great is suited to midday.

EXPLANATION

Richness is fullness and greatness; illumination and action balance each other, illumination is great and action is great—therefore it is called richness.

This hexagram represents operating the fire and preventing danger; it follows on the previous hexagram *gradual progress. Gradual progress* means stabilization and carrying out practice according to an initiatory process, whereby one gradually advances in an orderly manner, not letting the firing process go awry. "Fire" is a symbol of illumination; operating the fire means employing illumination. Illumination is the quality of awareness and perceptivity. If one can be aware, then one has the mind of Tao, and the spirit is knowing. If one can be perceptive, then there is no human mentality, and the mind is clear. With the spirit knowing and the mind clear, inwardly cultivating and subtly refining, clear about action and acting with clarity, one's illumination will grow day by day, and one's action will become greater day by day. When illumination and action are applied in concert, practice of the Tao is very easy. This is why *richness* is developmental.

However, though richness of illumination and action is developmental, it is necessary to know when to go forward and when to withdraw, to be able to be great or small, to forestall danger and foresee peril—only then can richness be enduring richness, can development be enduring development. This is like there being no "worry when the king is great." The king represents the ease of making works lofty and great when the accomplishment of the Tao is rich and full. When one is great and knows how to preserve it, there is no worry about greatness.

What path is the path of no worry? It is the path "suited to midday." Day represents illumination, the middle means freedom from partiality and bias. When development of illumination is rich and full, the firing process has been completed, and the medicine has been made, the kindling should be quickly removed from under the stove and the fire should be stopped. Stopping when it is appropriate to stop, illumination is not overused. When illumination is not overused, proceeding and withdrawing according to the time, firmness and flexibility balancing each other without partiality or bias, then that which is not yet rich can become so, while that which is already rich can be preserved. There is no further worry that richness may be lost.

■ *First yang:*   Meeting your director, even as equals there
is no blame. If you go on, there will be exaltation.

EXPLANATION
In the beginning of richness, when your illumination is not great, and it is
appropriate that you should foster richness, if there is communication
with a sage having the same virtues, this is meeting your director. Meeting
your director, you benefit each other, thus increasing understanding; even
though you are at the beginning of equality, it is possible to be blameless. It
is a logical certainty that if you go on using this strength there will be exaltation. This is being strong and producing richness in the beginning.

■ *2 yin:*   Increasing the shade, seeing stars at midday, if
you go on this way you will have doubt and affliction.
But if there is sincerity and it is acted on, it will bring
good fortune.

EXPLANATION
If you associate with the wrong people, you will not only be unable to
increase illumination, you will on the contrary block illumination. This is
like "increasing the shade, seeing stars at midday." Seeing stars at midday
means the light of the sun does not prevail over the light of the stars; illumination is blocked and does not get through. If one goes on this way to
operate the fire and carry out the convergence, right and wrong will be
indistinct, the practice will run into difficulty, and one will surely have
doubt and affliction. It is lucky if there is a true teacher in sight; if you
know you are not enlightened and sincerely seek enlightenment from another, borrowing strength to remedy weakness, arousing your spirit and
proceeding with vigor, not only will there be no doubt, but it will also
bring good fortune. This is borrowing strength when weak, to produce
richness.

■ *3 yang:*   Increasing shade, seeing glimmering
stardust at midday, one breaks one's right arm.
No one is to blame.

EXPLANATION
Using illumination too much, in desiring to enrich the illumination, instead one obscures the illumination. This is like seeing shimmering stardust at midday. When stardust is seen at midday, that means the light of the
sun does not prevail over the light of the moon; the damage to illumination is extreme. The reason for this is that one knows only how to use
strength and does not know how to use flexibility; one knows only how to
employ illumination and does not know how to nurture illumination.
When one advances too speedily, one will also regress rapidly; this is like
breaking one's right arm. This is bringing failure on oneself, and is not the
fault of anyone else. This is the richness of strength incapable of yielding.

■ *4 yang:*   Increasing shade, seeing stars at midday.
Meeting the hidden master is auspicious.

EXPLANATION
Here strength is in the body of movement (☵), near to yin: Not only is
it not possible to enrich illumination, there is also that which increases
obscurity. Again, this is like seeing stars at midday. But if one is strong yet
can be flexible and yielding, not using one's illumination actively, able to
nurture one's illumination, one thereby meets the hidden master, which is
auspicious. "Hidden" means unseen, concealed: Usually true practitioners
of Tao adopt a plain appearance even though they carry a treasure; many
of them conceal themselves in humble situations, and people cannot recognize them. When one is able to meet such a hidden adept, there is mutual inspiration; nurturing illumination and not employing it, illumination
is naturally not damaged, strength naturally does not fail. This is the
richness of strength able to be flexible and yielding.

■ *5 yin:*   Bringing beatification, there is glory; this is
auspicious.

EXPLANATION
With flexible receptivity in balance, by emptying the mind one can fill the
belly; therefore "bringing beatification, there is glory." "Bringing beatification" means that clarity arises in openness, so spiritual illumination comes
of itself. "There is glory" means that one's striving at the outset is not seen
by anyone, but then when one arrives at nonstriving, everyone knows.
This fifth line represents the very moment of richness, when emptiness
and fulfillment correspond, illumination and action are spontaneous, the
gold elixir has crystallized, and it is appropriate to take the path of nonstriving, using the "cultural fire" for incubation. This is the richness of
yielding and nonstriving.

■ *Top yin:*   Embellishing the room, shading the house;
peeking in the door, it is quiet, with no one there,
unseen for three years. Inauspicious.

EXPLANATION
When one is weak, without knowledge, not understanding the great Tao,
remaining at rest in solitary quietude, self-satisfied, thinking this is enough,
idly adorning the appearance of the house while going into a dark place
without illumination, this is like having a house with no one in it. Not
understanding in the beginning, one will see misfortune in the end; the
culmination of richness is an inauspicious culmination. This has been referred to as a magnificent buddha-shrine with no Buddha in it. This is the
richness of weak nihilism.

So in the path of richness, when not yet rich it is necessary to produce
richness by first understanding and then practicing. Once rich, it is neces-

sary to stop pouring on effort and to preserve richness. Producing richness and preserving richness, each follow its own appropriate timing: Forestalling danger, aware of perils, using illumination and operating the fire without erring either by excess or insufficiency, it is good to attain the proper balance.

56. *Travel*

Travel is developmental when small; if travel is correct, it leads to good fortune.

EXPLANATION

Travel means passing through and not lingering. As to the qualities of the hexagram, above is *fire* ☲, luminous, and below is *mountain* ☶, still: Using illumination with stability, illumination being based on stillness, one stabilizes the illumination and does not use it carelessly. Therefore this is called *travel*.

This hexagram represents nurturing the fire and transcending the world; it follows on the previous hexagram *making a young girl marry.* In *making a young girl marry,* there is uncontrolled action based on emotion, obeying the mundane energy of conditioning and burying the primal celestial energy, taking the artificial to be real, taking misery for pleasure. Practitioners of Tao should first see through worldly things, looking upon all conditions, all existents, as passing by, not injuring the real by delighting in the false, not disturbing the inward because of the outward. Understanding stillness and staying in the proper place, stabilizing illumination so that it is not damaged, when illumination and stillness are used together one can thereby transcend the world while in the world. Therefore travel is developmental when small, and travel leads to good fortune when correct.

"Small" travel means applying illumination with stillness, so that illumination is not used arbitrarily. The good fortune of correctness is when illumination is based on stillness, resting in ultimate good. Applying illumination with stillness, one forgets feelings in the face of objects. When illumination is based on stillness, one ejects extreme intellectualism. Unperturbed, like a mountain stably resting on the earth, unbefuddled, like the sunlight shining in the sky, inwardly there is no disturbance, outwardly there is no obscurity: When there is something to do, you use clarity to deal with it; when there is nothing to do, you use clarity to remain still. You are then free from greed and craving, not expecting or pursuing, not lingering or tarrying.

In general, *travel* as a path means just passing through once—you should not remain attached to the realm you pass through. If you are concerned with externals, you forget the inward; by pursuing ramifications you abandon the root. When illumination is called for, then be aware; but while aware still remain calm. When stillness is called for, be still; but while still, remain aware. When illumination and stability, awareness and stillness, are unified, how can there be failure to develop and prosper?

■ *First yin:*   **Restless in travel, this is the misfortune you get.**

EXPLANATION

When you are weak and unclear, unable to see through worldly things, not knowing where to stop, restlessly traveling here, traveling there, you bring misfortune on yourself. This is the travel of the weak and disoriented.

■ *2 yin:*   **Coming to a lodge on a journey with money in your pocket, you have attendants, yet are upright.**

EXPLANATION

Flexible receptivity in balance, staying in the appropriate place, is like coming to a lodge on a journey with money in your pocket. Having substance, yet you mix in with others, living with lesser people, while able to avoid being influenced by lesser people. This is what is called adapting to situations as they are, not letting people know what is hidden under your actions. This is travel with flexibility, balance, and rectitude.

■ *3 yang:*   **Burning the lodge on a journey, you lose your attendants. Even if righteous there is danger.**

EXPLANATION

When you are firm without flexibility, are unable to still inside and insist on stillness outside, totally cutting off social relations, upsetting the ignorant and ordinary, this is like burning the lodge on a journey, losing your attendants. On a journey on which you burn the lodge, though your travel may be correct, you arouse the hatred and suspicion of others, so this still is a road that brings on danger and disaster. This is travel in which firmness is excessive.

■ *4 yang:*   **Traveling in the right place, one obtains resources and tools, but one's heart is not happy.**

EXPLANATION

When one is strong and also illumined, it is like travelling in the right place; one is in control. After having completed oneself, one should also develop others; one may thus form relationships wherever one may be, build up virtue and accumulate good deeds, without difficulty. However, the correspondents are all negative (the fourth line corresponds with the first, which is yin)—even though one has resources and tools, if there are none who understand one cannot fulfill one's aspiration, and therefore one's heart is not happy. This has been the case time and again with those since ancient times who have had resources and tools but have been unable to carry forth the Path to any great extent. This is travel where one is strong but doesn't find the right time.

■ *5 yin:* **Shooting pheasant, one arrow is lost; eventually one is entitled, because of good repute.**

EXPLANATION

Being flexible and receptive, open and balanced, is like "shooting pheasant, one arrow is lost." "Shooting pheasant" means not using illumination; "one arrow is lost" means not using strength. Not using illumination, illumination is replete; not using strength, strength is complete—the whole psychophysical being is sublimated, and one lets things be as they are. Not losing oneself, neither does one turn away from others. One's virtue is sufficient to move people, and eventually one is entitled because of good repute. This is travel with flexibility and ability to integrate.

■ *Top yang:* **A bird turns its nest. The traveler first laughs, afterward cries. Losing the ox at the border, there is misfortune.**

EXPLANATION

When one presumes on strength in using intellect, aggrandizing oneself, knowing how to criticize others but not how to criticize oneself, not benefiting others and even harming oneself, this is like the travel of a bird burning its nest; first there is laughter, afterward weeping. Starting out by employing clarity, winding up by destroying clarity, and misfortune of "losing the ox at the border" is inevitable here. This is travel in which understanding is misused.

Of the travel indicated in the six lines, sometimes it is travel inside, sometimes it is travel outside; sometimes there is firmness in travel, sometimes there is flexibility in travel. Stillness within and travel without is found only in the yin in the second place. Emptying the self and traveling to others is only in the yin in the fifth place. Those who know this path can deal with the world without destroying the world, and can transcend the world while in the world.

57. *Wind*

Wind is small but developmental. It is beneficial to have somewhere to go. It is beneficial to see a great person.

EXPLANATION

Wind is penetration and laying low, meaning gradually making progress by flexible obedience. In the body of the hexagram, one yin lies below two yangs; traveling the path of firmness by means of the path of flexibility, not hurrying yet not lagging, gradually progressing step by step, obedient within and obedient without, obedient below and obedient above, going from near to far, rising from low to high, like the wind going farther and higher as it blows, reaching everywhere, therefore this is called *wind*.

This hexagram represents progressing on the path by flexible obedience; it follows on the previous hexagram *richness*. In *richness*, understanding and action are united, so that one can deal with things adaptively, passive or active at will, essence and life depending on oneself and not on fate. However, the path of uniting understanding and action is not easily accomplished; it cannot be done without the work of gradual progress by flexible obedience. If one is flexible and obedient, one can endure long; by gradual progress one can penetrate. Flexible obedience making gradual progress, getting stronger with persistence, working without slacking off, will eventually arrive at deep attainment of self-realization. Therefore "wind is small but developmental."

But though the ability to obey is a way of development, there are those who know about obedience but cannot practice it, there are those who can follow the low but not the high, there are those who can follow the high but not the low, there are those who can obey when it is pleasant but not when it is unpleasant, there are those who can obey in the beginning but not in the end—all of these are unable to really carry out the path of obedient progress, so even though they try to follow it they do not get through.

When we look for obedience in which knowledge and action are both effective, firmness and flexibility are employed together, able to be above and below, competent in both ease and adversity, effective both inwardly and outwardly, unified from start to finish, we find that only great people with balance and right orientation are capable of this. Therefore "it is beneficial to have somewhere to go," and "it is beneficial to see a great person."

A great person considers essence and life important, considers the Tao and its qualities valuable, looks upon the ephemeral body as like a dead tree, looks upon wealth and status as like floating clouds, is inwardly always more than fulfilled while outwardly appearing insufficient, truly applies real practical steps making gradual progress, mind firm and will far-reaching, determined not to rest until the great Path is completed.

Therefore there is benefit. Those who are not great people cling to partiality; they obey and follow without balance or correct orientation—how can they get anywhere, to any benefit? So the benefit of going somewhere is only for the great person.

■ *First yin:* Advancing and retreating, it is beneficial to be steadfast like a soldier.

EXPLANATION

When weak and hesitant, retreating as soon as one advances, one will never attain deeply. However, everyone has a share in the universal Tao; the only trouble is they lack will. If you can be determined, and approach true teachers, seeking personal instruction, striving mightily with the steadfastness of a soldier, you can enter the Tao beneficially. This is obedience by which the weak borrow strength.

■ *2 yang:* Obedient in the basement, frequently employing intermediaries, leads to good fortune, without blame.

EXPLANATION

Using strength with flexibility, not becoming inflated or complacent, humbling oneself to others, is like "obedience in the basement, frequently employing intermediaries." Not only does one govern oneself auspiciously, one also deals with other people blamelessly. This is the obedience of the strong who are able to be flexible and to yield.

■ *3 yang:* Redundant obedience is humiliating.

EXPLANATION

When one is self-satisfied, considering oneself while disregarding others, one cannot open the mind to ask for instruction, obeying those who are superior from an inferior position, and so one uses one's own intellectual brilliance to conform with the superior from a position of superiority; originally one wanted to go forward, but instead one falls behind. This is called redundant obedience. When obedience gets to redundancy, one can go along with those who agree, but not with those who disagree. Sometimes docile, sometimes not, one gets only humiliation. This is the obedience of the strong who cannot be flexible.

■ *4 yin:* Regret vanishes. The yield of the field is of three grades.

EXPLANATION

When one is only flexible and has no strength or firmness, it seems like one is too weak to reach deep attainment, and so there is regret. However, when flexibility is correctly oriented, near to superior strength, obedience following superiority gains balance thereby. This is one grade of "yield," the superior. When one approaches strength in a lower position, obedience following the strength below and being balanced thereby, this is the inferior grade of yield. As yin dwells in the midst of yang, not losing correctness regardless of accord or opposition is the middling grade of yield. When the three grades of great medicine, superior, middling, and inferior, return to the center, yin and yang merge, the gold elixir takes on form; this is purely the living potential. It is like planting crops in the fields, all of them maturing. What regret will not vanish? This is the obedience of balance and rectitude when weak.

■ *5 yang:*   It is good to be correct; regret vanishes. There is all-around benefit. There is no beginning, but there is an end. The last three days of the lunar cycle and the first three days of the lunar cycle are auspicious.

EXPLANATION

When one is strong and yet can still be obedient, being meticulous and single-minded, holding faithfully to the center, thereby whatever regret there was can vanish, and there is all-around benefit to the practice of Tao. That benefit is because the great person who is strong yet can yield is able to follow and also to lead. Starting out by obediently humbling oneself, it seems as if yielding injures strength—this is "no beginning." Having followed the way up, one is able to use flexibility to complete strength, so "there is an end."

The image of there being no beginning yet there being an end is as of the last three days and the first three days of the lunar cycle. The last three days start on the twenty-eighth of the lunar month, and first three days end on the third. On the twenty-eighth, the slight yang fades in the northeast, till the light finally becomes completely hidden on the thirtieth. At the new moon, the moon is tinged with the light of the sun; this is concealing yang within yin. By the third day, light like a wispy eyebrow appears in the west. The last three days of waning represent obedience concealing positive energy; the first three days of waxing represent obedience furthering positive energy.

The path of spiritual alchemy first follows lowliness to deep attainment, using flexibility and yielding, then follows the superior to self-realization, completing firm strength. Including yang within yin, using yin within yang, great and small are undamaged, completely balanced and correct, so the gold elixir crystallizes. The advantage of obedience in strength is most great. This is obedience using both strength and flexibility.

■ *Top yang:*   Obedient under the floor, one loses one's resources; even if faithful, there is misfortune.

EXPLANATION

At the culmination of obedience, the work of following lowliness is done, and one should withdraw from the path of yielding and proceed on the path of firmness, whereby to transmute all negativities. At this time one should not follow the low, but should follow the high, standing on top of the floor. If one clings and does not pass on, one who should be on top of the floor will wind up "under the floor." When yielding prevails over firmness, negative energy is not transmuted, and inevitably the great medicine obtained will be lost again, so that one's efforts will have been wasted. So it is logical that even if faithful, there will be misfortune. This is obedience in which yielding exceeds firmness.

So the path of progress through obedience gradually penetrating requires recognition of when to hurry and when to relax, discernment of what is conducive to good results and what leads to bad results, and the knowledge to stop at sufficiency. One must be firm when necessary, be flexible when necessary, using firmness and flexibility at the appropriate times, accordingly advancing to the balance of firmness and flexibility. This is the ultimate accomplishment.

58. Joy

Joy is developmental, beneficial if correct.

EXPLANATION

Joy is delight. In the body of the hexagram, two yangs are below, one yin is above; empty without, fulfilled within, it is represented as a body of water, and its quality is joy. As water provides moisture for myriad beings, joy develops myriad beings; joyful within and without, reaching the outer from within, communicating with the inner from without, inside and outside are conjoined, without separation between them—therefore it is called *joy*.

This hexagram represents joy in practicing the Tao; it follows on the preceding hexagram *travel*. *Travel* involves applying understanding with stability, so that understanding is not misused, having one's will on the Tao, so that no external things can move it. Having one's will on the Tao is finding joy in the Tao; when one delights in the Tao, then one can practice the Tao. This is why joy is developmental.

However, though joy is developmental on the path, it is only beneficial if correct. When it is correct, it is beneficial, and one consummates one's joy. If incorrect, it is not beneficial, and one loses one's joy. As in the image of the hexagram, with *joy* ☱ above and below, the six lines are parallel: The lower *joy* is inward joy, the upper *joy* is outer joy; when inward joy is fulfilled outer joy is also fulfilled, and when inward joy is empty outer joy is also empty. Fulfillment here means reality of joy, emptiness means falsehood of joy. Reality means joy endures; falsehood means joy does not last long. Herein lies the benefit of correctness.

People who practice the Tao really correctly do not delight in objects of the senses, in wealth and gain; they delight in benevolence, justice, and the qualities of the Tao. So naturally they have real joy and do not strive for artificial joy. Thus every step proceeds from the work they apply to the essence and life of body and mind; joyful in the beginning, they can naturally complete the end, so joy always develops, and the development is always beneficial.

■ *First yang:*   **The joy of harmony is good.**

EXPLANATION
When strong and firm and always correct and upright, joy comes forth naturally, without any effort; this is called the joy of harmony. When joy attains harmony, one can be great or small, without damaging one's strength, naturally producing good results. This is the joy of strength under control.

■ *2 yang:*   **The joy of truthfulness is good. Regret vanishes.**

EXPLANATION
True to the mean, having inner autonomy, delighting in the real and not in the false, unaffected by any illusions, good is therein; what regret would not disappear? This is the joy of strength attaining balance.

■ *3 yin:*   **Imported joy is not good.**

EXPLANATION
When weak, imbalanced, and not correctly oriented, one does not delight in the inner but delights in externals, giving up the real and pursuing the artificial. This is an obstacle to the practitioner of the Tao, who will thus never be able to enter the Tao; obviously it is not good. This is the joy of the weak who strive for externals.

■ *4 yang:*   **Joy after deliberation: If one is firm and wary without complacency, there will be happiness.**

EXPLANATION
Using strength flexibly, speaking only after deliberation, acting only after consideration, effecting the intended events with deliberation and consideration—this is called joy after deliberation. When joy is deliberate, one does not dare to submit to joy, but is careful and wary, not complacent, not acting improperly, as if seriously ill, eventually there will be happiness and one will be able to consummate one's joy.

■ *5 yang:*   **There is danger in trusting plunderers.**

EXPLANATION
If one is self-satisfied, able to find joy in strength but not in yielding, one will lose out in the end. Being strong but unhappy is the inevitable danger

in trusting plunderers. Generally speaking, people of natural brilliance can only receive benefit if they open their minds and approach people of the Tao with a humble attitude; if they presume upon their status or talent and like to be obeyed but hate to hear honest words, thus associating with petty people and avoiding superior people, their faults will increase day by day and their virtues will decrease day by day, their bad qualities will gradually grow and their good qualities will gradually vanish. Thus they bring danger on themselves even when they weren't in danger to begin with. This is what is meant by the saying that even if one has great talents, if one is haughty and jealous the talents are not worthy of consideration. This is the joy of the strong who are self-satisfied.

■ *Top yin:* Induced joy.

EXPLANATION
Delighting in outward appearances, using clever words and a commanding demeanor, not liked by others yet inducing others to like one, such people pretend to have what they have not, pretend to be fulfilled whereas they are empty; they are unwilling to think of their own errors, and also induce others to err. In the end they cannot make others joyful, and wind up being disliked themselves. This is the joy of the weak who concern themselves with externals.

So in joy there are differences between real and false, right and wrong; they are not the same in terms of leading to good or bad results, to regret or shame. In sum, it is important that joy be correct; if it is correct, it is developmental. If incorrect, it is not developmental. Those who would practice the Tao need the correct joy.

59. *Dispersal*

In dispersal there is development. The king comes to have a shrine. It is beneficial to cross great rivers. It is beneficial to be correct.

EXPLANATION
Dispersal means disorganization and disorder. In the body of the hexagram, below is *water* ☵, in which one yang is hidden between two yins, yang being trapped by yin; above is *wind* ☴, in which one yin enters under two yangs, yang being damaged by yin. Yin and yang do not interact, essence and sense are separated; so it is called *dispersal*.

This hexagram represents yin and yang being lost in confusion, then reordered; it follows on the previous hexagram *wind*. *Wind* involves gradually entering true eternity; because yin and yang are disordered, one progresses harmoniously to balance them. Once people's yin and yang are disordered, and essence and sense have shifted, the mind of Tao is obscured and the human mentality arises, the true sane energy is damaged and the false aberrant energy grows. This is like the one yang in the middle of *water* ☵, trapped by yin energy; the primordial is concealed inside acquired conditioning. Once the primordial is concealed, its vast energy is inhibited, and yin energy takes over affairs, insufficient to do good, excessive in doing evil, inevitably leading to total loss of natural innocence. This is like the one yin of *wind* ☴ insidiously rising under pure yang, subtly dispersing yang. This is why *dispersal* is so called.

However, even after dispersal, sages have a way to resolve dispersal, which is able to reorder that which is dispersed. What is the way to resolve dispersal? It is none other than the path of progress through obedience: The only distinction is that if you go one way, obeying invading conditioning, you disperse yang, while if you go the other way, obeying the primordial energy, you foster yang. If you can reverse obedience from acquired conditioning back to the primordial, gradually progressing, without hurrying or lagging, stopping falsehood and preserving truthfulness, mastering yourself and returning to appropriate order, that which is scattered can be assembled, that which is disorderly can be ordered, so that you can return to your original being. First dispersed, ending up not dispersed, there is thus paradoxically a way of development in dispersal.

Those who develop this have no danger in their hearts even when there is danger in events, are not imperiled inwardly even when there is outward peril; they make use of the path of flexibility to travel the path of firmness, and use positive energy to transmute negative energy. This is like a king coming to have a shrine, using sincerity to summon the spirit, so the spirit can be summoned. It is also like wood following the nature of water, "beneficial to cross great rivers," so that danger can be solved.

When people's yin and yang are scattered, it is always because of using the human mentality and abandoning the mind of Tao; every act, every step, is on dangerous ground. But if you use the mind of Tao and dismiss the human mentality, you can seek the jewel of life in a tiger's lair, search out the pearl of illumination in a dragon's abyss, progressing harmoniously in danger and getting through danger. With proper control according to events, whether agreeable or disagreeable, the mind of Tao is ever present, the human mentality passes away; the five elements aggregate, the four signs combine—what dispersal is there?

However, in the path of resolving dispersal, there is a process, there is a course of work, there is intensification and relaxation, there is stopping at sufficiency. The slightest deviation and you go far astray. It is only beneficial if you are correct. Accomplishing the work correctly, hastening and relaxing methodically, advancing and withdrawing at the proper times, there will surely be development and benefit.

■ *First yin:*   Act to save the horse; vigor will
have good results.

EXPLANATION
In the beginning of dispersal, before the mind of Tao is far gone, and the
human mentality has not yet grown to full strength, if you can exert a
powerful effort to save the mind of Tao, the goal is at hand, the true treasure is before you; if you go on this way, a good result can be attained. It is
a matter of applying vigor to quickly save it. This is resolving dispersal at
the beginning of dispersal.

■ *2 yang:*   Running to support upon dispersal,
regret vanishes.

EXPLANATION
When yang has fallen into yin, and one acts through the human mentality,
one is already in a state of dispersal, and should have regret; but as long as
one is strong and balanced, even though the human mentality arises, the
mind of Tao is stable; this is like running to support upon dispersal—
though there be regret, it can be eliminated. This is remaining secure even
in dispersal.

■ *3 yin:*   Dispersing the self, there is no regret.

EXPLANATION
At the extreme of danger, one regretfully walks on a precipice; but by
having correspondence with yang one follows the mind of Tao and not the
human mind—this is like dispersing the self. Regret derives from having
the human mentality; when there is the human mentality, there is self.
Dispersing the self is being selfless, nonegotistical, without the human
mentality. When there is no human mentality, the mind of Tao is not obscured; one does not cause regret, and has no regret oneself. This is being
able to escape dispersal on encountering it.

■ *4 yin:*   Dispersing the crowd is very auspicious.
On dispersal there is gathering, inconceivable
to the ordinary.

EXPLANATION
Yielding but maintaining correctness, refining the self and mastering the
mind, reaching utter emptiness and single-minded calm, dispersing the
crowd of negative forces and awaiting the return of positive energy, this is
incomparably auspicious. What makes this auspicious is that when one
can disperse false yin, one can recover and gather, so that what has been
deranged can return to order—after great dispersal is great integration, as
there is gathering of true yang on dispersal of false yin. True yin and true
yang unite, the five elements aggregate, the four signs combine; what was

scattered is gathered. This is not conceivable to the ordinary. This is return to nonfragmentation after dispersal.

■ *5 yang:*   **Dispersing defilement, that is a great directive. The dispersing king remains impeccable.**

EXPLANATION
Positive strength balanced and correct, perceiving when to hurry and when to relax, understanding what bodes well and what ill, getting rid of the false and restoring the true, one can thereby resolve dispersal. Therefore "dispersing defilement, that is a great directive; the dispersing king remains impeccable." The reason people cause dispersal of primordial positive energy and have faults is that they erroneously approve temporal artificial things, which have form, and abandon the primordial formless real treasure. If they can see through the artificiality of the temporal and not be burdened by acquired conditioning, that is like dispersing defilement. Having dispersed defilement, one promulgates a great directive, removing falsehood by truth, directly proceeding on the path of resolving dispersal. Thus by mastering oneself one can return to what is proper, thereby able to be humane. The mind-lord is peaceful and calm, integrated with natural principle, resting in the realm of ultimate good, without blame. This is dispersing the false and being able to complete the true.

■ *Top yang:*   **Dispersing the blood, going far away, there is no fault.**

EXPLANATION
At the end of dispersal, strength and flexibility are blended; this is "dispersing the blood, going far away." Dispersing the blood means the human mentality cannot injure the mind of Tao; going far away means the mind of Tao can repulse the human mentality. When the mind of Tao is present and the human mentality goes, then the human mind also sublimates into the mind of Tao; the gold elixir crystallizes, the spiritual embryo takes on form. At first yin and yang were fragmented and there was fault; finally yin and yang are blended and there is no fault. This is regaining integration when dispersal ends.

So when the human mentality arises, the mind of Tao leaves; when the mind of Tao arises, the human mentality leaves. The human mentality is enough to disperse and fragment yin and yang, while the mind of Tao can unite yin and yang. Being able to unite what has been dispersed, returning to the origin, reexperiencing the fundamental being, is the culmination of the path of resolving dispersal.

60. Discipline

Discipline is developmental, but painful discipline is not to be held to.

EXPLANATION

Discipline means having limits that are not to be exceeded. As to the qualities of the hexagram, above is *water* ☵, a pitfall, and below is *lake* ☱, joyous. Being capable of joy in danger, warding off danger by joyfulness, it is therefore called *discipline.*

This hexagram represents practicing obedience in unfavorable circumstances, adaptably keeping to the Tao; it follows on the previous hexagram *joy.* In *joy,* joyfulness reaches outside; one can delight in the Tao and practice the Tao. But if one can only be joyful in favorable circumstances and not in unfavorable circumstances, joy is not real, and ultimately it will be hard to get out of difficulty and danger, so one will not find joy.

Therefore those who practice reality and delight in the Tao do not let difficulty disturb their minds, and do not let peril and trouble affect their will; the situation may be dangerous, but their minds are not endangered, the times may be perilous but the Tao is not imperiled. Pleased with heaven and aware of the aim of life, they are at peace wherever they are: They use danger to nourish joy, and use joy to guard against danger. The situation may be up to others, but creation of destiny is up to oneself. Yin and yang cannot restrict such people, the created universe cannot bind them; whether in adversity or comfort, they do not lose their bearings. This is why discipline is developmental.

However, even though discipline can develop you, if you do not know how to adapt to changes, and cling fast to one discipline, that will become restrictive and stifling; this is called painful discipline. When discipline gets to the point of inflicting suffering, it brings on danger itself even where there was no danger; you will only suffer toil and servility, which is harmful and has no benefit. Not only does this not constitute discipline, it loses the appropriate measure. This is not joy in the midst of danger; it is enjoying the act of courting danger. Therefore it is not to be held to.

When superior people practice the Tao and establish virtue, they don't act in any way that is not just; their every step is orderly and regulated, their every word is timely and reasonable. In substance they are always calm, like a lake without waves; in function they act like water, which conforms to its environment. Their calmness does not reach the point of losing mindfulness, and their activity does not reach the point of straying from essence. There is a consistency about their movement and stillness, adjusted appropriately according to events, not restricted to a single pattern. When the time comes to stop, they stop; encountering danger, they deal with it. When the time comes to go on, they go on; getting out of danger, they do not bring on danger. Going along with the time, they deal with everything unminding, and therefore can get beyond yin and yang, not being constrained by yin and yang.

This is because heaven and earth can coerce what has form, but not what is formless; can coerce the minding, but not the unminding. Discipline is not according to mind but according to time; this is called discipline according to the time, having discipline yet according with the time. It is like the sections of bamboo; each section has a boundary, each section has a passage. In this way, how could one fail to develop?

■ *First yang:* **Not leaving home, there is no blame.**

EXPLANATION
In the beginning of discipline, firmly remaining upright, first becoming able to distinguish right and wrong and then after that acting—this is discipline not leaving home. "Not leaving home" means if one can be careful in the beginning one will naturally be blameless in the end. This is the discipline of the strong who are able to be upright.

■ *2 yang:* **Not going outside bodes ill.**

EXPLANATION
When firmness is led by weakness, one can only discipline inside and cannot discipline outside, and wind up living alone as quietists. This is called the discipline of not going outside. Not going outside, one may be disciplined, but one is ineffective. This bodes ill even when there is no adversity. This is the fixated firmness.

■ *3 yin:* **If one is not disciplined, one will lament.**
    It is no fault of others.

EXPLANATION
Imbalanced and disoriented, striving for externals and losing the inner, craving happiness without knowing it requires discipline, one will instead bring about unhappiness. This wound of lament is self-inflicted, and no fault of others. This is being weak and not knowing enough to have discipline.

■ *4 yin:* **Peaceful discipline is developmental.**

EXPLANATION
When receptive flexibility is correctly oriented, one borrows strength to eliminate weakness, so that even one incapable of discipline becomes capable of discipline. This is called peaceful discipline. When discipline reaches peace, it becomes spontaneous and does not come by forced effort. This is the discipline of the weak who are assisted by others.

■ *5 yang:*   Contented discipline is good: If you go on,
there will be exaltation.

EXPLANATION
Having inner mastery in a dangerous situation, one can be content in the
midst of suffering. When able to be content in the midst of danger and
difficulty, one can be disciplined in ordinary situations that are not hazardous. Also one can realize that there will be exaltation if one goes on. Consistent in appropriate measure in both easy and adverse situations, one
progresses to the unfathomable state of spirituality that is supremely balanced and correct. This is the discipline of being strong yet adaptable.

■ *Top yin:*   Painful discipline bodes ill if persisted in,
but regret vanishes.

EXPLANATION
At the end of discipline, being weak and infirm is called painful discipline.
When discipline becomes painful, and there is no sweetness in the bitterness, one is able to restrain oneself but not to reach out, like those
who forget about everything including their own bodies, those who stop
thoughts and extinguish their minds, those who meditate on the spirit and
enter trance; though they can be said to have discipline, they are courting
danger in hopes of good luck, with no benefit to essence and life. This is a
calamity in the path of discipline. However, insofar as they hold to one
discipline to the end and are not dragged down by human sentiments and
worldly affairs, they can be said to be freed from regret. As it is said, "If you
don't walk in the footsteps, you won't enter the room." This is the discipline of those who are weak and not thoroughly effective.

Of the six lines, only in the third is there ignorance of discipline: the other
five all have a path of discipline. Some are excessive, some insufficient—
they are not equal in terms of being right and wrong. Discipline able to be
careful at the outset is found only in the first yang. Discipline that is balanced and correct, that is developmental without fanatical adherence, is
found only in the fifth yang. Practitioners of Tao should first discern what
makes regulation of something discipline.

61. *Faithfulness in the Center*

**Faithfulness in the center is auspicious when it
reaches even pigs and fish. It is beneficial to cross
great rivers. It is beneficial to be correct.**

EXPLANATION
Faithfulness is truthfulness; faithfulness in the center means truthfulness
is within. The body of the hexagram has four yangs outside and two yins

inside: Open inside, solid outside, openness and solidity balance each other, inside and outside correspond. Also, the qualities of the hexagram are inner joy and outer accord; traversing the Path with joyful accord, not obsessed and not astray, it is therefore called *faithfulness in the center.*

This hexagram represents seeking fulfillment by being empty; it follows on the previous hexagram *dispersal.* In *dispersal,* yang is trapped by yin; yin sneaks in and yang gradually dissolves. If you want yin not to trap yang but to accord with yang, so that yin and yang conjoin, this is impossible unless you are seriously faithful to the Tao; without faithfulness to the Tao, practice is insubstantial and lacks power, inevitably leading to failure to complete what has been started. But if the mind is faithful and united, and thought is pure and true, myriad ruminations cease and sincerity within reaches outward, so that one can genuinely carry on true practice leading from lowliness to exaltation, from shallowness to depth, gradually enabling one to reach the state of profound attainment and self-realization.

Spiritual alchemy, the science of the gold elixir, uses the "yellow woman" as the go-between for yin and yang. The "yellow woman" is true intent; *faithfulness in the center* is truthfulness in the center—truthfulness is associated with earth, which is called the yellow woman. With the yellow woman in the center, it is possible to harmonize yin and yang, to communicate with self and others, to respond to myriad things—there is nothing that cannot be influenced. Therefore "faithfulness in the center is auspicious when it reaches even pigs and fish." Pigs and fish represent those without knowledge; when truthfulness can influence them, those without knowledge can harmonize themselves—how much the more so those with knowledge. If practitioners of Tao can apply the truthfulness that influences even "pigs and fish" to cultivation of essence and life, they will not fail to produce good results.

However, if faithfulness can be carried out in ease but not adversity, that faithfulness is not real, and will surely crumble in the end; even if one is faithful in this way, it does not bode well. There are people who believe in the Tao, and there are those who believe in the Tao and practice it regularly when all is well and comfortable; but there are hardly any who forget themselves for the Tao and do not lose control in situations of great difficulty and stress, when there are great obstacles, when things are topsy-turvy and in a shambles, and it is difficult to bear up patiently.

If one can remain unmoved and unperturbed in situations that are hard to endure, can go on through and get out, this alone is faithfulness that can move pigs and fish. This is why "it is beneficial to cross great rivers" for faithfulness in the center to bode well. Great rivers represent most hazardous places, adverse situations; if one can cross over adverse situations, needless to say one can cross over favorable situations. When able to pass through both favorable and adverse situations, that faithfulness is beneficial and suspicious wherever it goes.

However, the seventy-two aberrant schools, with their three thousand six hundred deviant practices, all cling to voidness or stick to forms; these are not studies that can fulfill our nature and lead to the meaning of life. The false distorts the real, the aberrant adulterates the correct; if you have faith without discriminating the false and real, the aberrant and correct, this is incorrect faithfulness, which is not beneficial and does not lead to good results. Therefore faithfulness is only beneficial if it is correct. Correct faith and correct practice meet with good results, unhindered in adversity or ease, entering from striving into nonstriving, thereby perfecting essence and life, completing beginning and end; of this one can be sure.

■ *First yang:* Forethought leads to a good outcome.
If there is something else, one is not at rest.

EXPLANATION
At the beginning of faithfulness, if one has faith only after forethought assessing what can be believed in, by being able to be careful in the beginning there is naturally a good outcome in the end. If one cannot assess whether something is so or not and carelessly believes now in this and now that, changing back and forth inconsistently, it will be difficult to make faithfulness complete; this is a case of where "there is something else," and so "one is not at rest." This means that faithfulness to the Path requires care in the beginning.

■ *2 yang:* A calling crane is in the shade, its fledgling
joins it; I have a good cup, which I will quaff
with you.

EXPLANATION
With true faithfulness in the center, knowing the white and keeping the black, subtly penetrating the barrier between yin and yang, spiritual illumination naturally comes: This is like "a calling crane is in the shade, its fledgling joins it; I have a good cup, which I will quaff with you"—mutual response with the same voice, mutual seeking in the same spirit, spontaneously being thus without aiming for it. This is faithfulness in hidden practice of inner refinement.

■ *3 yin:* Finding enemies, sometimes drumming, sometimes stopping, sometimes crying, sometimes singing.

EXPLANATION
Getting into aberrant practices, attached to your own body, attempting forced manipulations, is like faith in which one finds enemies—faith becomes enmity; after a time there inevitably comes a change, as one first believes in this, then that—when this practice doesn't work, one then tries that practice; "sometimes drumming, sometimes stopping, sometimes crying, sometimes laughing," vain and insubstantial, this is what is referred to by the statement, "It's easy to work with what is of the same species, hard to work with what is not of the same kind." Believing in what is not to be

believed will inevitably destroy faith. This is faith that takes the false to be true.

■ *4 yin:*   The moon approaches fullness. The pair of horses is gone. No fault.

EXPLANATION

In the space where above is yang and below is yin, yielding yet remaining upright, following the yang and not the yin, is like "the moon approaches fullness. The pair of horses is gone." The human body is pure yin, with no yang, just as the moon has no light of its own; it must borrow the gift of another before it can produce the elixir, just as the moon borrows the light of the sun. At the time of the new moon, it meets with the sun, and moonlight arises in the first three days of the lunar month. On the fifteenth, when it faces the sun, its light is round and full. This is yin following yang. On the sixteenth, one yin subtly arises, and increases until the thirtieth, when the moon turns away from the sun and has no light at all. This is yin turning away from yang. The science of the gold elixir begins with yin seeking yang, to return to pure heaven. This is like the moon approaching fullness. Having used yang to repel yin so as to transmute the temperament and constitution is like a pair of horses having gone. Following the yang to eliminate the yin, a precious pearl hangs in space, round and bright, clean and bare, illumining everything. Nothing can deceive it, so what fault could there still be that would not disappear? This is the faithfulness of weakness seeking strength.

■ *5 yang:*   With faithfulness that is firm, there is no fault.

EXPLANATION

Being strong and also balanced and correctly oriented, yin and yang blended, essence, feeling, vitality, and spirit all return to the center, benevolence, justice, courtesy, and wisdom all return to the mind; the five elements aggregate, truthfully unified without division. This is faithfulness that is firm; it is secure and cannot be dissolved. This is what is meant by the saying, "When a grain of gold elixir is swallowed into the belly, for the first time you know your destiny depends on you and not on heaven." When the work reaches this point, you are integrated with natural principle, the celestial design, and all entanglements are void; there is naturally no fault. This is faithfulness in which strength and flexibility are one.

■ *Top yang:*   The voice of a pheasant reaches the skies; even if devoted, the outlook is bad.

EXPLANATION

If one uses one's own intelligence to indulge in guesswork and personalistic interpretation, unable to humble oneself to seek from others and thoroughly investigate true principles, and plunges into practices impetuously, one who advances rapidly regresses swiftly; though one originally wanted to climb to the heights, instead one falls. This is just the call of a pheasant, incapable of soaring to the heavens to accomplish that which is rare in the world. This is faith that misuses intellect.

So the path of faithfulness in the center values faithfulness that is balanced, and above all faith that is correct. When faithfulness is balanced, the will is stable and endures unchanged; when faith is correct, right and wrong are clear, and practice of the Tao is very easy. Able to be balanced and correctly oriented, faithful to the Tao, one can then practice the Tao; by practicing the Tao one can attain the Tao. By this one faithfulness there is unfailing fortune and benefit.

62. *Predominance of the Small*

Predominance of the small is developmental, beneficial if correct. It is suitable for a small affair but not for a great one. The call left by a flying bird should not rise but descend. This is very auspicious.

EXPLANATION
Predominance of the small means that yin exceeds yang. As for the qualities of the hexagram, above is *thunder* ☳, active, and below is *mountain* ☶, still: Acting with restraint, basing action on stillness, stillness is stable and action is not on a large scale. Also, in the body of the hexagram, two yangs are inside four yins: Inwardly fulfilled, outwardly empty, inwardly firm, outwardly flexible, using the small to nurture the great, it is therefore called *predominance of the small.*

This hexagram represents being fulfilled and thus acting empty; it follows on the previous hexagram *discipline.* In *discipline,* one can be joyful even in danger, inwardly being autonomous, using things of the world to practice the principles of the Tao, using social activities to restore celestial qualities; the foundation of life stable, one can enter from striving into nonstriving.

In spiritual alchemy, before primordial true yang has been restored, one should empty the mind to seek to fill the belly. Once primordial true yang has returned, one should fill the belly and also empty the mind. The achievement of emptying the mind is the means to operate the natural true fire, to burn away the mundane energy of acquired conditioning until one is freed from it. This is why *predominance of the small* is developmental.

However, though *predominance of the small* is developmental, it is only beneficial if correct; if it is not correct, it is not developmental. The correct way of predominance of the small is that action not stray from tranquility, that action be carried out with tranquility; with movement and stillness as one, "the real person plunges into the profound depths, floating about yet keeping within the circle," neither indifferent nor obsessed, keeping a very subtle consistency.

This is suitable for a small affair, but not a great one, a small affair means nonstriving, a great affair means striving. Striving is the way to find yang, nonstriving is the way to nurture yang. Once one has filled the belly, it is appropriate that the small predominate to nurture yang. If you are capable of the great but not the small, you will not only be unable to preserve yang, yang will even be damaged.

Predominance of the small being beneficial when correct means it is beneficial in small action, not in great action, beneficial in small stillness, not in great stillness. When one acts yet is able to be still, being active in the midst of stillness, stopping in the appropriate place and acting on that, even as one acts one does not go beyond the appropriate position. This is like "the call left by a flying bird should not rise but descend." Though a bird flies up, its call goes down; this means action not straying from tranquility. Action not straying from tranquility should not rise but descend, the small predominating and nurturing the great; extracting lead and adding mercury, incubating for ten months, when the spiritual embryo is completely developed, with a thunderous cry the infant appears. When nurturance is sufficient, the auspicious outcome is great; the small predominates, but the good it does is great. Sublime and subtle indeed is the predominance of the small that is beneficially correct.

■ *First yin:* **A bird that flies thereby brings misfortune.**

EXPLANATION
In the beginning of predominance of the small, precisely when one should rest in the appropriate place and refine oneself, if one is weak and not firm in restraint, in a hurry to soar to the heights, one is like a bird flying without resting, in suspension, without stability; desiring to get ahead, instead one falls behind, suffering misfortune. One can be sure of this. This represents the small predominating yet vainly imagining predominance of the great.

■ *2 yin:* **Passing the grandfather, you meet the mother; not reaching the lord, you meet the retainer. No fault.**

EXPLANATION
With the constitution basically yin, if you abandon yang and respond to yin, this is like passing the grandfather and meeting the mother; yin is excessively predominant over yang. But if you are correctly oriented even though weak, do not use excessively high yin but take to low yang, that is like not reaching the lord but meeting the retainer; yin does not exceed yang. When you reach balance of yin and yang, so that firmness and flexibility are one energy, thoughts not coming out from within, outward things not penetrating, not letting any external influence at all adulterate

the contents of the crucible, you will not have the fault of losing what has been gained. This is predominance of the small not going to excess.

■ *3 yang:*   If you do not overcome and forestall it, indulgence will cause harm, which would be unfortunate.

EXPLANATION

When yang energy is replete, and it is time to forestall danger and foresee peril, if strength is imbalanced, knowing how to be great but not small, by not overcoming and forestalling it, indulgence will do harm; the celestial jewel that has been gained will be lost again. This is the great predominating and not knowing how to let the small predominate.

■ *4 yang:*   No fault. Do not dally with it too much; it is dangerous to go on. Caution is necessary. Don't persist forever.

EXPLANATION

Strong yet able to be flexible, already yin and yang have unified, the five elements have merged; now is when you should await the time to transcend being and nonbeing—you should not remain too yielding anymore. If you don't stop at sufficiency and still use the path of yielding to go ahead, this is excess of the small, and will invite the foreign energies of external influences, which is dangerous. This calls for caution. Being careful about this requires changing according to the time, not persisting in the same way forever. Stop when you should stop, rest and stop the work; act when you should act, to break the shell for spiritual transmutation. Proceeding from development to release, breaking through space, only then do you attain realization. This means predominance of the small should not be excessive.

■ *5 yin:*   Dense clouds not raining come from my neighborhood. The ruler shoots another in a cave.

EXPLANATION

Pure yin with no yang is like dense clouds not raining coming from one's own region. The path of cultivating reality forms an elixir of the polar energies of true yin and true yang; having only dense clouds, unable to produce rain, coming from one's own region and not reaching the region of others, self and others are separated. This is also like the ruler shooting another in a cave. The fifth line (yin) is close to the fourth (yang): A sage is in sight, but one cannot humble oneself to seek from another. Sitting quietly contemplating voidness, or forgetting things and even the body, this is wishing to complete the great work by voidness alone, shooting voidness with voidness, others void and self void, snaring others in a cave. Inside and outside one voidness, void without reality, how can you accomplish the work? This is predominance of the small without knowing to seek the great.

■ *Top yin:*   **Don't overstay here. The flying bird is gone. This is called calamity.**

EXPLANATION

When one is ignorant, this is already predominance of the small—one should not stay here any more. Excess in being ignorant and acting arbitrarily, listening to blind teachers, striving for elevation by conveying the vitality up to boost the brain, or conveying the energy up into the head, or keeping the thought on the point between the brows, or keeping the attention on the top of the brain, or silently paying court to the supreme god, or gazing into a mirror to get out of the body—knowing how to go ahead but not how to withdraw, one is like a bird flying to the greatest heights unable to stop itself, eventually experiencing calamity, from which none can rescue one. This is dwelling too long on a basis of predominance of the small.

So the path of predominance of the small requires seeking yang by yin before the elixir is obtained, then temporarily using yin to nurture yang after the elixir is obtained. In any case it requires that the small be correct. It will not do for the small to be either excessive or insufficient. Only then can it be developmental and beneficial.

63. Settled

Settlement is developmental, but it is minimized. It is beneficial to be correct. The beginning is auspicious, the end confused.

EXPLANATION

Settlement means the mutual completion of yin and yang: Being settled is the culmination of the mutual completion of yin and yang. As to the qualities of the hexagram, above is *water* ☵, a pitfall, and below is *fire* ☲, luminous. Using danger to nourish illumination, using illumination to guard against danger, understanding is born from difficulty and difficulty is passed through by understanding: As illumination and danger, understanding and difficulty, offset each other, this is called *settled.*

This hexagram represents forestalling danger, foreseeing perils, and stably completing the basis of the elixir; it follows on the preceding hexagram *faithfulness in the center. Faithfulness in the center* involves joyful, harmonious praxis leading to deep attainment of self-realization, so that any incompleteness of yin and yang can be settled. As long as there is incompleteness, one should seek completion; once complete, one should preserve completeness. Preserving completeness is the work of stabilizing and completing the basis of the elixir. Stabilizing the basis of the elixir is a matter of using illumination to guard against danger, holding off danger and nurturing illumination. Nurturing illumination means concealing illumination within, having knowledge but not using it, having ability but not employing it, clarifying the quality of illumination and resting in the ultimate good.

Forestalling danger involves being careful outwardly, not acting in any way that would be improper, not doing anything that would be unjust, living according to one's basic state and not wishing for anything else. Once one can nurture illumination inwardly, one can also ward off danger outwardly: Illumination has nourishment and is not damaged, danger dissolves on encountering illumination.

Illumination is the quality of *fire* ☲, positioned in the south; this is the spirit. Danger is the quality of *water* ☵, positioned in the north; this is the vitality. When the spirit is prone to activity, fire flames up; using vitality to nurture the spirit, fire is treated with water and irritation vanishes. When vitality leaks out easily, water flows downward; when vitality is governed by the spirit, water is treated with fire and thoughts of lust disappear. When irritation vanishes, the spirit is peaceful, so the mind is empty; when lust disappears, the vitality is whole, so the belly is full. When the mind is empty, the human mentality is absent and true yin appears; when the belly is full, the mind of Tao emerges and true yang arises. With true yin following true yang, true yang governing true yin, true yin and true yang conjoin, and in ecstasy there is form, in trance there is vitality, crystallizing into a tiny pearl: Swallow this, and it will extend life infinitely.

So it is that settlement is certainly developmental. But once yin and yang are complete, illumination is vigorous, and when illumination is vigorous it is easy to presume upon illumination and act arbitrarily. Unless one is very careful, one is likely to slip, and illumination, having culminated, will turn to darkness; the mind of Tao again obscured, the human mentality again arises, and in the middle of settlement and completion there is unsettling and incompleteness. This is the minimization of the development of settlement.

Generally speaking, as long as things are unsettled, most people are careful and conscientious, using lucidity to prevent danger. Once things are settled, people relax, thereby endangering themselves, obscuring lucidity and inviting peril. So when the development is small and not great, and what is gained is again lost, it is all for this reason.

Therefore the developmental aspect of settlement is only beneficial if correctness is preserved. Correctly nurturing illumination, correctly preventing danger, naturally clarity will not be damaged and danger will not arise.

But using illumination to forestall hazards is primarily beneficial in the beginning of settlement. The beginning is auspicious, the end is confused. That the beginning is auspicious means if one nurtures illumination early on, even if there is danger there is no peril. That the end is confused means that if you use clarity excessively, you invite danger where there is none. It is all this one clarity, all this one danger: If you can nurture clarity, there is no danger; if you use the clarity too much, there is danger. So practitioners of Tao should prevent the danger early on in the beginning of settlement.

■ *First yang:*   **Dragging the wheel, wetting the tail,**
there is no fault.

EXPLANATION
In the beginning of settlement, being strong yet keeping to what is right is like a cart dragging its wheels and not moving forward, like an animal getting its tail wet and drawing back. Being careful in the beginning, there is no fault in the end. This is prevention of unsettling at the moment of settlement.

■ *2 yin:*   **A woman loses her protection. Do not pursue;**
you will get it in seven days.

EXPLANATION
When weak and infirm, yin and yang incomplete, the great Tao is hard to practice. This is like a woman losing her protection and being in danger. However, if one is balanced and upright in spite of weakness, one refines oneself and waits for the time; light appears in the empty room, spiritual illumination comes of itself. Therefore, "Do not pursue; you will get it in seven days." The point of "seven days" is that seven is the number of fire; refining the self, fire reverts to reality, breaking through danger by illumination, using difficulty to develop understanding. Taking the yang in *water* $\equiv\!\equiv$ and filling in the yin in *fire* $\equiv\!\equiv$, water and fire settle each other; it happens naturally without forced effort. This is using yin to seek yang so that they complete, balance, and settle each other.

■ *3 yang:*   **The emperor attacks the barbarians, and**
conquers them after three years. Do not employ
inferior people.

EXPLANATION
At the peak of lucidity there is danger nearby; this is like the presence of barbarians. If one cannot take precautions early, settlement is liable to be unsettled. If those who are strong yet correct wish to avoid injury by danger, it is necessary to exert the utmost effort to preserve settlement, just as an emperor attacked barbarians and defeated them after three years. Even those who are strong and correctly oriented must exert themselves so; how much the more so the strong who are not correctly oriented. Therefore the text says "Do not employ inferior people." This represents settlement in which there is inability to forestall unsettling.

■ *4 yin:* With wadding to plug leaks, one is watchful all day.

EXPLANATION
When settlement is accomplished, one dismisses intellectualism and guards against danger, like preparing wadding to plug any leak that may appear in a boat, being watchful all day. This is settlement in which one can guard against any unsettling.

■ *5 yang:* Slaughtering an ox in the neighborhood to the east is not as good as the ceremony in the neighborhood to the west, really receiving the blessing.

EXPLANATION
When settlement is done, if one remains completely full, in the sense of the belly being full of energy without knowing how to empty the mind of thought, there is unsettling latent within settlement. This is like slaughtering an ox in the neighborhood to the east (yang) not being as good as the ceremony in the neighborhood to the west (yin), which really receives the blessing. This is because before settlement, when one is effecting settlement, one can do so by using emptiness to seek fulfillment. Once settlement is complete, at the culmination of completeness, fullness without emptiness is as before unsettling, incomplete. By emptiness one can be fulfilled; repletion invites error, as a matter of course. This is unsettling settlement.

■ *Top yin:* When the head gets wet, one is in danger.

EXPLANATION
If one does not understand the firing process and keeps going at full blast without stopping, unable to forestall danger in the beginning of settlement, one will naturally bring on danger at the end of settlement. This is like when the water reaches the head, one's whole body is sunk; yin and yang fragment, and the previous accomplishment all goes to waste. Danger is then unavoidable. This is winding up unsettled after having been settled.

When practitioners of the Tao get to the stage of taking (yang) from *water* ☵ and filling in (the yin) in *fire* ☲, so that water and fire settle each other, they are fortunate to accomplish this after untold exertion and toil; then when they seal it securely and guard against danger, they thereby complete the work that requires striving. Otherwise, if they relax and stop working, the firing process goes amiss, unsettling what has been settled, losing what has been attained. Therefore the methods of striving and non-striving are to be used according to the appropriate time. The ultimate accomplishment is when being and nonbeing are one, emptiness and fulfillment are both included, and essence and life are both comprehended.

64. Unsettled

Being as yet unsettled is developmental. A small fox, having nearly crossed the river, gets its tail wet, does not succeed.

EXPLANATION

Unsettled means yin and yang are not yet settled. As to the qualities of the hexagram, below is *water* ☵, a pitfall, and above is *fire* ☲, bright: Bright on the outside while dark on the inside, causing downfall by brightness, producing brightness because of danger, yin and yang are awry, and do not correspond; so it is called *unsettled*.

This hexagram represents refining the self and repelling yin, waiting for the appropriate time with suppressed yang; it follows on the previous hexagram *predominance of the small*. In *predominance of the small*, activity and stillness are as one; by smallness (yin) one cultivates the path of nonstriving. This is done after yin and yang complete and settle each other. Before they are settled, however, it is first necessary to reach all the yins that trap yang; only after that does true yin manifest and true yang return, so yin and yang balance each other and the gold elixir crystallizes. This is why the work that involves striving, refining the self and waiting for the time, is important.

Once people reach the age of sixteen, *heaven* and *earth* commingle: The yang in the middle of *heaven* ☰ enters the palace of *earth* ☷, so *earth* is filled and becomes *water* ☵; the yin in the middle of *earth* ☷ enters the palace of *heaven* ☰, so *heaven* is hollowed out and becomes *fire* ☲. The yin in *fire* receives the yang energy of *heaven*, yin and yang aggregate, and it turns into fire. The yang in *water* receives the yin energy of *earth*, yin and yang steam, and it becomes water. This fire and water are in the temporal mixing of yin and yang, the confusion of real and artificial; growing day and night, the warm gentle fire changes into violent hot fire, and the water of true unity changes into the water of unbridled lust.

Once the nature of fire erupts, the discriminatory consciousness takes charge of affairs, and the original spirit withdraws. Once the nature of water acts, the polluted vitality causes trouble and the original vitality is depleted. At this point people begin to vie for honor, plunder for profit, contest for victory, and seek power, depriving others to benefit themselves, using intellectual brightness outwardly; indulging in emotions, giving free rein to their desires, deluded by objects of sense, they ravage and abandon themselves, the danger of mundanity being stored within. Bright on the outside but dark on the inside, they bury the real and accept the false; the human mentality looms dangerously, the mind of Tao is now faint— essence is disturbed, life is shaken, yin and yang are out of harmony, the five elements injure one another. All sorts of emotions and cravings are in full force, all sorts of schemes and wiles are there. This is why being unsettled is unsettled.

However, being unsettled means not yet having reached settlement; it does not mean settlement is not possible, only that the person has not yet sought that settlement. If one seeks settlement, ultimately it will be possible to be settled. This is why there is a development aspect to being unsettled. But though there is a way of development in an unsettled state, nevertheless since the negative energy of acquired conditioning has been operative for so long, and the primordial true positivity has sunken so deeply, settlement cannot be effected immediately; the work of self-refinement is necessary before you can see an effect. Self-refinement means refining the human mind. The human mind is the progenitor of all mundanities; once the human mind is gone, accumulated mundanities evaporate, "light arises in the empty room," and true celestial energy gradually approaches restoration.

But before refinement of the self is perfected, the mind is not empty and the light is not true; negativity and mundanity still have not withdrawn completely, and one cannot seek their end in a hurry. If one does not know the firing process and rushes to achieve settlement, this is still the human mentality acting, working with false understanding. Then the unsettled will never be settled. This is like "a small fox, having nearly crossed the river, gets its tail wet and does not succeed." A fox is associated with yin, a creature known for its suspiciousness. Though a small fox is not very suspicious, it cannot be entirely free from doubts. As long as the human mentality is not gone, the mind of Tao does not become manifest; this is like the small fox—though nearly settled, before reaching settlement, if the refinement of the self is incomplete when settlement is nearly reached, though one wants to go ahead one instead falls behind.

Therefore practitioners of the Tao, in refining the self, must reach utter emptiness and tranquility, the yin trapping yang withdrawing completely, before the primordial yang energy comes from within nothingness, and true yin and true yang unite, able to settle what is unsettled. A classic says, "If refinement of the self is imperfect, the restored elixir does not crystallize." So we know refinement of the self is the first step in practicing Tao.

■ *First yin:* **Getting the tail wet, one is humiliated.**

EXPLANATION
A person of inferior qualities in deep danger must first refine the self and control the mind in order to practice the Tao; entering in gradually, one cannot seek completion all at once. But if one is then foolish and vain and seeks to emulate the way of those of lofty enlightenment and effect settlement, one will be trailed by danger before even moving. This is likened to getting the tail wet and being unable to go forward. One will only be humiliated. This is being unsettled and trying to force settlement.

■ *2 yang:* Dragging the wheels, it bodes well
to be upright.

EXPLANATION
Strength applied with flexibility, the wise one appears ignorant, the expert appears inept, refining the self and biding one's time; this is like a car
dragging its wheels. Nurturing strength for the time being, though in an
unsettled time, there is the good prospect of unseen settlement. This is
waiting while unsettled for the time to effect settlement.

■ *3 yin:* As yet unsettled, it bodes ill to go on an
expedition, but it is beneficial to cross great rivers.

EXPLANATION
At the culmination of unsettledness, when the possibility of settlement is
nearing, if one does not know the medicinal substances and the firing process but relies on the yin of oneself alone, vainly imagining settlement,
acting dangerously in hopes of good luck, the unsettled will never be
settled, and it will be unlucky to go to any lengths. It is lucky to live
among people imbued with Tao, however, because one can be aided by
others to complete oneself, so that yin can be converted and yang can be
restored; then even if one crosses perilous "great rivers" it will be auspicious and beneficial. This is seeking a teacher when unsettled and incomplete, to effect settlement and completion.

■ *4 yang:* Remaining correct brings good results, regret
vanishes; rising up to conquer the barbarians, in three
years one will have the reward of a great country.

EXPLANATION
When strength is in a weak position, it seems to have lost correctness, to
bode ill and cause regret; however, that whereby it can bring good results
and banish regret by remaining correct, is vigorous effort using strength
and firmness to rise up and conquer the barbarians, meaning to get rid of
the mundanity of acquired conditioning. Then, cultivating inner refinement privately, using flexibility, in three years one will have the reward of a
great country, meaning the restoration of primordial celestial energy. The
reason three years are needed to gain the reward is that the real will be
hard to restore, and the false will be hard to get rid of. It requires penetrating work over a long period of time before there can be completion.
This is gradually proceeding from unsettled incompleteness to settled
completion.

■ *5 yin:*   **Remaining correct brings good results, without regret; the light of a superior person has truth and goodness.**

EXPLANATION
Emptying the human mind and seeking the mind of Tao, not being led astray by false brilliance, is whereby "remaining correct brings good results." This line corresponds with the yang in the second place: Taking the fullness in the *water* ☵ of the other and using it to fill in the emptiness in the *fire* ☲ of the self, emptying the mind and being able to fill the belly, this is why there is no regret. Correctness bringing good results with no regret, yin and yang join, false brilliance leaves and true illumination arises, calm and undisturbed yet sensitive and effective, sensitive and effective yet calm and undisturbed: This is called the light of the superior person. Starting out unsettled, in the end there is a great settlement; its goodness is already truly in the empty mind. This is the ability of the unsettled to bring about settlement by emptying the mind.

■ *Top yang:*   **Having faith, one drinks wine without blame. When one gets one's head wet, having faith ceases to be right.**

EXPLANATION
At the end of being unsettled, when settlement is taking place, one can believe yin and yang will settle each other, this proceeding naturally and not depending on forced effort. So one can drink wine, have a party, without blame. However, although there is complete settlement in terms of celestial time, still human affairs cannot be neglected; one does one's best in human affairs, thereby assisting the Way of heaven. Then heaven and humanity act together; having faith in settlement, this faith is right. Otherwise, settlement in celestial time will be no more than a chance interval: Without the accomplishment of adjusting water and fire, the primordial treasure that has come will go again. When settling is unstable, it eventually becomes unsettled: This is like getting the head wet, having faith that is no longer right. This is effecting settlement by taking advantage of the time to use human power to accomplish it.

So the path of settling the unsettled has two aspects. When yang energy is trapped, one must refine the self, biding the time, thereby preventing danger. Once yang energy has emerged from the trap, one should use illumination to dispel darkness, thereby converting yin. Only when intensity and relaxation, advancing and withdrawing, are properly timed is this the path of twin cultivation of essence and life in which yin and yang settle and complete each other. So students who would practice the Tao should start by self-refinement.

Book II

The Commentary

1. *Heaven*

> heaven above,
> heaven below

**The activity of heaven is powerful; superior people
thereby strengthen themselves ceaselessly.**

Heaven is the celestial; its quality is power. In this image, heaven ☰ is
above and below; this is the image of the unified energy of heaven, which
flows ceaselessly above and below, acting powerfully. What superior people
see in this is that since humans originate from the energy of heaven, they
have this powerful quality of heaven. This power originally flows unceasing and uninterrupted, but because of mixture with acquired conditioning, people abandon the real and enter the artificial, strengthening what
should not be strengthened, so as a result there is at times interruption of
the flow of the original celestial power. Therefore superior people work on
the activation of the celestial power, temporarily using the artificial to
cultivate the real, restoring the primal while in the midst of the temporal,
strengthening themselves ceaselessly.

Strength means unbending firmness and strength, which myriad
things cannot move. If one can strengthen oneself ceaselessly, then wholesome energy is always present, and one has inner autonomy: Wealth cannot make one decadent, poverty cannot move one, authority and force
cannot suppress one. One does not act without propriety, one does not
abide in untruth, one does not wreak injustice. Whether in pleasant or
unpleasant circumstances, this strength is everywhere, never ceasing.
Such action is as it were celestial.

But there are people who are powerful in a worldly sense; there are
people who are powerful yet are drawn by things to use their power externally; there are also people who can sometimes strengthen themselves,
who start out diligently but end up slacking off, who follow the Path but
give up along the way. Genuine work of self-strengthening is all a matter of
not ceasing; if there is any slacking off, if there is any personal desire, it
cannot be called strength, it cannot be called self-strengthening. Only
ceaseless self-strengthening can reach total integration with the celestial
design, the indestructible, permanent state.

Heaven is the order of life; life is the quality of power, which is the original, vast, true energy. Because it has neither shadow nor form, yet is lively and active, flowing ceaselessly, it is called energy. Because it is most great and most strong, filling the universe, it is called power. Because it is the master of myriad beings, the progenitor of yin and yang, the root of creation, it is called the order of life. Energy, power, life—all are one strength. The work of life-building is consummated in self-strengthening without cease. This is the science of following the pattern of heaven.

2. *Earth*

earth above,
earth below

The configuration of earth is receptive; superior people support others with warmth.

Earth is the ground; its quality is receptivity. In this image, earth ☷ is above and below: The earth above is the high places, the earth below is the low places; this is the image of receptivity, the configuration of earth being high and low. What superior people see in this is that since humans are born with the energy of earth, they have this earthy quality of receptivity. Because of this, once their intellect is activated, they misuse intelligence and follow what should not be followed; obeying the temperament, they lose the essence of pure innocence. Inwardly unable to empty themselves, outwardly they cannot admit others; taking the artificial to be real, taking misery for pleasure, in the end they pass away.

Therefore, the wise take as their model the receptivity of earth, and bear others with warmth. Warmth is the quality of receptivity, which is inner openness and outward genuineness. Only by receptivity can one be open, only by warmth can one be genuine.

Inner openness means emptying the mind; by emptying the mind one can accept others. Outward genuineness means genuine action; by genuine action one can respond to others. Accepting others and responding to others is being able to support others. There being no end of people, there is no end to support; one becomes warmer the more support one gives, and one is able to be more supportive as one becomes warmer. The ability of superior people to support others means that superior people have the quality of warmth.

However, if one is supportive of others in favorable circumstances but not in adverse circumstances, this is not called warmth. Strong exertion outwardly without inner openness is not called warmth. The warmth that is supportive of others requires genuine practice, true application, bearing insult and attack, bearing all difficulty, hardship, sickness, and calamity, just as the earth bears the mountains, as the ocean takes in the rivers, as the plants and trees endure injury. Such is the warmth of the earth, such too is the warmth of superior people; this is how the earth bears things, and how the superior person bears things, too. The work of cultivating one's nature is summed up in warmth; this is the science of taking earth as a model.

3. *Difficulty*

water above,
thunder below

Thunder in the clouds is held back; the superior person orders and arranges.

Difficulty means being held back. The reason water ☵, on the top of the hexagram, is here referred to as clouds rather than water is that rain falls from clouds. When thunder ☳ rumbles in the clouds, and there is already the sense of rain, but the rain has not yet begun to fall, just when yin and yang have intertwined and are about to bring to pass what has not yet been possible—this is the image of *difficulty*.

What superior people see in this is that primordial celestial energy is trapped by the force of mundane conditioning, and though it occasionally becomes manifest, it is inhibited and cannot come forth freely: Without effort to foster the celestial and control the mundane, it is hard to gain access to this primal energy, and easy to lose it, missing it even when it is right there.

Therefore, based on its manifest action, the superior person "orders and arranges" the primordial celestial energy, in the sense of cultivating and maintaining it. To "order" means to harmonize the celestial and the earthly, to "arrange" means to adjust their relative proportions. Order without proper arrangement cannot perfect anything; knowledge of the ingredients without knowledge of the process cannot accomplish the Tao.

At the point where one yang arises on the ground of *water* ☵, the passage of contact of earth and heaven, the dividing bridge of life and death, the moment when both disaster and good fortune are possible, practitioners of Tao should quickly set to work, take command, carefully guard the budding awareness, and not let it be harmed by invasion of the force of mundanity.

When you gather the celestial energy as it grows, working uninterruptedly, ordering and arranging, promoting the primal and minimizing the secondary, knowing when to stop at sufficiency, if you do not slip up, even though the celestial energy does not come through at first, eventually it will unfold and expand, like thunder rumbling in the clouds, sweet rain falling of itself. This is what is meant by the saying "After a long darkness, the light is brilliant."

4. *Darkness*

mountain above,
water below

Under a mountain a spring is produced, in darkness.
A superior person nurtures character with fruitful
action.

Darkness means developmental nurturance without intellectualism. Above is *mountain* ☶, below is *water* ☵; here *water* is referred to as a spring and not water, because the spring under the mountain is water. When a spring is produced under a mountain, the spring is nurtured by the mountain, being water with a basis, flowing far from a deep source, going through without hindrance. This is the image of *darkness*.

What superior people see in this is that when those who practice the Tao want to exercise virtue outwardly, first they must develop character inwardly. If one acts without development, the action will have no basis; without inner mastery, action will injure character. This is the reason for emulating a spring emerging from a mountain, acting fruitfully without obstruction, taking as a model the mountain nurturing the spring, nurturing character with caring warmth.

The yang in the center of *water* ☵ refers to what is produced by celestial unity, the original generative energy that gives birth to beings. This is what is called the celestial virtue, or power. This virtue is hidden in the temporal; since ordinary people follow temporally acquired conditioning and abandon the primordial, most do not know how to develop, nurture, cultivate, and sustain this primal virtue, so as a result they gradually dissipate it and harm their own essence and life.

Those who awaken to this set aside acquired conditioning to practice inner development and outward action, using development to perfect action, using action to test development. Cultivating both inside and outside, nurturing character is developmental, and acting on it is developmental as well. Nurturing character means no worthy quality is left undeveloped, fruitful action demands that every act be fruitful. Nurturance of character demands that it be nurtured until it is stable as a mountain—only then is development complete. Fruitful action demands that it be effective as a spring flowing day and night—only then is fruition complete.

Action fruitful, character developed, one completes one's nature and understands the meaning of life, integrated with the celestial design, unconsciously following the laws of God. This is why *darkness* is valued.

5. Waiting

water above,
heaven below

**Clouds rise to heaven, waiting. The superior person
makes merry with food and drink.**

Waiting means there is something awaited. Above is *water* ☵, below is
heaven ☰; water vapor rises from earth to sky, where it condenses into
clouds. When clouds form in the sky, rain may be expected. This is the
image of *waiting*.

What superior people see in this is that when people are unable to
attain the universal Tao, it is because they are temperamental and unbalanced in action, because the earthly and the celestial are not in harmony.
Therefore superior people eat and drink to nourish the earthly, causing the
earthly to balance the celestial; they make merry to attune the celestial,
causing the celestial to join the earthly. When the earthly and the celestial
are in mutual harmony, living energy is stored within, producing being
from within nonbeing, spontaneously, without forced effort.

This happens because the sweet rain of life falls naturally through the
coalescing of the energies of heaven and earth; the sprouts of living potential grow when the energies of yin and yang commune. Here, food and
drink refers to nurturing the body, so that the body is sound; making
merry refers to nurturing the mind, so that the mind is unburdened.
When body and mind are nurtured, the restorative elixir is easy to crystallize. Herein lies what is known as refining the self and awaiting the
proper time.

6. Contention

heaven above,
water below

**When heaven and water go in different directions,
there is contention. Superior people plan in the beginning when they do things.**

Contention means argument over right and wrong. Above is *heaven* ☰,
below is *water* ☵; heaven is most high, water is most low, so heaven and
water go in different directions and do not meet. This is the image of
contention.

What superior people see in this is that aggressiveness and guile,
competitiveness and desire for power, are the beginnings of beckoning di-

saster in business and social relations. If one is not careful, one hurts others and damages oneself. Therefore superior people plan in the beginning when they do things; they do not contend with other people, they contend with themselves.

Doing things does not mean one particular action or deed, but all daily activities, practice of the Tao and establishment of inner character. If one does not plan in the beginning when doing things, one's perception of principles will not be clear, with the result that action will not be appropriate. Being temperamental or impetuous, being unbalanced in action, is accompanied by danger. Therefore one should plan in the beginning, doing what is to be done, avoiding what is not to be done, being careful in the beginning, so as to be able to complete the affair in the end.

Doing things means strong action; planning in the beginning means preventing danger. When one acts after planning, and is not careless in action, there is nothing in the world that cannot be done, nothing in the world that cannot be accomplished.

Impetuous action is aberrant action; to act dangerously is to beckon danger. In doing things, if one can plan in the beginning, the human mentality will gradually depart and the temperament will gradually sublimate. Joining oneself to others, looking upon others and oneself as the same, there will be no discordant action.

7. *The army*

earth above,
water below

There is water in the earth, the army. Thus does the superior person embrace the people and nurture the masses.

The army is one leading a multitude. Above is *earth* ☷, below is *water* ☵; this is the presence of water in the earth. The earth is broad, water is wet; in the earth there is water—one earth embraces myriad waters, myriad waters moisten one earth. This is the image of *the army.*

What superior people see in this is that the human body is like a country, and the mind is like the ruler; the vitality, spirit, nature, feeling, and energy in the body are like the people; the benevolence, justice, courtesy, knowledge, and truthfulness in the nature are like the masses. These people, these masses, are the basis of human life, and must be protected and cared for. Therefore the root is stabilized by embracing the people, external afflictions are prevented by nurturing the masses.

But it is first necessary to embrace the people, in the sense of first mastering oneself inwardly; after that one nurtures the masses, in the sense of managing externally. Inward mastery protects one from externals; managing externally affords one inner peace. When the inner and the outer balance each other, then everything follows the mind, whether in adversity or comfort. Such is the path of the leader of the army, and such is the path of the superior person embracing and nurturing.

8. *Accord*

water above,
earth below

There is water on the earth, in accord. Thus did the kings of yore establish myriad realms and associate with their representatives.

Accord means familiarity, association, closeness. Above is *water* ☵, below is *earth* ☷; water provides moisture without bound. This is the presence of water on the earth. Water is that which provides myriad things and beings with nutritive moisture; water travels on the earth, flowing without obstruction, the earth is boundless. This is the image of *accord*.

What the ancient kings saw in this was that the world is vast, and there is a limit to the exercise of government by one person, so that one person cannot associate familiarly with everyone. Therefore they established myriad realms and delegated representatives, instituting a system whereby the representatives came to court so that the king would be familiar with the representatives, and in turn had the representatives become familiar with the people of their realms. In this way government was able to reach where it otherwise could not, and be close to people who were far away and could not be otherwise approached. In other words, it was a matter of familiarity and association with the multitudes of people through familiarity and association with the representatives of government.

When practitioners of the Tao understand the principles of yin and yang, the earthly and the celestial, the five elements of vitality, spirit, nature, feeling, and energy, and the five virtues of benevolence, justice, courtesy, knowledge, and truthfulness, and cause them to dwell in their proper positions, this is like setting up realms and establishing government representatives. When yin and yang are harmonized, the five elements are a unified force and the five virtues are combined; this is like association with the representatives. When the five elements are united and the five virtues conjoined, all entanglements dissolve and all that is good reaches the same goal; this is like association with the people through association with the representatives.

In the body of the hexagram, the yang in the center of *water* ☵ is in the honored position of correct balance; this represents the mind of Tao, consciousness of reality. When the mind of Tao is manifest, benevolence, justice, courtesy, and knowledge are rooted in the heart, the tangle of myriad principles is integrated fully into the celestial design; the sprouts of living potential grow and fill the world, the golden flowers of spiritual energy bloom—you may gather them freely, they are spiritual medicines. This is like water flowing on the earth, reaching everywhere. The kings of yore associated with their representatives, practitioners of the Tao associate with all that is good—the principle is the same.

9. *Small Nurturance*

wind above,
heaven below

Wind blowing up in the sky is small nurturance; thus do superior people beautify cultured qualities.

Small nurturance is smallness of development. Above is *wind* ☴, below is *heaven* ☰; this is wind blowing up in the sky. When wind blows on the earth, by its circulation of air to myriad beings its nurturance is extensive; when it blows up in the sky, it can only relieve heat, so its nurturance is small. This is the image of *small nurturance.*

What superior people see in this is that the science of fulfilling nature and comprehending life is the great work of appropriating yin and yang, taking over evolution, reversing the process of life and death, taking charge of the pivotal mechanism; it cannot be carried out by those who have not received mental transmission of the science, but if great nurturance is impossible, then small nurturance is still called for, whereby to beautify cultured qualities.

Beautification means adornment; culture means the pattern of manners and conduct. Even though manners and conduct are not the great matter of cultivation of spiritual virtue, nevertheless those who cultivate spiritual virtue should not slight manners and conduct. Examples of cultured qualities are being equanimous and agreeable in dealing with people, being respectful and serious in performing service, being thorough and precise in activity, being careful and prudent in speech.

Concealing one's strength and acting with flexibility, observing what has gone before and being mindful of consequences, being serene and unhurried, one will naturally not act in any way that is impetuous or causes loss of character. This is like the wind blowing in the sky, relieving the heat. When one cultivates one's character to the point where irascibility and impetuosity vanish, then one is capable of small nurturance and also capable of great nurturance.

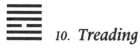

10. Treading

heaven above,
lake below

**Above is the sky, below is a lake: Treading. Thus do
superior people distinguish above and below, and
settle the will of the people.**

Treading means progressive ascent. Above is *heaven* ☰, below is *lake*
☱; the sky covers the lake, the lake looks up to the sky—so above and
below have fixed positions, which cannot be mixed up. This is the image of
treading.

What superior people see in this is that the metaphysical is called the
Tao and the physical is called the vessel; there is a distinction between the
greater and lesser, a difference between the noble and the base. The higher
is not to be considered lower, and the lower is not to be considered higher;
the greater is not to be considered lesser, the lesser is not to be considered
greater; the noble is not to be considered base, the base is not to be considered noble. This is whereby to distinguish above and below and settle the
will of the people, not allowing transgression through false ideas.

The celestial is the ruler; this is higher, above. The earthly is the citizenry; this is lower, below. When one can distinguish the higher and
lower, then right and wrong, sanity and aberration, are clear; not doing
anything inappropriate, sustaining the celestial and controlling the earthly,
cultivating the real and dissolving the false, thoughts not arising inwardly,
external things not entering the mind, myriad things are all empty of absoluteness, and all mundane feelings involved with objects are settled.

In the body of the hexagram, *lake* is the mundane, representing arbitrary feelings; *heaven* is the celestial, representing true sense. When the
mundane treads under the celestial and the celestial treads on top of the
mundane, then arbitrary feelings do not arise and true sense is always
present. True sense is unemotional sense; using unemotional sense to
control feelings is like a cat catching a mouse, like boiling water being
poured on snow—in a short time calamity turns to fortune, the "will
of the people" is settled, and there is nothing to thwart the Tao. Then
one gradually puts into practice the pure, unadulterated vitality of firm
strength in proper balance.

But settling the will of the people is all a matter of being able to distinguish the higher and the lower; the stability attained will be in proportion to the degree to which this distinction is successfully made. If there is
any lack of clarity in this distinction, there will be that much instability.
Therefore the sages' science of fulfillment of nature in comprehension of
life requires thorough investigation of principle as the first step.

11. *Tranquility*

earth above,
heaven below

**When heaven and earth commune, there is tranquility.
Thus does the ruler administer the way of heaven and
earth and assist the proper balance of heaven and
earth, thereby helping the people.**

Tranquility means success. Above is *earth* ☷, below is *heaven* ☰; the
energy of heaven rises from below, the energy of earth descends from
above—so the energies of heaven and earth, the celestial and the mundane, mix together, and myriad things are produced. This is the image of
tranquility.

What the ruler sees in this is that when heaven and earth, yin and
yang, mix together, myriad things are born, and when the celestial and
earthly elements in humans commune, everything is at peace; on this
basis does the ruler then administer the way of heaven and earth and assist
the proper balance of heaven and earth.

People are born with the energies of yin and yang and the five elements, so they have these energies of yin and yang and the five elements in
their bodies. When these energies are active in the body, they constitute
the five virtues. The five virtues in essence have a natural course, which
does not require forced effort; this is called the path of following nature.
The ruler who understands the principle of the mutual generation of the
five elements and causes humanity, justice, courtesy, knowledge, and
truthfulness to flow as one energy is administering the natural way of
heaven and earth giving life to humans.

The functions of the five virtues have their appropriate balance; it
will not do to cling to any of them at the expense of the others. This is
what is called the teaching of practicing the Tao. The ruler who understands the principle of the mutual overcoming of the five elements causes
benevolence, justice, courtesy, knowledge, and truthfulness each to attain
its appropriate proportion, assisting the proper balance of heaven and
earth as it endows humans.

Administering the way, assisting in its balance, is the means whereby
to accomplish the will of the world and achieve the work of the world,
thus helping the people, causing everyone to take the way of heaven and
earth as their way, and to take the balance of heaven and earth for their
balance, preserving universal harmony intact, each realizing one's true nature and purpose in life.

Who does not have the way of heaven and earth, who does not have
the balance of heaven and earth? The only problem is inability to administer and assist the way of its balance. If one can administer and assist the
way and balance of heaven and earth, then it is possible to preserve the

primordial complete and to dissolve acquired conditioning. When the primordial is complete and conditioning is dissolved, being is natural and action is appropriate; the five elements are one energy, the five virtues merge, nature and life are stabilized. What is more, one shares in the functions of heaven and earth, one shares the eternity of heaven and earth; what can compare to that tranquility?

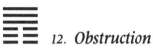

12. *Obstruction*

heaven above,
earth below

When heaven and earth do not commune, there is obstruction. The superior person therefore is parsimonious with power and avoids trouble, not susceptible to elevation by emolument.

Obstruction is blockage. Above is *heaven* $\equiv$, below is *earth* $\equiv\equiv$; the energy of earth rises up from below, the energy of heaven descends from above—the energies of heaven and earth, the celestial and the mundane, do not mix, and myriad things are stifled. This is the image of *obstruction*.

What superior people see in this is that heaven and earth, yin and yang, do not mix, myriad things are inert, and when the celestial and the earthly in the human being do not commune, natural reality is damaged. Therefore they are reserved and reclusive at the appropriate times, sparing with their powers and qualities, thus avoiding trouble, not susceptible to elevation by emolument.

To be parsimonious with power means to banish intellectualism, to conceal one's illumination and nurture it in secret, borrowing the temporal to preserve the primordial, not letting any external influences adulterate natural reality. This is because once people get mixed up in acquired conditioning, the false comes and the real departs; the mind is seduced by things, the nature is deranged and life is destabilized. No obstruction is more of a hindrance than this, no trouble is more of a problem than this. If one does not know to escape quickly, as soon as there is any ambition for honor or material gain, or any emotional feeling about objects of sense, this will cause even more obstruction—how can one then avoid injurious trouble? Not susceptible to being elevated to a high post in the world, one is not moved by glory or emolument, much less by petty gains.

The words "parsimonious with power" are very pregnant, involving many things and most detailed effort. Whatever talent or knowledge one has, one should hide it and be stolid as a monumental rampart, forgetting others and self, having power yet not being conscious of it. If one is conscious of one's power, that is not being parsimonious. Precisely because one is not conscious of one's power one cannot be elevated by emolument.

If emolument cannot elevate one, the trouble is no longer there, and the obstruction disappears of itself. Thus though the earthly and the celestial do not commune at first, they will inevitably join in the end; so the effect of avoiding trouble by being parsimonious with power is not small.

13. *Sameness with Others*

heaven above,
fire below

Heaven with fire, sameness with others; thus do superior people distinguish things in terms of categories and groups.

Sameness with others means being the same as other people. Above is *heaven* ☰, below is *fire* ☲. Fire is the sun; the sky covers everything, the sun shines on everything—the sky and the sun are in the same place, impartial and illuminating. This is the image of *sameness with others*.

What superior people see in this is that when practitioners of the Tao deal with people, it is important to be able to be the same as others, yet it is most important not to assimilate to them arbitrarily; so they distinguish them in terms of categories and groups. Categories and groups are internally similar and united, like different classes of people each having their own groups. Superior people see each group as a category in which all members are the same.

Distinguishing means differentiating; things are things that are right or wrong, good or bad. Superior people must distinguish things; they dare not arbitrarily consider all categories and groups the same. This is how they model themselves on the impartiality of heaven, and distinguish things in emulation of the illumination of the sun. When one is impartial and also lucidly aware, there is no one in the world one cannot be the same as, and there is nothing in the world that is arbitrarily considered the same as something different.

This is because superior people assimilate by means of the Tao, not in terms of mentality; they assimilate by means of reason, not in terms of personality. This is what is called harmonizing without being influenced, associating without becoming a partisan. This is how the sky and sun are the same toward things, and this is how superior people are the same with others.

14. Great Possession

fire above,
heaven below

**Fire is in the sky; great possession. Thus does the
superior person stop evil and promote good, obeying
heaven and accepting its order.**

Great possession means greatness of possession. Above is *fire* ☲, below
is *heaven* ☰; this is fire in the sky—when the sun is in the sky, much is
produced, the sun shines afar. Everything is under the sun in the sky. This
is the image of *great possession.*

What superior people see in this is that the nature of celestial order is
one integral principle, in which all that is good is ultimately assembled;
this is basic great possession. But because of mixture with temporal conditioning, once cognitive consciousness comes into play the primordial is
damaged. From this point on good and bad mix; those with great possession come to have little possession, and those with little possession come to
have nothing. Therefore, as soon as a bad thought arises, superior people
immediately stop it, and as soon as a good thought arises, they promote it,
obeying heaven and finding happiness in its order.

If one cannot find happiness in the celestial order, it is because of not
being able to obey heaven; not obeying heaven is due to not being able to
stop evil and promote good. If one can stop evil and promote good, eventually one will reach ultimate good without evil; with true sanity always
present, one returns to the pristine state of completeness, which is the
order of heaven. Then one goes from destitution to possession, from possession to greatness.

Human life in the world has a mission, which alone is important;
with this direction there is life, without it there is death. If one cannot find
happiness in this mission, this direction, this order, everything else is
empty and false. That to which heaven directs humanity is only good; if
one can find happiness in that command, then this is obeying heaven.
Obeying heaven is the way to obey the command; finding happiness in the
celestial mandate is the way to find happiness in heaven.

Having the direction of heaven is the greatest of possessions; but
having the direction of heaven lies entirely in stopping evil and promoting
good. Stopping evil and promoting good is illumination; obeying heaven
and finding happiness in its order is strength. Strength is the substance,
illumination is the function; open awareness unobscured embraces myriad principles and responds to myriad things.

Through clarification of the quality of illumination, one eventually
reaches ultimate good, wholly integrated with the celestial design, nature
and life stabilized. No possession is more substantial than this, no greatness is greater than this. No external possessions in the world can compare
with it.

15. Modesty

> earth above,
> mountain below

**There are mountains in the earth; modesty. Thus does
the superior person decrease the abundant and add to
the scarce, assessing things and dealing impartially.**

Modesty means to have endowments but not dwell on them. Above is
earth ☷, below is *mountain* ☶; this is the existence of mountains in
the earth. Originally, mountains are high and earth is low; inwardly concealing high attainments while in a state of lowliness, being outwardly
empty yet inwardly fulfilled, is the image of *modesty*.

What superior people see in this is that people have an abundance of
pride and a scarcity of humility; therefore they act presumptuously and
are never impartial. Therefore superior people decrease the abundant
pride and increase the scarce humility; when handling affairs and dealing
with people, they assess the relative importance of things, determine what
is appropriate according to the situation, and deal impartially with it.

Superior people capable of modesty have talent but do not presume
upon it; they have virtue, but do not dwell on it. They have no conception
of self, and no images of others. All pride and arrogance have vanished
from them, and their minds are always equanimous. When the mind is
equanimous, one is naturally also impartial in one's dealings. Inwardly
equanimous, outwardly impartial, one's virtue grows daily more lofty,
one's heart grows daily more humble, outwardly appearing to be lacking,
inwardly having more than enough. Many are the benefits of modesty.

16. Joy

> thunder above,
> earth below

**When thunder emerges the earth stirs; joy. Thus did
the kings of yore make music to honor virtue, offering
it in abundance to God, thereby to share it with their
ancestors.**

Joy is happiness. Above is *thunder* ☳, below is *earth* ☷; this is
thunder coming from the earth, stirring and rising up. When positive energy prevails harmoniously, all things are pleasantly uplifted by it; this is
the image of *joy*.

What the kings of yore saw in this was that virtue is what is commanded by heaven, and is the root of human life, so it should be a joy to cultivate and practice it. Therefore they made music to honor virtue. Joy is that whereby virtue is made harmonious, virtue is that whereby joy is made complete. If one creates enjoyments without honoring virtue, that is called creating enjoyment in the midst of misery. But by using joy to harmonize virtue, the virtue becomes more exalted; by using virtue to create joy, the joy becomes more harmonious. When virtue and joy coincide, this is called true happiness.

The richness of the music of that happiness and joy is sufficient to offer to God, and to share with the ancestors. Since what God likes is virtue, and what the ancestors like is virtue too, offerings to God and to the ancestors are offerings of virtue. When one creates enjoyment and happiness without losing virtue, this is obeying God and remembering the ancestors. Obeying God is answering heaven, remembering the ancestors is repaying our debt.

When people are born, they receive their lives from God and their bodies from their ancestors. The body is that whereby life is carried, life is that whereby the body is completed. Since the body and life are inseparable, repaying our debt is answering heaven, answering heaven is repaying our debt. When we answer heaven and repay our debt, we can be happy. Such is the effect of finding joy in honoring virtue; how can people be happy without honoring virtue?

17. *Following*

lake above,
thunder below

There is thunder in the lake, following. Thus do superior people go inside and rest when the sun goes down.

Following means adapting to the time. Above is *lake* ☱, below is thunder ☳; so there is thunder in the lake. Thunder stands for activity, lake stands for stillness; when activity enters into stillness, creative energy temporarily rests, and repose is necessary. This is the image of *following* the time.

What superior people see in this is that the primordial true positive energy in people is covered by the acquired force of mundane conditioning, and nature is moved by feeling. This is like that which is proper to *thunder* being appropriated by *lake*; if one wants to restore it, one cannot do so save by following the Tao. Therefore they "go inside and rest when the sun goes down," retreating into darkness at the hour of darkness, temporarily using stillness to nurture creativity, not daring to act arbitrarily, refining themselves and waiting for the proper time to emerge.

Resting when it is time to rest is what is referred to by the saying "If you want to take, you must give." This is particularly critical when *thunder* goes into *lake*, when the killing force is strong and the vivifying force is weak—this is the extreme of darkness. If you impetuously set to work at this juncture, not only will the vivifying force not return, but this will stimulate the killing force to go out of control.

So just "go inside and rest when the sun goes down," first be still before you act. The active follows the passive, the passive then follows the active; taking over this mechanism is imperceptible to anyone.

18. *Degeneration*

mountain above,
wind below

There is wind in the mountains; degeneration. Thus superior people rouse the people and nurture virtue.

Degeneration is when things fall apart. Above is *mountain* ☶, below is *wind* ☴; this is wind in the mountains. Mountains can nurture beings, wind can stir beings; stirring up and nurturing is the image of repairing *degeneration*.

What superior people see in this is that the vital spirit in humans is like the people, and the natural reality in humans is virtue; when there is degeneration in the natural reality, it is due to not knowing how to rouse the vital spirit to cultivate and nurture it. Therefore they rouse the "people" of the vital spirit, and nurture the "virtue" of natural reality.

Rousing the people must be like the wind gradually rising from below, ascending from lowliness to the heights. Nurturing virtue must be like the stability of a mountain as it nurtures beings, nurturing with richness and warmth. When one is able to nurture, the vital spirit becomes more and more active; when one is able to rouse, natural reality attains development. By rousing and nurturing, that which has not yet degenerated can be preserved, and that which has degenerated can be repaired. By gradual penetration, getting stronger with perseverance, one will eventually advance to the stage of ultimate good without evil, where there can be no degeneration.

19. Overseeing

earth above,
lake below

**Above the lake there is earth, overseeing. Superior
people use inexhaustibility of education and thought
to embrace and protect the people without bound.**

Overseeing means overseeing below from above. Below is *lake* ☱,
above is *earth* ☷; there is earth above the lake. Lakes make things wet,
earth supports things; widely providing water and support for the many—
this is the image of *overseeing*.

What superior people see in this is that education should be promoted and the life of the people should be stabilized; therefore they edu-
cate the people tirelessly, thinking of them and teaching them, guiding
them with virtue, equalizing them with etiquette, gradually influenc-
ing them.

Education is endless, and thought is also endless; the purpose is to
improve the morals and customs of the populace. The ground of ethics
gives abundant life, embracing the people without cruelty, protecting and
embracing them, minimizing criminal law, making taxes light, seeing to
sufficiency of food and clothing, like taking care of an infant, embracing
and protecting without bound.

When education and protection are done properly, there is harmony
between the leaders and the followers, a unity of will, resulting in an atmosphere of light and peace. This is the way it is when superior people are
in positions of authority; but superior people who have no position also
teach and protect people in the same way. When superior people instruct
others tirelessly, making speeches and writing books, they hope that everyone will become a sage, that every person will attain the Way. This too is
teaching and thinking inexhaustibly.

The mind of superior people embraces the whole universe, viewing
others and self as equals, accepting every being, loving every being; this
too is embracing and protecting without bound. Regardless of whether superior people have positions or not, they all aspire to foster life.

20. *Observing*

wind above,
earth below

Wind is over the earth, observing. Thus did the kings
of yore set up education after examination of the
region and observation of the people.

Observing is watching, looking. Above is *wind* ☴, below is *earth* ☷;
there is wind blowing over the earth. When wind blows over the earth,
wherever it goes everything sways and dances along with it; this is like
people being moved and influenced by what they observe. This is the image of *observing*.

What the ancient kings saw in this was that every particular region
has its own atmosphere, every particular region has its own character;
therefore it will not do to cling to one system to teach or rule them all.
Hence they examined the atmosphere of each region and observed the
character of the people, setting up education according to the region and
giving guidance according to the person.

Just as the wind blowing over the earth goes over hill and dale, east,
west, south, north, unhindered wherever it goes, so also was the teaching
of the kings of yore. All those who are invested with the responsibility of
teaching others should emulate the kings of yore and observe the locality
and the character of the people so as to be able to teach them effectively.

21. *Biting Through*

fire above,
thunder below

Thunder and lightning, biting through. Thus did the
kings of yore clarify penalties and proclaim laws.

Biting through is when the mouth closes in the process of eating something. Above is *fire* ☲, below is *thunder* ☳; the fire accompanying
thunder is lightning. This is thunder and lightning in the same place.
Thunder shakes things, lightning illumines things. Within punishment
there is reward, within killing there is vivifying. It is like when eating
something the mouth must close; it does not move at random, and when it
moves it discerns the flavor of the food. This is the image of *biting through*.

What the kings of yore saw in this was that when violent and vicious
people walk inescapably into the jaws of death, it is because they do not
know there is criminal law; therefore they established laws clarifying

major and minor penalties so that people would know that they should not commit crime. When there were those who did not accept the rule of the kings and intentionally transgressed even though they knew the laws, the kings assessed the gravity of their offenses, proclaiming uniform laws so that people would know the law cannot be escaped.

First informing people with clarifications, then punishing offenders with authority, life and death are clear, punishment and reward are both used. When those who execute the law do not impose unjust punishments, and those subject to the law accept the consequences of their deeds, there is no barrier between the two sides. This is represented as biting through.

Penalties and laws were explained and established by ancient kings for the sake of the world and the livelihood of the people. Those who administer laws should emulate the ancient kings in first clarifying them before executing them, in order to avoid mistakenly injuring life.

The people who have false ideas about attainment of the Tao, who are unable to first thoroughly examine its principles, but take up practice recklessly and get sidetracked in auxiliary methods, either clinging to emptiness or sticking to form, wishing to seek long life but instead hastening death, are like the criminals in the times of the ancient kings. They are chewing on nothing, they have nothing to get their teeth into—what is the benefit in fact?

22. *Adornment*

mountain above,
fire below

There is fire below the mountain, adorning it. Thus do superior people clarify government affairs, without presumptuous adjudication.

Adornment is beautification. Above is *mountain* ☶, below is *fire* ☲; there is fire below the mountain. When there is fire below the mountain, everything below the mountain is bathed in its light, and the fire illumines the mountain. This is the image of *adornment*.

What superior people see in this is that just as the light of a fire below a mountain is not great, when people are lacking in capacity their vision is not far reaching; therefore the superior people administer and clarify the simple matters of government affairs, and do not act presumptuously in difficult matters of adjudication.

Government affairs include such matters as the state of the manners and mores of the populace, finance, taxation, and civil proceedings. The thriving or decay of government affairs is obvious and easy to see; they are not difficult to manage, and can be changed when mistakes occur. When it comes to the matter and adjudication of criminal cases, however, where life is at stake, there are obscure factors that are difficult to discern; any lack of clarification can bring disaster on the innocent. Therefore only the wise and perspicacious can judge. Not judging presumptuously thus has the meaning of respect for life.

The use of illumination by practitioners of the Tao is also not beyond this principle. Social relations and daily activities are like the affairs of government; the profound and recondite science of fulfilling nature and arriving at the meaning of life is like adjudication. Social relations are the human Tao; fulfilling nature and arriving at the meaning of life are the celestial Tao. The human Tao is obvious and easy to see; anyone with a bit of capacity and intelligence can handle it. When it comes to the celestial Tao, however, it requires the verbal transmission and mental communication of a true teacher, great enlightenment and great penetration, before it is possible to manage it correctly.

When the celestial Tao is truly realized, whatever comes to hand is the Tao; benefiting oneself, one can also benefit others. This is the greatest accomplishment. If one does not have the transmission of a genuine teacher and imposes judgments by arbitrary guesswork, even the slightest error produces a great loss, and misapprehension of human nature and life. How can one judge presumptuously?

Not being presumptuous is the teaching of sages that enables people to nurture small understanding so as to gradually seek great understanding. It will not do to presume upon small understanding and thereby ruin the great work, deluding oneself and deluding others. Indeed, a little bit of knowledge can deceive people very much.

23. *Stripping*

mountain above,
earth below

Mountains are joined to the earth. Those above secure their homes by kindness to those below.

Stripping means removing. Above is *mountain* ☶, below is *earth* ☷; mountains are joined to the earth. Mountains are high, the earth is low; joining mountains to the earth, the excess of the high is removed and the insufficiency of the low is fulfilled. This is the image of *stripping*.

What those in high positions see in this is that just as mountains cannot be stable unless they are joined to the earth, those in high positions cannot be secure unless they are kind to those below them. Therefore they take away from the high and give to the low, to enable those below to find their places. This is because the people are the basis of the country; when the basis is secure, the country is at peace—then those in high positions can also live peacefully in their homes and administer noncoercive government.

Among practitioners of the Tao, those with capacity and knowledge are the high ones, and those without capacity or knowledge are the low ones. When those who have capacity do not presume upon it, and those who have knowledge do not depend on it, and they take their excess of capacity and knowledge and pass it on to those lacking in capacity and knowledge, joining the high to the low, being fulfilled but dwelling in emptiness, then elevation is true elevation, fulfillment is true fulfillment. They transform the artificial into reality, rest in ultimate good unwavering, and abide securely in their homes, invulnerable to external influences.

The secure home for humans is benevolence; taking from those above to give to those below, when the inversion is made, *stripping* changes into *return*. Having returned, it is possible to rely on benevolence; the mechanism of enlivening operates, and nature and life are secured. In securing "their homes by kindness to those below" the celestial mechanism is finally revealed.

24 *Return*

earth above,
thunder below

Thunder is in the earth; return. Thus did the kings of yore shut the gates on the winter solstice; caravans did not travel, the ruler did not inspect the regions.

Return means reversion and restoration. Above is *earth* ☷, below is *thunder* ☳; there is thunder in the earth. Thunder is something very active; when thunder stirs in the earth, the mechanism of enlivening operates, and myriad things are born.

What the ancient kings saw in this was that as everything revives when the positive creative energy operates, so does the living potential return to humans when their positive energy becomes manifest. So they closed the gates on the winter solstice, not allowing caravans to go forth and trade, not allowing the ruler to go out and inspect the regions. This was all to get people to emulate the restoration of heaven and earth, nurturing this point of living potential, not letting it be damaged.

What is the living potential? The potential is the natural innocent mind inherent in humans. This is the progenitor of life, the source of yin and yang. Once it falls into temporal conditioning, it becomes covered by temperament, and cannot be consistently manifest. When it occasionally does manifest, this is the time of the return of the celestial within the mundane.

This time, however, is hard to gain and easy to lose; most people do not know it, and miss it even when it is right there. Because of this, the mundane gradually grows and the celestial gradually wanes. When the celestial is exhausted and mundanity is complete, there is only death.

The shutting of the gates on the winter solstice is so that when the positive energy returns people will nurture it. Caravans not traveling means not allowing involvement with external artificialities to damage inner reality. The ruler not inspecting the regions means preventing keenness in criticizing others coupled with dullness in cultivating oneself.

Once the gates are closed, one is careful and strict; inwardly thoughts do not arise, external things do not enter. Thus the positive energy cannot leak out.

Thus it was that the ancient kings established their resolve for the sake of the world, and established order to enable the people to live. When superior people who practice the Tao refine themselves and master their minds, illumination arises in inner openness, and the living potential is activated; they should quickly gather it into the furnace of evolution, conscientiously forestall danger, carefully seal it and store it securely, fostering its growth from vagueness to clarity, until there is eventually a return of the celestial energy to pure completeness. This is the same idea as the ancient kings shutting the gates on the winter solstice.

This time when the positive celestial energy first returns is the passageway of life and death; if you can avail yourself of it, you enter the road of life, but if you lose it you wind up on the road of death. "Shut the gates" here means closing the door of death; when the door of death is closed, the door of life opens. Heaven borrows human power, humans borrow celestial power; when heaven and humanity work together, the elixir of immortality crystallizes in a short time, without requiring years of effort. Unfortunately, most people do not seek the personal instruction of a genuine teacher, and miss the opportunity that is right before them.

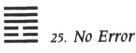

25. No Error

> heaven above,
> thunder below

Thunder moves under heaven, things accompany with no error. Thus did the kings of yore promote flourishing appropriate to the time and nurture myriad beings.

No error means no wandering mind and no arbitrary action. Above is *heaven* ☰, below is *thunder* ☳; thunder moves under heaven. When thunder is active in accord with the times of nature, myriad things stir with it; as long as the thunder is without error, myriad things also are without error. This is the image of *no error*.

What the ancient kings saw in this was that just as nature gives birth to beings with time, sages develop people with virtue; therefore they caused the Tao of perfect sincerity without error to flourish, fulfilling themselves and fulfilling others, responding to the times of nature, nurturing myriad beings, causing all to live according to their true natures, and to eventually be free from error.

By promoting flourishing appropriate to the time, so that the growth and the season are in harmony, thus nurturing beings so that all have their places, the activity of nurturing according to the time shares the function of heaven and the movement and stillness of thunder—how could there be error?

When practitioners of the Tao make no error in process or proportion, and advance and withdraw, hurry and relax, in the proper manner, this also promotes flourishing appropriate to the time. Unifying the elements of being into a single integral energy, so that myriad principles ultimately coalesce, is also nurturing myriad beings.

Developing beings according to the time, all beings are imbued with reality, and all ultimately are free from error. Thus it is that heaven and thunder have no error, thus it is that the ancient kings had no error, and thus it is too that practice of the Tao is without error. The way to be free from error is to act in a manner that is appropriate to the time.

26. *Great Accumulation*

mountain above,
heaven below

Heaven is in the mountains, great accumulation. Thus do superior people become acquainted with many precedents of speech and action, in order to accumulate virtue.

Great accumulation is extensive amassing and assembling. Above is *mountain* ☶, below is *heaven* ☰; this is heaven in the mountains. The sky is vast, mountains are small in comparison; being outwardly small yet inwardly great is the image of *great accumulation.*

What superior people see in this is that when people are unable to increase their virtue, it is because they presume upon their talent and knowledge, they aggrandize themselves, and do not know to emulate the sages of yore; therefore superior people become acquainted with many of the words and deeds of people of the past, recording them to foster expansion of consciousness and vision, thereby accumulating and storing their virtue.

The lifeline of the psychological teachings of the sages is stored in books. The speech and action of the ancient sages were speech and action of virtue. If one can study widely with serious intent, question earnestly and think for oneself, then one comes face to face with the sages, says what the ancients said and does what the ancients did. When speech and action are free from defect, one's virtue accumulates and grows day by day. Only then can one fulfill nature and reach the meaning of life. When both nature and life are comprehended, one is as permanent as heaven, as stable as the mountains. What can compare to the greatness of that accumulation?

27. *Jaws*

mountain above,
thunder below

There is thunder beneath the mountain. Superior people are careful about what they say, and moderate in eating and drinking.

Jaws has the meaning of taking nourishment. Above is *mountain* ☶, below is *thunder* ☳; there is thunder beneath the mountain. A mountain is still, thunder is active. Using stillness to nurture activity, activity being based on stillness, is like the upper jaw being still while the lower jaw moves, stillness awaiting movement. This is the image of *jaws*, meaning nourishment.

What the superior people see in this is that the mouth is a passageway through which things may exit or enter, and it is the door of right and wrong, the root of calamity, and fortune; therefore they are careful about what they say, and they are moderate in eating and drinking.

Speech is the voice of the mind; when speech is correct the mind is correct, and when speech is incorrect the mind is incorrect. Every word should be spoken only if it is of benefit to the course of the world and to people's minds. Speech should be guarded and not uttered at random.

Food and drink are important to the body; if food and drink are appropriate they benefit the body, and if food and drink are not appropriate they harm the body. Food and drink should be taken only after consideration of the reason. One should not crave too much, and should be moderate in eating and drinking.

When one is careful of speech, then the mind has nourishment; when one is moderate in eating and drinking, then the body has nourishment. When mind and body both have their nourishment, inside and outside are free from injury; then nature and life can be cultivated. This is what is meant by the saying "When one eats at proper times, the body is healthy; when one acts at the appropriate moment, the course of affairs runs smoothly."

28. *Great Excess*

lake above,
wind below

**Moisture destroys wood in excess. Thus superior
people stand alone without fear, and leave society
without distress.**

Great excess is excess of the great. Above is *lake* ☱, associated with
moisture, below is *wind* ☴, associated with wood. The nature of water
is to flow downward, the nature of wood is to float upward; when water
rises above wood, it can destroy wood, and when wood descends below
water, it can be destroyed by the moisture. This is the image of *great excess*.

What superior people see in this is that just as a great excess of
moisture can destroy wood, so can a great excess of talent and intelligence
in people destroy their character. Therefore they take the model of water
rising above wood in the sense of standing alone without fear, and take the
model of wood descending below water in the sense of concealing themselves and being free from distress; thus they accomplish the will of a person of exceeding greatness, and perfect the character of a person of exceeding greatness.

Because superior people who practice the Tao consider nature and
life to be the most important matter, they look down upon all existents as
empty of absoluteness, being like a clear lake unsullied by the dust of objects. They make use of the phenomena of the world to practice the principles of the Tao, playing a unique tune on an individual harp. Unmoved
by the prospects of life or death, they stand aloof of all things without fear.
Like the flexibility of wood, they have talent but do not presume upon it,
they have intelligence but do not rely on it. Though simple in appearance,
they hold a treasure; concealing their illumination and nurturing it in
obscurity, they do not seek to be known to others. They are hidden in a
profound privacy and have no distress.

Having no fear means that one cannot be constrained by things,
having will and energy far beyond that of others. Having no distress means
that errant thoughts do not arise, and one has cultivated development far
beyond that of others. Because of having no fear and no distress, one can
accomplish that which is rare in the world, and be beyond the perception
and beyond the reach of ordinary people.

29. Double Water

> water above,
> water below

Water travels, double water. Thus do superior people consistently practice virtue and learn how to teach.

Double water means water reaching from here to there. Above is *water* ☵, below is *water* ☵; this is water traveling from here to there, from there to here, traveling, flowing throughout. This is the image of *double water*.

What superior people see in this is that the work of sages is two-fold, involving both self-development and development of others. Self-development is the practice of virtue; development of others is teaching. If virtuous practice is inconsistent, it is hard to enter the universal Tao; if teaching is not learned, students will not understand.

Therefore they work on virtuous practice day by day and month by month, becoming familiar with the old and aware of the new, increasing their efforts as time goes on, aiming for profound attainment of self-realization. Then when it comes to teaching, they gradually develop guidance, making clear presentations and subtle indications, leading students further and further on until they penetrate thoroughly and are free from doubt.

The practice of virtue is the study of body and mind, nature and life. It is a very refined and subtle science, in which the slightest deviation can produce an enormous loss. It can be accomplished only by constancy and consistency, thoroughly investigating its principles, fulfilling nature and arriving at the meaning of life.

Teaching is a matter of receiving from forebears and educating successors. It is very urgent and necessary. If instruction is unclear, people will be misled as to the course they should pursue. One can develop others only if one learns how to teach, which involves searching out the profound and the recondite and clarifying that which is obscure.

The work of teaching is based on the practice of virtue; teaching means teaching the practice of virtue. Only if one is consistent and constant in the practice of virtue can one learn and practice teaching. If one cannot be consistent in the practice of virtue, then teaching will be baseless and unguided. When one is consistent in the practice of virtue and afterward learns how to teach, then what is consistent and constant in oneself is what is learned by others. This is like water traveling from here to there; it is all the same water, able to flow everywhere.

30. *Fire*

fire above,
fire below

**Light has dual function. Thus do great people illumine
the four quarters with continuing light.**

Fire refers to the light of the sun. Above and below is *fire* ☲, associated
with the sun. The sun goes in at night and comes out in the daytime; this
pattern represents inner illumination and outer illumination, one light
having a dual function. This is the image of *fire*.

What great people see in this is that if people are incapable of illuminating the inner, they will be incapable of illuminating the outward;
first illuminating the inner, then illuminating the outward, as is inner illumination, so also will be outward illumination. Therefore after they have
illumined the inward, they then continue the enlightenment to illumine
the four quarters.

"Light" is inner illumination, "continuing light" is outward illumination. What does light illumine? It simply illumines the inherent quality of
open awareness without obscurity. When one is open and aware, this
inner quality or virtue is already illumined, and truthfulness within reaches
outside, so that nothing can deceive one, nothing can burden one; one illumines the four quarters and sees everything as clearly as if it were in the
palm of one's hand. The "yellow sprouts" of living potential cover the
earth, the "golden flowers" of spiritual energy bloom throughout the
world. Whichever way one turns, everywhere is the Tao. Thoroughly lucid
inside and out, that illumination never ceases. Then one has clarified the
quality of illumination and rests in the highest good.

But continuing the enlightenment to illumine the four quarters cannot be accomplished by idleness and inaction; it involves adjustment
through effort. Illumination by enlightenment means perception with
clarity; if the enlightenment cannot illumine the four quarters, that light is
not great, and cannot be considered continuing light. Once one illumines
the inward and also illumines the outward, the light must be like the sun
climbing into space, illumining all things, such that nothing can block that
light. Only then is it true enlightenment, only then is it continuing light. If
there is any shortfall of perceptivity, that means the light is blocked to
some extent. When the light can illumine everywhere, and nothing can
obstruct that perception under any circumstances, so that it reaches everywhere without becoming defective anywhere, then the work of clarifying
the quality of illumination is complete.

31. *Sensing*

lake above,
mountain below

There is a lake on a mountain. Thus does the superior person accept people with openness.

Sensing means feeling. Above is *lake* ☱, below is *mountain* ☶; there is a lake on a mountain. A lake is open, a mountain is high; to be high yet capable of openness—this is the image of *sensing*.

What superior people see in this is that just as there can be no lake atop a mountain if there is no open space, similarly people can't be sensitive to anything if their minds are not open. Therefore they empty themselves of what they have, and receive enhancement from another.

The Taoist master Tz'u-yang said, "Stop exercising clever artifice as though it were effective practice; recognize the other's method of immortality." "The other" is another person, but it does not mean an ordinary person in the world—it means the original immortal true person inherent in oneself. Because of mixing with acquired conditioning, it has run away and become ineffective; long covered up and buried away, it is lost and does not return. Though it may show up occasionally, students who cling to the temporal, who stick to the conditioned, miss it even when it is right before them, and are unable to sense it.

This is all because of inability to refine the self. If one is unable to refine oneself, personal desires fill the being, and their sprouts clog the opening of awareness. Being filled and not open, whenever another comes there is no room for reception.

Superior people who practice the Tao refine themselves and master their minds, getting rid of all acquired pollutants, so that their minds are open. When the mind is open, the primordial energy comes from nothingness, so that one can receive enhancement from "the other" and become fulfilled. One senses by openness, the other responds with fulfillment; the small goes and the great comes, the gold elixir of immortality spontaneously crystallizes. This is like a high mountain being empty and open on top and receiving the moisture of a lake; it happens spontaneously, without any intention that it be so.

32. *Perseverance*

thunder above,
wind below

**Thunder and wind are perpetual. Thus does the
superior person stand without changing places.**

Perseverance is persistence. Above is *thunder* ☳, below is *wind* ☴;
when thunder is in motion, wind follows along. Thunder and wind grasp
each other; with wind the sound of thunder reaches afar, following thunder
the blowing of the wind is powerful. This is the image of *perseverance*.

What superior people see in this is that just as the nature of thunder is
strong while the nature of wind is gentle, strength and gentility balancing
one another so as to be able to stir myriad beings, in the same way there is
strength and gentility in people, which require one another so as to enable
people to persist in carrying out the Way. Thereby they stand without
changing places.

To stand means to be decisive, to have stability of concentration. One's
place means the path that is to be traveled, the Way that is to be carried out.
There are students who are decisive in doing things, there are those who
are decisive but do not know the proper way to go, and there are those
who know the way to go but eventually slack off after an earnest start,
alter their plans along the way, and change their places. All of them lack
the determination to persevere consistently, so they are unable to practice
the eternally unchanging Tao.

Superior people consider the nature and life of mind and body to be
the one important matter, and they know that to accomplish the Tao that is
eternally unchanging requires a permanently unchanging will. Emulating
the strength and vigor of thunder and the flexible gentility of wind, they
single out what is good and hold to it, gradually advancing in an orderly
manner, growing ever stronger the longer they persevere. Wealth and rank
cannot make them dissolute, poverty and ignominy cannot move them,
authority and arms cannot suppress them. Everything in existence being
void of absoluteness, they rest in the appropriate place, thus able to reach
profound attainment of self-realization, in which the earthly and celestial
are combined, lasting forever without corruption.

33. *Inaccessibility*

heaven above,
mountain below

**There are mountains under heaven, which is
inaccessible. Thus do superior people keep petty
people at a distance, being stern without ill will.**

Inaccessibility means no one can know you. Above is *heaven* ☰, below
is *mountain* ☶; there are mountains under the sky. The sky can contain
the mountains, but the mountains cannot get near the sky; this is the image of *inaccessibility*.

What superior people see in this is that when people bring trouble on
themselves, being injured by petty people, it is because of being narrow
and intolerant. Therefore superior people keep petty people at a distance,
being stern yet without ill will. To keep petty people at a distance does not
mean to avoid them but rather to cause petty people to keep their distance.
Not having ill will means to deal with people tolerantly and generously,
while being stern means to control oneself firmly.

Superior people who practice the Tao have minds as vast as the sky,
embracing all existence, yet aloof of it all. Tolerant of everyone, they live in
the world without destroying it, they are in the midst of the mundane yet
can transcend the mundane. They are not disliked by lesser people, yet as
their self-discipline and conduct are beyond the ordinary, and because
they are conscientious, lesser people avoid them even though they themselves do not try to avoid lesser people.

This is like mountains under heaven; no matter how high the mountains are, they cannot get close to heaven. Nothing under heaven is as high
or large as mountains are, yet heaven can contain even that which is as
high or as large as mountains—how much the more so that which is not
so high or large. Only when practitioners of the Tao have the capacity to
contain mountains, as it were, can they sustain the heavenly practice and
cultivate the heavenly Tao. Being inaccessible without hiding, they are
near to invulnerability.

False followers of Taoism in the world who are small-minded and intolerant and get irritated and angry at every encounter and confrontation
are naturally disliked and avoided by petty people, but they are never free
of obstacles.

34. Great Power

thunder above,
heaven below

**Thunder is up in the sky, with great power. Thus do
superior people refrain from what is improper.**

Great power means expansion of empowerment. Above is *thunder* ☳,
below is *heaven* ☰; this is thunder up in the sky. Thunder is something
strong and intense, its energy is very powerful; when it climbs up in the
sky, startling all with its vibration, its powerful energy expands even more.
This is the image of *great power.*

What superior people see in this is that just as when thunder ascends
into the sky in season it can thus vivify beings, so can people develop
character when they carry out their activities according to reason. Therefore superior people refrain from whatever is improper.

Propriety means the moderation of activity and repose, the ordering
of engagement and disengagement, guiding self-cultivation and social relations. When ordinary people follow their impulses and do whatever comes
to mind, perhaps greedily pursuing idle imaginations, indulging in emotions and giving free rein to desire, this is all improper.

Doing what is improper is not conducive to growth or empowerment.
Even if one becomes powerful, this is power that abandons the real and
enters the false, empowering that which should not be powerful. This is
really not power.

If one can avoid looking at what should not be looked at, avoid listening to what should not be listened to, avoid saying what should not be said,
avoid doing what should not be done, act properly and refrain from what
is improper, then whatever one does is proper.

Propriety is reason, reason is celestial. If one puts celestial reason
into practice, human desires do not arise; then every step one takes is in
accord with the sublime Tao. One is then a companion of heaven, with the
same achievement as thunder. Dwelling in the midst of the elements, one
is not constrained by the elements; living among myriad things, one is not
harmed by the myriad things. Is that power not great?

35. *Advance*

fire above,
earth below

**Light emerges over the earth, advancing. Thus do
superior people by themselves illumine the quality
of enlightenment.**

Advance is progress. Above is *fire* ☲, associated with the sun, and below is *earth* ☷; this is the sun emerging over the earth. The sun is light,
the earth is basically dark; when the light of the sun emerges over the
earth, it goes from darkness to light. This is the image of *advance.*

What superior people see in this is that just as the sun sets and also
rises, in the same way people can obscure their good qualities and also can
illumine them. Therefore superior people take it upon themselves to illumine the quality of enlightenment.

To illumine means to make manifest; the quality of enlightenment is
the spiritual nature of innate knowledge and innate capacity that is fundamental to humankind. This nature is originally truly open, subtly existing,
radiantly bright, without obscurity; but once it is mixed with acquired
temperament, it goes from clarity to obscurity and loses its basic nature.

But as unclarity comes from oneself, so also does clarity come from
oneself; it is just a matter of whether one illumines this nature by oneself
or not. If one actually knows how to illumine enlightenment, then one
can illumine it; one should set right to work to cultivate it, clearing away
all accumulated blockage, shed all kinds of feelings about things, and
work on the ground of reality.

Being careful and wary, nipping insidious inroads of conditioning in
the bud, the human mentality disappears of itself and the mind of Tao
manifests of itself. Temperament spontaneously sublimates, and the real
nature spontaneously is revealed. This then is the original open awareness without obscurity, round and bright, clean and naked, bare and
untrammeled.

36. Concealment of Illumination

earth above,
fire below

Light enters into the earth, illumination is concealed. Thus do superior people deal with the masses, acting unobtrusively while in fact illumined.

Concealment of illumination means being illumined but concealing it. Above is *earth* ☷, below is *fire* ☲, associated with the sun; this is light entering into the earth. When light enters into the earth, there is light within darkness. This is the image of *concealment of illumination.*

What superior people see in this is that when practitioners of the Tao are among the masses, if they use their illumination too much, they will startle the ignorant and amaze the worldly, easily bringing on abuse and slander. Therefore superior people deal with the masses by acting unobtrusively even though they are in fact illumined.

Dealing with the masses means facing the unenlightened with enlightenment; acting unobtrusively means concealing enlightenment and nurturing it. The beings produced by heaven and earth are not equal, the masses of people are not equal in terms of intelligence. There is a mixture of aberration and sanity, and everyone is an individual; how can every individual be totally good? Acting unobtrusively in dealing with people means dealing with them on their own terms, seeing the totality as one organism. This means having a quality of breadth like that of the earth, which supports everything and accepts everything, being responsive to everything in an adaptive way.

But acting unobtrusively does not mean that one does not use illumination at all. It means that one is outwardly unnoticeable but free from inward obscurity, so there is inner light within outer darkness. One is able to distinguish in every case who is wise and who is foolish, who is aberrated and who is sane. But though one harmonizes with others, one is not influenced, and though one associates with others, one does not become clannish. One's patterns of activity and passivity, absence and presence, are indiscernible to others; one is like the sun, which is bright when it rises, but also bright in secret when it has set. This is what is meant by the saying that a great hermit may well live in the city.

37. *Members of a Family*

wind above,
fire below

**Wind emerges from fire, members of a family. Thus
is there factuality in the speech of superior people,
consistency in their deeds.**

Members of a family means the people of one family. Above is *wind* ☴,
below is *fire* ☲; so fire is inside and wind is outside—wind emerges
from fire, when fire burns, wind spontaneously arises; wind and fire are
of the same family. This is the image of *members of a family.*

What superior people see in this is that just as wind and fire are in the
same place, wind rising from fire, similarly others and oneself live together, and so what one can do for others is based on oneself. If one is
upright oneself, others will naturally be influenced. Therefore when superior people speak, they do not speak in vain; there must be something factual for them to speak about. When they act, they do not do so at random;
there must be something consistent about their deeds. When one is careful
about one's words and prudent in one's acts, those with whom one lives
will also be factual in speech and consistent in deeds, and be members of a
family with oneself.

Members of a family does not only mean people of the same house;
it means all those among whom one lives and with whom one works.
When there is factuality in speech, words being based on actualities, then
there is a point, there is evidence—that speech will accord with reason.
When there is consistency in deeds, action having a conclusion, then there
is true practice and genuine application—those deeds will accomplish
something.

When one speaks factually and acts consistently, without flaw in
word or deed, inwardly not losing oneself, outwardly not hurting others,
then those with whom one lives and works will be influenced without
anything being said, just as wind spontaneously rises when fire burns.

Words are the voice of the mind, deeds are the tune of the body; if
practitioners of the Tao speak with factuality and act with consistency,
then the mind will be upright and the body will be disciplined, nature and
life will have a dwelling place. Furthermore, they will be in confluence
with heaven above and earth below, and will be members of a family with
heaven and earth.

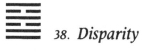

38. *Disparity*

fire above,
lake below

**Above is fire, below is a lake, disparate. Thus are
superior people the same yet different.**

Disparity means disjunction between one and another. Above is *fire* ☲,
below is *lake* ☱ : the nature of fire is to flame upward, while the nature
of water is to flow downward; when the fire is above, it cannot warm the
water, and when the water is below it cannot extinguish the fire. Thus
though the fire and the lake water are in the same place, their natures are
different; this is the image of *disparity*.

What superior people see in this is that practitioners of the Tao should
not fail to assimilate to others, yet should not be too much like others either. If they do not assimilate, they will startle and amaze the ignorant and
ordinary people, and will be disliked and suspected by others; if they become too similar, however, they will be caught up in their influence and
fall into mundane feelings. Therefore they are different in the midst of
sameness.

Emulating the way moisture permeates things, they merge with the
ordinary world and harmonize their illumination, responding to people
harmoniously, able to adapt without restriction, assimilating to everyone.
Emulating the way fire lights things up, they clearly distinguish truth and
falsity, dealing with people without confusion, inwardly autonomous,
having extraordinary self-control.

Outwardly the same yet inwardly not the same, inwardly different yet
outwardly not different, they are thus able to be very much like other
people while at the same time very much different from other people.
Outward sameness means going by worldly laws; inward difference is
practicing the principles of the Tao. This is what is meant by the saying "In
cultivating practice, one conforms and harmonizes, adapting to each individual situation as it is; nobody can fathom such changes, or see how one
acts or lies hidden."

39. Halting

water above,
mountain below

There is water atop a mountain, halting. Thus do superior people examine themselves and cultivate virtue.

Halting means there is difficulty and one cannot proceed onward. Above is *water* ☵, below is *mountain* ☶; there is water atop a mountain. A mountain is high and is very earthy; add water on top of that, and earthiness is strong while the celestial is weak. This is the image of *halting*.

What superior people see in this is that when people are unable to make progress on the path of sages, it is because they are competitive and contentious, emotional and greedy, not knowing how to improve themselves and correct their errors. Therefore superior people examine themselves and cultivate virtue.

If one is incapable of self-examination, one will not have self-mastery, and will be subject to manipulation; every act, every step, will entail danger and difficulty, will involve injury to life. Only by self-examination can one abandon the false and enter the real; not being deluded by externals, with every step one's feet then tread the real ground and virtue can be cultivated.

When virtue is cultivated, one's nature is stabilized and feelings are forgotten, so that one is unshakable and unwavering as a mountain. Not halted by obstacles, one cannot be injured by difficulties and troubles.

But the work of self-examination and cultivation of virtue requires clear knowledge of the image of the hexagram. The water is above, the mountain is below; the water being above means that the danger that causes halting is external, while the mountain being below means that developmental cultivation is internal. Seeing there is danger, if one can then use that danger to cultivate character, then even though the situation be dangerous the mind is not in danger. Outwardly there is danger, but inwardly it is not dangerous; the danger lies elsewhere, while cultivation of virtue and character lies in oneself. Using virtue to ward off danger, danger dissolves; using danger to cultivate character, virtuous action grows daily more lofty. So obstacles cannot faze one—indeed, it is after being halted by obstacles that one can cultivate character and virtue. If students can recognize the reality of self-examination, there is no need to worry about halting, and no need to worry about inability to develop virtue.

40. *Dissolution*

thunder above,
water below

**Thunder and rain act, dissolving. Thus do superior
people forgive faults and pardon crimes.**

Dissolution means shedding, dispersing. Above is *thunder* ☳, below is
water ☵; thunder rolls, rain falls, thunder and rain both act and the
celestial and earthly energies commune. This is the image of *dissolution*.

What superior people see in this is that when the force of mundanity
is congealed and stagnant, practitioners of the Tao should use intense
effort to burn it away; then when the celestial energy has returned, they
should use gentle effort to nurture it. Each phase has its proper time,
which does not allow deviation or delay. Therefore, after the force of mundanity has been dissolved, they "forgive faults and pardon crimes," going
along naturally to cause it to evaporate and disappear of itself, not allowing any force.

People have faults and commit crimes because of obeying acquired
conditioning, which obscures the primal; indulging emotions and giving
free rein to cravings, they will go to any lengths. This is why there needs to
be effort to attain self-mastery and self-control. Mastery and control
means correcting faults and eliminating misdeeds, using energy to transform the temperament. When the temperament has been sublimated, the
primordial comes back; with the mind of Tao always present, the human
mentality does not arise. Once faults and wrongdoings are eliminated,
there is no more need to work on mastery and control.

To forgive means to forgive past faults, to pardon means to pardon
past misdeeds. Forgiving and pardoning, sane energy grows strong and aberrant energy spontaneously disappears, the real remains and the false
does not come. Otherwise, if one does not know when to stop at sufficiency, and still keeps thinking about misdeeds and faults, after all this is
doing things with the human mentality, which again calls on faults and
errors after they had been eliminated. What had been dissolved now does
not dissolve; the danger of mundanity still remains, and celestial energy
is not pure. This is what is meant by the saying "To try to eliminate errant thoughts doubles the affliction; to aim for reality as it is also is
a mistake."

41. *Reduction*

mountain above,
lake below

**There is a lake under a mountain, reducing it. Thus
does the superior person eliminate wrath and cupidity.**

Reduction means decrease. Above is *mountain* ☶, below is *lake* ☱;
there is a lake under a mountain. The mountain is above, the lake is below; as the mountain is invaded by the moisture of the lake, it does not
rise high, and as the lake is limited by the mountain, it does not overflow—there is gain within reduction. This is the image of *reduction*.

What superior people see in this is that the violence in people erupts
as wrath, the self-interest in people emerges as cupidity; once wrath and
cupidity arise, they corrode natural reality, so their harm is very great.
Therefore superior people control their wrath, striving to change their
temperament, so that their nature and feelings are harmonious and peaceful, as steady as a mountain. They quell cupidity, striving to eliminate
wandering thoughts, so that their minds die and their spirits live, still and
clear as a lake without waves.

Wrath is something that impedes the Way, cupidity is a bandit that
disturbs the Way. If wrath and cupidity are not completely cleared up, even
if the great Way is in sight it cannot be fully accomplished. Therefore the
first step in practicing the Tao is to eliminate wrath and cupidity; when
one reduces away anger and desire, the work after that will be unobstructed, and there is hope for the way ahead.

This is why Confucians consider it essential to conquer the self and
return to propriety, Buddhists consider reduction of myriad phenomena to
emptiness fundamental, and Taoists consider self-refinement to set up the
foundation as primary. The sages of all three teachings first taught people
to get rid of personal wrath and cupidity.

The Taoist master Tz'u-yang said, "If you want to cultivate the restorative elixir to perfection, first you must refine yourself and master your
mind." Refining oneself means refining away this wrath and cupidity; mastering the mind means to control the mind and not give rise to wrath and
cupidity. If students are able, while in the midst of reduced reality, to reverse themselves and reduce falsehood, then it will not be difficult to practice the Tao.

42. *Increase*

wind above,
thunder below

**Wind and thunder increase. Thus do superior people
take to good when they see it, and correct whatever
faults they have.**

Increase is augmentation and enhancement. Above is *wind* ☴ and below is *thunder* ☳; this is wind and thunder meeting: When thunder
rolls, wind rises, the sound of wind enhances the thunder. This is the image of *increase*.

What superior people see in this is that to increase goodness it is necessary to reduce faults, and to reduce faults it is necessary to increase
goodness. Increase requires reduction, reduction complements increase,
so the increase has no end. Therefore when they see good they take to it,
and when they have faults they correct them.

When people are first born they are totally good, without evil; that
is, goodness is inherent in people, while faults are originally nonexistent
in people. It is because they are unaware of good that they have faults. If
they take to good when they see it, and continue to move toward goodness
until there is nothing they do that is not good, they will end up at ultimate
good. If they correct faults they have, and keep correcting them until there
is nothing faulty in them, they will finally become impeccable.

Taking to good means being able to be firm; correcting faults means
being able to be flexible. Firmness must be like the powerful, direct action
of thunder; flexibility must be like the gentle, gradual advance of wind.
Being vigorous, one can enter into goodness; being easygoing, one can be
without fault: Firmness and flexibility complement each other. What was
there before returns, and what occurred later disappears; the primal is
restored, and the acquired dissolves. By this enhancement one reaches
ultimate good with no evil, the stage of complete integration with the celestial design. So the work of taking to good and correcting faults is no
small matter.

43. *Parting*

lake above,
heaven below

Moisture ascends to heaven, which parts with it. Thus do superior people distribute blessings to reach those below, while avoiding presumption of virtue.

Parting is a bursting forth. Above is *lake* ☱ and below is *heaven* ☰; moisture ascends to heaven, then changes into rain and waters myriad creatures. It is as though heaven is being unselfish and parts with the moisture to let it flow down. This is the image of *parting*.

What superior people see in this is that just as myriad creatures grow when there is moisture in the sky, so are the people secure and peaceful when those above have benevolence. Therefore they distribute blessings to reach those below, causing everyone to benefit from their kindness.

To distribute to those below is to distribute blessings; if one distributes blessings unselfconsciously, then the giving is great, the generosity is real. This is like heaven covering everything and giving life to all creatures. This is what is meant by the saying "Those of great virtue do not consider themselves virtuous; they are companions of heaven."

If one is conscious of distribution of blessings being virtuous, this is presumption of virtue; there is still selfishness in the heart, and the distribution of blessings will not endure. This is not to be considered virtue; this is what those who distribute blessings are to strictly avoid.

Therefore superior people view others and self as the same; distributing blessings, they do not expect any reward. They have virtue but do not presume upon it, so their virtue grows day by day while their minds grow humbler day by day. They part with all self-satisfaction and self-importance. This comes about as inevitably as moisture in the sky falls to the earth.

Working on the Tao, accumulating achievement and building up practice, carrying out such and such expedients to benefit others, is like distributing blessings to people. But many who carry out expedients to benefit others do so without genuine sincerity; some do it for reputation, some do it for profit, some make an ineffective outward show of helping people based on ancient models and then blame others when things don't go quite as they wish. These are all cases of having no virtue yet presuming on virtue, and are not worthy of the name of benefiting others.

Observe how heaven bestows blessings on myriad creatures; does it expect any reward from them? Not expecting any reward from myriad creatures, heaven has virtue but does not presume upon it. If even heaven does not presume upon its virtue, how much less is the virtue of ordinary people to be presumed upon? Whenever one does anything for the benefit of others, if one can emulate heaven in not presuming upon virtue, one's virtue will not fail to be great.

44. Meeting

heaven above,
wind below

There is wind under heaven, meeting. Thus do rulers announce their directives to the four quarters.

Meeting is getting together. Above is *heaven* ☰, below is *wind* ☴; there is wind under heaven. Heaven creates myriad beings but cannot stir them; it is with the blowing of the wind that myriad beings stir. Thus heaven gets together with myriad beings through the agency of the wind. This is the image of *meeting*.

What rulers see in this is that just as heaven and myriad beings are far apart and cannot easily get together, but with the blowing of the wind those who have not gotten together do meet, in the same way rulers are far apart from their subjects and cannot easily get together, but with the announcement of directives, those who have not met can in fact meet. Therefore they give out directives for the education and guidance of the people, announcing them to the four quarters.

The four quarters are distant, and the local customs are not the same; how can everyone be taught personally? But when rulers give out directives, then everyone follows their direction, and those far and near are affected. This is like the wind under heaven, reaching everywhere, getting into everything. The ruler is heaven, the directive is the wind; where the wind reaches, things stir; where the directive reaches, the people are guided.

The way sages teach people is also like this. Just as rulers have directives that they announce to the four quarters, sages have classic writings that they use to teach later generations. They leave classic writings in the world for later generations, and students who hear them are stirred, those who read them are inspired. Even a hundred generations later people are roused and come face to face with the sages. The influence of the sages does not extend only to the four quarters of their own time. When rulers and sages love all beings and are in sensitive contact with all beings, they are upholding the practice of heaven.

45. *Gathering*

lake above,
earth below

**Moisture rises onto the earth, gathering. Thus do
superior people prepare weapons to guard against the
unexpected.**

Gathering is assembling. Above is *lake* ☱, below is *earth* ☷;
moisture rises onto the earth. When moisture is in the earth and rises
onto the earth, everything on the earth is nurtured by it and flourishes.
But there is a limit to water; it cannot always provide moisture for things.
Sometimes things flourish, and sometimes they don't. This is the image of
gathering.

What superior people see in this is that when practitioners of the Tao
get to where the five elements are assembled and have been returned to
the source, when everything acquired is obedient to their will, if they do
not know how to prevent danger and take perils into consideration, eventually what has been gathered will again disperse, and they will not be
able to avoid the trouble of losing what has been gained.

Therefore superior people prepare weapons to guard against the unexpected. "Weapons" means the tools of wisdom, the work of silent operation of spiritual awareness. When the primordial has been congealed, it is
not subject to injury by acquired conditioning, but it is still necessary to
dissolve the influences of personal history before nature and life can be
stabilized. If there is any remaining contamination, eventually conditioning will reassert itself and the primordial will again become fragmented.
Therefore this work of guarding is indispensible.

If one can prepare the weapons of wisdom to avoid being caught unawares, one will always have autonomous presence of mind, and the jewel
of life will not be damaged. After a long time, the five elements will merge
and sublimate, body and mind will both be refined, merging with the Tao
in reality, becoming eternally incorruptible. So the process of preserving
integration is important.

46. *Rising*

earth above,
wind below

**Trees grow on the earth, rising. Thus do superior
people follow virtue, accumulating the small to lofty
greatness.**

Rising is growth and ascent. Above is *earth* ☷, below is *wind* ☴,
which is associated with wood; this is trees growing on the earth. Trees
gradually growing up from the earth is the image of *rising*.

What superior people see in this is that when people are unable to
make their virtue lofty and great, it is because they do not know how to
follow virtue, and instead go against it. Not following virtue, abandoning
what is near at hand and pursuing what is far away, not having a substantial basis, they never will grow and rise. Therefore superior people follow
virtue and accumulate the small to lofty greatness.

Accumulation is gradual elevation, the small is the way to the great.
According with the time and according with reason is called following virtue. If one can follow such virtue carefully and conscientiously, doing
even a little good and getting rid of even slight faults, getting stronger with
persistence, working consistently, steadily accumulating effort, from the
small one will eventually reach lofty greatness.

This is like trees growing on the earth; first they are in the earth, then
they gradually emerge, gradually grow and branch out, and eventually become tall and stout, capable of serving as timbers. Tall stout timbers cannot
be produced in a day and a night. If students will not work steadily, imagining they have attained the Tao as soon as they make a little bit of progress, wanting to enter the inner sanctum before they have even gone
through the door, in this frame of mind they do not follow virtue but follow greed.

To reach a state of lofty greatness, the hexagram image indicates that
gradual progress and harmonious action develop together; herein lies
what is known as profound attainment of self-realization.

47. *Exhaustion*

> lake above,
> water below

**A lake with no water is exhausted. Therefore superior
people use life to the full and achieve their aim.**

Exhaustion means coming to an end. Above is *lake* , below is *water*
; this is the lake leaking, the water flowing away, so that there is no
water in the lake. This is the image of *exhaustion*.

What superior people see in this is that just as a lake without water is
empty, when people lack purpose their path is at an end. Therefore they
use life to the full to achieve their aim.

There is a life that consists of a quantity of energy, and there is a life
that consists of meaning of the Tao. The life that is a quantity of energy is
created by the universe, and is conditioned; the life of meaning of the Tao
creates the universe, and is primordial.

The primordial life is fundamentally something celestial, associated
with *heaven* ☰; because of mixture with acquired conditioning, it enters the realm of *earth* ☷ and changes into *water* ☵: this is the one
yang in the center of *water* ☵. Once this celestial yang falls, the jewel of
life is hidden, and the whole body is completely mundane. There is no
exhaustion more exhausting than this.

Using life to the full means to get to the end of conditioned life;
achieving one's aim means to achieve the primordial life. Establishing this
aim to use life to the full, using life to the full to achieve this aim, while the
amount of energy depends on something else, creating life depends on
oneself. Using the temporal to restore the primordial, ending false life and
establishing real life, producing being in the midst of nothingness, seeking
life within death, getting through an exhausting impasse, is like a lake
without water again being filled with water.

48. *The Well*

> water above,
> wind below

**There is water above wood, a well. Thus do superior
people comfort the people and urge reciprocity.**

The well has the meaning of nourishing people. Above is *water* ☵, below is *wind* ☴, associated with wood; there is water above wood. When

water rises above wood, the wood is moistened and becomes pliable, being nurtured by the water. This is the image of *the well*.

What superior people see in this is that the people must be nourished, and when they are nourished they must be educated. Therefore they teach them to work so as to have plenty of food and warm clothing, so as to nourish their bodies, and teach them to know courtesy and understand duty, to get along in harmony and help each other, so as to nourish their minds.

When body and mind are both nourished, people return to pristine simplicity and purity, forget their travail, become unified, and enter the realm of unconscious obedience to the laws of God.

The human body is the country, the human spirit is the people. To order the spirit and carry out the Tao day and night is to comfort the people; to take to good, correct faults, get rid of falsehood and keep truth, combine vitality, energy, and spirit, and join the earthly to the celestial— this is urging reciprocity. This kind of comfort is that whereby one forgets falsehood; this kind of urging is that whereby one cultivates reality. When falsehood leaves and reality remains, the path of nourishment is consummated.

49. *Change*

lake above,
fire below

There is fire in a lake, changing. Thus do superior people make a calendar and clarify the seasons.

Change is transformation. Above is *lake* ☱, below is *fire* ☲; there is fire in a lake. A lake is wet, fire is hot. If there is too much moisture, fire will dry it up; if there is too much heat, moisture will dampen it down. When moisture and fire are in the same place, the wetness and heat balance each other. This is the image of *change*.

What superior people see in this is that as people establish their careers in the world, when they cannot achieve proper adjustment based on actualities and cannot adapt to the times, it is because they do not understand the principle of change of the celestial Tao and the seasons of advance and withdrawal of yin and yang. Therefore superior people divide the various seasons of spring, summer, autumn, and winter, with their twenty-four energies and seventy-two periods, and thus make a calendar to show that the operation of the energies of the five elements each has its own time, to enable people to obey heaven and accord with the time, changing any element that is excessive so that it returns to correct balance.

Heaven has its times of operation, people have times when they should act; as the time changes, the way changes, so the way of change is the way of going along with the time. When one acts appropriately in concert with the time, action and inaction, preservation and elimination, will not lose their proper balance. This too is one kind of celestial practice.

50. *The Cauldron*

fire above,
wind below

**There is fire on top of wood; a cauldron. Thus do
superior people stabilize life in the proper position.**

The cauldron stands for the process of refinement by fire. Above is *fire*
☲, below is *wind* ☴, associated with wood; there is fire on top of
wood. Fire and wood in one place refining things by heating is the image
of *the cauldron.*

What superior people see in this is that just as a cauldron is a means
of cooking things but cannot accomplish this without the action of wood
and fire, in the same way that Tao is the means of bearing life, but stabilization of life cannot be accomplished without the work of entry and understanding. Therefore they gradually cultivate practice on the basis of the
proper standpoint to stabilize their life.

"Proper" means not being partial or biased, not being hypocritical or
dishonest; the "position" or "standpoint" is the opening of the mysterious
pass, the door of the earthly and the celestial. "Stabilization" means concentration without fragmentation. "Life" means the primordial generative energy.

If one can make one's standpoint correct, so that one's position is
proper, one enters the Tao gradually and practices it with understanding;
benevolence, justice, courtesy, and knowledge root in the mind, vitality,
spirit, the earthly soul, and the celestial soul combine, the elements of vitality, energy, spirit, essence, and intent integrate—energy becomes replete, the spirit becomes complete, and life is stabilized.

The path of stabilizing life lies entirely in work in the right place. To
be incapable of the proper position is to be ignorant of the mysterious
pass. To be ignorant of the mysterious pass is to be ignorant of life. Being
ignorant of life leads to attachment to voidness or clinging to form, taking
the false to be real, entering into the byways of auxiliary methods. Then
not only is one unable to stabilize life, one is even prone to injuring life.

Life is the primordial sane energy. Life is what is correct, what is correct is life. The correct standpoint, the proper position, is carefully preserving the sane energy in the mysterious pass, maturing and refining it
with both gentle and intense effort, working by day, cautious by night, not
letting any external energy contaminate the cauldron and furnace. Aiming to correct that which is not correct, aiming to stabilize that which is

unstable, proceeding from effort to finally reach spontaneity, returning from confusion to order, the work of stabilizing life in its proper position is consummated.

51. *Thunder*

thunder above,
thunder below

Traveling thunder reverberates. Thus superior people cautiously practice introspection.

Thunder is movement. Above and below is *thunder* ☳☳; this represents the movement of the sound of thunder, traveling from here to there, from there to here. When the thunder here stops, thunder elsewhere erupts; thunder continuing upon thunder is the image of *thunder.*

What superior people see in this is that errant thoughts arise wildly, another thought arising before one thought is ended, thought after thought continuing, like the movement of traveling thunder, reverberating unceasing. So if people are unable to practice introspection, they will injure nature and reason, abandon the real and enter the false, ultimately destroying their own essential life.

Therefore superior people cautiously practice introspection, striving to cause true mindfulness to grow and errant thought to vanish, not allowing the slightest defect to remain in the heart. This is because good and evil, fortune and calamity, depend on the movement of a single thought, which makes the difference between heaven and hell. One can only sustain good thoughts and get rid of bad thoughts if one is able to be cautious before the movement of thought and introspective after the movement of thought, guarding against dangers, aware of perils, not daring to slack off at any time.

Sustaining good thoughts and getting rid of bad thoughts until all bad thought is gone and all thought is purely good, ultimately wholesome without any ill, then thought may be active all the time without one being hindered by its activity, that activity returning to the state of total integration with the celestial design.

52. *Mountains*

mountain above,
mountain below

**Joining mountains. Thus do superior people think
without leaving their place.**

Mountains symbolize stability. With *mountain* ☶ above and below, one
mountain joins another, and so on, so that a thousand mountains, ten
thousand mountains, present a single image of stability.

What superior people see in this is that the inherent goodness in
people is the "place" wherein people are human, where they should remain all their lives and never leave for a moment; therefore they emulate
the image of joining mountains, and think without leaving their place.

In both social and spiritual life, investigating truth and distinguishing
right from wrong, people cannot dispense with thought; but if the thought
is right, then they are in their place, while if the thought is wrong they are
out of place. It is important that all thoughts stop in their proper place,
and do not lose their original reality.

If practitioners of the Tao are able to think in their place, the mind of
Tao is ever-present and the human mentality is forever quiescent; no external objects can influence them, so there is no harm to thought.

Do-nothing quietists may say they forget about things and forget
about their own bodies, not thinking at all; but this has nothing to do with
the Tao of nature and life of body and mind, and is also one form of being
out of place.

Being in place means being immutable, stabilized in the right way.
Thought that is properly stabilized encompasses all reason and responds to
all things. Though one thing all day, never being out of place, it is as
though there were no thought. Indeed, when you know the One, all tasks
are done; if you do not know the One, then thought is out of place. How
many students in the world know the One?

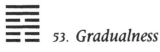

53. *Gradualness*

wood above,
mountain below

**There are trees on the mountain, growing gradually.
Thus do superior people abide in sagacity and improve
customs.**

Gradualness means going slowly. Above is *wood* ☴, below is *mountain*
☶; there are trees on the mountain. Trees on a mountain will grow

great and tall; but great and tall trees do not reach their full growth in a day and a night. This is the image of *gradualness*.

What superior people see in this is that virtue is the root of human beings, goodness is the most precious treasure of human beings; if they cannot maintain their virtue, they are not sagacious, and if they cannot transform their temperament, their goodness will not be great. Therefore they emulate the stability of a mountain in abiding immutably in sagacity, and emulate the gradual growth of trees, not rushing or lagging, gradually sublimating the force of customary mundanity so as to return to ultimate goodness.

Sagacity is the fundamental nature of ultimate goodness; custom is the mundane force of accumulated influences. Custom here does not mean only people's customs in the usual sense, but includes all mundane feelings and desires, including greed, anger, and folly. When one abides in sagacity and applies it to daily affairs, one is sagacious in everything and virtuous in every situation. Abiding in sagacity, the person becomes one with the virtue of sagacity, and so rests immutable and unwavering in ultimate good. When the character is good, all the accumulated influences of mundane feelings gradually disappear, turning into true sense, without hypocrisy or deceit, so that customs return to goodness.

Once the real is restored, the false evaporates of itself. The real is thus within the false, and the false is not outside the real. With sagacity, customs must improve, as a matter of course. The reason gradualness is applied in both abiding in virtue and improving customs is that since the human mentality has been in charge of affairs for so long, the mind of Tao is not apparent; even though one abide in virtue, one cannot immediately do so securely, and even though one improve customs, one cannot immediately do so completely.

When abiding in virtue is insecure, this is not called sagacity; when improvement of customs is incomplete, this is not called customary goodness. Abiding in the virtue of sagacity must reach the point where one is sagacious in all respects; only then is the abiding secure. Improvement of customs must reach the point where all customs are good; only then is improvement complete.

When one's character is sagacious and one's customs are good, the primal is complete and the secondary sublimates; there is only goodness, nothing else. Returning to pristine purity, steady as a mountain, upstanding as a tree, the business of doing is completed and the business of nondoing comes to the fore. From now on one practices in a different mode, using the natural fire of reality to incubate the spiritual embryo, whereby it is possible to enter the realm of unfathomability of spiritual transformation.

54. *Making a Young Girl Marry*

thunder above,
lake below

There is thunder above a lake, making a young girl marry. Thus superior people persist to the end and know what is wrong.

Making a young girl marry means that intercourse is not proper. Above is *thunder* ☳, below is *lake* ☱; there is thunder above a lake. Thunder stands for agitation, movement; lake stands for calm, stillness: Thunder agitating a lake, movement disturbing the stillness, the water of the lake overflows, the intercourse of yin and yang is not proper. This is the image of *making a young girl marry.*

What superior people see in this is that there are true and false yin and yang, there is right and wrong practice; the intercourse of true yin and yang comes about naturally, and thus can endure, while the intercourse of false yin and yang comes about through forced effort, and hence ultimately cannot last long. Therefore superior people want to persist to the end, yet first should know what is wrong.

Persisting to the end means to persist to the end of eternity. To know what is wrong means to know the degeneracy of what is incorrect. The Tradition of Connected Sayings of the I Ching says, "By finding out truth and fulfilling one's nature, one arrives at the meaning of life." The Tao of nature and life is all a matter of determining right and wrong by finding out truth. Finding out truth means finding out the principle of communion of yin and yang.

The dividing line between the primordial and the conditioned is but a hairbreadth; on one side is the primordial, on the other side is the conditioned. Conditioned yin and yang always interact, but their intercourse is not correct; it has no conclusion, and goes wrong. For example, there are ignorant people in the world who join the energies of heart and genitals, or join the active and passive energy channels up and down the back and front of the body, or cause energy to rise up the spine at midnight and descend down the front of the body at noon, or gather energy from sexual intercourse, or heat lead and mercury together, or regulate their exhalations and inhalations—all of these are recognizing the artificial as real, and trying to force communion; imagining that they will thereby live long, instead they are hastening death. This is quite wrong, a serious degeneration. If practitioners of the Tao want to persist to the end, they should first know what is wrong; if they know what is wrong, they will not be deluded by the depraved words of false teachings. Then if they seek to persist to the end, there is hope they will be closer.

55. *Abundance*

thunder above,
fire below

**Thunder and lightning both arrive, abundant.
Thus do superior people pass judgment and execute
punishment.**

Abundance is fullness and vigor. Above is *thunder* ☲☲, below is fire
☲☲; this is the arrival of both thunder and lightning. Thunder shakes,
lightning illumines; thunder and lightning complement each other, power
and intelligence act together. This is the image of *abundance*.

What superior people see in this is that when people in the world
accept the false and abandon the real, take misery for pleasure, crave possessions and sensual stimulation, ruin their character and conduct, mis-
behave in a hundred ways, and enter a state of benightedness, they are like
criminals in prison awaiting the time when they will be executed. Looking
into the source of this, it is because of not knowing how to distinguish the
real from the false. Therefore superior people emulate the shining illumination of lightning, thoroughly investigating the recondite principles of
nature and life, distinguishing right and wrong, like passing judgment
in court.

Once they have discerned the real within the false, they also distinguish the false within the real; with genuine knowledge and certain insight, they do not mistake the seeming for the true. Emulating the power
of thunder, they extirpate implanted aberrating influences and clean up
their spirits, like executing punishment of criminals. Liberating the innocent, executing the guilty, acting decisively and directly, they do not grant
respite to insidious ills.

Passing judgment means applying flexibility to minute discernment,
effecting knowledge. Execution means applying firmness to decisive power,
acting with strength. The sages' science of nature and life of body and
mind is twofold, involving knowledge and action. If one knows but does
not act, one cannot attain the Tao; if one acts without knowledge, one
mistakes nature and life. Knowing and then acting, completing knowledge with practice, proving understanding in action, some day one will
master oneself and return to what is right, and all the world will revert to
goodness. If students are able to judge truth and act effectively, there is no
doubt that they will reach the state of abundance of qualities of the Tao,
where wealth is daily renewed.

56. *Transience*

fire above,
mountain below

There is fire atop a mountain, transient. Thus superior people apply punishment with understanding and prudence, and do not keep people imprisoned.

Transience means passing on, not remaining. Above is *fire* ☲, below is *mountain* ☶; there is fire atop a mountain. Fire atop a mountain does not burn for long; it passes through once and is over. This is the image of *transience.*

What superior people see in this is that the penal system relates to human nature and life; if judgment is passed without understanding, the falsely accused cannot receive justice, and if punishment is inappropriately applied, the innocent are harmed. Therefore superior people emulate the illumination of fire to clearly discern what is unjust and what is just, to affirm what is right and repudiate what is wrong. For those who have done wrong, this means to accept punishment with good grace. Superior people also emulate the caring warmth of mountains, being careful and prudent about punishment, making it light where possible, reducing it where possible. For those in charge of applying the law, this means not being arbitrary in punishment. With understanding and prudence, matters are settled as they are dealt with, and people are not kept imprisoned with suspicion and doubt and treated cruelly.

In practice of the Tao, the use of understanding is to break through delusion; being prudent and not overusing that understanding is the way to nurture reality. Through understanding and prudence, falsehood is done away with and truth is kept; then one can stop striving and take to nonstriving. This is like applying punishment with understanding and prudence and not keeping people imprisoned. If you do not know to stop at sufficiency, but keep on fussing, you will again call on delusion where there is no delusion, and produce mental illness. How then can you attain the state where one comprehension applies to everything?

In the image of the hexagram, there is fire on a mountain. The mountain is the substance, the fire is the function: Understanding what should be understood, stopping when one should stop, clarity is not separated from stillness; one clarifies the quality of illumination, and rests in the highest good.

57. *Wind*

> wind above,
> wind below

**Wind following wind. Thus do superior people
articulate directions and carry out tasks.**

Wind symbolizes gradually entering. Above and below is *wind* ☴; one wind arises first, another wind follows after. Wind following wind is the image of harmonious progress.

What superior people see in this is that since practitioners of the Tao live with people, they cannot but have tasks, and since they have tasks they must carry them out. Generally speaking, to carry out tasks calls for serenity, without rush. If one carries out tasks hurriedly and without first articulating directions for those who share in the tasks to clarify why they are thus and so, then people will not follow along, and the tasks will not be fulfilled. Therefore superior people first articulate directions and then carry out tasks.

Articulation means clarification; directions are instructions. Tasks are whatever people should do, things like cultivating character, accomplishing works, accumulating achievements and deeds, taking burdens upon oneself for the benefit of others. Directions are not only the orders of the rulers to the ruled; the instructions given by the honorable and experienced people who exercise leadership in affairs to less developed people are all called directions. If directions are articulated before tasks are carried out, then the people will know those tasks are to be done; one person takes the lead, and many people follow behind, so that all tasks are successfully carried out. This is like wind following wind, the two winds continuous, going together without mutual interference. This is the way superior people do good with others.

58. *Joy*

> lake above,
> lake below

**Joined lakes are joyful. Thus do superior people
explain and practice with companions.**

Joy means the joy of harmony. Above and below is *lake* ☱; this is two lakes joined together, providing each other with water. This is the image of *joy.*

What superior people see in this is that the Tao of nature and life is most profound, and the slightest slip causes a tremendous loss, so they expound and practice it with companions.

Companions are people of like mind on the same path. Principles are not clear without explanation, explanation is not thorough without practice. Companions explain to each other, and practice what is explained by each other, discussing back and forth, pursuing their investigation into the Tao in the process of this interaction, entering deeply into it and advancing far on it, finally reaching attainment.

The reason for this is that the knowledge of one person is limited, whereas the views of many people are endless. When there is something one does not know oneself, one needs companions to explain and clarify it. By this mutual explanation and practice, those who do not know will come to know, and those without mastery will gain it. Inwardly understanding and outwardly acting in accord with that understanding, there is no doubt that one will reach the stage of profound attainment of self-realization.

59. *Disintegration*

wind above,
water below

**Wind blows above water, unintegrated. Thus ancient
kings honored god and set up shrines.**

Disintegration means scattering in confusion. Above is *wind* ☴, below is *water* ☵; this is wind blowing above water. The nature of wind is to penetrate, but it cannot get into water; the nature of water is to flow downward, and it does not take in the wind. One another not joining is the image of *disintegration*. However, even though wind cannot enter water, it can go along with water as it blows; and even though water cannot take in wind, it can rise up along with the blowing of the wind. So there is also the image of resolving disintegration here.

What ancient kings saw in this was that people receive their nature and life from heaven, and receive their bodies from their parents; though there may be differences in social status and differences in goodness and evil, in sanity and aberration, nevertheless the source of everyone's endowments is the same. Therefore the ancient kings honored God and respected heaven, and set up shrines to pay respect to their ancestors, so as to cause everyone to know to honor God and respect their ancestors, not forgetting their roots.

When the roots are not forgotten, the basis is established and the path develops; correcting faults and pursuing goodness, manners and morals change, so that what had disintegrated can be reunited. Great indeed was the ancient kings' way of resolving disintegration.

If practitioners of the Tao can realize the intention of the ancient kings in resolving disintegration, respect heaven and not oppose it, requite their origins and not forget them, seek life within death, seek blessing within injury, then the four forms can be combined and the five elements can be assembled; this then is the original self, without any disintegration.

60. *Regulation*

water above,
lake below

**There is water over a lake, regulated. Thus superior
people determine measures and discuss virtuous
actions.**

Regulation means having limits. Above is *water* ☵, below is *lake* ☱; there is water over a lake. There is a limit to which a lake can hold water; if there is too much water, the lake overflows. This is the image of *regulation.*

What superior people see in this is that establishment of virtue is the basis of everything that people should do or not do, and they should not act arbitrarily. This is called regulation. However, there is a way of changing adaptively according to the situation; if one holds to one regulation to the end, one's practice will not be successful, but will instead damage one's character. Therefore regulations must be distinguished, so superior people determine measures to discuss virtuous actions.

The three hundred sixty-five days of a year is one of four ways of measurement; the yearly cycle is also divided into four seasons, eight divisions, and seventy-two periods, each with its boundaries. These are "measures." People are born with certain measures of earthly and celestial energies of the five elements, so they have the virtues of the five elements; when they act without losing those virtues, that is virtuous action.

Superior people determine the measures of waxing and waning of the earthly and celestial five elements and discuss the virtuous actions of benevolence, justice, courtesy, knowledge, and truthfulness; this is to cause people to be benevolent when it is appropriate to be benevolent, to be just when it is appropriate to be just, to be courteous when it is appropriate to be courteous, to be knowing when it is appropriate to be knowing, and to be truthful when it is appropriate to be truthful. They also discuss how the five virtues are one energy, how the earthly and the celestial work together, without bias or partiality.

This is because they want people to embody the virtues of heaven and earth as their own qualities and the processes of the four seasons as their own conduct. The science of nature and life is a process of work that is entirely a matter of the measure of evolution; if you conform to the appropriate measure, you can cultivate celestial qualities—this is virtuous action. If you lose the proper measure, you turn away from celestial qualities—this is the demise of virtue. Actions that destroy virtue are actions without regulation, taking the false to be real, taking what is wrong to be right. Even if you can hold fast to one regulation, this still is sticking to voidness or clinging to form, and ultimately is of no benefit to nature and life. The intention of superior people in determining this and discussing this so as to enlighten people and fulfill their work was profound indeed.

61. *Truthfulness Within*

wind above,
lake below

There is wind above a lake, with truthfulness between them. Thus superior people consider judgments and postpone execution.

Truthfulness within means there is sincerity in the center. Above is *wind* ☴, below is *lake* ☱; there is wind above a lake. The form of a lake is facing upward, the nature of wind is penetrating; wind blows on the lake, the lake receives the wind, as though there is feeling between them. This is the image of *truthfulness within.*

What superior people see in this is that adjudication of criminal cases concerns people's nature and life, and if there is any carelessness the innocent are harmed; therefore after a conviction is established, they do not immediately carry out the sentence—even if the crime is unpardonable, they still postpone execution and reconsider the case, seeking a way of life in the midst of death.

Practitioners of the Tao search out the recondite and find out the hidden, fish out the profound and reach the remote, so as to thoroughly investigate the abstruse and subtle truth; this requires genuine knowledge and clear vision, without the slightest trace of confusion in the mind. In this sense it is like adjudication of criminal cases. When one understands truth in the mind and puts it into actual practice, the mind dies and the spirit comes to life; gradually cultivating this without seeking immediate results is like postponing execution.

Consideration is whereby life is sought in the midst of death, freeing the innocent and condemning the guilty, enlivening what should be alive and killing what should be dead. If consideration is not thoroughgoing, one has no independent perception, and one does not have too much self-confidence, how could it be appropriate to "kill" rashly? Postponement means reconsideration of whether or not "death" is appropriate.

Inasmuch as the way of life is perforce difficult, the way of death is not easy either. If one does not postpone death but rather hastens death, hoping for quick accomplishment, one may become a nihilistic quietist. So it is a matter of "death" after consideration, and then reconsideration at the time of death whether it is right or wrong, true or false. Only when this is perfectly clear in one's mind will one avoid the mistake of taking the spurious for the genuine.

In the image of the hexagram, above is *wind*, representing gradual advance, while below is *lake*, representing harmonious and joyful action. Gradualism means one can avoid haste, harmony means one can be considerate. With consideration and relaxation, truthfulness within being put into practice outwardly, an all-out effort will dissolve away all the pollution of conditioning and expose the primordial original being, so that one will surely reach the realm of eternal life.

62. *Excessive Smallness*

thunder above,
mountain below

There is thunder over a mountain, excessively small. Thus superior people are excessively deferential in conduct, excessively sad in mourning, excessively frugal in consumption.

Excessive smallness means excess in being small. Above is *thunder* ☳, below is *mountain* ☶; there is thunder over a mountain. When thunder is up in the sky, its sound reaches afar, but when thunder is over a mountain, its sound is muffled. This is the image of *excessive smallness*.

What superior people see in this is that practitioners of the Tao should minimize themselves in their daily activities, and not become too grand. This is because it is permissible to go to excess in being small, but not in being grand. Therefore superior people are excessively deferential in conduct, excessively sad in mourning, and excessively frugal in consumption.

It is not right to be too deferential in conduct, but when one is deferential one does not look down on people or become arrogant, so there is no harm in being excessively deferential. It is not right to be too sad in mourning, but when one is sad there is grief in the heart and one esteems nature and life, so there is no harm in being excessively sad. It is not right to be too frugal in consumption, but when one is frugal one does not waste natural resources and is content with what one has, so there is no harm in being excessively frugal.

These three things are all examples of excessive smallness, excessive without being too extreme. This is how it is with such small matters; when it comes to the great matter of nature and life, one must know the appropriate moments to advance and withdraw, to sustain and negate, one must know the principles of filling and emptying, effacing and fostering— since even the slightest miss can result in an enormous loss, no excess is permissible.

In the image of the hexagram, there is thunder over a mountain. The mountain is still, the thunder is in movement. Action is carried forth by means of stillness, action is based on stillness. Obviously the small may be excessive but the great may not be excessive.

63. *Settled*

water above,
fire below

**Water is above fire, settled. Thus superior people
consider problems and prevent them.**

Settled means a matter is already settled. Above is *water* ☵, below is *fire* ☲; the water is above fire. Water is cold, fire is hot: When water is heated by fire, its coldness vanishes, and when fire is controlled by water its heat stops; water and fire in the same place is the image of being *settled*.

What superior people see in this is that practitioners of the Tao invert the earthly and the celestial, taking the celestial element wrapped up in the earthly (represented by the yang in the center of *water* ☵) and fill in the earthly element mixed in with the celestial (represented by the yin in the center of the *fire* ☲); the earthly vitality transforms and the true vitality is born, the conditioned spirit dies out and the original spirit remains. Using the vitality to nurture the spirit, using the spirit to concentrate the vitality, the vitality and spirit cling to each other and congeal inseparably; returning to the original, going back to the fundamental, that which was unsettled is now settled.

But returning to the original and going back to the fundamental just completes the preliminary stage of work; if one does not use the natural "fire" of reality to forge this attainment into reality, when settlement culminates it will become unsettled again, and the work that has been done hitherto will all go to waste. Therefore superior people consider problems and prevent them beforehand.

"Problems" means the problems of the earthly and the celestial not being settled. At the moment of settlement, the true earthly and the true celestial are united, invulnerable to external influences. However, even though invulnerable to external influences, the acquired energy of conditioning in the person has still not disappeared, so if one does not know how to purify oneself and gently nurture the spiritual essence, thereby to prevent acquired energies from acting up in moments of carelessness, there will surely be problems later on.

Considering the existence of problems and preventing them beforehand, applying the work of increasing spiritual awareness while decreasing mundane conditioning, rooting out the accretions that have accumulated in the mental faculties through personal history, mundanity will end and the celestial will become pure and incorruptible; finally when you break through space, that is comprehensive attainment. Until you reach the stage of breaking through space, there will still be problems. Therefore practitioners of the Tao must consider that the state of great repose comes only upon breaking through space and freeing the real body.

64. *Not Yet Settled*

fire above,
water below

Fire is above water, not yet settled. Thus superior people carefully discern things and keep them in their places.

Not yet settled means something has not yet reached settlement. Above is *fire* ☲, below is *water* ☵; the fire is above water. When fire is above water, the fire cannot heat the water and the water cannot control the fire; water and fire in separate places is the image of being *not yet settled*.

What superior people see in this is that once people get mixed up in temporal conditioning, the real is obscured and the artificial comes forth, body and mind are unstable, vitality and spirit are clouded, volatility erupts and greed arises; taking misery for pleasure, they go to any lengths, and become extremely unsettled.

Nevertheless, sages have a way of restoring the primordial within the temporal; it is just that people have never thought of this settlement. If they wanted this settlement, they would be capable of settlement. Therefore superior people carefully discern things and keep them in their places.

"Things" here means the primordial and the temporal, the real and false earthly and celestial; "place" means where these things abide. Carefully discerning whether things are real or false, it is necessary to be perfectly clear in mind, with genuine knowledge and perception, free from any doubt or confusion whatsoever. This is the work of investigating things to produce knowledge. In respect to the reality or falsehood of things, keeping them in their places, so that the real is recognized as real and the false is recognized as false and the two are not mixed up, is the science of rectifying the mind and making the intent sincere.

When one discerns things and understands truth, and also keeps things in their place and does not act recklessly, the mundane and the celestial are not mixed up, the real and the false are distinguished; then there is settlement in the midst of the unsettled. This is like water conveying moisture and fire conveying heat, each accomplishing what it can accomplish, each on a separate path.

The primordial is that whereby the real body is made, the temporal is that whereby the phantasmic body is made. Before the primordial and temporal are settled, the mundane and the celestial are mixed up, the real and the false are confused. If one can distinguish the real from the false, one will know the places of the primordial and the temporal. The temporal has its place in the temporal, which is clearly obvious; one should not mistake something temporal for something primordial and forcibly seek settlement.

The words "carefully discern" have a most profound meaning. Discernment requires investigation and penetration of every subtlety, without any carelessness allowed. This is particularly so because the primordial and the temporal are so close that it is easy to mistake them; only by careful, minute discernment is it possible to recognize truly and know clearly that each has its place. When one knows that each has its place, then one can keep each one in its place. When one can keep each in its place, then the primordial can be preserved and temporal conditioning will not act up. Then the unsettled can be settled; the true earthly and the true celestial conjoin, water and fire commingle, and the spiritual embryo forms. The reasons the sages put the hexagram *not yet settled* at the end was so that when people are not yet settled they will investigate the truth and hasten to seek settlement.

Mixed Hexagrams

 1. Heaven   *2. Earth*

Heaven is firm, earth is flexible.

Heaven is strength; stronger than strong, it is the ultimate of firmness. Of that which is firm, nothing is firmer than heaven. Heaven as the Tao is the unceasing circulation of one energy, above and below, eternally so. Its essence is strong, so it can create all things with ready knowledge. Since humans are endowed with the energy of heaven, they are imbued with this quality of firmness and ready knowledge.

Firmness is sanity; life dwells therein. For practitioners of the Tao, the science of creating life consists of nourishing this firm strong sanity. Nourishing sanity requires ready knowledge like heaven, not being constrained by things; only then does sanity always remain present, so the jewel of life is secure, and one is a companion of heaven.

Earth is receptivity; harmonious and submissive, it is the epitome of flexibility. Nothing is more flexible than earth. Earth as the Tao is ultimate breadth and calm, ultimate lowliness and humility, never changing. Its essence is flexible, so it can give life to all things with simple capacity. Since humans are endowed with the energy of earth, they are imbued with this quality of flexibility and simple capacity.

Flexibility is the true mind; nature dwells therein. For practitioners of the Tao, the science of cultivating nature consists of cultivating this flexible, receptive true mind. Cultivation of the true mind requires simple capacity like earth, able to bear anything; only then is the ground of mind clear and calm, so the true nature is not obscured, and one is a companion of earth.

What in heaven is ready knowledge is in humans innate knowledge. What in earth is simple capacity is in humans innate capacity. If one can be firm, innate knowledge is ready at hand, and not obtained by thought. If one can be flexible, innate capacity is simple, and not reached by effort. When innate knowledge and innate capacity, firm and flexible, join together, the qualities of strength and receptivity are complete, and the work of nature and life is done. This is why people of old called spiritual alchemy the most simple and most ready of paths.

8. Accord   **7. The Army**

Accord is pleasant, the army is miserable.

Accord is close association, associating the earthly with the celestial. When the earthly does not bring about the downfall of the celestial, but obeys the celestial, preventing danger by this obedience, this is the way to bring about happiness. Those who cannot have happiness cannot have it because they throw down the real and obey the false. If one can obey the real and thus sublimate the false, the false too will return to reality; how can this not be pleasant?

The army is the militant path, stopping aberration by means of rectitude. When the celestial leads the earthly, the celestial is not overcome by the earthly but rather controls the earthly. Practicing obedience in danger is the way to prepare against misery. The reason people have misery is that they are able to handle favorable situations but not unfavorable situations. If one can deal with unfavorable situations harmoniously, then even unfavorable situations become acceptable, and there is no misery.

Accord means obeying the celestial with the earthly; by obeying the celestial, one does not bring about the fall of the celestial. The army means practicing obedience in unfavorable situations; through obedience, the celestial does not fall. Falling or not falling depends on whether or not one is obedient to the celestial; so obedience, receptivity to the celestial, brings about happiness and defends against misery, beneficial wherever one goes.

 19. Overseeing   **20. Observing**

The obligation of overseeing and observing is sometimes giving and sometimes seeking.

Overseeing is closely approaching. Within conformity there is joy; the joy lies in harmony. If you want to take it, first you must give it. Giving without giving is "sometimes giving."

Observing is examination. Proceeding gradually in accord with the time, by being gradual the action is harmonious. Following what is desired, you gradually introduce guidance. Seeking without seeking is "sometimes seeking."

Giving must accord with likes, seeking requires harmony. Giving and seeking are both harmony, the only difference being between inner harmony and outer harmony. By outer harmony one can approach people and win their approval, using the artificial to cultivate the real. By inner harmony one can watch oneself and enhance one's spiritual character, using the real to transmute the artificial.

Through approaching people considerately one gives, through observing oneself watchfully one seeks. When others are joyful, one is joyful oneself. First giving, after that one seeks. This is why harmonization is valuable.

 ## 3. *Difficulty*

 ## 4. *Darkness*

In difficulty, see without losing bearings; in darkness is adulteration and attachment.

Difficulty is having trouble making progress. When the celestial becomes active in the midst of peril, when the mind of Tao becomes manifest, one has inner autonomy, does not act dangerously but rather prevents danger, and even though active does not lose one's bearings. When the celestial first becomes active on the earthly plane, when celestial energy is first restored, earthly energy is strong, and one should not act at random; not losing one's bearings, one should await the right time to get out of danger.

Darkness is obscurity, lack of clarity. When the celestial is fallen into the earthly, when the human mentality has already arisen, right and wrong are mixed up, and the human mind does not obey the celestial but rather overrules it. Therefore it is adulterated and ignorantly becomes attached to externals. However, even though the celestial energy has fallen into the earthly plane, still the celestial energy has not yet disappeared; when mundanity becomes manifest, one should stop danger according to the time.

When the celestial becomes active in the midst of peril, one awaits the time to foster the celestial. When the mundane traps the celestial, one accords with the time to repel the mundane. Each has its own time. Whether activating or stilling, if one does not miss the right timing, one can actively get out of danger and neutralize danger by stillness; then the celestial energy will not be damaged by the force of mundanity.

 ## 51. *Thunder*

 ## 52. *Mountain*

Thunder is arising, mountain is still.

Thunder represents the celestial coming to the fore from beneath the earthly, celestial energy arising with time. This is symbolized by thunder. When the sound of thunder arises, it booms irrepressibly. The *thunder* hexagram is made of two *thunder* trigrams; there is thunder outside thunder, one thunder reaching another thunder, a thousand thunders, ten thousand thunders, all in one thunder. When practitioners of the Tao activate the energy of will and go directly forward, arriving at the remote by way of the near at hand, this should be like the movement of thunder; only then can they rise up with firmness, and not be subject to compulsion by human desires.

Mountain represents the celestial resting on top of the earthly, celestial energy becoming still with time. This is symbolized by a mountain. The stillness of a mountain is quiet and steady, forever immovable. The *mountain* hexagram is made of two *mountain* trigrams; there is a mountain outside a mountain, one mountain linking with another mountain, a thousand mountains, ten thousand mountains, all one stillness. When practitioners of the Tao concentrate and store their spirit and energy, unstirring and unwavering, reaching without from within, this should be like the stillness of a mountain; only then can they be firm in stillness, and not be moved by the conditions of the environment.

Using firmness, one rises up like thunder and acts with efficacy and decisiveness. Nurturing firmness, one is still as a mountain and calmly concentrates with tranquil stability. If one can act or be still in accord with the time, one can use firmness wherever one goes, and nothing can damage that firmness.

 ## 41. Reduction   ## 42. Increase

Reduction and increase are the beginnings of strength and debility.

Reduction is lessening. Delighting in stillness and stilling delight, stopping delight that is not right, stopping in the proper place—this is reduction of excessive yielding.

Increase is augmentation. Harmony of action making action harmonious, fostering action of which one is incapable so as to gradually become capable of the action—this is increase where firmness is insufficient.

By reducing excessive yielding, one can be flexible without the tendency to yield becoming too strong. By increasing firmness where it is insufficient, one can be firm without debility. But reduction and increase are aimed at restoring proper balance of firmness and flexibility; if reduction and increase go too far, that which is excessive is reduced to the point of debility, while that which is insufficient is increased to the point of becoming too strong. So reduction and increase are the beginnings of strength and debility.

Therefore practitioners of the Tao should consider proper balance of firmness and flexibility to be the goal to aim for when they apply effort to increase or reduce. When firmness and flexibility are in proper balance, there is flexibility within firmness and firmness within flexibility; firmness and flexibility are one energy, the earthly and the celestial combine harmoniously, and the golden elixir of spiritual immortality crystallizes.

26. *Great Accumulation*

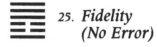 25. *Fidelity* (No Error)

Great accumulation is timely, fidelity is disastrous.

Great accumulation means development in great measure. Strong in stilling, stilling one's strength, not using strength arbitrarily but rather in accord with the time, being strong when strength is appropriate, being still when stillness is appropriate, resting in the highest good and not wavering—this is great accumulation, having great development, and being able to accord with the time.

Fidelity is boldness in affairs. Strength of action being adamant in action, action is too aggressive; arbitrary strength is strong when it is not appropriate to be strong, acts when it is not appropriate to act, acting obsessively, without flexibility, bringing on disaster through fidelity.

Those whose strength is within are strict in governing themselves, outwardly appearing deficient while inwardly having more than enough. The more they accumulate development, the greater they become. Filled with immense energy, they nurture it to repletion and exercise it efficiently. Having no error within, they naturally have no error without.

Those whose strength is external are rash in dealing with others, outwardly having more than enough while inwardly being deficient. They err in action, disrupt harmony and lose balance, get involved with the false and damage the real. As their development is not great, their activity is not effective.

So only those with great accumulation of development can be free from error; those who wish to be free from error must first accumulate great development. If one's development is not great but one wishes to put it into practice without error, even with fidelity one actually is in error; this is the disaster.

Practitioners of the Tao should carefully develop immense energy, and combine duty with right direction, so that they may attain to perfect truthfulness without error.

 45. *Gathering*

 46. *Rising*

Gathering masses and rising does not allow coming.

Gathering is massing. Inwardly docile while outwardly joyful, by docility human desires sublimate, by joyfulness irritability vanishes. When human desires sublimate, the true yin is manifest; when irritability vanishes, the true yang comes back. When the earthly and the celestial combine, sane energy solidly masses and the gold elixir forms.

Rising is ascending. Inwardly obedient and outwardly harmonious, being obedient, one gradually advances in the Tao, being harmonious, one is respectfully careful in action. Gradually advancing without going to excess in firmness, being respectfully careful without going to excess in yielding, firmness and flexibility balance each other, external influences do not come, and the gold elixir can be preserved.

However, if you want the sane energy to mass solidly, you must harmonize with its joy, first gaining the good will of the other. If the other is not joyful, one cannot obtain the true reality of the other. Harmonizing with its joy is simply a matter of appropriating living energy within the death-dealing mechanism.

If you want external influences not to come, you must be obedient and harmonious, first overcoming your own self-importance. If the self is not overcome, one cannot remove the past conditioning of the self. Being obedient and harmonious is simply a matter of reversing the usual course of conditioning.

By appropriating living energy, one can gather; by reversing the course of conditioning, one can rise. When one is able to gather and to rise, the real gathers and the false does not come. When gathering reaches the point of the unification of the five elements, one rises to the ultimate good without evil, where being and nonbeing are one, and nature and life are both comprehended.

 ## 15. Modesty   ## 16. Delight

Modesty can lead to depreciation, delight to laziness.

Modesty is making naught of what one has; still within, conforming without, one does not use strength at all. However, when stilling strength and yielding, it is easy to become overly modest, making light of oneself without knowing how to esteem oneself. This results in damage to one's strength. So it is very important to know when to stop being submissive and conformist; stopping at the appropriate point, one is outwardly modest, yet does not despise oneself inwardly.

Delight is taking pleasure in what one has; submitting inside and acting outside, one submits to and acts on one's strength. However, when one submits receptively and acts dynamically, it is easy to indulge in delight too much, becoming lazy and not knowing how to prevent it. This results in damage to one's flexibility. So it is very important to apply obedience in action, according with and keeping to what is right, delighting outwardly without becoming lazy inwardly.

Modesty without self-depreciation is true modesty; delight without laziness is true delight. Not depreciating, not becoming lazy, by modesty one brings about delight, in delight one can be modest. Then in action and stillness one can be in harmony wherever one may go.

21. Biting Through   *22. Adornment*

Biting through is eating, adornment is without color.

Biting through means that when eating something the mouth must close. The hexagram consists of the trigrams for fire and thunder, representing illumination and action. Action requires understanding to prevent any activity from violating true reason. This is like the mouth closing and the teeth moving when eating something; the movement must be properly timed.

Adornment is embellishment. The hexagram consists of the trigrams for fire and mountain, representing illumination and stillness. Employing stillness with understanding, one does not allow one's nature to be obscured or confused at any time. This is like adornment without color; simplicity is realized by embellishment.

When action is not done without understanding, action does not go awry; when illumination is always combined with stillness, the illumination is nurtured. Action must be based on understanding; action is understanding. Stillness comes from illumination; stillness is illumination. When action and stillness are both enlightened, one spontaneously clarifies the quality of illumination and rests in the highest good, with enlightenment present everywhere.

 58. Joy   *57. Following*

When joy appears, following submits.

In the trigrams forming the hexagram *joy*, one yin appears above two yangs; creativity is balanced by receptivity, so that one is strong but does not become arrogant. This quality is one of harmony and joyfulness, symbolized by a lake. A lake is open above and closed below, full but not overflowing. In this hexagram there are two *lake* trigrams, representing lakes joining each other, providing much moisture. When practitioners of the Tao have equanimity of mind, in a state of mental harmony, inside and outside are as one; having yet appearing to lack, fulfilled yet appearing empty, not complacent or self-satisfied, they should be like lakes conjoining, their influence soaking into all beings—this finally may be called outward manifestation of harmony.

In the trigrams forming the hexagram *following*, one yin lies beneath two yangs; the celestial is exalted and the earthly is abased, but though yielding one does not become too weak. This quality is one of ability to penetrate, symbolized by wind. The energy of wind is strong, but its action is gentle; gradually arriving without speeding, it penetrates deeply without vehemence. In this hexagram there are two *wind* trigrams, wind following after wind in a continuum, proceeding in an orderly manner. When practitioners of the Tao have stable minds and far-reaching wills, working in an orderly fashion, they penetrate by sincerity and act with flexibility; neither obsessed nor negligent, they should be like the continuum of wind after wind, reaching everywhere—then they will finally be able to arrive at deep attainment of self-realization.

Flexibility appearing outwardly is harmonization of strength; flexibility submitting below is advancement of strength. If one can harmonize strength, then strength will be concealed within flexibility, and one will be strong without it becoming excessive. If one can advance strength, then flexibility seeks that strength, and one can be flexible without becoming ineffective. This is using flexibility without damaging strength.

 17. Following   *18. Degeneration*

Following, there is no fault; upon degeneration, repair is done.

Following means two things going along with each other. When the celestial acts and the earthly rejoices in it, the celestial accords with the earthly and the earthly accords with the celestial. When the earthly and the celestial go along with one another, those who had faults can be without fault.

After the primordial in people is lost to fragmentation, the true nature is obscured and emotional cravings arise at random, so there is fault. Now when one actively seeks harmony, appropriating the living potential within the death-dealing potential, feeling returns to essential nature; this then is the original state, which is without fault.

Degeneration means corruption. When the earthly advances but the celestial halts it, when the earthly damages the celestial but the celestial stops the earthly, the earthly is controlled by the celestial, and that which had degenerated is repaired and so does not degenerate any more.

Once people act through acquired conditioning, external influences enter, and there is a loss of autonomy. This is degeneration. Now when one uses strength to control yielding, restoring the primordial within the temporal, one clarifies what is good and returns to the beginning; this is the natural innocence of basic nature, which is not degenerate.

The faultless applying following is the celestial seeking earthly reception; repairing where there is degeneration is the earthly according with the celestial. The celestial seeks earthly reception, using the earthly as a means to restore the celestial; the earthly accords with the celestial, using the celestial as a means to sublimate the earthly. The consummation of the path of following and repairing degeneration is in the restoration of the celestial and the sublimation of the earthly.

23. Stripping Away   *24. Return*

Stripping away is decay, return is restoration.

Stripping away is dissolving away; five yins have stripped away the yang down to one last yang. This is like when people submit to conditioned mundanity, so that it has stripped the celestial almost completely away; this momentum will inevitably lead to continued stripping, causing the body to decay.

Return is restoration; one yang returns below five yins. This is like when people restore the primordial celestial, so that the living potential again appears; gradually they can restore the celestial to purity, and cause the original state to reappear.

So stripping away is the forerunner of return; restoration is the presage of incorruptibility. When stripping away occurs, if one can halt it and not let the celestial be completely stripped away, then use the slight remaining celestial to reestablish the universe and again set up the crucible and furnace, causing the celestial to return in time, then what has been lost can be regained, what has gone can be recovered. When the primordial is pure and conditioning is dissolved, then there is no more worry of stripping away and decay.

 35. Advance   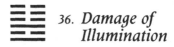 *36. Damage of Illumination*

Advance is daytime, damage of illumination is destruction.

Advance is progress of illumination. Producing illumination by way of accord, where there is illumination darkness disappears. This is like the sun rising in daytime, gradually ascending, the light increasing with its ascent, its illumination growing as it rises.

Damage of illumination is when illumination is injured. Ruining illumination by accord, light disappears into darkness. This is like the sun going down at night, the darkness increasing as it gradually descends, its illumination being destroyed.

In one case, light emerges from darkness; in the other, light disappears into darkness. The difference between them lies in the difference between accord with the inner and accord with the outer. When accord is within, then errant thoughts do not arise and the mind is sincere; when sincere, one is capable of illumination. When accord is outside, then the spirit is dimmed by the shroud of material desires; being dimmed, it loses illumination.

Inner accord is the path of reversal of conditioning; outer accord is the path of submission to conditioning. By reversal, illumination is produced, and that illumination is penetrating and effective. By submission, illumination is destroyed, and thus illumination is obscured. So the gain or loss of illumination is a matter of reversal or submission to conditioning. Therefore practitioners of the Tao should know how to apply the path of reversal in the midst of the flow of conditioning.

 48. The Well　　　　　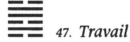 *47. Travail*

The well is a matter of mastery, travail is a matter of encounter.

The well is the path of developing people. It is the time of mastery because mastery is the means of arriving at the Tao. Before one can improve other people, one must improve oneself; only when there is no danger in oneself can one solve others' problems. If self-development is not complete, this is going into danger willingly; when self-development is complete, one gets out of danger. Having gotten out of danger, having completed one's own self-development, if one then also develops other people, there will be no end to the development.

Travail means situations of toil and difficulty. To say it is a matter of encounter means that travail is that whereby character is tested. Before one can eliminate danger, it is first important that one can handle danger. If one can be joyful even in danger, then eliminating danger will consummate that joy. When one encounters travail but cannot accept it, this is willfully going into danger. When one encounters travail and can accept it, this is being capable of joyfulness even in danger. In the latter case, the body may be exhausted, but the mind cannot be exhausted, so even in travail one develops and gets through.

When one has reached mastery, one develops others; when one encounters travail, one develops oneself. Those who can develop others when they reach mastery will be able to develop themselves in times of travail; those who are able to develop themselves in times of travail will be able to develop others when they reach mastery. In the encounter between travail and mastery, as the time changes development also changes. Only when there is development in both comfort and adversity can one be called a practitioner of the Tao.

31. Sensing   *32. Perseverance*

Sensing is swift, perseverance is long.

Sensing is the sensing of the original mind. When one is inwardly still, outwardly joyous, joyfulness is based on stillness, stillness is used to seek joy. Being still, one is capable of nurturance; being joyful, one is capable of action: Joyfulness and stillness need each other. Tranquil and unstirring, yet sensitive and effective, communing spiritually rather than physically—the barrier between the earthly and the celestial is subtly penetrated. This bespeaks the swiftness of sensing.

Perseverance is constancy of mind. Inwardly docile, outwardly active, acting with gentleness, one is gentle without being weak, active without being aggressive. When docility and action are united, the mind is stable and the will is far-reaching; neither rushing nor lagging, one enters from striving into nonstriving, the effect goes from gradual to immediate. This bespeaks the length of perseverance.

What is referred to as mindlessness is absence of the human mentality; what is referred to as mindfulness is mindfulness of the Tao. When one is free of the human mentality, the mutual sensing of the earthly and celestial is swift; when one is mindful of the Tao, effective practice endures. Swiftness of sensing comes about spontaneously, without cultivation, without striving; long perseverance comes about through effort, and involves action and striving. Striving and nonstriving each has its secret; the distinction is all a matter of the absence of the human mentality and the presence of mindfulness of the Tao. After one has reached complete realization of the universal Tao, neither existence nor nonexistence remain; others and self are ultimately empty, and one enters the state of ultimate truthfulness, like a spirit. Here, it is not only the human mentality that cannot be applied; even the mindfulness of Tao is not applicable.

 59. Disintegration   *60. Regulation*

Disintegration is separation, regulation is stillness.

In disintegration, yang energy falls down while yin energy rises up, so they are separated from one another. In regulation, danger lies outside while joy resides within; one is able to be still when thwarted by circumstances.

Yet when yin and yang are separated, there is still a way to make them join; this lies in dealing with the situation in which yang has fallen in a harmonious and gentle fashion, so as to resolve the situation.

If one is able to be still when thwarted, one has an opportunity to get through the impasse; this lies in managing troubles correctly in a congenial manner.

Gradually resolving disintegration, at first there is separation but finally there is union. Correctly establishing regulation, though there is danger one can get through it.

But disintegration is always due to not knowing there is regulation; if one knows regulation, one will not do anything improper, will not abide anywhere but on the path of the Tao, will not do anything unrighteous. The situation may be up to others, but creation of life is up to oneself. Therefore there is no disintegration.

So in the qualities of the hexagrams, the danger (*water* ☵) in *disintegration* is on the inside, while the danger in *regulation* is on the outside.

 40. Liberation   *39. Halting*

Liberation is relief, halting is difficulty.

Liberation means the celestial energy gets out of danger, and there is relief. When the celestial energy gets out of danger, it starts by stirring into activity within the mundane. When the force of mundanity is dispelled and the repression of the celestial energy is relieved, being relieved, the celestial energy is no longer damaged by the force of mundanity, and can be used to transmute accumulated mundanity.

Halting means the celestial energy is having difficulty within the mundane. Celestial energy being in danger, the incipient celestial is still hidden within the mundane. When the force of mundanity is powerful and the celestial energy is thwarted, while the celestial energy is in difficulty, it will not do to hurriedly seek to get out of this danger; one should quietly nurture the faint celestial energy.

The reason for transmutation of accumulated mundanity after liberation is that even though the celestial energy has gotten out of danger, the force of mundanity still has not yet disappeared entirely, and the root of calamity is still there; though one may obtain relief for a time, before long one will again be trapped by mundanity and will no longer be free. So it is most important to act in such a way as to get out of danger and apply the work of increase and decrease, using the celestial to repel the mundane. When the force of mundanity has been thoroughly repelled and the celestial energy completely restored, only then is this genuine liberation.

The reason it is necessary to quietly nurture the faint celestial energy when halted is that when the celestial energy is surrounded by mundanity, the force of mundanity inhibits the celestial; if you try to forcibly free it from danger, not only will you not be able to free it from danger, you will in fact bring on danger and be in even more difficulty. So it is most important to be still in danger, applying the method of guarding, temporarily using passivity to preserve the creative. When the celestial energy is not lost and the force of mundanity gradually recedes, only then can one be free from trouble and not be halted.

When the celestial is emerging from danger, one should promote the celestial and repel the mundane; when the celestial is in danger, one should nurture the celestial and guard against the mundane. Repelling mundanity and guarding against mundanity each has its own process; if you apply them with the proper timing, then and only then will you avoid going wrong.

 ## 38. Disparity

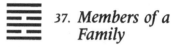 ## 37. Members of a Family

Disparity is external, members of a family internal.

Disparity means separation, obstruction of one from another. In the hexagram, *fire* is above and *metal* is below; metal and fire do not combine. This represents the spirit running to externals and feelings stirring within, losing the real because of the false. This is to say that the function of awareness is applied to externals.

"Members of a family" means union. In the hexagram, *wood* is above and *fire* is below. Wood is produced within fire. This represents the original spirit staying within and the flexible nature adapting externally, using openness to seek fulfillment. This is to say that the function of awareness is applied inwardly.

When awareness is applied to externals, its light does not return to the root; arbitrary feelings stir and true sense is obscured. When awareness is applied within, its light has returned to the root; the artificial changes into the real, the temperament dissolves and the true nature appears. Depending on whether awareness is internal or external, there is a difference between disparity and nondisparity, between unity and disunity. Practitioners of the Tao should turn their attention inward to nurture the light of awareness.

 ## 12. Obstruction

 ## 11. Tranquility

Obstruction and tranquility are opposite.

Obstruction is blockage. Strong energy exercised outwardly, flexible nature concealed within—sanity disintegrates and aberration accumulates; personal desires that fill the being block off the opening of awareness. Flexibility being damaged by strength is the source of obstruction.

Tranquility is mastery. Strong energy being within, flexible nature is applied outwardly; strict in governing oneself, generous in dealing with others, the mind grows daily more humble while the character becomes daily more noble. Strength used with flexibility is the sign of tranquility.

External strength with internal weakness causes obstruction, external flexibility with internal strength causes tranquility. So the difference between obstruction and tranquility is a matter of whether strength and flexibility are inside or outside. We cannot take lightly the functions of strength and flexibility.

 ## 34. Great Power

 ## 33. Inaccessibility

With great power, be still: To be inaccessible, withdraw.

Great power is excess of strength. Strong on the inside and active on the outside, already strong and yet still promoting strength, strong but acting arbitrarily, the action will harm strength. This is magnitude of power. To be still means to be still when it is appropriate to be still, using stillness to nurture power, not letting strength become too adamant.

Inaccessibility is concealment of strength. Stilling strength and being strong in stillness, already strong and so stilling that strength, strength stops in its proper place, so that the strength is not ruined. This is being inaccessible at the right time. To withdraw means to withdraw when it is appropriate to withdraw, withdrawing so as to avoid fault, not letting the force of mundanity arise insidiously.

Generally speaking, the path of using firmness or strength is to foster strength when one is not yet strong, then to nurture strength once one is strong. Fostering strength is using power; nurturing strength is storing power. When you should act, act, furthering power in action; when you should be still, be still, storing power in stillness. If the timing is correct, action will be powerful, and stillness too will be powerful; inaccessibility will be developmental, and power will be developmental too. Then you can be strong wherever you go, and there will be no damage to your strength anywhere.

To understand when to proceed and when to withdraw, to know when to stop at sufficiency, is not something of which the ignorant are capable. To know when to hasten and when to relax, to be aware of what bodes well and what bodes ill, calls for the judgment of an adept.

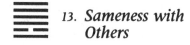

14. *Great Possession*

13. *Sameness with Others*

Great possession is abundance, sameness with others is closeness.

Great possession is abundance of possession. Strong on the inside and lucid on the outside, after filling the belly one can empty the mind; able to empty the mind, thus the original spirit stays in its abode, refining gold with fire, the gold returning to its original state upon meeting fire and becoming bright. When the great elixir is completed, myriad principles are ultimately united, and wherever one goes is the Tao. Completing strength with lucidity, one has great possession that continues to increase; what one possesses is very abundant indeed.

Sameness with others is being close to people. Lucid inwardly and strong outwardly, after emptying one's mind one then fills the belly; able to fill the belly, thus sanity is ever-present, feeding the fire with gold, fire returning to its origin upon meeting gold and not being hot. With receptivity and creativity in harmony, the inward and the outward join, tranquil and unstirring yet sensitive and effective. Completing lucidity with strength, one assimilates to others and others assimilate to oneself; that sameness is very close.

To be strong and lucid is to refine gold with fire; to be lucid and strong is to return fire with gold. When gold is restored and fire has returned, gold and fire are in the same abode; gold is fire, fire is gold, in the sense that strength and lucidity are as one.

When one has certain endowments, one is able to assimilate to others; assimilating, one's endowments increase. This is called great possession; this is called great sameness. Great possession and great sameness involve receptivity and creativity, emptiness and fullness, others and self; great and small are unflawed, firmness and flexibility are both complete. Completely integrating with the celestial design, one's energy flows, and the path of twin cultivation of nature and life is complete.

49. *Change*

50. *The Cauldron*

Change gets rid of the old, a cauldron obtains the new.

Change means getting rid of the old and not using it. The way of getting rid of the old has gold on top and fire below, using fire to refine gold, getting rid of the pollutants in gold and restoring the celestial. The arbitrary feelings of people are mundane gold, the true sense in people is celestial gold. Using the true fire of the original spirit to burn away the mundane gold of arbitrary feelings, when arbitrary feelings are gone true sense appears;

this is called unemotional sense, which is permanently incorruptible gold. This is what is meant by "gold becoming bright when refined by fire."

A cauldron is that wherein something is refined to obtain the new. The way to obtain the new has fire on top and wood below, perfecting wood in fire, changing its polluted substance and returning it to reality. Human temperament is mundane wood, the true nature of humanity is celestial wood. Using the true fire of the original spirit to burn away the mundane wood of temperament, when the temperament vanishes the true nature appears; this is called impersonal nature, which is wood without smoke or flame. This is what is called "producing wood in fire."

Change and renewal, the false departing and the real arriving, is the uniting of nature and sense, returning to the origin and going back to the fundamental. However, it is necessary first to change the old, in the sense of refining the self, emptying the mind, and biding the time. After that, the cauldron obtains the new, in the sense of subsequently gathering the medicine and filling the belly, so as to form the elixir. Obviously, as long as one has not yet emptied the mind, one cannot fill the belly and also empty the mind then. In the hexagram *change*, illumination (*fire* $\equiv\equiv$) is inside, in the hexagram *the cauldron* illumination is outside; nature and sense both become real, and one illumination pervades both striving and nonstriving.

 62. Excessive Smallness   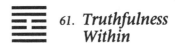 **61. Truthfulness Within**

Excessive smallness is excess, truthfulness within is sincerity.

Excessive smallness means that which is small is excessive. Using stillness to motivate action, action always based on stillness, outwardly empty yet inwardly fulfilled, the small is excessive but the great is not excessive. Still when it is appropriate, active when it is appropriate, action does not become divorced from stillness, stopping in the realm of utter goodness without evil.

Truthfulness within means having sincerity within. Joyfully practicing in a gradual manner, gradually consummating joy, outwardly full, inwardly empty, using emptiness to seek fulfillment, sincere within and active without, penetrating by truthfulness and functioning flexibly, one gradually advances to the realm of profound attainment of self-realization.

However, those who cannot minimize themselves and start from smallness also cannot be truthful within; and those who cannot be faithful and sincere also cannot be exceedingly small. With excessive smallness and truthfulness within, empty yet full, full yet empty, emptiness and fullness both employed, action and stillness require one another, joyfulness and pliability are as one. When one is excessive without extremism, and truthfulness is within, there is no worry that practice of the Tao will not succeed.

55. Abundance *56. Transience*

**With abundance there are many mishaps,
transience lacks familiars.**

Abundance is flourishing greatness. Once one has understanding and also acts on it, putting understanding into practice in action, understanding and action sustain one another; sufficiency of understanding and greatness of action is the height of abundance. At the height of abundance, it is easy to become self-satisfied and complacent; if one is unable to guard against it, excess in understanding damages its clarity, while excess in action ruins one's practice—therefore there are many mishaps. Because there are many mishaps, things may be reversed and practice will be upset.

Transience is passing through once and not staying long. Once one is still and also lucid, lucidity based on stillness, lucidity and stillness need each other, stillness providing nurturance, lucidity remaining intact. Myriad things are transient; by regarding things as transient, one is able to act simply, without seeking anything extraneous. Still within but not stopping without, one is clear to oneself but not to others; therefore there are no familiars. Lacking familiars, one adjusts to things as they come, not tarrying too long over anything.

For those who are preserving abundance, this is a matter of making their understanding abundant, yet also taking care to keep their understanding fluid, with understanding not acted on arbitrarily. For those practicing transience, this is a matter of keeping understanding fluid yet also taking care to enrich their understanding, with understanding not being too stationary.

Transience is the function of abundance, abundance is the body of transience. Whether applying understanding in action, or nurturing lucidity in stillness, if action and stillness are properly applied, one can keep lucid understanding intact.

 30. Fire *29. Water*

Fire rises, water descends.

In fire, one yin is stuck in between two yangs; outwardly full while inwardly empty, the body is firm while the function is flexible. The nature of fire is to flame upwards, so it is said that fire rises.

In water, one yang is fallen in between two yins; outwardly empty while inwardly full, the body is flexible while the function is firm. The nature of water is to flow downwards, so it is said that water descends.

Irascibility in people is like fire. Becoming contentious and aggressive whenever provoked, aggrandizing oneself, and acting willfully without restraint, is like the flaming up of fire.

Greed in people is like water. With random thoughts arising in profusion, abandoning the real and getting into the false, going along with the wind arousing waves, sinking into debasement, is like water flowing downwards.

When the sages teach people to subdue anger, this is to subdue this irascibility. When they teach people to quell desire, this is to quell this greediness. When irascibility is subdued and the fire returns to the origin, then the mind is empty and produces light, so the original spirit is not obscured. When greed is quelled and the water returns to the source, then the belly is full and there is no danger, so the original vitality does not drain away.

When the spirit is illumined and the vitality is purified, as true water and true fire they balance each other; the earthly and the celestial join, and the primordial energy comes forth from nothingness.

 ## 9. *Small Nurturance*   ## 10. *Treading*

Small nurturance is poverty, treading is not staying put.

Small nurturance means poverty of development. Yielding docilely to accumulate strength, though firm one is still weak; the development is not great, the action is not far-reaching.

Treading means not staying in a lowly position. Joyful in practicing strength, though weak one is still firm; the determination single-minded, the action grows powerful spontaneously.

In small nurturance, the strength (*heaven* ☰) is inside, true positivity is still intact; as a person of superior virtue, one should therefore be purposefully active— so if one then tries to develop by passivity, not using one's abundant energy, willingly abiding in lowliness, throwing oneself away, sitting idly and watching how things turn out, one will surely come to the point where positivity culminates and negativity arises, hidden strength is overcome by weakness, and one becomes debilitated.

In treading, the strength is outside. True positivity already defective; as a person of inferior virtue, there is nothing one can do—but if one is yet able to joyfully practice strength, seeking the guidance of others, calmly progressing, persisting in the path without obsession or indifference, one will eventually be able to reach from the near at hand to the remote, to gradually rise from lowliness to the heights. Weakness overcome by strength, those without ability become capable.

So in the path of practice of the Tao, it is not a matter of the level of people's talents or qualities, but of whether or not they have determination. Without determination, even talented and intelligent people are incapable of attaining the Tao; with determination, even ignorant men and women are capable of attaining it. As it is said, those who realize it immediately ascend to the rank of sages, while those who miss it sink in the stream forever.

 ## 5. *Waiting*

 ## 6. *Contention*

Waiting, one does not go forward. Contending, one is not friendly.

Waiting means awaiting the proper time. Strong in the midst of danger, able to be strong when encountering danger, danger is in others, strength is in oneself; wanting to take from others without losing oneself, therefore one waits and does not go forward. The purpose of not going forward but awaiting the proper time is just to take the true celestial out of the mundane.

Contention is a contest for victory. Danger is in strength, there is danger because of strength, inwardly one is poisoned with mundanity, outwardly one is vicious and violent; not only does one hurt others, one also injures oneself, therefore in contention one is not friendly. Not being friendly, tending toward aggression, eventually one will bring about the downfall of true positivity into mundanity.

When one is not pushing strength forward, strength remains intact; instead one uses danger to nourish strength. Not being friendly to others, one will not be befriended by others; instead one beckons danger by exerting strength. It is the same strength and the sane danger, but when strength is internal, one can be out of danger even when there is danger, and when strength is external, one beckons danger even when there is no danger. In one case it is internal, in one case it is external; accordingly there is fortune or calamity. So practitioners of the Tao should secretly nurture celestial qualities so as to prevent danger.

 ## 28. *Great Excess*

 ## 27. *Jaws*

Great excess overturns, jaws nourish correctness.

Great excess is excess of positivity. Inwardly pliable while delighting in externals, when positivity culminates negativity enters. Once negativity enters, the human mentality arises; seeing objects, one gives rise to feelings, following desires, so that one's nature is deranged and one's life is destabilized. This is what is meant by "overturns."

Jaws refers to taking nourishment. Inwardly active while outwardly still, when negativity culminates positivity returns. Once positivity returns, the mind of Tao becomes active, so that one has inward autonomy, moves toward what is good and corrects faults, resting in the proper place. This is what is meant by "nourishes correctness."

The path of cultivating reality is from beginning to end the path of nourishing correctness. Filling the belly and being able to empty the mind, nourishing fulfillment with emptiness, one can be correct without overturning. Emptying the mind and being able to fill the belly, consummating emptiness by fulfillment, one can return to correctness after overturning.

Therefore the image of great excess is full on the inside and empty on the outside, showing that fullness must seek emptiness. The image of jaws is full on the outside and empty on the inside, showing that emptiness must seek fulfillment. One may first fill the belly and after that empty the mind, or one may first empty the mind and then fill the belly. When emptiness and fulfillment are both used, the paths of doing and nondoing are consummated, the work of nourishing correctness is completed.

 ## 53. Gradualness

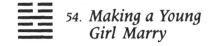 ## 54. Making a Young Girl Marry

Gradually a woman marries, waiting for the man to go.
Making a young girl marry is the end of the girl.

Gradualness means going slowly, without hurry. In practicing the Tao it is important to go gradually, without hurry, so as to rest in the proper place, calmly, without compulsion, proceeding step by step in an orderly fashion, refining the self and awaiting the proper timing. This is like in the image of the hexagram, where the youngest son (*mountain* ☶) is paired with the eldest daughter (*wind* ☴)—the woman waits for the man to go, and after that gets married. This is correct communion of yin and yang; eventually there is success, sense and nature are as one, the earthly and the celestial combine.

Making a young girl marry means haste. Practice of the Tao should not be hasty, for when one rushes one indulges in arbitrary guesswork and personalistic interpretation, recklessly forcing the issue without thoroughly investigating the true principles of the Tao, seeking to attain it all at once. This is like in the image of the hexagram, where the youngest daughter (*lake* ☱) is paired with the eldest son (*thunder* ☳)—the girl is forcibly wed before her time. This is incorrect communion of yin and yang; eventually there is failure, and one winds up alone in solitary quietism.

The Tao of practice of reality is the science of discovery of truth, consummation of nature, and arrival at the meaning of life. It involves particular processes and courses of work; it requires gradual practice in order to reach profound attainment of self-realization. If you rush, eager for attainment, setting about impetuously, you may proceed quickly but will regress rapidly. How then can you corral the earthly and celestial energies into the center of your being, unite sense, nature, and intent in the original state? If you want to attain the Tao, there is no other way to do so save by the achievement of gradual cultivation.

 ## 63. Settled

 ## 64. Not Yet Settled

Being settled is stabilization, being unsettled is the end of a man.

Being settled means the earthly and the celestial are completed. In the hexagram, *water* ☵ is above and *fire* ☲ is below; with fire, water is not cold, and with water, fire is not hot. Heaven and earth constitute the body, water and fire constitute the function; innate knowledge and innate capacity, creativity and receptivity, are as one, spirit and vitality cleave to each other, and the celestial and the earthly combine—thus it is called stabilization.

Not yet settled means the earthly and the celestial are separated. In the hexagram, *fire* ☲ is above and *water* ☵ is below; fire and water are in different places. Water flows downward and fire flames upward, so water cannot control fire and fire cannot heat water—innate knowledge turns into artificial knowledge and temper flares; innate capacity turns into artificial capacity and greed arises.

The temper is fire, greed is water; when the temper is exercised outwardly and greed is stored within, one's nature becomes deranged and life is destabilized, the earthly and the celestial are incomplete and imbalanced. Therefore it is called the end of a man. The end of a man means that the celestial is overcome by the mundane; the artificial takes over affairs and the real is buried away, not coming to the fore.

Yet even when settled, when the completion of the earthly and the celestial is consummated, the consummation of balance may become unsettled, so it is necessary to use the path of nonstriving in order to preserve completion and balance. The work of preserving completion and balance is to use the natural real fire to burn away all the pollutants of conditioning; when the force of mundanity is sublimated and the celestial energy is unadulterated, the great elixir is perfected and one is liberated, spiritually transformed, entering into the realm that is unborn and undying.

As for the path to take when unsettled, as long as the earthly and the celestial are not yet settled, one should seek to balance, complete, and settle them, and apply striving to bring about this settlement. After all, the true celestial energy that has become overcome and trapped in the mundane is originally of the celestial realm, and the earthly energy hidden in the heart is originally of the earthly realm; now if you take the bit of celestial water of true unity from the water of desire on the earthly plane and use it to extinguish the raging fire of temper in the heart, and take the real fire of open awareness out of the temperamental fire in the heart and use it to burn away greed on the earthly plane, thus the true earthly and the true celestial will combine harmoniously, real water and real fire will not be separated, and from not being settled one can arrive at settlement. This will restore the original being, in which the celestial is strong and the earthly obeys it, endowed with innate knowledge and innate capacity.

But preserving settlement and bringing about settlement, striving and nonstriving, involve different methods, with distinct approaches. Therefore the meaning of being settled is the prevention of danger by illumination, and the meaning of not yet being settled is the extraction of illumination from danger. Preventing danger by illumination, warding off peril to nurture illumination, repelling conditioning within the primordial, is the means to preserve settlement. Extracting illumination from danger, using illumination to break through danger, retrieving the primordial within the temporal, is the way to bring about settlement.

The secrets of preserving settlement and bringing about settlement are no more than this. Going along with conditioning produces humans, reversing conditioning produces sages. It is not easy to understand what is meant by this reversal.

 ## 44. *Meeting*   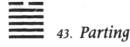 ## 43. *Parting*

Meeting is encounter; the weak meets the strong.
Parting is separation; the strong parts with the weak.

Meeting is encounter, as one weak line encounters five strong lines, representing the insidious arising of the mundane on the culmination of the celestial. The encounter is unexpected; the force of mundanity enters through heedlessness.

Parting is separation, as five strong lines part with one weak line, representing the imminent purity of the celestial and the imminent disappearance of mundanity. The parting is spontaneous, without forced separation; the celestial energy grows with time.

After people are born, the primordial celestial energy is stored in the ephemeral body; growing day and night, by the age of sixteen the primordial energy is replete. This is called the state in which the celestial is unadulterated; at this stage one is a person of superior quality. At this time, if one meets an enlightened teacher and is guided to practice the Tao of nonstriving spontaneity, thereby accomplishing temporal achievement so that nature is comprehended and life is perfected, then one becomes an impeccable personification of reality.

Otherwise, without this guidance and practice, the culmination of the celestial will inevitably give way to mundanity; mundanity arises isidiously under the celestial, so the mundane joins the celestial, and conditioning begins to take charge. Thereafter mundanity grows day by day and the celestial wanes day by day, until the celestial is finally extinguished. Though that first bit of mundanity be slight, its deleterious effects are powerful.

The Tao of striving for the gold elixir has in fact been set up for middling and lesser people, in whom the joining of the mundane to the celestial has already taken place. Striving means to foster the celestial and detach from the mundane. Detaching from the mundane by means of the celestial requires that one first foster the celestial while within the mundane; fostering the celestial is just a device to repel mundanity.

When the celestial energy has been fostered to the point of correct balance, represented by the fifth line from the bottom of the hexagram, this is stabilizing life in the proper state. Celestial energy is already sufficient, and the force of mundanity is now weak; the mind of Tao is in charge of affairs, and the gold elixir has formed. At this point one has transformed all mundanity, like a cat catching mice, except for the root of mundanity, which has not yet vanished and is still capable of being a burden on the path. Though the spiritual embryo has formed, it cannot be free. When an ancient Taoist said, "As long as there is any force of mundanity that has not been exhausted, one does not become immortal," he was referring to this root of mundane elements.

What is this root of the aggregate of mundanity? It is the discriminating spirit of the human mentality. The discriminating spirit is the seed of endless routine, the root and stem of personal history; its authority is very great, its roots are very deep. At the time of "meeting," it is the first bit of mundanity to arise, and at the time of "parting" it is the last bit of mundanity to leave. It is that which gives birth to people, and it is that which kills people. People are very attached to it, and are unwilling to part with it, so even if they want to get rid of it, it is not easily gotten rid of.

The way to get rid of the discriminating spirit of the human mentality is to be firm yet capable of harmony, to be strong but flexible, neither obsessed nor indifferent, neither forgetful nor insistent, waiting for it to lose support and wane in power, so that it can be removed by detachment. Extirpating the root of misfortune, bringing forth the original state before personal history, round and bright, clean and naked, bare and untrammeled, unborn and undying, this is something indestructible and incorruptible.

The path of superior people is eternal, the path of inferior people is miserable.

The path of the *I Ching* is the Tao of balance of the earthly and the celestial. The earthly is flexible, the celestial is firm. The quality of firmness is based on strength, the quality of flexibility is based on receptivity. Strength is ready knowledge, receptivity is simple capacity. Ready knowledge is the innate knowledge in people, simple capacity is the innate capacity in people.

Innate knowledge is rooted in heaven, and belongs to the order of life; innate capacity is rooted in earth, and belongs to nature. People are endowed with the ready and simple qualities of heaven and earth; knowledge and capacity are both innate, firmness and flexibility are both included, nature and life reside in one body.

Subsequently, upon mixture with temporal conditioning, innate knowledge turns into artificial knowledge, innate capacity turns into artificial capacity; the earthly and the celestial out of harmony, firmness and flexibility are out of balance, so nature becomes deranged and life is destabilized, losing the natural endowment of simplicity and readiness of heaven and earth, losing the innate goodness of knowledge and capacity.

This is what Mencius referred to when he said, "The difference between humans and beasts is very slight; inferior people lose it, superior people keep it." If one keeps this innate knowledge and innate capacity, one then is a superior person; if one loses this innate knowledge and innate capacity, one then is an inferior person. "The path of superior people is eternal" means superior people keep this; "the path of inferior people is miserable" means inferior people lose this. This is because the path of superior people is to restore this innate knowledge and innate capacity and to repel artificial knowledge and capacity; therefore it is eternal. The path of inferior people follows artificial knowledge and artificial capacity and abandons innate knowledge and capacity; therefore it is miserable.

Innate knowledge and innate capacity are primordial, while artificial knowledge and artificial capacity are conditioned. When you recover the primordial reality, then you comprehend nature and realize the meaning of life, and so enter the road of life; this is the eternity of the path. If you follow conditioned artificialities, you obscure nature and damage life, and so enter the road of death; this is the misery of the path.

Of the sixty-four hexagrams of the *I Ching*, the reason *heaven* and *earth* are the gate and door is to show people the path of firmness and flexibility, simplicity and readiness. The other sixty-two hexagrams show people the path of modification of simplicity and readiness. The three hundred eighty-four lines of the sixty-four hexagrams all teach people how to know when they are not simple and ready, and to modify this so that they may eventually become simple and ready.

Modification to simplicity and readiness means that knowledge and capacity are in their innate condition of innocence, and one is a superior person. If one does not change to simplicity and readiness, then knowledge and capacity are faulty, and one is an inferior person. The difference between superior people and inferior people is simply a matter of whether or not they know how to make this change.

The path of superior people is the path of the gold elixir, the spiritual alchemy, the science of reversing the overtaking of the celestial by the mundane. The gold elixir is the nature in which simple and ready innate knowledge and innate capacity are merged. The restored elixir is the restoration of the original state of this simple and ready innate knowledge and innate capacity. The great elixir of gold liquid is the refining of this nature consisting of a combination of simple and ready innate knowledge and innate capacity into something forever incorruptible. The firing process is the sixty-four hexagrams, indicating modification of simple and ready knowledge and capacity to restore them to their innate goodness. The medicinal substances are the firm and flexible, simple and ready qualities of knowledge and capacity in their innate innocence. The spiritual embryo is the return of firm and flexible, simple and ready knowledge and capacity to innate innocence. Liberation is when firmness and flexibility combine, simplicity and readiness are uninhibited, knowledge and capacity enter the spiritual, and neither being nor nonbeing remains.

The alchemical classics and writings of the adepts, amounting to thousands of volumes, do not go beyond the principles of the *I Ching*, and the principles of the *I Ching*, its sixty-four hexagrams and three hundred eighty-four lines, do not go beyond this path of firm and flexible, simple and ready knowledge and capacity, which are both innate. The *I Ching* is for the consideration of superior people, not for the consideration of inferior people. This is because superior people can cultivate this path of firm and flexible simplicity and readiness, reverse the overtaking of the celestial by the mundane, and restore the original innate knowledge and innate capacity. Inferior people, on the other hand, obey conditioning, which obscures their celestial roots, and bring destruction upon themselves; how can they know how to practice this great Tao, the path back to the primordial?

Appendix

Using *The Taoist I Ching*

For practical use of *The Taoist I Ching,* a number of steps have been found helpful by both newcomers to the *I Ching* and those experienced in other traditions on the *I Ching.*

Because the *I Ching* is treated as an integrated system in Liu I-ming's Taoist commentary, any approach to its contents will yield results limited to the degree that knowledge of the system is limited. This is especially true of a random approach. Therefore, the first step is to read the book in its entirety, without pausing to judge or question, just going along with the flow of its images and ideas. A few things to be noted at this stage:

In the Introduction
- the quotations from Confucian and Taoist literature
- the explanations of yin and yang
- the explanations of the eight trigrams
- the names of the sixty-four hexagrams

In the Text
- the double helix structure
- the combination of trigrams
- the transformations of yin and yang

Ancient literature suggests reading one hexagram in the morning and one at night. At this rate, this initial phase of consultation can be completed in approximately one month. This may have to be repeated one or more times at intervals to effectively set the basic program into the mind.

The reader might then proceed to consult the *I Ching* on specific matters in the following ways, suggested by commentarial analysis and found useful by contemporary experimenters.

Trigram method: Regard the bottom trigram as the subject of the reading, the top trigram as the object of that subject. This object could be a person, a job, a situation, an event, and so on. The subject is yourself or the person you are reading for.

Focus on the meanings of the trigrams, and read for a particular quality in a particular situation. If, for example, someone is restless, that would indicate a reading for thunder, movement. If the external situation is perilous, that would indicate a reading for water, danger. With movement on the inside/bottom and danger on the outside/top, the hexagram is *Difficulty.* The statements and commentaries on this hexagram then go on to discuss this situation and how to handle it to the best advantage.

Analytic method: The trigram is composed of three lines, traditionally representing heaven, humanity, and earth. The heavenly, or celestial, is associated in humans with the spiritual, or reason or the ideal. The earthly is associated with the mundane, with desire and passion. The human or social is characterized by its balance of reason and desire, or of the spiritual and the mundane. Reviewing the meanings of yin and yang, analyze the subject and object, build a trigram for each, then consult the resulting hexagram. People often find it very useful to make two hexagrams from two trigrams, to consult from both points of view.

An alternative method of generating trigrams is to use a time scale. The lower trigram represents the beginning, middle, and end of the effort or process that goes on within the subject. The upper trigram represents the beginning, middle, and end of the effect of that effort or process on the environment, social or material. This method can be used in up-to-the-moment retrospectives, where the top line is the present or visible future. It might also be used to assess picturings of the future.

In either method, since there are many alternative meanings of yin and yang under the opposing categories of true and false, the commentarial reading may be found to have shifted from the meaning used by the reader to derive it. This often provides useful insight through juxtaposition of antithesis, and it also helps to compensate for the shifts that take place in ambiguous situations, where a line could be yin in one sense and yang in another. Because of this, and because of the fact that yin and yang always imply one another in some sense, people generally seem to find it useful to also read the hexagram that would be formed by the opposite of each line derived by each method. In cases where there is substantial ambiguity, hexagrams generated by varying the ambiguous lines also have proved useful.

I Ching reading can be refined into an affair of endless complexity because of the nuances of situations and the complicated interrelation of the elements of *I Ching* polar analysis. The simple methods outlined here have been tested with remarkable results and can easily be used by anyone. From beginning to end, however, there is no way to escape the effect of the reader on the reading.

For those who wish to become experts in the use of the *I Ching*, or who wish to make sophisticated, in-depth readings on situations of great complexity, my forthcoming volume on the *I Ching* mandalas, to be published by Shambhala Publications, provides traditional programs for further study. These programs can be used with any tradition and any translation of the *I Ching*.

Glossary

A

aberrant energy   Energy deriving from, or affected by, external influences or internal habit; compulsive and impulsive behavior; unruly thought and emotion.

aberrant fire   Volatility, passion; especially anger and aggression. Also, unstable consciousness, conditioned consciousness.

aberrant schools   Schools of practice fixated either on form/matter or on voidness. Those fixated on form are those that mechanically or obsessively practice physical exercises, concentration on the physical or imaginary body, rituals, asceticism, or other formal practices. Those fixated on voidness are the quietists, for whom tranquility is the goal. These schools are called aberrant because they do not transcend their own limitations, they mistake means for ends, and thus they cannot reach the Tao. In Taoism, the definition of aberrant schools dates back at least to Chuang-tzu and the *Triplex Unity,* works of the third century B.C. and second century A.D.

adding and subtracting   Increasing conscious access to the mind of Tao, decreasing domination by the human mentality. See the Introduction for further clarification of these terms.

adding mercury   Increasing objective consciousness by removing conditioned subjectivity. See *extracting lead.*

advancing the fire   Promoting illumination, enhancing awareness; see *advancing yang.*

advancing yang   Fostering the mind of Tao, primal unconditioned awareness, in order to bring it to the fore of consciousness and overmaster the inhibited consciousness of the human mentality.

assembling the five elements   The process of internal unification of the human being. This is sometimes described in terms of basic awareness, basic vitality, intellect, and emotion being yoked to will, all being in harmony under the control of the unifying cohesive force of will. It is also described in terms of the qualities of benevolence, justice, courtesy, and wisdom being unified in proper proportion by the central quality of truthfulness or sincerity.

B

bamboo Drumming on bamboo to call a phoenix means emptying the human mind to evoke the mind of Tao; bamboo stands for emptiness and flexibility.

bellows In the imagery of alchemy, the bellows is what fosters the fire; hence it means the effort to concentrate. On an elementary yogic level, the bellows means the breath, which is used as an aid to concentration.

black Symbol of the state of profound tranquility and detachment.

body outside the body A stage of practice when the consciousness has expanded beyond the personal individuality to merge, spacelike, with the universe, which becomes as it were the greater body. The expression is also used by some Taoists to refer to the concentrated projection of consciousness in psychic travel, the ability to form a mentally produced body outside the physical body.

building life Taoist arts of energy circulation and storage for physical well-being and the capacity to sustain higher levels of consciousness. In general, there are three types of such arts: physical exercises, such as T'ai Chi Ch'uan; psychophysical exercises, such as inner visualization and circulation of psychic heat; and mental exercises involving conservation of psychic and physical energy by control of senses, intellect, and emotions.

C

cangue A large square of wood locked on the neck as a punishment in old China; hence it means something that inhibits, obstructs, deprives one of freedom.

celestial decree The fundamental human nature before it is shaped by temporal conditioning into fixed personality and temperament.

celestial energy The primal energy of living consciousness, which is prior to, and underlies, mundane conditioned awareness.

center The center is the balance point of the human being, sometimes defined as the state before emotions arise. It also refers to will, intent, attention, concentration, truthfulness, sincerity, around which the state of mind and actions of the individual are centered.

cinnabar The energy of open consciousness. Cinnabar is red, associated with fire, which is associated with awareness. From cinnabar comes mercury, which stands for the essence of consciousness.

combining the four signs Unification of mind; joining feeling and essence (q.v.), real knowledge and conscious knowledge. Also sometimes defined as combination of strength, flexibility, awareness, and love.

congealing Stabilization of consciousness.

crucible Or cauldron; the vessel in which the alchemical "cooking and refining" is done: It is sometimes used to refer to open awareness, sometimes to the combination of the qualities represented by the eight *I Ching* trigrams.

crystallization Stabilization of consciousness.

culling Being alert to make conscious contact with the celestial energy, or mind of Tao, when it emerges from behind the veils of conditioning and mundane preoccupations, then exerting effort to sustain and expand this contact, to accumulate and store this energy. The metaphor comes from the act of "culling" or gathering medicine/elixir in the "crucible."

cultural fire The practice of "nondoing"—inner alertness without overt effort.

D
dark yellow A general term for sickness.

deviant practices Practices that lead those who become obsessively immersed in them astray from the Tao; generally speaking, they are techniques that induce ecstasy or other extraordinary sense experiences. Also, practices that are useless or harmful. Many of these are listed in Taoist texts.

discriminatory consciousness Consciousness fixed in habitual patterns of thought; consciousness unaware of unity underlying diversity.

dragon's pool Symbol of the world, in the sense that enlightenment is to be developed in the midst of the world, partly through dealing with the problems of life in the world.

E
elixir The innate knowledge and capacity of mind; also said to be a compound of vitality, energy, and spirit, the productive, kinetic, and conscious forces of life.

enter the lair looking for the tiger Using difficulty and danger, the challenges of life in the world ("the lair") to develop strength and firmness ("the tiger").

essence The essence of consciousness, held to be formless, ineffable, ungraspable, accessible only to "true feeling" or "true sense," a property of the real knowledge of the mind of Tao.

extensive observation Observation of objective situations. See also *spiritual observation.*

external furnace The world and outer life of the individual, used as a means of refining the mind and developing character.

extracting lead Removing the accretion of subjectivity polluting the real consciousness, or mind of Tao; goes with *adding mercury,* q.v.

F

false energy   The energy of conditioning, habit; the energy of external influences, or the thoughts and emotions stirred by such influences.

feeling   True feeling, or true sense, is regarded as a faculty of the mind of Tao, the accurate sensing of the essence of mind and the nature of reality.

firing process   The process of refinement of consciousness.

five elements   See *assembling the five elements.*

five virtues   Benevolence, justice, courtesy, wisdom, truthfulness.

four signs   Or four forms; see *combining the four signs.*

furnace   The mind of Tao; see Introduction.

G

genuine intent   Focus of attention, or will, or mental concentration, uninfluenced by external circumstances or by thoughts and emotions. This is the "medium" through which yin and yang, the conscious human mind and the subconscious mind of Tao, are united, so that real knowledge may become conscious and conscious knowledge may be attuned to reality.

gold   Symbol of incorruptibility, purity, illumination.

gold elixir   Symbol of enlightenment, the product of the spiritual alchemy; sometimes referred to as a refinement of a compound of vitality, energy, and spirit, the productive, kinetic, and conscious forces that animate living beings.

golden blossoms/golden flowers   According to one interpretation, golden flowers stand for true feeling, true sense, the capacity of the mind to intuit its essence. Another interpretation refers to golden flowers as the result of the combining of primordial energy, the original force of life, with primordial spirit, the original essence of consciousness. Thus in general golden flowers represent the awakening of the original mind.

great and small   Yang and yin; see Introduction.

great river   Symbol of difficulty, danger, hardship, obstacles, the trials and toils of life.

H

hauling a boat through mud and water   Action in the world.

I

incubation   Calmly nurturing stored energy and awakened consciousness within; development of the *spiritual embryo,* q.v.

intent   See *genuine intent.*

J

jade mushrooms   Symbol of yielding, flexibility, long life; a tortoise swallowing a jade mushroom represents flexibility in the human mind being governed by the firmness of the mind of Tao.

K

killing   Killing has several senses in Taoism. One is the sense of suffocation of the living potential by keeping it encased in habit and mundane preoccupations. Another is the sense of destroying this living potential by wasting energy through unruly physical and mental activity. A third meaning of killing is "killing" the ego; there is a common slogan, "kill the mind, enliven the spirit," meaning to conquer the cruder aspects of consciousness in order to bring to light the more subtle aspects.

killing energy   The force of impermanence and mortality: According to Taoist teaching, people have the option of using this positively to motivate transcendence.

L

lead   Symbol of real knowledge; see *metal, true lead.*

lead meets winter   Real knowledge awakening upon attainment of utter quiescence and emptiness.

living midnight   The state of mental quiescence combined with keen awareness, threshold of the dawn of the awakening of the original mind after the acquired mentality is silenced.

M

mercury   Symbol of flexible consciousness.
metal   Symbol of the firm, unequivocal feeling or sense of real knowledge.

midnight   See *living midnight.*

moon reaching fullness   The full awakening of the mind of Tao.

N

negative energy   The energy of mundanity, the force of habit; fixation on, or emotional and intellectual disturbance by, things of the world, including the body and self.

nihilism   In the context of Taoism, nihilism is denial of or withdrawal from the world, when this withdrawal is kept as a policy or fixed state rather than a temporary device; intoxication with detachment or obsession with the idea or experience of "nothingness" are manifestations of nihilism in this sense.

nonbirth   The nonarising of the impulses and compulsions characteristic of the human mentality.

O

original face   The fundamental wholeness of the human being as it is before being shaped by conditioning through external influences; the real self.

other   This term has several points of reference. It can refer to a teacher, in which case "taking" or "getting" from the "other" means receiving the verbal instruction and mental transmission of a teacher. Also, the "other" can be used to refer to feeling, which becomes "other" when it has become estranged from inner awareness of the essence of consciousness to become agitated by or fixated on externals; in this case, taking from the other means recovering true feeling of the inner essence of mind. "Other" also means everything and everyone outside oneself, in which feelings are involved; then taking from the other means to recover the energy invested in people and things by maintaining inward autonomy. "To get, first you must give," a common dictum used in reference to the "other," means that in order to receive from the other it is necessary first to develop a certain attitude or orientation, a certain harmonization, on one's own part.

P

pearl   Symbol of clarified awareness.

planting lotuses in fire   Being in the world and acting efficiently in the world without being coerced by the influences of the world.

polar energies   Yin and yang.

positive energy   The primordial or "celestial" energy of life, which is not trapped by mundane feelings or fixations; the energy of the mind of Tao.

Q

quietism   Attachment to tranquility; adoption of the life of a recluse as an end in itself; attachment to meditation exercise stilling the mind, without corresponding dynamic action following a climax of stillness.

R

rectitude   Though this can in general mean correctness of action or orientation, it often has the special meaning of restraint, stillness, when in a position of weakness; the term "chastity" is used in this same way.

refinement   Purification of consciousness.

releasing   Freeing mind from the enclosure of mundane conditioning.

restored elixir   Consciousness returned to reality from restrictive mental habit and attachment to conceptual constructs; feeling returned to essence from agitation over externals.

reversing   Reversing the process of conditioning by withdrawing from fixations and obsessions so that the mind cannot be manipulated by external or internal events. Returning to the "innocent" state represented by the "infant."

S

sane energy   The primal, unconditioned energy of the mind of Tao, "sane" in the sense of being whole, unscattered, aligned with the celestial design of reality and not enslaved by the demands of the ego.

seeds of vicious circles   Configurations of habit energy, through the force of which repetitious patterns of thought, being, and action become fixed in the conditioned personality.

seven-times restored elixir   Seven is the number associated with yang fire; this elixir means consciousness without volatility, stabilized awareness.

shell   The boundaries of the sense of individuality.

small vehicle   Quiescent detachment practiced alone; called a small vehicle because it serves only as a means of personal comfort or release, and lacks the dynamic capable of benefiting others.

spiritual embryo   A term for the initial coalescing of the unified being in which consciousness and reality, feeling and essence, vitality and spirit, are joined in one energy. It is also defined as the quality of correct balance of flexible receptivity, the beginning of conscious development. This is the embryonic form of the "new human" to be produced by Taoist practice.

spiritual observation   Inner contemplation, awareness of the mind; goes with *extensive observation* (q.v.) or observation of the objective situation.

suchness   Being as is; spontaneity; reality unmasked by subjective projections.

T

ten months' work   The period of *incubation* (q.v.) of the *spiritual embryo* (q.v.). The term "ten months" is a figurative expression based on the image of human gestation, which lasts ten lunar months, and is not literal: It means the period of stabilization of the state in which the human mind and the mind of Tao are united, taking care to avoid fragmentation through succumbing to inner or outer agitation.

tiger's lair   Symbol of the world: see *dragon's pool* and *enter the lair looking for the tiger.*

true energy   See *sane energy.*

true fire   Stable awareness and attention, not influenced by ordinary intellection or emotion.

true intent   See *genuine intent.*

true lead   Symbol of the real knowledge of the mind of Tao; see *metal* and *lead.* The image is of firmness and gravity, which stabilizes the volatile "mercury" of the human mind.

U

usurping creation   Or "taking over evolution"; recovering autonomy, becoming free from the compelling force of habituation, and taking the initiative in continuing conscious development unhindered by the limitations of personality or culture. This is the work of creating the "new human."

W

winter   The climax of the practice of quiescence; see *lead meets winter*. See also *living midnight*. Winter followed by spring, like midnight followed by dawn, symbolizes the culmination of yin followed by arising of yang. See Introduction.

Y

yellow woman   The "go-between" of yin and yang, through which the human mind and mind of Tao are mated: a symbol of the *genuine intent* (q.v.), the power of stable concentration.

yellow sprouts   Symbol of the "living potential," the basic life energy when freed from the domination of conditioning; the original creative potential of being.

Key for Identifying the Hexagrams

TRIGRAMS UPPER ▶ / LOWER ▼	Ch'ien ☰	Chên ☳	K'an ☵	Kên ☶	K'un ☷	Sun ☴	Li ☲	Tui ☱
Chi'en ☰	1	34	5	26	11	9	14	43
Chên ☳	25	51	3	27	24	42	21	17
K'an ☵	6	40	29	4	7	59	64	47
Kên ☶	33	62	39	52	15	53	56	31
K'un ☷	12	16	8	23	2	20	35	45
Sun ☴	44	32	48	18	46	57	50	28
Li ☲	13	55	63	22	36	37	30	49
Tui ☱	10	54	60	41	19	61	38	58

I CHING MANDALAS
A Program of Study for
The Book of Changes

Preface

The *I Ching*, or *Book of Changes*, is an ancient book of omen and advice that has gained such popularity in both East and West that it hardly needs any introduction. Less well known is the esoteric lore of the *Changes* relating to higher education and intellectual development. This volume contains readings of this classic book of consultations specially structured according to traditional programs of study and training, with additional programs for analytic consultation, programs for specialized patterns of focus on *Changes* omens and advice, and programs for the mechanisms of meditation.

This book is presented as a companion volume to my other *I Ching* translations—*The Taoist I Ching*, *The Buddhist I Ching*, and *I Ching: The Tao of Organization*—to enable the serious student of this ancient classic to develop a comprehensive, in-depth understanding of the book according to the three Ways of Chinese thought and to provide a series of analytic methods by which the *I Ching* in any of these three versions, or in any other translation, may be deliberately and systematically consulted.

The open publication of such study programs in China seems to date back about one thousand years, to the time of paramount Chan Buddhist influence on the study of ancient Chinese lore, both Taoist and Confucian. As a whole, the programs reflect the Buddhist practice of striving for enhanced objectivity through deliberate consideration of multiple points of view. The effect of this approach to *The Book of Changes* is to produce a sense of intensity combined with seemingly unlimited extension, one familiar in Chan studies of literature.

It may seem tautological to say that the pervasive feature of the structure of *The Book of Changes* is that it changes, but this point nevertheless requires deliberate attention because the format of the written text is more or less fixed, due to the nature of writing itself. Very different impressions are derived not only from different traditions of *Changes* commentary, but also from different patterns of reading. Thus a special literature developed to illustrate specific patterns that highlight certain aspects of the *Changes* teaching while maintaining its overall coherence.

In modern terms, these are programs for *Changes* study and consultation, originally designed to open up the inner and outer world of those who use the written *Changes* to learn to perceive the unwritten changes. In Buddhist and Taoist terms, this means learning to see the times within each time, the possibilities in every potential. In ordinary terms, it means using a tool that itself changes as perception develops in order to keep that development evolving to the point where the tool is no longer needed.

Historical Introduction

The Sanskrit word *mandala*, well known in English through classic studies of Indian religion, has the meanings of a circle, a sphere, a territory, a group, a society, and a collection. In Buddhism the word is applied to certain forms of sacred art designed to present compendia of teachings. Mandalas may consist of patterns of symbolic letters, abstract designs, or figures of beings and objects. In most cases their advantage as educational tools lies in their immediate, nonlinear presentation of interrelated ideas to be held in mind together. In the context of the *I Ching*, diagrams, or mandalas, are similarly used to group the symbols and readings of the text in certain specific ways, as well as to represent fundamental ideas and structures underlying the culture of the *I Ching*.

While there survive a few very ancient Chinese equivalents of the mandalas of Indian spiritual traditions, more of them are left from the Taoist schools of the early centuries CE, when Buddhism was entering China. Even more of them remain from the records of Taoist schools of the eleventh century CE onward. Generally speaking, they tend to be more abstract than the magnificent fine arts associated with Tantric Buddhist traditions, and their popular use as talismans has tended to obscure other ranges of function, in the absence of general knowledge of the totality of the mechanism of talismans.

The original trigrams and hexagrams of the *I Ching*, which could be called mandalas in the classical sense, date from long before Buddhism came into China, but the esoteric mandalas associated with the *I Ching* and its inner teachings are said to have originated among the Taoist methodologists (*fang-shi*) of the Han dynasty, which began in the late third century BCE and formally ended in the early third century CE.

By all accounts, the *I Ching* mandalas came into the public domain during the Sung dynasty, which began in the latter tenth century CE and ended in the latter thirteenth century. The Sung dynasty was a time of reamalgamation of spiritual teachings in China, when increasing numbers of Confucian scholars sought out the Taoist and Chan Buddhist teachings. Many Confucians of the more pedestrian variety, however, were scandalized by the notion that Taoists had held secrets about the *I Ching* for a thousand years and rejected the claim that the *I Ching* mandalas were among the devices of the ancient Taoist methodologists.

Nevertheless, some of the *I Ching* teachings of the Taoist Shao Ying of the Hundred Sources school filtered into Confucianism through Zhou Dunyi and Cheng Yi in the eleventh century, permanently changing the face of Confucianism. Cheng, a distinguished Confucian scholar and educator, was a student of Taoism and Buddhism, though he opposed certain formalities and aberrations associated with monastic elaborations of the latter. His famous interpretation of the *I Ching* is translated in my *I Ching: The Tao of Organization*.

The neo-Confucian movement known to its practitioners as the study of Inner Design was strongly influenced by Zhou and Cheng, and thus came to bear the indelible marks of Taoism and Buddhism. The emergence of this new Confucianism took place at the same time as the emergence of new Taoism, which included what were believed to be revelations of the ancient traditions through reexperience of the source of the teachings. Part of this new Taoist lore was the genre of *I Ching* mandalas. An interpretation of the text of the *I Ching* according to the teachings of new Taoism is presented in my earlier translation entitled *The Taoist I Ching*, while teachings of the same school on the inner meanings of the mandalas are contained in this present volume.

There are various sets of *I Ching* mandalas, with common and different designs. Generally speaking, there are two major functions associated with these mandalas. One is to encapsulate the foundation of the ideas underlying the *I Ching*, the other is to encapsulate models of *I Ching* organizational patterns or study courses. As certain mandalas illustrate, a basic characteristic of these functions is that they are interdependent, as are all of the teachings of the *I Ching* itself. This volume uses both of these functions: the Readings chapter, on the outer teachings, employs programs abstracted from the mandalas with readings of the text of the *I Ching* as tools for consulting, coordinating, and augmenting my earlier translations from Taoist, Buddhist, and Confucian interpretations; the Arcana sections, on the inner teachings, presents a series of essays on the foundation of ideas represented by the mandalas, based on the teachings of Liu I-ming, master of Taoism, Confucianism, and Chan Buddhism.

Consulting the I Ching

The *I Ching* is commonly thought of as having originally been an oracle or book of divination that was later philosophized. This popular conception is partly based on archaeological evidence demonstrating the existence of oracles and divination practices in remote antiquity and partly on the assumption that superstition antedates philosophy. It is true that there is an overt allusion to divination procedure in the core text of the *I Ching* and that reference to divination is made in the earliest known strata of commentary; and it is also true that the book has been popularly regarded and used as an oracle since time immemorial. There are, however, dissenting voices from each of the three main traditions of Chinese thought, stimulating further examination into the nature of the *I Ching* and the possibility of more complete and coherent use of the *I Ching* than that available within the framework of divination techniques.

Simply to call a book an oracle does not, of course, explain either the book or what an oracle is. The fact that divinatory use of the *I Ching* is still practiced—not only by people steeped in ancient beliefs but also by people acculturated to modern scientific beliefs—does at least demonstrate that if divination is to be regarded as a more pristine or primitive level of understanding than philosophy, the development of understanding represented by transition from divination to philosophy cannot be regarded as necessarily parallel with a forward movement in time. The popular use of certain famous Persian poetry for divination provides an excellent example, more easily verified historically than that of the ancient *I Ching*, of what might be called a regressive use of literature never intended by its author.

There are, in short, no grounds for assuming that more and less sophisticated understandings and applications of the *I Ching* did not exist side by side from remotest antiquity. Indeed, objective studies of religions comparing the teachings and methods of founders with the dogmas and rites of institutionalizers would suggest in fact that the customary conception and use of the *I Ching* as an oracle for divination may very likely have been a later development. In Buddhist terms, it might be theorized that *I Ching* divination represents an imitation or a relic of the original use of the teaching.

In my introduction to *The Taoist I Ching*, I cited several Chinese sources presenting a view of the *I Ching* that basically rejects the idea of the classic as an oracle. These arguments bear repeating, not because they are necessarily truer than any other but because the popularity of the view that the *I Ching* was and is an oracle is such that it is easy to take it for granted as true and thus to leave unexamined the possibility that the *I Ching* is not a mystery but a system, a system that can be seen whole and whose workings can be deliberately understood and applied.

These arguments may be summed up as follows:

1. Skillful *I Ching* use does not involve divination, in the sense of picking out chapters to read according to yarrow stick drawings or tosses of coins.

2. The early commentaries traditionally ascribed to the great sixth-century BCE educator Confucius, while recognizing the currency of divination and speaking of it as a means, nevertheless were written for the express purpose of bringing out the pragmatic psychology, sociology, and metaphysics of the *I Ching* in a time when the use of the already-ancient classic had degenerated into divination.

3. After the final degeneration of that protracted phase of Chinese civilization marked by the emergence and elaboration of the *I Ching* in what was to be its final form, when the founder of a new order attempted a radical cultural revolution in which all records of the old civilization were to be destroyed, it was the association with divination that spared the *I Ching* from the fire, suggesting the use of this format as a protective coating, much as popular forms of literature such as proverbs, poetry, fiction, and humor served as protective coating for developmental teachings in postclassical China.

4. The purpose of the written *I Ching* is to reveal the principles whereby human beings can understand their minds and thus learn to improve their ability to adapt to external change, so that they can be more effective and enjoy greater peace of mind.

The premise that the *I Ching* is a system that can be understood and operated also implies that its oracular function can be deliberately understood and applied quite apart from the question of whether or not it is primary or an imitation of something more real. According to the commentator of *The Buddhist I Ching*, the practice of divination is legitimately used in working with the *I Ching* in the sense that divination is popular and thus can be used as a means of communicating with people. According to Buddhist teaching, wisdom can only be conveyed directly without signs to those who already have wisdom, in proportion to the wisdom they already have; while wisdom can only be communicated to those without wisdom through some sort of functional medium.

While the idea and practice of divination are in fact often accepted, even enthusiastically, by modern products of Western civilization, modern presentations of the *I Ching* in connection with divination ordinarily go to some lengths to make rational accommodations, in the interest of communicating with those who feel the need for rational explanations. Underlying these rational accommodations is the recognition of cognitive limitations.

Recent progress in physics and psychology has prepared the well-informed modern mind to accept the ancient Taoist and Buddhist proposition that there is more to reality than what we perceive and how we construe our perceptions. While this view allows room for the idea of invisible connections, however, it still does not clarify the nature of the link between these invisible connections and relationships among events as they are ordinarily perceived. Recognition of limitations does not in itself demonstrate the means of transcending limitations, nor does it provide a method of determining the reality or otherwise of what may be attributed to inspiration, intuition, or revelation, such as do in fact seem to leap over the boundaries of ordinary perception.

One theory that has proven most attractive to modern Westerners is the idea of synchronicity, or relationships between simultaneous events that are not susceptible to ready explanation in terms of ordinary conceptions of causality. Here again, while this concept may be useful in relaxing the compelling force of habitual associations and allow for a wider range of awareness of potential significance, it fails to clarify the nature of relations and leaves room for virtually unlimited imagination. Popular literature, from pseudooccultism to financial forecasting, abounds with examples of attempts to draw conclusions about the possible meanings behind coincidences of all sorts.

Application of the idea of synchronicity does not, therefore, guarantee a broader perspective or deeper understanding if there is no change in a pattern of rationalization other than to apply the same pattern to a larger field of possibilities. More modern thinking about thinking pioneered by the brilliant work of Edward DeBono, on the other hand, provides us with a more operative conceptual vocabulary for understanding practical potential in the use of *I Ching* readings drawn by a method that is from the ordinary point of view a random one, such as the yarrow stick procedure traditionally used in divination.

Using DeBono's model of lateral thinking, it is easy to conceive of the process of *I Ching* divination as a means of expanding thought or opening up new perceptions, without the immediate intrusion of subjective expectations. Since the inherent structure of the *I Ching* involves focus on polarity—opposition and complementarity—which are found in some form in any situation, relevance at some level seems to come naturally. Then the associations surrounding the link between the subject of the consultation and the reading that is chosen foster what might be called centrifugal thinking. In contrast to centripetal thinking, which contracts around—and attempts to draw conclusions towards—a point of assumed relevance, centrifugal thinking expands outwards—and extracts latent possibilities—from a point of perceived relevance.

In Buddhist terms, the infinite complexity of the universe as a web of relationships is referred to as the inconceivability of cause and effect. Buddhist philosophy acknowledges that everything is inextricably related to everything else, but while it consequently insists that the totality of relationships cannot be exhaustively defined except by the totality itself, Buddhist philosophy does not therefore abandon analytic reason but recognizes different levels of intellectual understanding, including the purely fictitious and the relatively true.

Buddhism commonly takes a twofold approach to distinguishing levels of fiction and truth, reducing subjectivity and increasing objectivity. Generally speaking, subjectivity is reduced by stilling arbitrary trains of thought, while objectivity is increased by broadening the scope of comprehensive examination. According to the model of the Flower Ornament school of Buddhism, noted for its extraordinary teachings on time and causality, this is done by dissolving the fixation of attention on ordinarily perceived externals, then restructuring the attention in such a way as to balance the need for perceptual order with the possibility of deliberately creative extension and enhancement of life experience.

One of the best-known structures used by the Flower Ornament school to reorient awareness may be visualized through one of its classical metaphors, an immense circular net of jewels or mirrors, each of which contains the reflections of all the other jewels or mirrors, all of which already have within them the reflections of all the other jewels or mirrors. It is enough to summon this image mentally for just a brief moment to see the infinity of infinities implied in the simultaneous interreflections; in practice, this visualization is used to arrest the linear movement of the conceptual faculty and suggest an impression of multidirectional perception and thought in the inconceivably complex web of events.

There is a further pragmatic issue here, in that the nature of the link between the inconceivable and the conceivable, the mysterious and the manageable, may be generally intuited but not specifically defined just by drawing attention to the existence of the gap. To assist in clarifying this link, the Buddhist Flower Ornament teaching applies practical steps to understanding events on different scales at one and the same time. An event may be seen as a composite of a number of smaller events, for example, and as itself one element of a larger event. Furthermore, events that may appear very different in fact may be very similar in principle. By balancing different points of view, seeing them not only as individual perspectives but as parts of a more comprehensive perspective that includes the ways in which different viewpoints reflect upon each other and are reflected in each other,

Flower Ornament Buddhist thought prepares the mind for enlarged perception and enhanced objectivity.

Considered in this light, the *I Ching* also serves as a tool for the practical development of normal consciousness, and this is the spirit in which it has been approached by leading thinkers of all three traditions of Chinese thought. Not only does its structure illustrate the interdependence of its elements as well as the interdependence of the parts and the whole, its archaic language is so pregnant with potential meaning in the total context of Chinese thought and symbolism that the same text can produce several different readings. The effect of these characteristics of the *I Ching* is to produce an integrated array of images and insights permeated with central themes arising from the interaction of tension and complementarity in relationships.

The existence of interpretations of the *I Ching* so different as often to demand variant translations of the text itself—indeed, even of the names of numerous hexagrams—was the basis of my decision to render the *I Ching* in three different versions, according to readings and understandings deriving from Taoism, Buddhism, and Confucianism, the three leading traditions of Chinese practical philosophy. Furthermore, the enormous amount of attention ordinarily devoted to divination and the preponderance of commentary based on limited Confucian concepts stimulated my interest in tradititonal uses of the *I Ching* beyond these parameters.

The conception of the *I Ching* as an oracle is understandable in terms of the long-standing popularity of divination and its traditional association with the *I Ching*. There are also obvious historical reasons for the predominance of certain Confucian concepts in the general understanding of the *I Ching*. To begin with, the original words of the *I Ching* are attributed to two of the most revered figures in Confucian historiography, and the earliest commentaries—now ordinarily embedded in the *I Ching*, or appended to it—are attributed to Confucius or his school. Regarded as a classic in its Confucianized form, the *I Ching* thus became a standard subject for study by all Confucian scholars seeking public office through the civil service examination system. When the works of Chu Hsi (1130–1200) were chosen for the basis of the examinations in the fourteenth century and retained as orthodox for six hundred years, this naturally had a long-term effect on the study of the *I Ching*. Chu Hsi's commentary on the *I Ching* is unfortunately cursory and hackneyed, and it fixates on divination practice without balancing this by attention to the need for total or holistic understanding.

Given the influence of political history and historical politics on the study of the *I Ching*, it is not surprising to find a modern Chinese interpreter, ostensibly writing on scientific aspects of the classic, pausing in his discussion to affirm the Confucian identity of the text and deny that there is any relation between the *I Ching* and Taoism—or to find a modern Western translator state that Taoists simply ignored the classic. Yet Taoist literature, especially the literature of spiritual alchemy, abounds with references to, and material from, the *I Ching;* and there are a number of works devoted completely to its interpretation, such as the one translated in my earlier volume entitled *The Taoist I Ching.*

My purpose in producing new translations of the *I Ching* according to commentarial traditions as yet little known or unexplored in the West (and in large segments of its readership in the East) was to broaden the scope of *I Ching* studies beyond the realm of official Chinese orthodoxy and indeed beyond the realm of Chinese culture and history. Even in the Confucian field, there are commentaries on the *I Ching* far more illuminating than the pedestrian work of Chu Hsi, whose talents are hardly commensurate with the politically enforced popularity of his writing. After completing translations of Taoist and Buddhist interpretations of the *I Ching,* therefore, I turned to a Confucian commentary that was not confined to the arid pedantry so commonplace in official Confucianism or to the popular notion of the *I Ching* as a tool for divination.

At present there is, to be sure, a dedicated effort by some modern scholars to leave the rut into which *I Ching* studies so easily fall due to the weight of historical circumstances. An approach that has drawn considerable attention in the academic world is that of textual criticism, involving the search for ancient variants and the question of the original form of the text. My own interest, on the other hand, is not particularly academic or historical but, rather, practical and thus has led to issues of interpretation that are not primarily philological but psychological.

Before going into the specifics of the programs for *I Ching* study presented in this volume, it will be useful to review the structure and contents of my three translations of the *I Ching* in order to clarify the operative relation of this volume with these translations. While the present volume is arranged so that it can be used alone or in conjunction with virtually any translation of the *I Ching,* nevertheless it draws on and coordinates the interpretations of the text given by the commentators in my earlier translations, so it is to these that I will now turn to illustrate something of the different ways in which the *I Ching* can be presented and how this volume may be used to integrate them.

The first translation in this series, entitled in English *The Taoist I Ching,* is based on a text divided by the Taoist commentator into explanations of the *I Ching* proper and explanations of two major additions attributed to Confucius. The *I Ching* proper, in this context, means the sayings on the hexagrams attributed to King Wen of the twelfth century BCE, plus the sayings on the individual lines of the hexagrams attributed to King Wen's son, the Duke of Chou. The Confucian additions treated in this particular text are the sayings known as the Great Images associated with the hexagrams, and the sayings on pairs of hexagrams in the commentary known as the Mixed Hexagrams.

In most texts, the Great Images are inserted directly into the *I Ching* proper, so this Taoist arrangement, allowing as it does for greater interpretative scope, is of considerable interest. Like many Taoists, the expositor of *The Taoist I Ching* regarded original Confucianism as a branch of Taoism, and even the Confucian commentaries are given Taoistic interpretations dealing with the use of this classic as a guide to the development of vitality, energy, and spirit.

The second translation in the series, entitled in English *The Buddhist I Ching*, is based on a text that inserts several of the ancient Confucian commentaries directly into the *I Ching* proper. The first of these is that known as the Overall Judgment, an analysis of the symbolism of each of the hexagrams in terms of the trigrams of which it is composed. Following each Overall Judgment is the Great Image, a brief statement on the hexagram; this is the commentary that the aforementioned Taoist interpreter isolates into a separate section. There is also a comment on the image of each individual line of each hexagram.

Like the Taoist interpreter, the Buddhist interpreter was also learned in Confucianism; the Buddhist commentary goes somewhat further, however, in discussing the social and institutional dimensions of its sphere of interest, aided by the use of the text in closer conjunction with the pristine Confucian commentaries. The Buddhist balances this, on the other hand, with extensive teachings on inner workings of the mind. Where this latter dimension is concerned, the interpretation focuses on a harmonious balance of factors essential to the understanding, practice, and experience of higher psychological evolution; and it also analyzes the causes and effects of defective or distorted developments.

The third translation in the series, entitled *I Ching: The Tao of Organization*, is based on the famous commentary of a major figure among the founders of the neo-Confucian movement, which integrated Taoist and Buddhist practices with Confucian social science. Since this commentary closely follows the pristine Confucian interpretations found in the commentaries on judgments and images, already included in *The Buddhist I Ching*, these latter additions and the recapitulations of the commentator have been used only to translate the original text of the *I Ching* and the essential explanations thereof given in the commentary. The third translation thus represents a streamlined version of the original, focusing on use of the *I Ching* in analyzing group and individual psychology and behavior in organizations.

The object of this fourth work is twofold: to relate the teachings found in the *I Ching* through the perspectives of the three traditions of Chinese thought and to map out specific patterns of study as indicated by the sequences and sets of hexagrams contained in the *I Ching* mandalas. This twofold object is in turn approached in two ways: first, three levels of readings are arranged according to three specific patterns, yet in such a way as to link each level; second, certain programs of consultation based on associations and constructions indicated by the mandalas are defined in conjunction with the interlocking readings.

As a first step to using this book, therefore, one could peruse the included Readings—of the images, themes, and lines of the *I Ching* according to their individual sets: in the Images section, this means the set of images in each series; in the Themes section, the set of readings of each pair of signs; in the Lines section, the sets of readings for the lines in each quantity of yin or yang. The meditations in the Arcana sections now show ways of deepening consciousness more directly; the preceding readings of the *I Ching* provide something like an outer framework that contains the energy of deep inner work and prevents it from leaking out in random or idiosyncratic ways, while the inner work deepens the understanding and application of the outer teachings.

This procedure familiarizes the reader with the general contents of the text and some of the basic structures of its traditional presentation. Starting with the arcana and starting with individually chosen hexagrams would produce correspondingly different effects, equally valid according to the use made of them. If the book is approached through chosen readings eventually followed by total systematic readings, going from the part to the whole, again the compound effect would cast a different impression than would proceeding from the whole to the parts. Ultimately, of course, the goal is to integrate specific, or local, perception and understanding with total, or global, perception and understanding, so the final result of all methods should be the same complete understanding.

One way to understand the existence of *I Ching* mandalas, or groups of sets, is in terms of the limitations inherent in linear writing and ways of overcoming this hurdle. The sequence of hexagrams in the traditional text of the *I Ching* is just one way of reading the book; and even this one order can be understood in radically different ways, a shown in the contrast between the method of *The Taoist I Ching* and that of *I Ching: The Tao of Organization*. Since the written text has a fixed shape, other sequences are therefore mapped in various mandalas to guide the reader through other programs of study that yield further insight into the integrity of the total system of the *I Ching*. This is something that cannot be done by reading only according to a divination technique or only according to the standard order of the written text.

In this volume, the readings of the *I Ching* are arranged first of all according to several of these alternate programs, geared towards magnification of understanding not by elaboration of individual elements but by elaboration of their effects through specific combinations. Therefore just by reading each set of each section in the order presented, it is possible to enter a new frame of mind. After this introduction, other arrangements conducive to further expansion of perceptions are mapped out for use in exploring the readings in this volume as well as those in my other three translations of the *I Ching*.

The Images section of the Readings of this volume is arranged in the order specified by several interrelated diagrams illustrating the *primal* order of the trigrams and hexagrams (illustrations 4–6). The hexagrams are arranged in eight series, based on the bottom trigrams. This order is quite different from the *temporal* sequence of the trigrams and hexagrams that is ordinarily used in the written form of the text of the *I Ching*, and a distinctly different impression is obtained from reading the hexagrams in this primal order rather than in the temporal order.

Before turning to the themes and lines of the hexagrams, however, it will be of great interest to read each sequence of images both forwards and in reverse; this can be done comparatively rapidly, and the impressions created by this practice illustrate something of the potential the text has for generating different perspectives and perceptions according to the order in which it is studied. There are, no doubt, among the readers of my earlier translations those who have applied this principle of reversal to note the dramatically different effects according to the order in which the Taoist, Buddhist, and organizational commentaries are read.

Those who have read *The Taoist I Ching, The Buddhist I Ching,* and *I Ching: The Tao of Organization* will have noticed that each of these commentaries is individually designed to be read straight through, revealing a coherent system of practice. In terms of the totality of these three versions, representing as they do the three main traditions of Chinese thought, when they are read in the order in which they have appeared, a certain pattern emerges that is more than the sum of its parts; when they are read in the reverse order, another dimension of that pattern becomes evident. A similar, if less dramatic, effect can be had in working with individual hexagrams or pairs of hexagrams, using the readings and maps in this volume in conjunction with the readings in the other three volumes.

The Themes section of this book is designed to coordinate and harmonize the Taoist, Buddhist, and Confucian understandings, summarizing basic points illustrated in the themes of the hexagrams according to each tradition. This part is arranged according to three interwoven plans: first, based on the temporal order of the hexagrams, it follows the order of the standard written text; second, based on the mandala known as the complete map of the sixty-four hexagrams in the process of spiritual alchemy (illustration 2), the hexagrams are paired, following the same order but in twos, each pair consisting of one hexagram from the odd, or yang, sequence and one hexagram from the even, or yin, sequence; third, based on a Taoist model, the entire text is divided into upper and lower courses, each course then being divided into beginning, middle, and end.

The Lines section of this book arranges the readings of the lines of the hexagrams according to a map known as the diagram of the changes of the hexagrams, which in turn is a variant of a Taoist mandala called the complete map of the Six Yangs and Six Yins of the Yang Fire and Yin Convergence (illustration 3). The design of this program facilitates study of lines in sets according to specific concentrations of yin or yang.

The last chapter of the book is a series of essays on the foundation of ideas and practices for producing the heightened awareness that is supposed to empower the use of the *I Ching*.

Directions

Hexagrams can be consulted deliberately according to certain traditional models, based on trigrams and lines. Even though they are chosen according to the associations in the mind of the reader projected through the programs, nevertheless the resulting readings under ordinary circumstances always contain an element external to the expectations of the reader. Thus the reading is useful in analyzing perceptions from given points of view, based on the selections they elicit from the *I Ching* system, with the added vantage point of extra perceptions outside those points of view.

TRIGRAM SYSTEMS

Several trigram association systems are found in *I Ching* mandalas. The basic principle is that the lower, or base, trigram represents the inside or beginning and the upper, or shifting, trigram represents the outside or the end. Therefore a hexagram can be chosen to represent the inner state and outward manifestations of an individual, a pragmatic inspiration and its outcome, the relationship between two individuals, or an individual and a group or general environment.

In the system outlined in a mandala of the trigrams representing the primal integration of yin and yang, the associations of the trigrams are as follows:

Heaven: yang, strength, life, justice and duty
Lake: yin, harmony, sense and feeling, justice and duty
Fire: yin, understanding, spirit, courtesy
Thunder: yang, action, nature, humanitarianism
Wind: yin, obedience, nature, humanitarianism
Water: yang, severity, vitality, wisdom
Mountain: yang, restraint, vitality, wisdom
Earth: yin, conformity, nature, courtesy

EXAMPLES

The qualities of the relationship between someone who is good-natured and actively helps fellow human beings, and someone who is intelligent, aware, and tactful can be represented by the hexagrams *Richness* (55) and *Biting Through* (21). These hexagrams depict the qualities that the relationship brings out in the person symbolized by the bottom hexagram.

The good-natured, active humanitarian, represented by the trigram *Thunder*, in association with an intelligent, aware, and tactful partner, represented by the trigram *Fire*, is successful in doing what is right in the world at large, as symbolized by the hexagram *Biting Through*.

The intelligent, aware, and tactful person, represented by the trigram *Fire*, in association with the good-natured, active humanitarian represented by the trigram *Thunder*, can successfully make full use of intelligence to accomplish great deeds without anxiety, as represented by the hexagram *Richness*.

The advice of the lines of the hexagram are specific directions for fulfilling the potential of these qualities in the relationship, by avoiding pitfalls, heeding warnings, following directions, and taking advantage of opportunities.

For the purpose of selecting readings, individuals are described in terms of the qualities that bear on the situation or relationship concerned. There are four qualities in this scheme, each represented by two trigrams, according to different modes of acquisition and exercise of these qualities.

The quality of justice represented by *Heaven* acts from the energy of identification with life; the quality of justice represented by *Lake* is informed by sensitive harmonization.

The quality of courtesy represented by *Fire* is that of someone in the position of an outsider or guest, who is able to treat others as they would be treated, by being perceptive. The quality of courtesy represented by *Earth* is that of someone on home ground, in whom customary courtesy has become naturalized by ordinary conformity with the environment.

The quality of humanitarianism represented by *Thunder* is that of the natural activist. The quality of humanitarianism represented by *Wind* is that of the natural pacifist.

The quality of wisdom represented by *Water* is characterised by ability to master the passions in action. The quality of wisdom represented by *Mountain* is characterised by ability to restraint the passions in stillness.

The reader who has thus chosen a pair of hexagrams now turns to the Images section of the Readings in this volume. The hexagrams can be found easily by reference to the base trigram, since the Images section is divided into eight subsets, each one based on a single trigram. The sets are in the standard sequence of the primal order:

1. Heaven
2. Lake

3. Fire
4. Thunder
5. Wind
6. Water
7. Mountain
8. Earth

Within each subset, the sequence of the shifting upper trigrams also follows this order.

When the target hexagrams are located, the images are read along with the neighboring images located directly above and below.

Each hexagram is numbered according to the regular sequence of hexagrams used in the standard written *I Ching*. This number is now used to locate the thematic reading of the target hexagram in the Themes section of the book. The group of readings in the Themes section is divided into six subsets:

Hexagrams 1–8 are in the beginning of the upper course.
Hexagrams 9–16 are in the middle of the upper course.
Hexagrams 17–30 are in the end of the upper course.
Hexagrams 31–42 are in the beginning of the lower course.
Hexagrams 43–50 are in the middle of the lower course.
Hexagrams 51–64 are in the end of the lower course.

In this reading, each hexagram is paired with a neighbor in this sequence, with which it is related. Thus the scope of the original reading is further enlarged.

Each thematic reading is followed by a note on the number of yang and yin lines in each hexagram. The reader then turns to the Lines section, in which readings of the lines are grouped in sets of hexagrams with the same number of yang and yin lines. A hexagram with one yang line and five yin lines will thus be found in two sets: the two sets have the same members, but they are in different orders, according to whether the hexagrams are being defined by their yang lines or their yin lines. In this arrangement, different configurations of the same concentrations of lines of one pole, yin or yang, can be seen together, thus expanding the original reading yet further by analogy.

Another way of choosing hexagrams is outlined in two diagrams representing the trigrams in temporal processes (illustrations 9, 10). One is called the diagram of *following* temporal creation, the other is called the diagram of transformation by *reverse* operation within the temporal. Since the trigrammatic associations in these diagrams are simply the reverse of one another, it is easy to treat their systems in tandem. The correspondences here are as follows:

HEAVEN   *Following: True strength shifts, false strength emerges.*
                Reversal: False strength dissolves, true strength returns.
Here, true strength means strength of character, firmness of will, decisiveness in action. False strength means aggressiveness, stubbornness, belligerence.

LAKE   *Following: True yin submerges, false yin advances.*
              Reversal: False yin submerges, true yin advances.
Here, true yin means flexibility, false yin means weakness; these associations are closely related to the true and false obedience symbolized by the trigram *Earth*.

FIRE   *Following: The original spirit is obscure, the conscious spirit*
              is bright.
              Reversal: The conscious spirit is silenced, the original spirit
              is manifest.
Here, the original spirit means the primal subtle function of awareness; the conscious spirit is temporally conditioned consciousness.

THUNDER   *Following: True yang stops, false yang appears.*
                 Reversal: False yang stops, true yang appears.
Here, true yang is strength or firmness, false yang is obduracy or aggressiveness; these associations are closely related to the true and false strength symbolized by the trigram *Heaven*.

WIND   *Following: Attraction of arbitrary emotions, concealment*
              of original sense.
              Reversal: Sublimation of arbitrary emotions, revelation of
              original sense.
Here, original sense refers to an objective sense of reality; arbitrary emotions are subjective feelings about objects.

WATER   *Following: The original vitality is submerged, turbid vi-*
               tality is born.
               Reversal: The original vitality is stabilized, turbid vi-
               tality disappears.
Here, the original vitality refers to the pure essence of life energy; turbid vitality refers to personal passion.

MOUNTAIN   *Following: The original nature becomes defective,*
                  temperamental nature acts.
                  Reversal: The original nature lives, temperamen-
                  tal nature fades away.
Here, original nature means the basic essence of consciousness, temperamental nature means the shifting array of moods and feelings that characterize the personality.

EARTH   *Following: True obedience shifts, false obedience arises.*
Reversal: False obedience transforms, true obedience
remains.

Here, true obedience means that which follows direct perception of what is right, good, or necessary; false obedience means that which follows someone or something simply out of weakness, or for purely personal advantage.

In terms of external qualities, *Fire* is associated with courtesy and pleasure. *Water* is associated with wisdom and sadness. *Wind* is associated with justice and anger. *Mountain* is associated with kindness and joy.

Yet another trigrammatic system is represented in a diagram depicting the generation of the trigrams as "being produced from nonbeing." The correspondences indicated in this program are as follows:

Heaven means activity of sense or feeling.
Lake means tranquillity of sense or feeling.
Fire means activity of spirit.
Earth means tranquillity of spirit.
Water means activity of vitality.
Mountain means tranquillity of vitality.
Thunder means activity of nature.
Wind means tranquillity of nature.

Sense or feeling is associated primally with intuition and temporally with emotion.
Spirit is associated primally with pure awareness and temporally with cognition and intellection.
Vitality is associated primally with generative energy and temporally with sexuality.
Nature is associated primally with the essence of consciousness and temporally with temperament and personality.

This diagram thus generates readings in terms of active or passive states in primal and/or temporal psychological faculties and functions. The crucial point of interest in alternating associations chosen to derive readings is the distinctive character of the way the reader interprets passages. This enhances awareness of the effect of the observer on the observed, in accordance with the level of participation of the observer in the observed.

HEXAGRAM CONCENTRATIONS

There are several sets of concentrations of hexagrams generated by the diagrams of the primal and temporal orders of the trigrams, both separately and superimposed. An ancient diagram of the primal order says that each trigram is to be joined with the one standing opposite to it in the arrangement (illustration 7). The diagram of the primal order is drawn thus:

Heaven

Lake   Wind

Fire   Water

Thunder   Mountain

Earth

According to the directions of the ancient diagram, this produces the following set of hexagrams:

 Obstruction (12) and Tranquillity (11) from Heaven and Earth
 Sensing (31) and Reduction (41) from Lake and Mountain
 Unsettled (64) and Settled (63) from Fire and Water
 Constancy (32) and Increase (42) from Thunder and Wind

The diagram of the temporal order of the eight trigrams is drawn thus:

Fire

Lake   Earth

Mountain   Wind

Thunder   Heaven

Water

By the same process, this produces the following set of hexagrams:

 Unsettled (64) and Settled (63) from Fire and Water
 Parting (43) and Treading (10) from Lake and Heaven
 Gradual Progress (53) and Degeneration (18) from Mountain and Wind
 Joy (16) and Return (24) from Thunder and Earth

In study of the sets of hexagrams generated by these diagrams, note the relationship between the meanings of the hexagrams in each pair; in study of the sets of hexagrams generated by the combination of the two orders shown next, note the sense of progression in the meanings of the hexagrams as a sequence. The combination of the primal and temporal orders, in which the temporal is by definition placed outside the primal, is drawn thus:

                    Fire

                  Heaven

        Wind   Earth

            Lake   Wind
Thunder Fire   Water   Lake

        Thunder   Mountain

    Mountain   Heaven

                  Earth

                  Water

These pairs form the following hexagrams:

> Great Possession (14) from Fire over Heaven
> Faithfulness in the Center (61) from Wind over Lake
> Richness (55) from Thunder over Fire
> Nourishment (27) from Mountain over Thunder
> Accord (8) from Water over Earth
> Rising (46) from Earth over Wind
> Exhaustion (47) from Lake over Water
> Withdrawal (33) from Heaven over Mountain

The final concentration group of hexagrams is a set of twelve hexagrams representing the rise of yang and descent of yin through each line of the structure of a hexagram. This group is commonly arranged in a linear fashion in Taoist alchemical texts, and it also forms the circumference of a circular arrangement of hexagrams according to increasing and decreasing concentrations of yang and yin. These twelve hexagrams, and the hexagram clusters associated with each one, are as follows:

1. Return (24) This hexagram contains all hexagrams with yang in the first place, to be read with the first line of the total yang hexagram *Heaven.* The hexagrams with yang in the first line are all those in the *Heaven, Lake, Fire,* and *Thunder* series, as given in the Images section of the Readings.
2. Overseeing (19) This hexagram contains all hexagrams with yang in the second place, to be read with the second line of the total yang hexagram *Heaven.* The hexagrams with yang in the second place are all those in the *Heaven, Lake, Wind,* and *Water* series.

3. Tranquillity (11) This hexagram contains all hexagrams with yang in the third place, to be read with the third line of the total yang hexagram *Heaven*. The hexagrams with yang in the third place are all those in the *Heaven*, *Fire*, *Wind*, and *Mountain* series.

4. Great Power (34) This hexagram contains all hexagrams with yang in the fourth place, to be read with the fourth line of the total yang hexagram *Heaven*. The hexagrams with yang in the fourth place are the first, second, third, and fourth hexagrams in each series as given in the Images section of the Readings.

5. Parting (43) This hexagram contains all hexagrams with yang in the fifth place, to be read with the fifth line of the total yang hexagram *Heaven*. The hexagrams with yang in the fifth place are the first, second, fifth, and sixth hexagrams in each series.

6. Heaven (1) This hexagram contains all hexagrams with yang at the top, which are the first, third, fifth, and seventh hexagrams in each series.

7. Meeting (44) This hexagram contains all hexagrams with yin in the first place, to be read with the first line of the total yin hexagram *Earth*. The hexagrams with yin in the first place are all those in the *Wind*, *Water*, *Mountain*, and *Earth* series.

8. Withdrawal (33) This hexagram contains all hexagrams with yin in the second place, to be read with the second line of the total yin hexagram *Earth*. The hexagrams with yin in the second place are all those in the *Fire*, *Thunder*, *Mountain*, and *Earth* series.

9. Obstruction (12) This hexagram contains all hexagrams with yin in the third place, to be read with the third line of the total yin hexagram *Earth*. The hexagrams with yin in the third place are all those in the *Lake*, *Thunder*, *Water*, and *Earth* series.

10. Observing (20) This hexagram contains all hexagrams with yin in the fourth place, to be read with the fourth line of the total yin hexagram *Earth*. The hexagrams with yin in the fourth place are the fifth, sixth, seventh, and eighth hexagrams in each series as given in the Images section of the Readings.

11. Stripping Away (23) This hexagram contains all hexagrams with yin in the fifth place, to be read with the fifth line of the total yin hexagram *Earth*. The hexagram with yin in the fifth place are the third, fourth, seventh, and eighth hexagrams in each series.

12. Earth (2) This hexagram contains all hexagrams with yin on top, which are the second, fourth, sixth, and eighth hexagrams in each series.

These twelve hexagrams can be studied together as a set in themselves or individually in association with other hexagrams in their respective groups. Another version of the complete array of hexagrams surrounded by these twelve gives rise to the organization of hexagrams in terms of similar concentrations of yin or yang; this is the order on which the Lines section of the Readings is based.

The practice of categorizing hexagrams according to whether they have yin or yang in any given line is also useful for consulting hexagrams for individual lines, to study the implications of a given quality in a specific position. This naturally leads to the question of the qualities and positions of lines in constructing hexagrams for analytic consultation.

HEXAGRAM SYSTEMS

The methods using lines to call hexagrams are somewhat more complex than those using trigrams. Each line position is given a specific association, according to the framework of interpretation; the reader then assigns yin or yang to each position as it applies to the situation under consideration.

THE TAOIST I CHING

There are several methods of line association in constructing analytic hexagrams. In *The Taoist I Ching*, there are two basic synchronic systems, which may be defined as follows:

first line: inner desire
second line: inner human feeling
third line: inner reason
fourth line: outer desire
fifth line: outer human feeling
top line: outer reason

Desire is the expression of vitality, and may be more or less selfish or unselfish. Human feeling is the expression of energy, in which the forces of desire and reason are mixed. Reason is an expression of intelligence, which may be more or less coherent or fragmentary.

In this scheme, the juxtaposition of inner and outer may be placed on different axes. "Inner" can be assigned to the private feelings and thoughts of the individual, with "outer" assigned to the individual's expressed feelings and thoughts. In this way a hexagram is used to represent a single person.

Example

An individual who is inwardly angry, is motivated by resentment, and habitually rationalizes personal bitterness but nevertheless puts on the appearances of affection, community, and idealism, can be represented by yin in the first or inside three places and yang in the last or outside three places. This produces the hexagram *Obstruction*.

The Taoist reading for the hexagram says, "Obstruction's denial of humanity does not make the superior person's rectitude beneficial. The great goes and the small comes." Viewed in the light of the characterization of the person it is drawn to represent, this reading gives a psychological and social analysis of the situation of such a person. People who are inwardly angry generally feel that they have not been given their due. Frustration turns the need for self-esteem into self-aggrandizement; people like this are inclined to resort to feelings of superiority and self-righteousness, which they use to rationalize their bitterness. But since this whole process only exacerbates the original problem of alienation, no amount of justification is of any benefit except to mask the original feelings. In this sense, when the small concerns of the individual ego come into play, the larger concerns of overall harmony go into eclipse.

The inner and outer lines can also be associated with a subject and another person or an environment, in order to construct a hexagram through analysis of a relationship. In this system, the line positions may be construed in the following manner:

first line: the emotional life, quality, or state of the subject
second line: the social activity of the subject
third line: the intellectual activity and psychological state of the subject
fourth line: the emotional life, quality, or state of the partner in the relationship or the group or society at large.
fifth line: the social activity of the partner in the relationship or the group or society at large
top line: the intellectual activity and spiritual state of the partner in the relationship or the group at large.

When the reader has drawn a hexagram with these structures according to the ways in which the individual, relationship, or situation is reflected in him or her, the hexagram can be found by referring to the series based on its inner trigram in the Images section of the Readings. The image reading then leads to the location of the hexagram in *The Taoist I Ching* and to the thematic readings and the line readings in the present volume.

Another method of hexagram construction by line position used in *The Taoist I Ching* in tandem with the synchronic methods outlined above is the diachronic method, in which the line positions are associated with phases of a process. In this system, the lines of the inside trigram represent the beginning, stabilization, and consummation of the causal factors or internal effort involved in a particular undertaking; the lines of the outside trigram represent the beginning, stabilization, and consummation of the results or external manifestations of the undertaking.

Each of these line analysis methods calls for a choice between yin and yang at each position. In *The Taoist I Ching*, both yin and yang are dual in the sense that both have positive, or developmental, associations—called true yin and true yang—as well as negative, or involutionary, associations—called false yin and false yang. These associations may be summarized as follows:

True Yang	*True Yin*
firmness	flexibility
strength	docility
durability	yielding
decisiveness	self-mastery
power	self-restraint
energy	selflessness
keenness	humility
fearlessness	simplicity
objectivity	openness
consistency	courtesy
	contentment
	detachment

False Yang	*False Yin*
aggressiveness	weakness
stubbornness	shallowness
hypertension	pliability
hyperactivity	quietism
fanaticism	passivity

There are also yin-yang associations that cut across these axes, as follows:

Yang	*Yin*
enlightened mind	human mentality
original mind	conditioned mind
energy	spirit
intuitive knowledge	cognitive knowledge
fullness	emptiness
activity	stillness

THE BUDDHIST I CHING

Several more line position analysis systems are contained in *The Buddhist I Ching*. Two of these systems are for general application and simply take the progression of the positions from the first to the top line to represent successive phases of progressions of time and depth. In addition, there are three special systems applying Buddhist concepts and practices to questions of social, organizational, and personal evolution.

One such method is based on six stages of experience ranging from ordinary mundane consciousness to transcendence of meditation:

first line: mundanity, attachment to the items of the ordinary world
second line: meditation in the midst of the world yet purified enough to perceive underlying reality
third line: meditation that is at once both in the world and beyond the world
fourth line: meditation that is beyond the world
fifth line: meditation that is neither in the world nor yet beyond the world
top line: end of subtle attachments to the experiences of meditation

Another system is based on a somewhat different six-step progression from ideal to actualization:

first line: potential
second line: consciousness of potential
third line: cultivation of potential
fourth line: experiential intimations of possibilities ·
fifth line: conscious expressions of developed potential
top line: ongoing unfolding of potential

The third system follows a set of fundamental practices that may start diachronically but are consummated synchronically:

first line: generosity
second line: self-discipline
third line: patience
fourth line: diligence
fifth line: meditation
top line: insight

In these systems, yin may be associated with openness, flexibility, humility, or weakness; it also has the special associations of stillness and concentration. Yang may be associated with fruition, firmness, ardor, or strength; and it also has the special associations of action and insight.

In all of these systems, the thoughts and perceptions generated by the readings derive from the interaction of the text with the premises of the reader's analysis. Thus the use of different systems of line associations and different values of yin and yang produce correspondingly different effects on the understanding and application of the readings taken by these systems and values.

When line programs are used to consult *The Taoist I Ching* or *The Buddhist I Ching*, they often yield associations beyond those with which the reader has approached the construction of the hexagram. This is normal, in that commentators ordinarily do not analyze each hexagram according to every system, and they proceed from the hexagram to the analysis rather than from the analysis to the hexagram. Thus the reader can often find more in a line than is made explicit by any given commentator, because the situation to which the reading is being applied is known directly to the reader.

Due to the inherent nature of the text, therefore, a reader may draw a hexagram according to one system, and find that the commentator has explained it according to another. This has the effect of delivering input from beyond the realm of subjective expectation, presenting a new angle on the question at hand, stimulating broader development of thought. Since expectations may subconsciously confine the perspective of the reader, the use of variable analytic systems by commentators is one of the most powerful tools of living *I Ching* reading.

I CHING: THE TAO OF ORGANIZATION

The system used in *I Ching: The Tao of Organization* uses the line positions of hexagrams to construct models of groups. Because of its philosophical background in social studies, this system tends to be used more uniformly than those used in the Taoist and Buddhist commentaries; like these other methods of explanation, however, it embodies the internal principle of change in the shifting of the values of yin and yang.

Thus in using any commentary the reader may choose a line in terms of a particular association of yin or yang, and then find an explanation in terms of another association of yin or yang. This has the specific effect of considering an attribute from the point of view of transmutation, from good to bad and bad to good. Anger and justice, for example, are both yang, signifying that the same basic force can fuel one or the other. Thus the reader looking for a consultation on justice may find a reading on anger, while the reader looking for a consultation on anger may find a reading on justice. The reader looking for a consultation on weakness may find a reading on flexibility, while the reader looking for a consultation on flexibility may find a reading on weakness. This puts the entire reading in a larger and more complete context.

In the basic system of line associations used in *I Ching: The Tao of Organization*, the inner, or lower, trigram of a hexagram is taken to represent the lower echelons of a society or organization, while the outer, or upper, trigram is taken to represent the upper echelons; the lines then represent corresponding positions within their respective echelons. Essentially, the associations of the individual lines in this scheme are as follows:

first line: the common person, the broad base of society
second line: the expert, in a position of service
third line: the middle manager or local leader

fourth line: the direct assistant to the overall leadership
fifth line: the overall leadership
top line: the experienced consultant

This scheme can also be cast diachronically to represent an individual career, as follows:

first line: childhood or youth
second line: practical education
third line: social independence
fourth line: professional development
fifth line: social and professional success
top line: retirement and old age

THE PARENT LINE SYSTEM

Hexagrams can also be construed by analogy with the corresponding lines in the parent hexagrams, *Heaven* and *Earth,* or *The Creative* and *The Receptive.* That is, each line of a target hexagram can be chosen according to the meaning of the corresponding line in the *Heaven* or *Earth* hexagram. Since the values of each line in the parent hexagrams are taken to be broadly representative, it is useful to take the interpretations of all three traditions into account for the purposes of using this system.

HEAVEN

First Yang

Confucianism: The first yang represents the beginning of creation, when positive energy has just sprouted, when the sage is in a lowly position. At this stage one cannot act on one's own; one should work on oneself privately while awaiting the proper time to act.

Taoism: In the beginning of strength, when the quality of strength is activated, this is the time to nurture healthy energy; one should not yet rely on this strength or presume upon it.

Buddhism: This refers to discovering great potential yet working quietly and unassumingly to develop it inwardly.

Second Yang

Confucianism: One's inner qualities become outwardly apparent. Public presence is advantageous.

Taoism: When strength is in balance and not exaggerated, firmness and flexibility match. The living energy is always there, natural goodness is apparent, the spiritual potential takes shape.

Buddhism: When one has intellectual understanding of potential, it is beneficial to see real teachers.

Third Yang

Confucianism: At the top of the bottom echelon, where leadership qualities are evident yet the position is still that of a subordinate to the upper echelon, it is best to work hard and be wary of the danger of failing or abusing the trust of others.

Taoism: This represents being filled with an abundant flow of energy yet controlling and guiding it deliberately by the force of will and attention.

Buddhism: This is a dangerous position of strength with great responsibility, in which it is necessary to work and watch, not forgetting danger when secure, being humble and circumspect in discharging great responsibility.

Fourth Yang

Confucianism: This is the position of mastery of the option of whether to act or not, as a matter of appropriate timing; the activities of sages are designed to suit the needs of the time.

Taoism: The quality of strength has developed, the spiritual potential is complete, awaiting the appropriate time for a forward evolutionary step, examining the climate and taking precautions against danger.

Buddhism: This means retreating in order to advance, stepping back to go ahead.

Fifth Yang

Confucianism: This is the position of leadership, in which it is beneficial to see worthy people in the lower echelons.

Taoism: This is the stage of mental and physical sublimation, union with objective reality, evolutionary transformation of self and others.

Buddhism: This is the noninvasive government of enlightened leaders.

Top Yang

Confucianism: To go beyond what is timely leads to an impasse.

Taoism: When strength goes to excess, one will fail in one's task; pride leads to regret.

Buddhism: Regret is the way to deal with arrogance.

EARTH

First Yin

Confucianism: Incipient negative qualities should not be encouraged, lest they harden into habits.

Taoism: Carelessness leads to invasion of external influences.

Buddhism: Accumulated good and evil lead to resulting joy and sorrow.

Second Yin

Confucianism: Be honest, upright, and magnanimous, and there will be benefit without even trying.

Taoism: The balanced mind is inwardly straightforward, the balanced person is outwardly upright, thus able to do good naturally.

Buddhism: Harmonious adaptability in accord with the design of reality is correct.

Third Yin

Confucianism: This line represents being faithful to one's responsibilities while keeping one's merits concealed, not taking credit for achievements.

Taoism: This represents flexibility of nature with firmness of will, hiding one's excellence and conforming to the external order.

Buddhism: This represents being in the world and beyond the world at the same time.

Fourth Yin

Confucianism: This represents hiding knowledge to avoid attention.

Taoism: This represents acceptance of fate, neither causing trouble nor seeking good.

Buddhism: This represents individual liberation, unaffected by the praise or blame of society.

Fifth Yin

Confucianism: This represents humility in leadership.

Taoism: This represents spontaneous manifestation of virtue, so that one is trusted implicitly and is taken as an example by others.

Buddhism: This represents objective awareness of both absolute and ordinary reality.

Top Yin

Confucianism: This represents the culmination of the growth of yin, with excess leading to confrontation and struggle.

Taoism: This represents wanting to make others follow without being able to follow others.

Buddhism: There is inevitably a battle at an impasse.

Using this scheme, the reader constructs hexagrams by considering each position and choosing either a yang line from *Heaven* or a yin line from *Earth* by drawing analogies between the positional line themes and the subject of the consultation. This method is particularly effective in combination with the line position system in which a yin or yang line in a specific place in any hexagram is amplified by the readings for yin or yang lines in that place in other hexagrams.

TOTAL READING: THE PRIMAL ORDER

The primal order of the hexagrams, based on permutations of the trigrams according to their primal order, is used in the Images section of the Readings. This order is also traditionally arranged in a circle, in which all the hexagrams with yang in the first place are on the left half-circumference and all the hexagrams with yin in the first place are on the right half of the circumference (illustration 4). Using 1 for yang and 0 for yin, if this circle is divided into its halves, straightened into two parallel lines, and lain on its side, it produces an arrangement useful for yet another system of *I Ching* reading:

```
1 0 1 0 1 0 1 0 1 0 1 0 1 0 1 0 1 0 1 0 1 0 1 0 1 0 1 0 1 0 1 0
1 1 0 0 1 1 0 0 1 1 0 0 1 1 0 0 1 1 0 0 1 1 0 0 1 1 0 0 1 1 0 0
1 1 1 1 0 0 0 0 1 1 1 1 0 0 0 0 1 1 1 1 0 0 0 0 1 1 1 1 0 0 0 0
1 1 1 1 1 1 1 1 0 0 0 0 0 0 0 0 1 1 1 1 1 1 1 1 0 0 0 0 0 0 0 0
1 1 1 1 1 1 1 1 1 1 1 1 1 1 1 1 0 0 0 0 0 0 0 0 0 0 0 0 0 0 0 0
1 1 1 1 1 1 1 1 1 1 1 1 1 1 1 1 1 1 1 1 1 1 1 1 1 1 1 1 1 1 1 1

  1 0 1 0 1 0 1 0 1 0 1 0 1 0 1 0 1 0 1 0 1 0 1 0 1 0 1 0 1 0 1 0
  1 1 0 0 1 1 0 0 1 1 0 0 1 1 0 0 1 1 0 0 1 1 0 0 1 1 0 0 1 1 0 0
  1 1 1 1 0 0 0 0 1 1 1 1 0 0 0 0 1 1 1 1 0 0 0 0 1 1 1 1 0 0 0 0
  1 1 1 1 1 1 1 1 0 0 0 0 0 0 0 0 1 1 1 1 1 1 1 1 0 0 0 0 0 0 0 0
  1 1 1 1 1 1 1 1 1 1 1 1 1 1 1 1 0 0 0 0 0 0 0 0 0 0 0 0 0 0 0 0
  0 0 0 0 0 0 0 0 0 0 0 0 0 0 0 0 0 0 0 0 0 0 0 0 0 0 0 0 0 0 0 0
```

In this diagram, each column of six figures represents a hexagram. The top section is the yang half-circumference, beginning with *Heaven;* the bottom is the yin half-circumference, ending with *Earth.* After separating out *Heaven* and *Earth* on the top left and bottom right—the two parent hexagrams joining each other at the beginning and end of the total cycle—alignment of hexagrams in corresponding positions in the twin arrays according to the primal order yields a coherent system of study by pairs of hexagrams with complementary themes. Following the top-down order of the circle, pairing the hexagrams in sequence going from the top to the bottom on both yang-based and yin-based halves simultaneously, this generates the following reading system:

Parting (43) and Meeting (44)
Great Possession (14) and Excess of the Great (28)
Great Power (34) and the Cauldron (50)
Nurturance of the Small (9) and Constancy (32)

Waiting (5) and Wind (57)
Great Accumulation (26) and The Well (48)
Tranquillity (11) and Degeneration (18)
Treading (10) and Rising (46)
Delight (58) and Contention (6)
Disharmony (38) and Exhaustion (47)
Marrying a Young Woman (54) and Unsettled (64)
Faithfulness in the Center (61) and Solution (40)
Discipline (60) and Dispersal (59)
Reduction (41) and Water (29)
Overseeing (19) and Darkness (4)
Sameness with Others (13) and The Army (7)
Revolution (49) and Withdrawal (33)
Fire (30) and Sensing (31)
Richness (55) and Travel (56)
People in the Home (37) and Predominance of the Small (62)
Settled (63) and Gradual Progress (53)
Adornment (22) and Halting (39)
Concealment of Illumination (36) and Mountain (52)
No Error (25) and Humility (15)
Following (17) and Obstruction (12)
Biting Through (21) and Gathering (45)
Thunder (51) and Advance (35)
Increase (42) and Joy (16)
Difficulty (3) and Observing (20)
Nourishment (27) and Accord (8)
Return (24) and Stripping Away (23)

If the yang-based side and yin-based side of the circular arrangement are read consecutively instead of simultaneously, following the circle all the way around down from the top and up from the bottom, the straight representation looks like this:

```
1 0 1 0 1 0 1 0 1 0 1 0 1 0 1 0 1 0 1 0 1 0 1 0 1 0 1 0 1 0 1 0
1 1 0 0 1 1 0 0 1 1 0 0 1 1 0 0 1 1 0 0 1 1 0 0 1 1 0 0 1 1 0 0
1 1 1 1 0 0 0 0 1 1 1 1 0 0 0 0 1 1 1 1 0 0 0 0 1 1 1 1 0 0 0 0
1 1 1 1 1 1 1 1 0 0 0 0 0 0 0 0 1 1 1 1 1 1 1 1 0 0 0 0 0 0 0 0
1 1 1 1 1 1 1 1 1 1 1 1 1 1 1 1 0 0 0 0 0 0 0 0 0 0 0 0 0 0 0 0
1 1 1 1 1 1 1 1 1 1 1 1 1 1 1 1 1 1 1 1 1 1 1 1 1 1 1 1 1 1 1 1

0 1 0 1 0 1 0 1 0 1 0 1 0 1 0 1 0 1 0 1 0 1 0 1 0 1 0 1 0 1 0 1
0 0 1 1 0 0 1 1 0 0 1 1 0 0 1 1 0 0 1 1 0 0 1 1 0 0 1 1 0 0 1 1
0 0 0 0 1 1 1 1 0 0 0 0 1 1 1 1 0 0 0 0 1 1 1 1 0 0 0 0 1 1 1 1
0 0 0 0 0 0 0 0 1 1 1 1 1 1 1 1 0 0 0 0 0 0 0 0 1 1 1 1 1 1 1 1
0 0 0 0 0 0 0 0 0 0 0 0 0 0 0 0 1 1 1 1 1 1 1 1 1 1 1 1 1 1 1 1
0 0 0 0 0 0 0 0 0 0 0 0 0 0 0 0 0 0 0 0 0 0 0 0 0 0 0 0 0 0 0 0
```

This arrangement produces a set of thirty-two pairs of antithetically structured hexagrams, in which one member of each pair has yin where the other member has yang and yang where the other has yin. This produces the following study program:

Heaven (1) and Earth (2)
Parting (43) and Stripping Away (23)
Great Possession (14) and Accord (8)
Great Power (34) and Observing (20)
Nurturance of the Small (9) and Joy (16)
Waiting (5) and Advance (35)
Great Accumulation (26) and Gathering (45)
Tranquillity (11) and Obstruction (12)
Treading (10) and Humility (15)
Joy (58) and Mountain (52)
Disharmony (38) and Halting (39)
Marrying a Young Woman (54) and Gradual Progress (53)
Faithfulness in the Center (61) and Predominance of the Small (62)
Discipline (60) and Travel (56)
Reduction (41) and Sensing (31)
Overseeing (19) and Withdrawal (33)
Sameness with Others (13) and The Army (7)
Revolution (49) and Darkness (4)
Fire (30) and Water (29)
Richness (55) and Dispersal (59)
People in the Home (37) and Solution (40)
Settled (63) and Unsettled (64)
Adornment (22) and Exhaustion (47)
Concealment of Illumination (36) and Contention (6)
No Error (25) and Rising (46)
Following (17) and Degeneration (18)
Biting Through (21) and The Well (48)
Thunder (51) and Wind (57)
Increase (42) and Constancy (32)
Difficulty (3) and The Cauldron (50)
Nourishment (27) and Excess of the Great (28)
Return (24) and Meeting (44)

In both of these total orders it is often possible to see a connection between the themes of the paired hexagrams from the names alone. When used for reading guides, these study sequences link each hexagram into several different families, enlarging a chosen reading according to a multidimensional pattern that yields a critical yet manageable mass of the entire system of the *I Ching*.

DIVINATION METHODS

In some other volumes in this series of *I Ching* translations, there is included a publisher's note on the well-known coin-throwing system of *I Ching* consultation. For instruction in the more complex milfoil stick, or yarrow stick, method, see *The Authentic I Ching* by Henry Wei. This modern Confucian treatment of the classic uses the diagrams for mathematical deductions and speculations and explains the practice of milfoil divination as given in *Guidance for the Ignorant* by the twelfth-century writer Chu Hsi, who was famous for compiling and annotating selections of the early literatures of both Confucianism and neo-Confucianism (see above, page 351). On the subject of the general principles of divination, Wei's book presents modern Occidental and Oriental views together. Wei's treatment of the milfoil system is superior to that of Wilhelm, especially in that it includes the association or visualization system of the correspondences between the manipulations of the stalks and the cycles of nature.

Wei advances the theory that the milfoil system is superior in that the length of the procedure allows more time for meditation on the question concerned, which added concentration will increase sensitivity to relevant messages in the reading. It seems quite reasonable that the procedure will work in this way when it is applied in this way, but it is also possible to reverse this.

According to Taoist interpretations, the design of ritual invocation of certain associations, such as the ceremonial of traditional *I Ching* consultation, is to produce a mood of seriousness and respect, a condition of alertness. Given that one approaches the *I Ching* in this way (that is, by divination) only with a serious question, the mind of the seeker of omen and advice is already under the influence of its own thoughts on the matter. The quiet interlude of silence, the burning of incense, the grouping and regrouping of stalks in concert with thoughts of the cycles of day and night, seasons and years, origination, elaboration, and return provide a means of switching the mind off the track of its thoughts hitherto, refreshing the attention in such a way that it may be awake to un-thought-of possibilities. This may be thought of as much like the experience many people seem to have when they think very deeply and intensely about a question, only to have it resolved through an apparently irrelevant impact or interaction. It is not that the thought had no potential but that it needed more room to sprout.

The use of the *I Ching* for regular reading, on the other hand, is geared more toward solving questions before they become questions, and preventing problems before they happen. The *I Ching* is written and interpreted to cover the bases of the inner and outer life or how people relate to their own inner and outer worlds and even how they relate to the subjective and objective qualities of these relations themselves. As the different programs of study illustrate, the book is like a hall of mirrors at the end of a giant kaleidoscope; the total effect of this system is to create a fluid yet orderly complex of connections matching the complexity of ordinary real life but having greater total coherence. The complexes of readings approached in this way yield ordinarily invisible or unthought of perspectives on the reasons and consequences of the ways that people deal with life, so that people can have the opportunity to consider their possible relevance to their existing perceptions of the nature, quality, and meaning of their lives and actions.

SUMMARY

The Images section of the Readings in this book is on the images of the hexagrams of the *I Ching*, arranged in groups according to their base trigram, following the sequence of the primal trigrammatic order transposed onto a linear basis by a Taoist operation known as "reversal of the temporal."

Several sets of notation are used for the trigrams and hexagrams to facilitate reference to other systems. For reference to systems of reading by trigrammatic analysis, the hexagrams in each group are referred to in terms of the name of the changing outer trigram over the group base trigram. The sequence of the changing of the outer trigram over each base trigram is the same as that of the succession of base trigrams according to the primal order.

For reference to positional analysis, the line structure of the trigrams and hexagrams is indicated by a three- or six-digit notation mark composed of 1s and 0s. This notation device is obtained by setting a trigram or hexagram on its side, so that left = bottom and right = top, and replacing solid, yang lines and broken, yin lines with 1 and 0 respectively. For example, the trigram *Thunder*, which is one yang under two yins, is represented by 100, and the hexagram *Thunder*, thunder over thunder, is represented by 100100.

For reference to the section of this book on the meanings of the themes of the *I Ching* hexagrams, the hexagrams are also noted by name and number in the conventional order used in standard written texts of the *I Ching* proper. This number is also given for easy reference to other translations of the *I Ching*. In addition, an alphabetized list of numbered hexagram names and variants is provided in an index for reference to the citations in different sections of this book as well as to *The Taoist I Ching*, *The Buddhist I Ching*, and *I Ching: The Tao of Organization*.

The image readings are thus a guide to the orders of other systems of readings as well as being an entire system in themselves. Ordered by base trigram, they are arranged in series as follows:

1. Heaven 111
2. Lake 110
3. Fire 101

4.   Thunder   100
5.   Wind   011
6.   Water   010
7.   Mountain   001
8.   Earth   000

The concise image readings are particularly useful for study in terms of groups. Each series yields a coherent pattern of processes, phases, or aspects of social development. As shown in the classic *Great Learning*, these are to be read both forward and in reverse, to produce a balanced image of the reverberation of individual and group development.

This grouping can also be used as a guide to study of the themes or lines of hexagrams with the same base trigrams. This style of study enlarges upon the inner dimensions of each of the human processes pictured in the images. When used in this way, this primal grouping is of particular interest in opening up Book II of *The Taoist I Ching*.

There is another very interesting system of reading the images, which again is designed to create a balanced outlook. The easiest way to represent this system is to refer to the trigrams by ordinal number 1 through 8, and again let left = base and right = top. The system of parallel readings from the yang and yin sides of the primal circle would then be described as follows:

1 : 1 is read with 8 : 8 (Heaven with Earth).
1 : 2 is read with 8 : 7,

and so on, to produce the following scheme, reading left to right:

1:1 + 8:8, 1:2 + 8:7, 1:3 + 8:6, 1:4 + 8:5, 1:5 + 8:4, 1:6 + 8:3,
1:7 + 8:2, 1:8 + 8:1
2:1 + 7:8, 2:2 + 7:7, 2:3 + 7:6, 2:4 + 7:5, 2:5 + 7:4, 2:6 + 7:3,
2:7 + 7:2, 2:8 + 7:1
3:1 + 6:8, 3:2 + 6:7, 3:3 + 6:6, 3:4 + 6:5, 3:5 + 6:4, 3:6 + 6:3,
3:7 + 6:2, 3:8 + 6:1
4:1 + 5:8, 4:2 + 5:7, 4:3 + 5:6, 4:4 + 5:5, 4:5 + 5:4, 4:6 + 5:3,
4:7 + 5:2, 4:8 + 5:1

The symbol + means that the images of the two hexagrams in each pair are to be read together. This method of reading is very useful for those who wish to see the reality underlying Confucianism, apart from historical imitations and bastardizations of Confucianism. As in all total system reading programs, this program for the images is to be read through in this order. This is an exercise in thinking about one's general perception and experience of life, including mental images of past, present, and future.

In this sense, starting from the total *I Ching* system as a basis and reaching out mentally to events in time, it is a reversal of the divination method, which proceeds from a past, present, or future event to the *I Ching* and then back to the event. Of course, in traditional practice there is a well-traveled bridge between these two approaches, since skilled readers of the *I Ching* were those who had mastered the total system in principle, had applied it to themselves the way psychoanalysts and Zen teachers apply psychoanalysis or Zen to themselves before they practice on others, and had subsequently had a great deal of experience with people.

The Themes section of the Readings in this book presents a summary of Confucian, Taoist, and Buddhist views of the meanings of the hexagrams. These interpretations are given in concise abstracts in order to facilitate study of hexagram themes in sets. The order in which the hexagrams are listed is that of the conventional written *I Ching*, but they are treated in thirty-two pairs and six groups, according to Taoist models.

It is also useful to read these themes in the primal order indicated by the arrangement of the reading on the images. The hexagrams in this format may also be grouped in pairs, as explained above, resulting in the following study program (with hexagrams listed by their numbers in the conventional order).

1 + 2	17 + 12	33 + 49	49 + 33
2 + 1	18 + 11	34 + 50	50 + 34
3 + 20	19 + 4	35 + 51	51 + 35
4 + 19	20 + 3	36 + 52	52 + 36
5 + 57	21 + 45	37 + 62	53 + 63
6 + 58	22 + 39	38 + 47	54 + 64
7 + 13	23 + 24	39 + 22	55 + 56
8 + 27	24 + 23	40 + 61	56 + 55
9 + 32	25 + 15	41 + 29	57 + 5
10 + 46	26 + 48	42 + 16	58 + 6
11 + 18	27 + 8	43 + 44	59 + 60
12 + 17	28 + 14	44 + 43	60 + 59
13 + 7	29 + 41	45 + 21	61 + 40
14 + 28	30 + 31	46 + 10	62 + 37
15 + 25	31 + 30	47 + 38	63 + 53
16 + 42	32 + 9	48 + 26	64 + 54

Using this list, the reader can readily find the primal associate of any hexagram from the standard order of the written text. Another transformation of the Primal Round Diagram (illustration 4), from which this program is derived, produces another set of thirty-two pairs of hexagrams, the hexagrams in each pair now being structural opposites. This latter program is useful for studying hexagrams from the point of view of the inevitable transformation of yang into yin and yin into yang. Again using the ordinal numbers of the hexagrams according to the conventional sequence of the written *I Ching*, this system may be summarized as follows:

1 + 2	17 + 18	33 + 19	49 + 4
2 + 1	18 + 17	34 + 20	50 + 3
3 + 50	19 + 33	35 + 5	51 + 57
4 + 49	20 + 34	36 + 6	52 + 58
5 + 35	21 + 48	37 + 40	53 + 54
6 + 36	22 + 47	38 + 39	54 + 53
7 + 13	23 + 43	39 + 38	55 + 59
8 + 14	24 + 44	40 + 37	56 + 60
9 + 16	25 + 46	41 + 31	57 + 51
10 + 15	26 + 45	42 + 32	58 + 52
11 + 12	27 + 28	43 + 23	59 + 55
12 + 11	28 + 27	44 + 24	60 + 56
13 + 7	29 + 30	45 + 26	61 + 62
14 + 8	30 + 29	46 + 25	62 + 61
15 + 10	31 + 41	47 + 22	63 + 64
16 + 9	32 + 42	48 + 21	64 + 63

Using these lists, any hexagram drawn by any method can at once be elaborated systematically for further clarification and elucidation of relevant themes.

The Lines section of the Readings deals with the sayings associated with the individual lines of the hexagrams. These are organized according to a diagram in the Taoist tradition representing the total process of physical, mental, and spiritual refinement. Originally a circle in the Taoist tradition, this diagram is made linear in neo-Confucian tradition, where it is called the Diagram of the Transformations of the Hexagrams.

Since this treatment is based on the sayings, it must be given in a linear form in writing, so to this extent I have used the neo-Confucian design; according to the pattern of the Taoist process, however, the yang phase precedes the yin phase, so I have incorporated this order into the reading.

In terms of format, the reading is divided into sections based on numbers of yang and yin lines. Each section is headed by a list of the hexagrams in that set, with their numbers according to the conventional written order. In each section the line readings are numbered according to position within the indicated hexagram. This system enables the reader to extend attention to patterns of ideas recurring in specific concentrations of yang and yin or in specific positions of yang and yin.

Like the other readings, on the images and the themes, the system of line sayings can also be viewed as both complete in itself and as part of the total statement of the *I Ching* science of human behavior. In one sense, it could be said that the images set forth certain ideals, the themes present the vagaries of conditions and circumstances, and the lines disclose the pragmatic steps toward handling conditions and circumstances in such a way as to draw closer to ideals in a rational and deliberate manner.

Again like the other readings, there are different procedures that may be used together in order to derive the optimum advantage from the sayings on the lines. One procedure is to read straight through in the order of the written text here, that is, to read the yang lines from one to five, then read the yin lines from one to five. The complementary method is to read both yang and yin by category, that is, to read the yang lines in each category followed by the yin lines in each category. The readings for six yang or yin lines are given separately, however, in the directions on line programs, as these are the parent hexagrams, with general applications, whose line readings form an abstract model of a total positional analysis system.

The Arcana sections of the book are on Taoist ideas of human development relating to the use of the *I Ching* for psychological studies.

The Mandalas

1. Unification of the River Diagram, Lo Writing, and Primal and Temporal Eight Trigrams

The River Diagram, Lo Writing, and their combination are explained in the first three Arcana sections in this volume. In this diagram, the sets of dots within the circle comprise the River Diagram, while the sets of curved lines surrounding the circle comprise the Lo Writing.

Surrounding the Lo Writing are the *I Ching* trigrams in their primal order surrounded by the trigrams in their temporal order. These are given in translation on page 362.

2. The Cauldron, Furnace, Medicines, and Firing Process

The *cauldron, furnace, medicines,* and *firing process* are Taoist alchemical terms for the structure of the *I Ching.* The cauldron and furnace are the hexagrams *Heaven* and *Earth,* symbolizing energy and spirit, firmness and flexibility, set on the top and bottom of the circle in the diagram. The medicines are the hexagrams *Water* and *Fire,* symbolizing real knowledge and conscious knowledge, set to the right and left of the circle in the diagram.

The firing process is illustrated by the rings of hexagrams in the circle. This representation shows how the hexagrams in the standard sequence of the written *I Ching* go in pairs. Twenty-eight pairs consist of hexagrams that are upside-down reversals of each other; the other two pairs are, like the cauldron and furnace pair and the medicine pair, yin-for-yang-and-yang-for-yin reversals of each other.

This arrangement produces the standard sequence of the hexagrams in the conventional written text of the *I Ching*, as well as the double-ring sequence within that sequence, used in the interpretation of *The Taoist I Ching*. The order and pairing of the hexagrams in the Themes section of the Readings in this volume are generated by this system.

Further explanation of this scheme is given in one of the Arcana sections.

3. The Six Yangs and Six Yins of the Yang Fire and Yin Convergence

The six yangs and six yins of the yang fire and yin convergence demonstrates two ways of ordering and studying hexagrams, using a basic structure of Taoist practice expressed in terms of the *I Ching*. The hexagrams here are arrayed according to the number of yang lines and the number of yin lines composing them. This scheme is used to study yang and yin in specific positions and to study yang and yin in specific concentrations. It generates the order used in the Lines section of the Readings in this volume. Further explanation is given in one of the Arcana sections.

4. The Primal Round Diagram

The Primal Round Diagram of the structure of the sixty-four hexagrams is derived from the primal order of the trigrams. This round arrangement can be straightened into parallel sets of hexagrams in two ways, as illustrated on pages 373–375, producing two systems of *I Ching* study by hexagram pairs.

5. The Primal Square Diagram

The Primal Square Diagram is also derived from the primal order of the trigrams. Using ordinal numbers for trigrams—1 for *Heaven*, 2 for *Lake*, 3 for *Fire*, 4 for *Thunder*, 5 for *Wind*, 6 for *Water*, 7 for *Mountain*, and 8 for *Earth*, the hexagrams can be represented by pairs of numbers. Putting the bottom trigram to the left and the top trigram to the right, the Primal Square Diagram can be represented as follows:

8:8	8:7	8:6	8:5	8:4	8:3	8:2	8:1
7:8	7:7	7:6	7:5	7:4	7:3	7:2	7:1
6:8	6:7	6:6	6:5	6:4	6:3	6:2	6:1
5:8	5:7	5:6	5:5	5:4	5:3	5:2	5:1
4:8	4:7	4:6	4:5	4:4	4:3	4:2	4:1
3:8	3:7	3:6	3:5	3:4	3:3	3:2	3:1
2:8	2:7	2:6	2:5	2:4	2:3	2:2	2:1
1:8	1:7	1:6	1:5	1:4	1:3	1:2	1:1

6. The Primal Horizontal Diagram

The Primal Horizontal Diagram demonstrates the derivation of trigrams and hexagrams through bifurcation and permutation, to show the generation of the primal linear order of trigrams—*Heaven, Lake, Fire, Thunder, Wind, Water, Mountain,* and *Earth*—and the primal linear order of hexagrams resulting from permutation of the trigrams in this sequence.

The primal linear order of the hexagrams is used in the Images section in the Readings. Given by ordinal numbers according to the standard sequence of the *I Ching,* the primal linear order is as follows:

> 1, 43, 14, 34, 9, 5, 26, 11, 10, 58, 38, 54, 61, 60, 41, 19, 13, 49,
> 30, 55, 37, 63, 22, 36, 25, 17, 21, 51, 42, 3, 27, 24, 44, 28, 50, 32,
> 57, 48, 18, 46, 6, 47, 64, 40, 59, 29, 4, 7, 33, 31, 56, 62, 53, 39,
> 52, 15, 12, 45, 35, 16, 20, 8, 23, 2

Information on the Taoist "reverse operation" of the Primal Horizontal Diagram is given in one of the Arcana sections. It is also used to derive a trigram association system, as described on pages 359–361.

7. An Ancient Picture of the Eight Trigrams in Their Primal Arrangement

The ancient picture of the primal eight trigrams indicates the pairing of the trigrams in opposite positions in the arrangement. This procedure is applied on pages 362–363, generating sets of hexagrams representing certain major aspects of the total system.

8. Diagram of the Primal Integration of Yin and Yang

The diagram of the Primal Integration of Yin and Yang gives the trigram system given on page 362. In the diagram, the term "mysterious female" is written in the center of the trigram ring, while at the zenith and nadir are written the characters of the term "valley spirit." These are Taoist terms for sustained open awareness. Around the perimeter are the words, "When yang energy is strong and active, yet harmonious and clear, there is yin within yang. The yin nurtures the yang, your destiny accords with your nature; then destiny is nature. When yin energy is docile and restrained yet can also restrain, there is yang within yin. The yang balances the yin, your nature accords with your destiny; then nature is destiny."

9. Diagram of Following Temporal Creation

10. Diagram of Transformation by Reverse Operation within the Temporal

Diagrams 9 and 10 generate a tandem trigram association system for deriving hexagrammatic descriptions of relationships and situations, as described on pages 359–361. The formulas for the attitude of mind in which *I Ching* reading is to be done using this method are written around the circumference of the trigram arrangements in these diagrams (translated as follows on page 387).

Following

When the primal recedes and conditioning takes over, strength and obedience lose normality, the forces and elements of the human being are out of harmony and antagonize each other, destroying the natural reality of the human being. Reality is eventually buried by falsehood. If you follow the temporal combinations of yin and yang, whatever comes to be passes away—life and death go on and on.

Reversal

Make the door of death into the door of life; do not take the gate of life for the gate of death. If you understand what kills you and know how to reverse it, you will finally know that benefit can arise from harm.

11. The Center

The Diagram of the Center is explained in one of the Arcana sections. Names of the center written around the bisected circle are there translated (page 445). Below the circle is this description of the center: "Supremely effective, supremely sacred, supremely spiritual, it produces heaven, earth, and humanity. When you look at it, you do not see it; when you listen for it, you do not hear it; when you grasp it, you do not find it; when you aim for it, you lose it. When you discuss it, that is not it; and when you look for it, it is not there."

12. The Gold Pill

The Diagram of the Gold Pill is explained in one of the Arcana sections. Inside the circle of the pill are the words "essence" and "life." Surrounding the perimeter of the pill are "the absolute," "the infinite," "one energy," and "open selflessness."

Above the pill is the poem, "There is something before heaven and earth; it is nameless, originally silent and peaceful. It is the master of myriad forms, which doesn't wither through all seasons."

Below the pill, it says, "It walks with you, sits with you, and also sleeps with you. Vaguely, subtletly, obscurely, dimly, it is right before you. If you can recognize it, take it into the furnace and refine it. When the work is done in ten months, it transforms into a gold cicada."

Readings

THE IMAGES

Heaven Series
Lake Series
Fire Series
Thunder Series
Wind Series
Water Series
Mountain Series
Earth Series

HEAVEN SERIES 111

1. Heaven over Heaven: Heaven (1) 111111
2. Lake over Heaven: Parting (43) 111110
3. Fire over Heaven: Great Possession (14) 111101
4. Thunder over Heaven: Great Power (34) 111100
5. Wind over Heaven: Nurturance of the Small (9) 111011
6. Water over Heaven: Waiting (5) 111010
7. Mountain over Heaven: Great Accumulation (26) 111001
8. Earth over Heaven: Tranquillity (11) 111000

Heaven Series Images

Heaven: Ideal people strengthen themselves ceaselessly.

Parting: Ideal people distribute blessings to reach those below them, while avoiding presumption of virtue.

Great Possession: Ideal people stop evil and promote good, obeying Heaven and accepting its order.

Great Power: Ideal people refrain from what is improper.

Nurturance of the Small: Ideal people beautify cultured qualities.

Waiting: Ideal people enjoy life.

Great Accumulation: Ideal people become acquainted with many precedents of speech and action in order to accumulate virtue.

Tranquillity: The ruler administers the way of heaven and earth and assists the proper balance of heaven and earth, thereby helping the people.

LAKE SERIES 110

1. Heaven over Lake: Treading (10) 110111
2. Lake over Lake: Joy (58) 110110
3. Fire over Lake: Disharmony (38) 110101
4. Thunder over Lake: Marrying a Young Woman (54) 110100
5. Wind over Lake: Faithfulness in the Center (61) 110011
6. Water over Lake: Discipline (60) 110010
7. Mountain over Lake: Reduction (41) 110001
8. Earth over Lake: Overseeing (19) 110000

Lake Series Images

Treading: Ideal people distinguish above and below and settle the ambitions of the people.

Joy: Ideal people form associations for education and action.

Disharmony: Ideal people assimilate yet are different.

Marrying a Young Woman: Ideal people persist to the end and find out if something is wrong.

Faithfulness in the Center: Ideal people consider judgments and postpone executions.

Reduction: Ideal people eliminate wrath and cupidity.

Discipline: Ideal people determine measures and discuss virtuous conduct.

Overseeing: Ideal people use inexhaustibility of education and thought to embrace and protect the people without bound.

FIRE SERIES 101

1. Heaven over Fire: Sameness with Others (13) 101111
2. Lake over Fire: Revolution (49) 101110
3. Fire over Fire: Fire (30) 101101
4. Thunder over Fire: Richness (55) 101100
5. Wind over Fire: People in the Home (37) 101011
6. Water over Fire: Settled (63) 101010
7. Mountain over Fire: Adornment (22) 101001
8. Earth over Fire: Concealment of Illumination (36) 101000

Fire Series Images

Sameness with Others: Ideal people distinguish things in terms of categories and groups.

Revolution: Ideal people make calendars and clarify the seasons.

Fire: Great people illumine the four quarters with continuing light.

Richness: Ideal people make judgments and execute punishments.

People in the Home: Ideal people are factual in their speech, consistent in their deeds.

Settled: Ideal people consider problems and prevent them.

Adornment: Ideal people clarify governmental affairs without presumptuous adjudication.

Concealment of Illumination: Ideal people deal with the masses, acting unobtrusively while in fact illumined.

THUNDER SERIES 100

1. Heaven over Thunder: No Error (25) 100111
2. Lake over Thunder: Following (17) 100110
3. Fire over Thunder: Biting Through (21) 100101
4. Thunder over Thunder: Thunder (51) 100100
5. Wind over Thunder: Increase (42) 100011
6. Water over Thunder: Difficulty (3) 100010
7. Mountain over Thunder: Nourishment (27) 100001
8. Earth over Thunder: Return (24) 100000

Thunder Series Images

No Error: Ancient kings promoted growth appropriate to the time and nurtured myriad beings.

Following: Ideal people go inside and rest when the sun goes down.

Biting Through: Ancient kings clarified penalties and proclaimed laws.

Thunder: Ideal people cautiously practice introspection.

Increase: Ideal people take to good when they see it and correct whatever faults they have.

Difficulty: Ideal people order and arrange.

Nourishment: Ideal people are careful about what they say and moderate in eating and drinking.

Return: Ancient kings shut the gates on the winter solstice; caravans did not travel, the ruler did not inspect the provinces.

WIND SERIES 011

1. Heaven over Wind: Meeting (44) 011111
2. Lake over Wind: Excess of the Great (28) 011110
3. Fire over Wind: The Cauldron (50) 011101
4. Thunder over Wind: Constancy (32) 011100
5. Wind over Wind: Wind (57) 011011
6. Water over Wind: The Well (48) 011010
7. Mountain over Wind: Degeneration (18) 011001
8. Earth over Wind: Rising (46) 011000

Wind Series Images

Meeting: Rulers announce their directives to the four quarters.

Excess of the Great: Ideal people can stand alone without fear and can leave society without distress.

The Cauldron: Ideal people stabilize life in the proper position.

Constancy: Ideal people stand without changing places.

Wind: Ideal people articulate directions and carry out tasks.

The Well: Ideal people comfort others and urge reciprocity.

Degeneration: Ideal people inspire others and nurture virtue.

Rising: Ideal people follow virtue, accumulating the small to lofty greatness.

WATER SERIES 010

1. Heaven over Water: Contention (6) 010111
2. Lake over Water: Exhaustion (47) 010110
3. Fire over Water: Unsettled (64) 010101
4. Thunder over Water: Solution (40) 010100
5. Wind over Water: Dispersal (59) 010011
6. Water over Water: Water (29) 010010
7. Mountain over Water: Darkness (4) 010001
8. Earth over Water: The Army (7) 010000

Water Series Images

Contention: When they do things, ideal people plan first.

Exhaustion: Ideal people use life to the full and achieve their aim.

Unsettled: Ideal people carefully discern things and keep them in their places.

Solution: Ideal people forgive faults and pardon crimes.

Dispersal: Ancient kings honored God and set up shrines.

Water: Ideal people consistently practice virtue and learn how to teach.

Darkness: Ideal people nurture character with fruitful action.

The Army: Ideal people embrace the people and nurture the masses.

MOUNTAIN SERIES 001

1. Heaven over Mountain: Withdrawal (33) 001111
2. Lake over Mountain: Sensing (31) 001110
3. Fire over Mountain: Travel (56) 001101
4. Thunder over Mountain: Preponderance of the Small (62) 001100
5. Wind over Mountain: Gradual Progress (53) 001011
6. Water over Mountain: Halting (39) 001010

7. Mountain over Mountain: Mountain (52) 001001
8. Earth over Mountain: Humility (15) 001000

Mountain Series Images

Withdrawal: Ideal people keep petty people at a distance, being stern without ill will.

Sensing: Ideal people accept others with openness.

Travel: Ideal people apply punishment with understanding and prudence and do not keep people imprisoned.

Preponderance of the Small: Ideal people are excessively deferential in conduct, excessively sad in mourning, excessively frugal in consumption.

Gradual Progress: Ideal people live wisely and improve customs.

Halting: Ideal people examine themselves and cultivate virtue.

Mountain: Ideal people think without leaving their place.

Humility: Superior people decrease what is too much to add to what is too little, assessing things and dealing impartially.

EARTH SERIES 000

1. Heaven over Earth: Obstruction (12) 000111
2. Lake over Earth: Gathering (45) 000110
3. Fire over Earth: Advance (35) 000101
4. Thunder over Earth: Joy (16) 000100
5. Wind over Earth: Observing (20) 000011
6. Water over Earth: Accord (8) 000010
7. Mountain over Earth: Stripping Away (23) 000001
8. Earth over Earth: Earth (2) 000000

Earth Series Images

Obstruction: Ideal people are parsimonious with power and avoid trouble; they are not susceptible to material inducements.

Gathering: Ideal people prepare weapons to guard against the unexpected.

Advance: Ideal people shine with the quality of enlightenment themselves.

Joy: Ancient kings made music to honor virtue, offering it in abundance to God; thereby they share it with their ancestors.

Observing: Ancient kings set up education after examination of the region and observation of the people.

Accord: Ancient kings set up myriad realms and associated with their representatives.

Stripping Away: Those above secure their homes by kindness to those below.

Earth: Ideal people support others with warmth.

THEMES

Upper Course

> beginning: hexagrams 1–8
> middle: hexagrams 9–16
> end: hexagrams 17–30

Lower Course

> beginning: hexagrams 31–42
> middle: hexagrams 43–50
> end: hexagrams 51–64

BEGINNING OF THE UPPER COURSE

> 111111 Heaven (1)
> 000000 Earth (2)
>
> 100010 Difficulty (3)
> 010001 Darkness (4)
>
> 111010 Waiting (5)
> 010111 Contention (6)
>
> 010000 The Army (7)
> 000010 Accord (8)

Themes of the Beginning of the Upper Course

1. Heaven *and* Earth

Confucianism: *Heaven* is creativity, *Earth* is receptivity.

Taoism: *Heaven* is firmness, *Earth* is flexibility; *Heaven* is knowledge, *Earth* is capacity; *Heaven* is energy, *Earth* is spirit.

Buddhism: *Heaven* is knowledge, *Earth* is obedience.

The combination of *Heaven* and *Earth* is held to produce the complete human being.

Lines: *Heaven* is six yang lines; *Earth* is six yin lines.

2. Difficulty *and* Darkness

Confucianism: *Difficulty* is sluggishness and congestion in the beginning of an undertaking; *Darkness* is immaturity and ignorance of the way out of difficulty.

Taoism: *Difficulty* is trouble making progress, *Darkness* is obscurity. Also, *Difficulty* means being held back, *Darkness* means inner development without rationalization.

Buddhism: *Difficulty* is hardship at the beginning of an age, the beginning of a lifetime, the beginning of a task, the beginning of a thought; *Darkness* is ignorance and lack of development.

Together, *Difficulty* and *Darkness* represent the first stirrings of the evolutionary instinct in the conditioned mind; it is this very instinct toward development that forces the individual to confront the reality of the stifling effect of conditioning.

Lines: *Difficulty* and *Darkness* are two yang lines and four yin lines.

3. Waiting *and* Contention

Confucianism: *Waiting* means nurturing strength when at an impasse, awaiting an appropriate time to go into action; *Contention* represents a combination of desire and strength.

Taoism: *Waiting* means awaiting the right time to proceed; *Contention* means deciding right and wrong.

Buddhism: *Waiting* means waiting for the proper conditions under which people can be educated; *Contention* means self-criticism.

Contention tends to result from failure in waiting, but positive, effective contention may follow from sufficient waiting.

Lines: *Waiting* and *Contention* are four yang lines and two yin lines.

4. The Army *and* Accord

Confucianism: *The Army* represents conflict, *Accord* represents harmony.

Taoism: *The Army* represents repulsion of falsehood, *Accord* represents association with truth.

Buddhism: *The Army* represents the battery of educational methods used to overcome ignorance; *Accord* represents coordination of these methods.

The Army and *Accord* are complementary in the sense that conflict is fundamentally aimed at removal of conflict and establishment of harmony.

MIDDLE OF THE UPPER COURSE

111011 Nurturance of the Small (9)
110111 Treading (10)

111000 Tranquillity (11)
000111 Obstruction (12)

101111 Sameness with Others (13)
111101 Great Possession (14)

001000 Humility (15)
000100 Joy (16)

Themes of the Middle of the Upper Course

1. Nurturance of the Small *and* Treading

Confucianism: *Nurturance of the Small* is read as *Small Development;* it represents individuals nurturing one another by grouping together, or the use of flexibility to nurture strength. *Treading* refers to conduct, the manners developed by people in mutual association.

Taoism: *Nurturance of the Small* here means nurturance by smallness; in other words, this refers to development through minimization of the self, as, for instance, humility may be used as a means of self-development. *Nurturance of the Small* may also mean small development, such as the development of manners and conduct in people who are not yet ready for higher spiritual development. *Treading* means progress, ascent towards higher attainment.

Buddhism: *Nurturance of the Small* is also read as *Small Obstruction;* the two meanings are combined in the sense of using obstruction positively, as a means to develop oneself. Here smallness also refers to flexibility. *Treading* means carrying out the process of mental transformation.

These two hexagrams are both connected with the idea of development. The former focuses primarily on yin—the small, the humble, the flexible, the recessive. The latter focuses primarily on yang—the strong and progressive. Their order reflects two logical forms of progression of personal development: in one, confrontation with external obstruction and internal weakness leads to positive action; in the other, social cultivation is required before spiritual cultivation can be effective.

Lines. *Nurturance of the Small* and *Treading* are five yang lines and one yin line.

2. Tranquillity *and* Obstruction

Confucianism: *Tranquillity* refers to the serenity that results from conduct that is appropriate to the situation and therefore successful. *Obstruction* results from lack of communication between those in high positions and those below them. *Tranquillity* also represents harmonization of firmness and flexibility, while *Obstruction* represents lack of harmonization.

Taoism: *Tranquillity* represents the combining of yin and yang, resulting in mastery and success. *Obstruction* represents the opposite, blockage and failure due to separation of yin and yang.

Buddhism: *Tranquillity* represents integration of transcendent enlighten-

ment and work in the world. *Obstruction* refers to contamination of
teachings through religious attachment and spiritual egoism.

Tranquillity and *Obstruction* are ordinarily used proverbially to represent
success and failure. They are the archetypes of communion and alienation; Confucians, Taoists, and Buddhists alike use this pair in
particular to illustrate the principle that truly successful government is
government in the service of the people.

Lines: *Tranquillity* is classified under three yang lines; *Obstruction* is classified under three yin lines.

3. Sameness with Others *and* Great Possession

Confucianism: *Sameness with Others* (*Association with Others*), following
immediately upon *Obstruction*, refers to the need for people to get together and cooperate in order to resolve social problems. *Great Possession* refers to the wealth—material and psychological—that comes
through cooperative association.

Taoism: *Sameness with Others* refers to the practice of illuminates mixing
with ordinary society, concealing their enlightenment. *Great Possession*
refers to the growth of personal power and enlightenment.

Buddhism: *Sameness with Others* refers to the experience of universal
compassion, the realization of unity with all life. *Great Possession* refers
to the attainment of higher qualities after enlightenment.

These two hexagrams are also closely related, representing a logical progression from attainment of social/psychological integration to attainment of the organic growth naturally consequent upon this
integration.

Lines: *Sameness with Others* and *Great Possession* are five yang lines and
one yin line.

4. Humility *and* Joy

Confucianism: *Humility* means remaining modest even though one may
have the personal wealth—material or psychological—represented by
great possession. *Joy* (*Delight*) represents the happiness that results
from the ability to be humble in spite of great possession.

Taoism: *Humility* means not dwelling on what one has; *Joy* is the happiness that comes from acting in accord with the time.

Buddhism: *Humility* means not presuming upon one's enlightenment;
Joy is the bliss of realization of openness.

Humility and *Joy* also go hand in hand, for without humility, great possession—whether it be material or metaphysical—results in disharmony with the human environment and consequent unhappiness.

Lines: *Humility* and *Joy* are one yang line and five yin lines.

END OF THE UPPER COURSE

100110 Following (17)
011001 Degeneration (18)

110000 Overseeing (19)
000011 Observing (20)

100101 Biting Through (21)
101001 Adornment (22)

000001 Stripping Away (23)
100000 Return (24)

100111 No Error (25)
111001 Great Accumulation (26)

100001 Nourishment (27)
011110 Excess of the Great (28)

010010 Water (29)
101101 Fire (30)

Themes of the End of the Upper Course

1. Following *and* Degeneration

Confucianism: *Following* refers to a group following its leader, and to people following a course appropriate to their situation. *Degeneration* refers to deterioration and disorder, such as may come about through misguided following.

Taoism: *Following* may mean expediently going along with desires in order to introduce guidance gradually, or it may mean adaptation to the conditions of the time, or it may mean seeking true perception by focusing on the essence of consciousness, or it may mean the earthly following the celestial. *Degeneration* means deterioration, corruption of the human mind by artificial conditioning, but it is taken to include the meaning of repairing degeneration by abandoning the false and returning to the true.

Buddhism: *Following* means widespread absorption of enlightening influence, and it also means harmonization with the real character of things after realization of truth. *Degeneration* refers to the deterioration of Buddhism that results from development of a following motivated by personal ambitions, and it also refers to deterioration of the individual through the exercise of sentimental compassion.

Following and *Degeneration* form a reverberating pair. The quality of following depends on what is followed; degeneration results from wrong following. Conversely, degeneration can be remedied by the right following.

Lines: *Following* is classified under three yang lines; *Degeneration* is classified under three yin lines.

2. Overseeing *and* Observing

Confucianism: *Overseeing* refers to supervision of subordinates by superiors. *Observing* means watching, particularly in the sense of subordinates watching superiors in order to observe their example.

Taoism: *Overseeing* means watching over the process of inner concentration in order to foster the development of positive energy. It also has the meaning of education. *Observing* means careful attention to the timing of the developmental process.

Buddhism: *Overseeing* refers to elimination of imbalances in meditation. *Observing* refers to examination of the mind in order to cut off delusions.

The general themes of *Overseeing* and *Observing* are much the same; the differences are only in terms of what is overseen and observed. Sometimes the contrast is made between those above overseeing those below and those below observing those above; sometimes the contrast is made between overseeing others and observing oneself. In either case, the central point is ongoing attention.

Lines: *Overseeing* and *Observing* are two yang lines and four yin lines.

3. Biting Through *and* Adornment

Confucianism: *Biting Through* refers to the joining of the separated. *Adornment* refers to culture, order, and organization necessary when people join to form a community.

Taoism: *Biting Through* represents the combination of understanding and action. *Adornment* refers to inner personal cultivation.

Buddhism: *Biting Through* refers to correcting immorality and mental disease. *Adornment* means establishment of regulations in the exoteric sphere, adornment of the mind with concentration and insight in the esoteric sphere.

Biting Through and *Adornment* are complementary in that the result of the reconciliatory or corrective process represented by the former becomes the basis of the latter, and the beautification process represented by the latter consolidates the gains of the former.

Lines: *Biting Through* and *Adornment* are classified under three yang lines.

4. Stripping Away *and* Return

Confucianism: *Stripping Away* takes place when petty people tear down enlightened people; *Return* is the restoration of enlightened leadership.

Taoism: *Stripping Away* refers to acquired conditioning stripping away primal energy; *Return* refers to the first restoration of primal energy.

Buddhism: *Stripping Away* can refer to the proliferation of formalities defeating real practice or to imitation's taking the place of real practice; in a positive sense, it can mean stripping away the shell of the ego to reveal the true reality that lies beyond subjectivity. *Return* can refer to the restoration of true teaching, return to normality, or return to the essence of reality. In terms of meditation, *Stripping Away* refers to proceeding from contemplation of conditionality to contemplation of emptiness, stripping away emotional clinging to appearances; *Return* refers to proceeding from contemplation of emptiness to contemplation of conditionality, returning to the nonduality of form and emptiness.

In general terms, *Stripping Away* and *Return* represent the culmination of waning and the beginning of waxing.

Lines: *Stripping Away* and *Return* are one yang line and five yin lines.

5. No Error *and* Great Accumulation

Confucianism: *No Error* means accord with true reason unaffected by subjective desire. *Great Accumulation* means building up learning and virtue.

Taoism: *No Error*, also read as *Fidelity*, means fostering the original creative energy innate in human beings. *Great Accumulation*, also read as *Nurturance of the Great*, means developing the "spiritual embryo" formed by this original energy. Also, *No Error* means freedom from errant thought and arbitrary action, while *Great Accumulation* means accumulation of virtue.

Buddhism: *No Error* means restoration of a true path and also return to the true essence of mind. *Great Accumulation* means development of adepts and buildup of provisions of enlightenment on a large scale.

Overall, *No Error* is the necessary precondition for *Great Accumulation*.

Lines: *No Error* and *Great Accumulation* are four yang lines and two yin lines.

6. Nourishment *and* Excess of the Great

Confucianism: *Nourishment* refers to provision of material and psychological needs, of oneself and others. *Excess of the Great* is read as *Great Surpassing*, and refers to what is surpassing in greatness, something that is not ordinarily seen.

Taoism: *Nourishment* means discerning what is good and cleaving to it, becoming empty in order to seek fulfillment, using stillness to nurture activity. *Excess of the Great* means being too strong and hence in need of openness to balance this.

Buddhism: *Nourishment* means developing virtue for the benefit of all; it also means nurturing the seed of enlightenment. *Excess of the Great* is read as *Passing of the Great*, and refers to when practice is becoming effective; it can also refer to being prone to contamination and decline after initial success.

Nourishment and *Excess of the Great* also reverberate, in that success in the former leads to success in the latter yet success in the latter, if carried too far, again necessitates the former.

Lines: *Nourishment* is two yang lines and four yin lines; *Excess of the Great* is four yang lines and two yin lines.

7. Water *and* Fire

Confucianism: *Water* is read as *Double Pitfall,* and refers to danger within danger. *Fire* has the meanings of clinging and illumining.

Taoism: *Water* is read as *Mastering Pitfalls,* and refers to getting through danger; it also refers to self-development and development of others. *Fire* means inner and outer awareness.

Buddhism: *Water* is read as *Multiple Danger,* and refers to contamination of a teaching after it has become a fad; it also refers to arousal of past mental habits in those prone to intellectualism. *Fire* means cleaving to true teaching and accurate observation.

Water and *Fire* are so-called timeless hexagrams, which, along with *Heaven* and *Earth,* are considered to be in some sense applicable to all situations because of the scope of their meanings. Put simply, *Water* has the sense of danger and the sense of getting through danger; *Fire* has the sense of the awareness needed to get through danger successfully. Therefore *Water* and *Fire* form a pair.

Lines: *Water* is two yang lines and four yin lines; *Fire* is four yang lines and two yin lines.

BEGINNING OF THE LOWER COURSE

001110 Sensing (31)
011100 Constancy (32)

001111 Withdrawal (33)
111100 Great Power (34)

000101 Advance (35)
101000 Concealment of Illumination (36)

101011 People in the Home (37)
110101 Disharmony (38)

001010 Halting (39)
010100 Solution (40)

110001 Reduction (41)
100011 Increase (42)

Themes of the Beginning of the Lower Course

1. Sensing *and* Constancy

Confucianism: *Sensing* refers to communion of complementary opposites. *Constancy* refers to consistency and continuity in this interaction.

Taoism: *Sensing*, read as *Sensitivity*, refers to harmonization of yin and yang, to opening the mind in order to become sensitive, and to sensing the original mind. *Constancy* refers to persistence in application to spiritual development.

Buddhism: *Sensing* refers to interaction between the enlightened and the unenlightened; it also refers to interaction between mind and objects. *Constancy* refers to the permanence of eternal principles.

Constancy underlies *Sensing*, both in terms of its basis and its ideal; *Sensing* actualizes *Constancy*, in terms of bringing it into actual consciousness and practice.

Lines: *Sensing* and *Constancy* are classified under three yin lines.

2. Withdrawal *and* Great Power

Confucianism: *Withdrawal* means retreat or escape, as when enlightened people conceal themselves when petty people become dominant in society. *Great Power* means progress and growth, such as takes place after undisturbed accumulation of strength in seclusion.

Taoism: *Withdrawal* means keeping energy in check, controlling one's strength and not presuming on it. Also read as *Inaccessibility*, it refers to the enlightened ones' keeping away from petty people, concealing their strength. *Great Power* means expansion of positive energy, which, if excessive, again requires withdrawal.

Buddhism: *Withdrawal* refers to self-development, in the sense that it may represent a temporary withdrawal of focus from society at large to the individual. Focus on individual development, of course, is ultimately for the benefit of society at large, but under certain circumstances it can best be accomplished by withdrawal from unmanageable involvement in externals. *Great Power*, also read as the *Power of the Great*, refers to the strength developed through individual self-work in a state of withdrawal.

Withdrawal and *Great Power* are another reverberating pair of hexagrams. Withdrawal may be a prelude to great power, as power is built up in seclusion (which seclusion may or may not be overt, as there is internal seclusion and external seclusion). Then again, withdrawal may be a concomitant or an aftermath of great power, as withdrawal and inaccessibility may be needed to safeguard power or to prevent it from becoming overbearing.

Lines: *Withdrawal* and *Great Power* are four yang lines and two yin lines.

3. Advance *and* Concealment of Illumination

Confucianism: *Advance* refers to progress toward complete fulfillment after the attainment of power. *Concealment of Illumination,* read as *Damage to Illumination,* refers to a reversal taking place after the climax of rising. In *Advance,* enlightened leadership is at the head; in *Concealment of Illumination* (*Damage to Illumination*), ignorant leadership is in power.

Taoism: *Advance* means progress in illumination, using sincerity and clarity of mind to promote enlightenment. *Concealment of Illumination* means stopping intensive effort when illumination is sufficiently advanced and concealing enlightenment when in the midst of ordinary people. Failing these results in injury or damage to illumination, an alternate reading of the hexagram theme.

Buddhism: *Advance* refers to the emergence of knowledge and the growth of virtue. *Concealment of Illumination* refers to inward development of enlightenment unbeknownst to others; read as *Damage to Illumination,* it refers to inability to withdraw in a timely manner.

Advance and *Concealment of Illumination* are complementary in that advance will eventually necessitate concealment of illumination in order to prevent damage to illumination, while concealment of illumination will facilitate higher advancement.

Lines: *Advance* and *Concealment of Illumination* are two yang lines and four yin lines.

4. People in the Home *and* Disharmony

Confucianism: *People in the Home* refers to order in family life and, by extension, to social obligations in general. *Disharmony,* in contrast, refers to alienation and discord.

Taoism: *People in the Home* refers to inward mastery of mind and self refinement. *Disharmony* means opposition, but the emphasis is on reconciliation of discord.

Buddhism: *People in the Home* refers to realization that subjective experience is only consciousness. *Disharmony,* or opposition, refers to the disparity between mundane and transmundane meditations.

Lines: *People in the Home* and *Disharmony* are four yang lines and two yin lines.

5. Halting *and* Solution

Confucianism: *Halting* means being obstructed by danger, *Solution* means resolution of trouble.

Taoism: *Halting* represents preserving the primal in the midst of the temporal. *Solution,* or *Liberation,* refers to taking advantage of the right time to gather primal energy.

Buddhism: *Halting* refers to obstruction due to unreconciled differences, *Solution* refers to resolution of difficulties.

Lines: *Halting* and *Solution* are two yang lines and four yin lines.

People in the Home, Disharmony, Halting, and *Solution* can be seen as two pairs of opposites or as a circular series. When the order represented by *People in the Home* breaks down or fails to be established, this results in disharmony, which causes obstruction and halting; halting is a result of discord, but it is also an opportunity to regroup one's resources and find a solution, enabling harmony to be reestablished.

6. Reduction *and* Increase

Confucianism: *Reduction* is when those in lower positions benefit those in higher positions; this may take the form of subordinates willingly serving superiors, or it may take the form of superiors exploiting subordinates. *Increase* is the opposite, when those in higher positions benefit those below them.

Taoism: *Reduction* refers to lessening what is excessive, while *Increase* refers to augmenting what is deficient.

Buddhism: *Reduction* means reducing mundanity, *Increase* means increasing enlightenment.

In each case, *Reduction* and *Increase* are complementary opposites; in the political sphere represented by Confucian tradition, they tend to be cyclical, while in the higher psychological realms treated in Taoist and Buddhist traditions they are carried on simultaneously.

Lines: *Reduction* and *Increase* are classified under three yang lines.

MIDDLE OF THE LOWER COURSE

111110 Parting (43)
011111 Meeting (44)

000110 Gathering (45)
011000 Rising (46)

010110 Exhaustion (47)
011010 The Well (48)

101110 Revolution (49)
011101 The Cauldron (50)

Themes of the Middle of the Lower Course

1. Parting *and* Meeting

Confucianism: *Parting,* read as *Removal,* refers to a time when enlightened people are on the ascendant and petty people are about to go into eclipse. *Meeting* refers to the joining of the parted.

Taoism: *Parting* refers to repulsion of external influences by healthy inner energy. *Meeting* refers to preserving primal energy against the insidious inroads of external influences.

Buddhism: *Parting* refers to elimination of residual confusion after preliminary attainment of selflessness. *Meeting* refers to use of inherent evil after enlightenment in order to contact mundane people.

Generally speaking, *Parting* and *Meeting* represent successive phases of development, wherein the positive aspects of meeting can only be realized after parting has been successful.

Lines: *Parting* and *Meeting* are five yang lines and one yin line.

2. Gathering *and* Rising

Confucianism: *Gathering* represents formation of a social group or community. *Rising* represents growth and upward progress, such as is made possible by collective effort.

Taoism: *Gathering* refers to recovery and concentration of dissipated vitality, energy, and spirit. *Rising* refers to orderly progress in the process of restoring primal wholeness.

Buddhism: *Gathering* represents grouping of resources, *Rising* represents receptively following the path of spiritual development.

Gathering and *Rising* also represent successive phases in the developmental process, first assembling the appropriate elements, then proceeding on that basis in an orderly fashion.

Lines: *Gathering* and *Rising* are two yang lines and four yin lines.

3. Exhaustion *and* The Well

Confucianism: *Exhaustion* refers to the depletion of strength and end of rising momentum. It also represents a time when enlightened people are eclipsed and worn out by petty people. *The Well* represents a return to the bottom, which also carries the suggestion of a reservoir to which one returns after exhaustion.

Taoism: *Exhaustion* represents being at an impasse, and also resolving an impasse through self-refinement. *The Well* has the sense of nurturance, meaning development of personal virtues in order to nourish others.

Buddhism: *Exhaustion* refers to mental exhaustion due to rising without stopping. *The Well* refers to the constancy of inherent virtues underlying changes in cultivated qualities.

Exhaustion and *The Well*, taken as a pair, represent the need for balance. Lofty development depends on deep reserves, just as a high building must have a sturdy foundation.

Lines: *Exhaustion* and *The Well* are classified under three yin lines.

4. Revolution *and* The Cauldron

Confucianism: *Revolution* means change, reform, renewal; *The Cauldron* represents the means or ability to effect this change.

Taoism: *Revolution* (or *Change*) means refinement of personal desires so as to become unselfish; it also means changing adaptively according to the time. *The Cauldron* represents sublimation of mundane energy and stabilization of higher energy.

Buddhism: *Revolution,* read as *Change,* refers to change of character as preparation for higher studies. *The Cauldron* represents the path by which people are transformed into buddhas.

In terms of their general themes, *Revolution* and *The Cauldron* are intimately associated, representing the process and means of change from a lower to a higher state.

Lines: *Revolution* and *The Cauldron* are four yang lines and two yin lines.

END OF THE LOWER COURSE

100100 Thunder (51)
001001 Mountain (52)

001011 Gradual Progress (53)
110100 Marrying a Young Woman (54)

101100 Richness (55)
001101 Travel (56)

011011 Wind (57)
110110 Joy (58)

010011 Dispersal (59)
110010 Discipline (60)

110011 Faithfulness in the Center (61)
001100 Predominance of the Small (62)

101010 Settled (63)
010101 Unsettled (64)

Themes of the End of the Lower Course

1. Thunder *and* Mountain

Confucianism: *Thunder* has numerous associations: succession, upward mobility, self-mastery, and progressive leadership of the body politic. *Mountain* has the meaning of stillness, stability, stopping and resting at the appropriate place.

Taoism: *Thunder* means action, specifically in the sense of activity, inner and outer, carried out in order to progress along the path of transformation and development. Inner activity, the practice of introspection, is especially emphasized. *Mountain* represents inward and outward stillness, using quietude to nurture energy.

Buddhism: *Thunder* represents the stirring of thought or the objectification of mental habits; in terms of Buddhist practice, this calls for the active exercise of insightful examination. *Mountain* represents stopping and stilling thoughts and emotions, so as to maintain tranquillity in the midst of events.

Thunder and *Mountain* are complementary opposites, the one necessitating the other for the attainment of balance.

Lines: *Thunder* and *Mountain* are two yang lines and four yin lines.

2. Gradual Progress *and* Marrying a Young Woman

Confucianism: *Gradual Progress* represents progress that is carried out in an orderly manner, at an appropriate pace. *Marrying a Young Woman*—meaning the marriage of a young woman—is an example and a representation of orderly procedure.

Taoism: *Gradual Progress* refers to progress on the path of spiritual development according to the appropriate order, without rushing. *Marrying a Young Woman,* read as *Making a Young Girl Marry,* represents improper interaction, seeking the essence of consciousness through arbitrary emotion rather than using the essence to seek true sense; it also represents undue haste.

Buddhism: *Gradual Progress* means gradually clearing up confusion about specific phenomena in the realm of causality; *Marrying a Young Woman* refers to the practice of gradual meditation.

Gradual Progress and *Marrying a Young Woman* both emphasize the need for appropriate order and pace in purposeful activity.

Lines: *Gradual Progress* is classified under three yin lines; *Marrying a Young Woman* is classified under three yang lines.

3. Richness *and* Travel

Confucianism: *Richness,* or *Abundance,* refers to flourishing resulting from the proper combination of understanding and action. *Travel* refers to destabilization.

Taoism: *Richness* represents a balance of illumination and action. *Travel* represents nondwelling, transcending the world.

Buddhism: *Richness* represents inclusion of meditation on phenomena to foster the path of enlightenment. *Travel* represents enlightening work in transient worlds.

Here it is instructive to note that in the Taoist and Buddhist traditions, which include both worldly and world-transcending outlooks and practices, *Richness* and *Travel* are complementary, whereas in the Confucian tradition, which is ordinarily worldly and has generally had the defect of attempting to ignore certain important implications of transience, *Richness* and *Travel* are contrasting opposites.

Lines: *Richness* is classified under three yang lines; *Travel* is classified under three yin lines.

4. Wind *and* Joy

Confucianism: *Wind* represents adaptability, obedience, following, and entry. *Joy*, read as *Pleasing*, refers to people's pleasing each other in their mutual association.

Taoism: *Wind* represents progress through flexible obedience. *Joy* refers to joy in following the Tao.

Buddhism: *Wind* represents following true insight in concentration practice in order to penetrate essential truth. *Joy*, read as *Delight*, refers to the satisfaction of fulfillment.

Wind and *Joy* are closely related in that both represent harmonization, particularly harmonization of the inward and the outward.

Lines: *Wind* and *Joy* are four yang lines and two yin lines.

5. Dispersal *and* Discipline

Confucianism: *Dispersal* refers to dissolution, but the emphasis of the hexagram is on the remedying of dissolution, just as the emphasis of the hexagram *Degeneration* is on remedying degeneration. *Discipline* refers to measures adopted to restore and maintain coherence in groups and their undertakings.

Taoism: *Dispersal* refers to disorganization and disorder, but here again the emphasis is on reestablishment of order. *Discipline* represents the practice of obedience in unfavorable circumstances.

Buddhism: *Dispersal* is interpreted as disbursal, meaning sharing. *Discipline*, read as *Regulation*, refers to the control of dispersal in order that it not become excessive.

While *Dispersal* is given a negative interpretation in Confucian and Taoist readings, the theme of the hexagram actually revolves around the remedy. *Discipline* then takes up this theme and deals with the practicalities of order. The Buddhist interpretations of *Dispersal* and *Discipline* refer respectively to centrifugal and centripital forces in communal organization and order.

Lines: *Dispersal* is classified under three yin lines; *Discipline* is classified under three yang lines.

6. Faithfulness in the Center *and* Predominance of the Small

Confucianism: *Faithfulness in the Center*, read as *Sincerity in the Center*, refers to the sincerity or truthfulness of the individual as the focal point of trust reposed in the individual by other members of society. *Predominance of the Small* is read as *Small Excess*, which means going beyond the norm in small things and also means being minimal in excess; but here again the emphasis is on remedy, regarding small excess as an inspiration or opportunity to correct excess.

Taoism: *Faithfulness in the Center* represents seeking fulfillment by emptying oneself, as is done in the process of seeking full awareness by
emptying the mind of restrictive thoughts and attitudes. *Predominance
of the Small* refers to acting as if one were empty after having attained
fulfillment.

Buddhism: *Faithfulness in the Center*, read as *Sincerity in the Center*, refers
to sensitive response and integration emanating from the true core of
the being. *Predominance of the Small*, read as *Small Excess*, refers to
minor excesses occurring through intensity of good intentions; here,
again, the emphasis is on regarding this as a stimulus to perfection.

Faithfulness in the Center (or *Sincerity in the Center*) and *Predominance of
the Small* (or *Small Excess*) are another reverberating pair of hexagrams, in that the former is regarded as the cause or reason of the
latter, while the latter calls for return to the former.

Lines: *Faithfulness in the Center* is four yang lines and two yin lines; *Predominance of the Small* is two yang lines and four yin lines.

7. Settled *and* Unsettled

Confucianism: *Settled* represents a time when matters are settled, but it
also carries the sense of warning against complacency. *Unsettled* represents the fact there is never an end to change, that the settled again
becomes unsettled; but it also carries the idea of an unsettled state as a
stimulus to seek settlement.

Taoism: *Settled* represents the mutual completion of the earthly and the
celestial, the integration of vitality and spirit; it also carries the sense
of guarding against the danger of destabilization. *Unsettled* means that
the earthly and the celestial are not yet settled, and represents the
need to refine the self and stand apart from mundane conditioning in
order to seek settlement.

Buddhism: *Settled* refers to the use of compensating factors to resolve
imbalances in all situations. *Unsettled* refers to the fact that there is no
end to things and also stands for the original impetus to seek settlement and harmony.

Settled and *Unsettled* are another reverberating pair of hexagrams, and
their place at the conclusion of the *I Ching* proper is regarded as
highly significant in that they provide a final illustration of the way in
which opposites can work together and flow into each other. The reason *Unsettled* rather than *Settled* is the last hexagram—contrary to the
automatic assumption of linear thinking—is to emphasize that the
finite number of hexagrams in the *I Ching* is not intended to represent
a closed system, and that the process of change is never ending.

Lines: *Settled* is classified under three yang lines; *Unsettled* is classified
under three yin lines.

Each of these themes has a number of nuances and may change radically according to the situation. This, of course, is one meaning of the name of the classic, *The Book of Changes*. For more thorough studies of individual themes, see my previous volumes, *The Taoist I Ching*, *The Buddhist I Ching*, and *I Ching: The Tao of Organization*. Each of these volumes presents a new translation of the text of the *I Ching*, with commentaries from each of the major traditions of Chinese thought. For further study of the hexagrams in pairs as presented here, see especially the Mixed Hexagrams section in *The Taoist I Ching*.

LINES

One yang line
Two yang lines
Three yang lines
Four yang lines
Five yang lines
One yin line
Two yin lines
Three yin lines
Four yin lines
Five yin lines

HEXAGRAMS WITH ONE YANG LINE

100000 Return (24)
010000 The Army (7)
001000 Humility (15)
000100 Joy (16)
000010 Accord (8)
000001 Stripping Away (23)

Indications of the Yang Lines in Hexagrams with One Yang

Return (24)

1 It is very lucky if you return to truth immediately.

The Army (7)

2 It is lucky if there is no error at the central core.

Humility (15)

3 Humble workers who accomplish their end will be lucky.

Joy (16)

4 Truthfulness in doing good bodes well.

Accord (8)

5 Manifestation of accord with others, with leniency and naturalness, bodes well.

Stripping Away (23)

6 Those effectively aware of an incorruptible inner core get help, those not effectively aware of it lose everything.

HEXAGRAMS WITH TWO YANG LINES

110000 Overseeing (19)
101000 Concealment of Illumination (36)
100100 Thunder (51)
100010 Difficulty (3)
100001 Nourishment (27)

011000 Rising (46)
010100 Solution (40)
010010 Water (29)
010001 Darkness (4)

001100 Predominance of the Small (62)
001010 Halting (39)
001001 Mountain (52)

000110 Gathering (45)
000101 Advance (35)

000011 Observing (20)

Indications of the Yang Lines in Hexagrams with Two Yangs

Overseeing (19)

1 Sensitivity is good if it is correct, intention and action bode well if correct.

2 Sensitivity is good if it is in harmony with the good of the whole.

Concealment of Illumination (36)

1 It may be necessary to conceal oneself and flee in order to preserve one's uprightness.

3 When it is nearly time to emerge from concealment, it will not do to try to effect a hasty correction of affairs.

Thunder (51)

1 A stir or a shake-up causes alarm; but if it is used as a stimulus to improve, it has good results.

4 Incautious action is ineffective.

Difficulty (3)

1 Remain correct, establish stability and control.

5 Correctness has good results in small matters, but self-righteousness is bad in great matters.

Nourishment (27)

1 Ignoring your own endowments and seeking elsewhere bodes ill.

6 When in charge of taking care of others, it is good to be diligent and enterprising.

Rising (46)

2 Communicate with sincerity, and you will be blameless.

3 If there is no resistance, there is no questioning.

Solution (40)

2 Balance and correctness bring good fortune.

4 When not positioned rightly, wait for peer support before acting.

Water (29)

2 When in a dangerous position, only small gains can be made.

5 Avoid faults by remaining stable.

Darkness (4)

2 It is good to share and cooperate with others.

6 Oppose ignorance or avoid it—do not allow yourself to become infected by it.

Predominance of the Small (62)

3 Unless precautions are taken, one in the ascendancy is attacked, bringing misfortune.

4 Do not act from a position of disadvantage—be cautious and correct.

Halting (39)

3 Turn back on seeing danger.

5 Peer support is available in trouble if you are balanced and moderate.

Mountain (52)

3 Inflexibility in middle management is fatal, overweening ambition is dangerous.

6 Prudent self-restraint bodes well.

Gathering (45)

4 If you overstep your authority in an undertaking, you will avoid blame only if you are very successful.

5 Be correct but don't take yourself seriously, and you will have no regrets.

Advance (35)

4 Trying to advance beyond your capabilities is dangerous even if you are determined and sincere.

6 Avoid fault by self-mastery; do not be proud even though correct.

Observing (20)

5 Observe your personal growth so as to be impeccable.

6 Observe what you produce and see that it is blameless.

HEXAGRAMS WITH THREE YANG LINES RISING FROM BELOW

111000 Tranquillity (11)
110100 Marrying a Young Woman (54)
110010 Discipline (60)
110001 Reduction (41)

101100 Richness (55)
101010 Settled (63)
101001 Adornment (22)

100110 Following (17)
100101 Biting Through (21)

100011 Increase (42)

Indications of the Yang Lines in Hexagrams with Three Yangs

Tranquillity (11)

1 Collective effort to make progress leads to good luck.

2 Be tolerant and supportive of others, without partisanship, and you can act seriously in a balanced way.

3 Things cannot always remain comfortable—be steadfast when hard times come.

Marrying a Young Woman (54)

1 Constancy and service bring good luck.

2 Single-minded reserve is beneficial.

4 Wait for the right time.

Discipline (60)

1 If you know when to avoid action, you will avoid mistakes.

2 You will be unlucky if you miss the right timing and opportunity.

5 You will be lucky if you can be content under unfavorable conditions and will make progress if you act on this basis.

Reduction (41)

1 There is no blame if you drop what you are doing to help others who are not as capable as you are, but be sure to assess proper measure and avoid excess.

2 It is beneficial to remain firm in abstinence when action would lead to bad luck; stay even.

6 Don't be overbearing, be supportive; then you won't be faulted. Be faithful, and you will be lucky—benefiting from having an aim— because you will have helpers without partisanship.

Richness (55)

1 Partnership as equals leads to raising of level.

3 Too much use of strength is counterproductive.

4 Conceal your abilities and be unobtrusive even while in command of the situation.

Settled (63)

1 Be careful in the beginning so as to be faultless in the end.

3 Strive to overcome negative influences, using the best of yourself.

5 Don't be complacent when you have accomplished something—remain humble, and you will really reap the rewards of your achievement.

Adornment (22)

1 Be down to earth, without artifice.

3 When successful, it is good to be always upright.

6 Adornment by simplicity is impeccable.

Following (17)

1 Standards change—choose wisely. It is effective to communicate with society.

4 When the strong follow the strong, they can attain their aim; but it is not necessarily good. If you are faithful to the right way, and act with understanding, you can be blameless.

5 Be truthful in goodness, and you will be lucky.

Biting Through (21)

1 There is no blame if trouble is stopped right away.

4 Find out your ingrained faults; work hard and be upright.

6 If you are so set in your ways that you cannot listen to anyone or anything else, that is unlucky.

Increase (42)

1 There is profit in undertaking great work, but you will only avoid blame if it turns out very well.

5 Don't seek the rewards of sincerity, for sincerity brings its own rewards.

6 Keep up the pressure when you're on top, and you may invite attack. Persisting in this is bad luck.

Indications of the Yang Lines in Hexagrams with Three Yins

Obstruction (12)

4 There is no blame in acting according to a higher order. Those of like mind cleave to good fortune.

5 Stopping obstruction, great people are fortunate; but they still arrange security against loss.

6 If there is obstruction at first, there will be joy when it is overturned.

Gradual Progress (53)

3 Strength without balance leads to action without reflection. Inappropriate associations produce unmanageable results. It is beneficial to guard against enemies.

5 Gradually progressing to the peak of attainment, avoid making improper liaisons in haste, and you will ultimately be invincible.

6 When you transcend ordinary affairs, you can be an example for others.

Travel (56)

3 It is dangerous to alienate those above and below you.

4 If you have resources and tools but cannot use them, you will not be happy.

6 You may be happy if you are highly placed; but if you become haughty, you will come to grief. If comfort makes you careless, you will suffer loss and misfortune.

Sensing (31)

3 When persistence turns to indulgence, it is shameful to go on.

4 Be upright, and you will be fortunate and have no regrets. If your mind is unstable, this will influence your associates.

5 If you are sensitive in an impersonal way, you will have no regrets.

Dispersal (59)

2 When isolated, seek support; and regrets will vanish.

5 In a time of dissolution and incoherence, order should be made to extend everywhere; the position of the ruler who accomplishes this is blameless.

6 Avoid harm, and there is no blame.

Exhaustion (47)

2 One is ennobled through hardship. It is beneficial to convey true sincerity. It is unlucky to be aggressive; if you are aggressive and therefore experience misfortune, you have no one to blame but yourself.

4 When bereft of firm support, you can only progress slowly; this is humiliating, but you will eventually reach your end.

5 When at an impasse because of lack of cooperation from those around you, pursue a balanced course and there will be a gradual improvement in the situation. It is beneficial to be sincere and serious.

Degeneration (18)

2 It will not do to be adamant in situations that call for gentleness and flexibility.

3 When you are adamant in correcting someone who is also strong, there is a little regret but no great blame.

6 When you are unconcerned with reputation or material advantages, you can set your mind on higher things.

The Well (48)

2 You cannot be of much help to others before you have developed yourself.

3 When you have much to share with others but no opportunity to do so, this grieves you. Others should benefit from what you have within you, but they will be able to do so only when someone in a position of power or authority is aware enough to recognize your worth.

5 When your personal development is complete, then you can nourish others.

Constancy (32)

2 If you are strong yet flexible and balanced, you have nothing to regret.

3 If you are not constant in virtue, you may be disgraced. It is shameful to persist in being this way.

4 Just because you take action does not mean you will get results.

HEXAGRAMS WITH FOUR YANG LINES

111100 Great Power (34)
111010 Waiting (5)
111001 Great Accumulation (26)

110110 Joy (58)
110101 Disharmony (38)

110011 Faithfulness in the Center (61)

101110 Revolution (49)
101101 Fire (30)

101011 People in the Home (37)

100111 No Error (25)

011110 Excess of the Great (28)
011101 The Cauldron (50)

011011 Wind (57)

010111 Contention (6)

001111 Withdrawal (33)

Indications of the Yang Lines in Hexagrams with Four Yangs

Great Power (34)

1 Impulsive presumption of power makes it bad luck to act on conviction.

2 Be correct, and you will be lucky.

3 Immature people exploit power, mature people do not. Persistence can be dangerous—rambunctious people get stuck.

4 Be correct, and you will be lucky and free from regret; getting through impasses, you will not be burdened but will be empowered.

Waiting (5)

1 When waiting on the fringes of a situation before the appropriate time to act has arrived, be steady and avoid giving in to impulse—then you won't go wrong.

2 When you are on the brink of a difficult situation, people will talk a little; but if you remain centered and relaxed, it will turn out well in the end.

3 Standing around in the thick of things brings on enemies.

5 When comfortably situated, you will be lucky if you are upright and true.

Great Accumulation (26)

1 Help yourself out of danger.

2 Strength in balance is stabilized.

3 When you are ready to act, it is beneficial to struggle for right. If you practice offensive and defensive arts, they are useful when you have somewhere to go.

6 At the peak of attainment you find freedom.

Joy (58)

1 Enjoyment in harmony with others is lucky.

2 Sincere delight is auspicious; it removes regret.

4 Uncertainty about attraction makes you uneasy. Be firm and swift, and you will be happy.

5 It is dangerous to trust plunderers.

Disharmony (38)

1 Don't mull over the past. If you have lost yourself, don't pursue a false image—only then can you spontaneously recover. Seeing bad people, be blameless.

2 See the truth in all situations, and you will be impeccable.

4 Opposition isolates you. When you meet good people, cooperate sincerely and diligently, and there will be no blame.

6 When isolated by opposition, people appear to each other in a hostile

light. At first they may nearly come to strife; but if they later give up antagonism and work as partners, they can complement each other in a productive way that ends up well.

Faithfulness in the Center (61)

1 Be prepared, and you will be lucky. If you are distracted, you will be uneasy.

2 Keep working sincerely even though you may not be recognized, and your heart's desire will come to you. When you are fulfilled, you share with others spontaneously.

5 Be firm in sincerity, and you will be impeccable.

6 If you get proud and try to go beyond your real capabilities, your self-righteousness will bring you misfortune.

Revolution (49)

1 Be balanced and stable.

3 If you are too adamant, action is unlucky, even if you are right. Change yourself first before you tell others to change, and eventually they will trust you if you are consistent.

4 Regret disappears if you are sincere; you can change your fate for the better.

5 Great people make clear changes, resulting in unambiguous certainty.

Fire (30)

1 Be careful when you are mixed up, to avoid fault.

3 It is bad luck to be a diehard.

4 If you are too hasty and too intense, you will burn out.

6 To master a situation well, grasp the critical point, don't bear down on peripherals.

People in the Home (37)

1 Guard the home and there is no regret.

3 When people in the home are strict, conscientious diligence leads to good results. When the women and children are frivolous, it will end in humiliation.

5 Regard all the world as your family, without giving in to anxiety. Then you will be lucky.

6 To have truthfulness gives you an air of dignity, which is eventually lucky.

No Error (25)

1 Proceed without error, and you will be lucky.

4 Be correct, and there will be no error.

5 When there is superficial malaise without fundamental error, do not go about trying curatives, and you will be happy.

6 You may be unsuccessful in what you do even if you are not in error.

Excess of the Great (28)

2 It is beneficial for an old and enfeebled organization to get an infusion of fresh life.

3 It is unlucky to be stubborn in the face of insurmountable odds.

4 It is lucky to be tempered in firmness, but there are still other concerns as well.

5 An infusion of new life into a fundamentally sterile organization results only in a temporary flowering.

The Cauldron (50)

2 If you are inwardly secure, even if people are jealous, luckily they cannot affect you.

3 Even if you are inwardly fulfilled, you need means to employ this outwardly to be completely useful. When mutually completing factors are effectively present, all is finally well.

4 If you take on too much without a solid foundation, you will eventually be drained, leaving embarrassment and bad luck.

6 It is very lucky and beneficial to have a balance of firmness and flexibility.

Wind (57)

2 In a position of subordinate responsibility, it is good to maintain frequent and honest communications.

3 It is embarrassing to have to try over and over again.

5 Be correct and you will be lucky and free from regret—everyone else will benefit too. You may start from nothing, but you will wind up somewhere. Luck is in the time immediately preceding, and immediately succeeding, a change.

6 If you follow people inferior to you, you will lose your tools and resources—even if you are faithful, you will be unlucky.

Contention (6)

2 When your ambitions are thwarted, if you go back home and live unobtrusively, you will escape calamity.

4 If you are unsuccessful in your suit, accept fate and change yourself so as to live rightly—then you will be lucky.

5 Contention bodes well when it is balanced and correct.

6 If you are too adamant, before long you will lose what you have gained.

Withdrawal (33)

3 It is hard and dangerous to be too inaccessible. It is a good idea to take care of your family.

4 Mature people are well able to be inaccessible to those whom they like; immature people are not.

5 Be inaccessible at the right time, and you will be lucky.

6 Magnanimous withdrawal is beneficial to all.

HEXAGRAMS WITH FIVE YANG LINES

111110 Parting (43)
111101 Great Possession (14)
111011 Nurturance of the Small (9)
110111 Treading (10)
101111 Sameness with Others (13)
011111 Meeting (44)

Indications of the Yang Lines in Hexagrams with Five Yangs

Parting (43)

1 If you act impulsively and fail, this constitutes a fault.

2 If you are really alert, there is no worry even if people try to take you unawares.

3 It is unlucky to show too much emotion. Mature people are decisive and independent. If something holds them up, they may get irritated but do not make mistakes.

4 When you are restless but unable to get anywhere, your regret would disappear if you had followers; but no one will believe in your word.

5 Cutting through resolutely, balanced action is impeccable.

Great Possession (14)

1 Do not associate with what is harmful, and you will be faultless. Realize the danger, struggle against it, and you will be blameless.

2 When you have great capacity for bearing responsibility, if you have an aim, you will be blameless.

3 Impartial action is public service, of which petty people are incapable.

4 Refuse to aggrandize yourself, and you will be blameless.

6 Good fortune that is a blessing from heaven is beneficial to all.

Nurturance of the Small (9)

1 If you use the appropriate means to return to normality, what blame is there? This is lucky.

2 It is lucky for people to lead each other back to normality.

3 An organization cannot make progress without cooperation.

5 When you are sincere, that is attractive; share the wealth with the neighbors.

6 Once you have been successful in developing excellent qualities in yourself, it is dangerous to let the feeling of ease thus engendered assert itself because this would result in overweening pride, which makes action unlucky.

Treading (10)

1 Act plainly, and there is no blame.

2 If the course of action you have taken turns out to be smooth, you will be lucky only if you remain chaste in the sense of being inwardly undisturbed by externals.

4 Be extremely cautious when dealing with dangerous forces, for final good luck.

5 Decisive action is dangerous even if correct.

6 Watch what you do, consider what is best, and you will get back your luck.

Sameness with Others (13)

1 Be impartial with people, and you will be blameless.

3 Forced assimilation to others does not work, even if you persist in trying.

4 If you are an obstinate type of person, you will be lucky if you know when to hold back.

5 When enlightened people share a time and a place with ordinary society, at first this causes a disturbance but later has a felicitous effect. The enlightened have to win others over before they can get together.

6 Associating with others while maintaining a distance involves no regret.

Meeting (44)

2 When you need to work on your self alone, there is no blame in that; but it does not help those around you then.

3 When your autonomy is not well developed, you have trouble accomplishing things. If you are diligent when you have trouble, you will at least make no serious mistakes.

4 It is unlucky to alienate people.

5 Keep your brilliance concealed, and you will be inspired.

6 Obstinacy can lead to humiliation. You have no one but yourself to blame for this.

HEXAGRAMS WITH ONE YIN LINE

011111 Meeting (44)
101111 Sameness with Others (13)
110111 Treading (10)
111011 Nurturance of the Small (9)
111101 Great Possession (14)
111110 Parting (43)

Indications of the Yin Lines in Hexagrams with One Yin

Meeting (44)

1 Be restrained, careful, and correct in worldly encounters.

Sameness with Others (13)

2 Factionalism leads to regret.

Treading (10)

3 Undertaking more than one is really capable of leads to trouble and bad luck. This means trying too hard, without complementary leisure and enjoyment.

Nurturance of the Small (9)

4 Be truthful, and you will be impeccable.

Great Possession (14)

5 Power arising from mutual trust and cooperation bodes well.

Parting (43)

6 Petty people ultimately have no authority and cannot prevail in the end.

HEXAGRAMS WITH TWO YIN LINES

001111 Withdrawal (33)
010111 Contention (6)
011011 Wind (57)
011101 The Cauldron (50)
011110 Excess of the Great (28)

100111 No Error (25)
101011 People in the Home (37)
101101 Fire (30)
101110 Revolution (49)

110011 Faithfulness in the Center (61)
110101 Disharmony (38)
110110 Joy (58)

111001 Great Accumulation (26)
111010 Waiting (5)

111100 Great Power (34)

Indications of the Yin Lines in Hexagrams with Two Yins

Withdrawal (33)

1 Be conservative when weak in ability.

2 Be firm in will; don't be influenced by externals.

Contention (6)

1 Criticism without contentiousness is useful to clarify situations.

3 If you are resting on your laurels, you will have good luck only if you remain upright in hard times—don't try anything great.

Wind (57)

1 When you are vacillating and wavering, it would be beneficial for you to become steadfast and get your mind under control.

4 When you are powerless, correct orientation flexibly following the more-developed leads to freedom from regret.

The Cauldron (50)

1 In order to follow what is good, first get rid of what is bad.

5 Balanced in the center, you will benefit from single-mindedness.

Excess of the Great (28)

1 Be flexible when in a low position, and there is no blame.

6 Going too far leads to misfortune, even if you are not at fault.

No Error (25)

2 It is beneficial to act purposefully if it is not just out of greed or other selfish reasons.

3 Obsession or dogmatic clinging brings misfortune even to innocent bystanders.

People in the Home (37)

2 It bodes well to be single-minded and undistracted when all you can practically do is work on your present condition.

4 A rich home is lucky.

Fire (30)

2 Balanced awareness is very good.

5 You will be lucky if you take note of your shortcomings and avoid presumption and complacency.

Revolution (49)

2 The actual consequences of a change are only realized after the fact; then people accord with it willingly.

6 Mature people renew themselves at a deep level, while superficial people change only on the surface.

Faithfulness in the Center (61)

3 Fickleness in relationships causes vacillation in the hearts of the fickle, producing a vicious circle.

4 When your inward development has matured, you must withdraw from intimacy with those who will drag you down because of their personal whims.

Disharmony (38)

3 Act arbitrarily, and you will eventually be thwarted.

5 Even if weak, you can be free from regret if you cooperate unselfishly with those who are more powerful.

Joy (58)

3 Self-serving pretense leads to bad luck.

6 Seducing people by flattering them is not enlightened.

Great Accumulation (26)

4 Budding strength is auspicious in the docile if it is flexible and correctly oriented.

5 Strength and firmness should be tempered by gentility.

Waiting (5)

4 Listen with an open mind, come out of the shell of self-absorption.

6 When in a restrictive situation, do not rush to exercise your abilities but do recognize them and treat them with care.

Great Power (34)

5 If you are easygoing and not aggressive, you will have no regret.

6 When at an impasse, unable either to go ahead or turn back, work hard, and you will be lucky.

HEXAGRAMS WITH THREE YIN LINES RISING FROM BELOW

000111 Obstruction (12)
001011 Gradual Progress (53)
001101 Travel (56)
001110 Sensing (31)

010011 Dispersal (59)
010101 Unsettled (64)
010110 Exhaustion (47)

011001 Degeneration (18)
011010 The Well (48)

011100 Constancy (32)

Indications of the Yin Lines in Hexagrams with Three Yins

Obstruction (12)

1 A weak person put in a position of leadership needs allies but will be lucky and successful only if personally upright.

2 Weak people are lucky if they work for the right people. Strong people are not deranged by the crowd.

3 Sometimes it is appropriate to endure disgrace willingly.

Gradual Progress (53)

1 If humble people are diligent and express themselves, there is no blame on them. Foolish people blame others for their troubles, but this is no fault of others.

2 Proceed gradually, enjoy the fruits of your labors, and you will be lucky.

4 In uncertain situations, you will avoid trouble only if you cleave to people who are better than you are.

Travel (56)

1 Petty fussing on a journey is unlucky.

2 When you have material means, people will surround you—remain upright.

5 Don't exploit your power and you will gain anyway, through good repute.

Sensing (31)

1 External stimulus to action demands no prejudgment.

2 It is unlucky to get stirred up when you should be impassive—it is lucky to stay put then.

6 Speaking a lot may be good or bad or neither.

Dispersal (59)

1 If you seek help, seek it from those who can really help you.

3 Be selfless and you will have no regrets.

4 If you get rid of factionalism, you can experience a sense of community that is ordinarily not even dreamed of.

Unsettled (64)

1 It is humiliating to be thwarted right at the outset.

3 It is unlucky to act adventurously when your mind is unsettled; it is beneficial to get involved in serious affairs.

5 Be correct, and you will be lucky and have peace of mind. The enlightenment of developed people is truthful and leads to good luck.

Exhaustion (47)

1 If you give in to temporary exhaustion, you may needlessly become further debilitated.

3 When you get yourself into an impasse and are in an uncomfortable position, it is unlucky to pursue externals at the expense of content.

6 When exhausted at an impasse, in distress you regret your actions, but it is better to work for the future than to mull over the past.

Degeneration (18)

1 The degeneration of one generation can be remedied by the next— you will have good luck if you are wary of the danger.

4 If you indulge—and indulge in—the degeneration of the preceding generation, you will experience shame.

5 If you remedy the degeneration of the preceding generation, this action will be praised.

The Well (48)

1 If you let your bad habits stagnate and clog your personality, others will find you unpleasant and useless.

4 Keep your inner reserves in good repair, and you will be impeccable.

6 Share your inner wealth with others if it nourishes them, and you will be very fortunate.

Constancy (32)

1 Persist too intensely at what is currently beyond your depth, and your fidelity to that course will bring misfortune, no gain.

5 While single-mindedness may be good for an individual, it may be inauspicious in a larger context.

6 It is unlucky to be excited all the time.

Indications of the Yin Lines in Hexagrams with Three Yangs

Tranquillity (11)

4 When you are unsettled, you do not prosper. Work with those around you; be honest without being admonished.

5 In a position of authority, you will be very fortunate if you do not try to monopolize authority but seek alliances with wise people even if they are of lower status.

6 When things are falling down around you, do not be belligerent. If you try to assert yourself within your own circle, you will be humiliated even if you are right.

Marrying a Young Woman (54)

3 If you seek something based on subjective expectations, you may wind up with a lesser substitute.

5 Be humble when you are about to reach your peak, and you will have good luck.

6 When partners cannot fulfill their duties to one another, nothing is gained by their association.

Discipline (60)

3 Without discipline, you will come to grief. You have no one to blame but yourself for this.

4 Discipline is successful if exercised calmly.

6 Discipline should not be masochistic.

Reduction (41)

3 Excess should be reduced. You gain by single-mindedness.

4 Reduce what ails you, and you will be joyful and blameless.

5 Reduce your egotism, and you will gain support such that none will oppose you.

Richness (55)

2 If you proceed without clear awareness, you will be afflicted by doubt. If you are demonstrably sincere, you will have good luck.

5 If you are able to bring out the excellent, there will be joy and celebration.

6 If you are ostentatious and proud, you will be isolated and unfortunate.

Settled (63)

2 When you are vulnerable, remain balanced and upright, in control of yourself, and you will eventually succeed.

4 Be prepared against danger and maintain diligence.

6 It is dangerous to go to extremes.

Adornment (22)

2 Improve yourself by seeking what you lack.

4 To improve yourself, innocently seek appropriate associates as soon as possible.

5 Improve yourself through association with those who are better than you. It may be embarrassing to humble yourself, but the result is good.

Following (17)

2 If you concern yourself with trivialities, you will miss what is important.

3 If you concern yourself with what is important, you will not be bothered with trivialities. You gain by following higher aims and profit by steadfast rectitude.

6 Solidarity in following good leads to empowerment.

Biting Through (21)

2 Faults are easy to correct if you are balanced and upright.

3 If you try to correct others when you yourself are out of place, there will be bitter resentment. This is somewhat embarrassing but not completely wrong.

5 When you are in a position of authority and punish subordinates, be balanced and correct; there will be no mistake if you are upright, careful, and diligent.

Increase (42)

2 Common consensus cannot be gainsaid. Always be upright, and you will have good luck. Leaders should serve universal law.

3 There is no blame in using unfortunate events in a beneficial way. Being sincere and balanced in action, one presents impartial use of authority.

4 Balanced action openly expressed is followed impartially; it is advantageous to use this as a basis to move the center of operations.

HEXAGRAMS WITH FOUR YIN LINES

000011 Observing (20)
000101 Advance (35)
000110 Gathering (45)
001001 Mountain (52)
001010 Halting (39)
001100 Predominance of the Small (62)
010001 Darkness (4)
010010 Water (29)
010100 Solution (40)
011000 Rising (46)
100001 Nourishment (27)
100010 Difficulty (3)
100100 Thunder (51)
101000 Concealment of Illumination (36)
110000 Overseeing (19)

Indications of Yin Lines in Hexagrams with Four Yins

Observing (20)

1 Uncultivated people are not blamed for naive observations, but it is a disgrace for cultivated people.

2 When observation is limited, restraint is beneficial.

3 Observing your personal growth, proceed or withdraw accordingly.

4 Observing the flourishing of a nation, it is beneficial to be a guest of the ruler.

Advance (35)

1 If you run into obstacles to progress, it is to your benefit to be steadfast. If people do not trust you, be easygoing, and there will be no blame.

2 If you experience grief in the course of progress, be steadfast and upright, and you will have good luck.

3 Regrets disappear when there is group approval.

5 When you have nothing to regret, do not worry about loss or gain. It bodes well to proceed, for this will benefit everyone.

Gathering (45)

1 If there is trust but it does not last, there will be disorder and mobbing. If you lament this, you will later laugh over it, so do not worry, for it is blameless to proceed.

2 When attraction is good and blameless, as long as you are sincere, simplicity in relationships is beneficial.

3 Association that brings sadness gains nothing. There is no fault in going on, but there is some regret.

6 Those who are in high positions but are weak may sigh and weep, but that is no fault of others.

Mountain (52)

1 Stop impulsive behavior at the outset, and there will be no harm. It will benefit you to be always correct.

2 When you try to stop something but cannot help the consequences, you are unhappy.

4 Control your behavior so as to be impeccable.

5 Speak in a controlled, orderly manner, and you will be free from regret.

Halting (39)

1 When it would cause trouble to go on, it is laudable to wait and review the situation.

2 When leaders and followers both recognize trouble as trouble, they do not work for personal interests alone.

4 When action would bring on trouble, restraint wins support.

6 When you have trouble getting anywhere, you will be very lucky if you reflect and examine yourself. It is beneficial to see a great person.

Predominance of the Small (62)

1 It is unlucky to try to make progress too rapidly.

2 If you are not up to a position of leadership, stay in a subordinate position and be blameless.

5 You cannot be completely effective by yourself; you still remain isolated if you only find your associates among people like yourself.

6 When you surpass others and do not meet them on their own level, they feel alienated from you. This is unlucky. This is called calamity.

Darkness (4)

1 When use of punishment is necessary to awaken the ignorant, easing restrictions leads to regret.

3 The weak should not be exposed to sources of temptation that would make them uselessly lose themselves.

4 It is regrettable to be stuck in ignorance.

5 Ignorance in the sense of innocence is lucky.

Water (29)

1 Going from one perilous situation to another is unlucky.

3 When you are insecure and restless, you go from pitfall to pitfall, imperiled and thwarted, until you wind up in a rut—don't act this way.

4 With the same resources you could be good or bad; be simple, sincere, and open, and eventually you will be faultless.

6 It is unlucky to get inextricably tied up in a thorny situation.

Solution (40)

1 Even if you are weak and lowly, you can be blameless if you harmonize with those of greater attainments.

3 Acting opportunistically with only your own agenda in mind brings on enemies; even if you are righteous about what you are doing, you will be humiliated.

5 Enlightened people are liberated in a positive way and are sincere towards the unenlightened.

6 The unruly are brought down for the benefit of all.

Rising (46)

1 It is very auspicious to rise truthfully to a higher aim.

4 Form truthful alliances wherever you are, and you will be lucky and safe.

5 You will be lucky if you are correct, rising step by step.

6 When you rise into the unknown, it is to your advantage to be unrelentingly correct.

Nourishment (27)

2 Weak overclasses feeding off strong underclasses is an abnormal system; it will run out of luck if it tries to rely on a weak leadership above it.

3 If you refuse what will really benefit you, you will be unlucky if you are steadfast. Avoid doing this, because you will gain nothing by it.

4 It is lucky when overclasses nourish the underclasses, watching them and bringing out their talents.

5 If you are in a position of leadership but are powerless, you will be lucky if you remain upright. You had better not try to undertake a major project.

Difficulty (3)

2 When you are on hard ground and still powerless yourself, you may have at hand the means to proceed yet be unable to use them yet. Your present activity does not imply that you refuse to participate in society, rather the reverse—you are simply being true to principles and not making premature commitments.

3 Ambition without preparation and direction gets you lost. A true leader would turn back, seeing that this would only lead to regret if pursued.

4 When you have means but are not getting anywhere, seek appropriate associates, and you will be lucky, to everyone's benefit.

6 If you cannot pull your own weight, you won't make any progress, to your great dismay.

Thunder (51)

2 When there is a shake-up, there is danger. This makes you aware that normality has been lost, and impels you to seek it from on high. Don't confuse this with compulsive search. Reversion to normality takes some time.

3 When in a slump, you can avoid trouble if you stir yourself into vigorous action.

5 When your actions are erratic, that is dangerous. Reflect on what you have not lost, and you will find something to do.

6 When you are weak in your actions and unstable in your perceptions, you will be unlucky in a major undertaking. You may not be shaken up yourself, but there will be shake-ups near you. People may not be to blame, but you will be criticized if you associate with them.

Concealment of Illumination (36)

2 When you cannot reveal what you are thinking because of oppression, if you try to remedy the situation, you will be lucky if you can avail yourself of power.

4 When you find deep understanding hidden in your heart, you depart from the shell of superficial views.

5 When just heirs of a corrupt regime conceal their understanding, this is beneficial and correct.

6 In ignorance we become emotionally uplifted by a flash of insight; without guidance, this eventually leads to depression.

Overseeing (19)

3 If you are being presumptuous in thinking you can oversee others, there is no benefit in that. If you reject presumptuous supposition, you can eliminate trouble.

4 Consummate overseeing is impeccable.

5 Knowledgeable overseeing, appropriate for a great leader, is lucky.

6 Be attentive in overseeing, and if you have good luck there will be no fault.

HEXAGRAMS WITH FIVE YIN LINES

000001 Stripping Away (23)
000010 Accord (8)
000100 Joy (16)
001000 Humility (15)
010000 The Army (7)
100000 Return (24)

Indications of the Yin Lines in Hexagrams with Five Yins

Stripping Away (23)

1 Nothing good is achieved without a sound foundation.

2 Nothing good is achieved without the right materials.

3 Shed fixations, and you will be blameless.

4 It is unlucky to let yourself be divested of means of support.

5 Even if people are ignorant, if they can be induced to follow good advice in an orderly manner, this can benefit them all.

Accord (8)

1 Accord with truth is blameless. When you are sincere and uncontrived, you will eventually have good luck.

2 Accord from within bodes well if it is correct.

3 Association with the wrong people is injurious.

4 You will be lucky if you associate with wise people in the right way.

6 Accord without guidance bodes ill.

Joy (16)

1 When you're happy, it's unlucky to crow about it.

2 It is lucky to be firm and steadfast and not procrastinate.

3 Looking to others for happiness leads to regret if persisted in.

5 Remain upright in spite of insecurity, and you will not be overwhelmed.

6 Though you may lose yourself in joy, this must eventually change. Do not blame anyone for this.

Humility (15)

1 It is lucky if leaders use humility as a means of travel.

2 Expressing humility is good if correct.

4 The exercise of humility is beneficial to all.

5 When you do not aggrandize yourself but share with those around you, it is good to extend this to strangers and enemies as well—it is beneficial to all.

6 If you are proud of your humility, you have yet to really overcome yourself.

The Army (7)

1 Collective action must be done in an orderly manner, otherwise even a good cause produces bad results.

3 Arbitrary actions may result in harm and bad luck.

4 If you don't know what to do, you can at least avoid blame if you refrain from impulsive action.

5 It is beneficial to catch predators—there is no blame in that. But the leader of such an action must be mature; if the leadership is immature there will be casualties, and the outlook is bad even if the cause is right.

6 In a large community, order is established through successive levels of organization.

Return (24)

2 It is lucky when what is good returns.

3 Repeatedly attempting to restore the good is diligence. This is blameless.

4 Be centered and independent.

5 Reflect clearly on yourself, so as to be free from regret.

6 Reform gone awry is unlucky—if it becomes aggressive, the results will be shattering.

Arcana

THE RIVER DIAGRAM

The Ho-t'u (Hotu), or River Diagram, is one of the oldest artifacts of Chinese civilization. It is traditionally said to have been found by Fu Hsi (Fu Xi), the most ancient ancestor of Taoism, believed by Taoists and Confucians to be the originator of the *I Ching* itself.

According to Chinese lore, Fu Hsi examined the patterns of heaven, earth, and living creatures, and this was the foundation of his knowledge. An auspicious event, the appearance of a "dragon horse" that emerged from a river, drew the attention of Fu Hsi to the pattern on its back.

Both the dragon and the horse are symbolic of nobility and leadership. In *I Ching* terms, the horse represents the yin factor, temporal, mundane guidance, while the dragon represents the yang factor, celestial guidance. The "dragon horse," a combination of these two, produces what Confucians call "the mandate of heaven," by which people rise to human leadership through their attunement to higher meaning.

In simplified modern Taoist terms, Fu Hsi was a student of psychological, physical, and social events. Each of these domains, according to Taoist analysis, is further divided into higher and lower dimensions.

The celestial, or psychological, plane is divided into the dimension of direct objective perceptions, of the kind that are sometimes called "higher perceptions" or "enlightenment," and the dimension of self-conditioned intellectual activity, the psychology of the everyday world.

The earthly or physical plane is divided into the domain of the animate and the domain of the inanimate, physiological laws and material laws.

The plane of beings, the social plane, is divided into reason and desire, specific combinations of reflections of the celestial and earthly planes.

The River Diagram is said to show the way to the higher dimension of these realms, called the "natural, uncontrived Tao." In human terms, it may be thought of as an abstract model of a human being.

The diagram is composed of fifty-five dots, in five sets (included in illustration 1). As a whole, these five sets represent the so-called five elements or five forces—water, wood, earth, fire, and metal—that compose the abstract structure. Each of these sets is composed of two subsets, representing higher and lower manifestations of these elements or forces.

The first set consists of one dot and six dots. These stand for so-called yang water and yin water. Yang water symbolizes the "original vitality," described as nonsensual vitality, also as the original, universal, creative force. Yin water symbolizes "turbid vitality," described as a combination of emotion and sensuality.

Opposite this first set is a set of two and seven dots, standing for yang fire and yin fire. Yang fire symbolizes the "original spirit," described as the fundamental subtlety in all awareness. Yin fire stands for ordinary awareness, conditioned by the mundane environment.

To the left is a set of three and eight dots, standing for yang wood and yin wood. Yang wood symbolizes "essence" or "nature," sometimes called the original human nature, also associated with the essence or nature of life, or consciousness itself. Yin wood symbolizes temperament, the commanding mood or habit of life or consciousness developed through environmental conditioning.

To the right is a set of four and nine dots, standing for yang metal and yin metal. Yang metal symbolizes "original sense," or the "basic feeling" of reality, described as unemotional sense, that intuits the essence of consciousness and therefore is more objective in its sense of reality than the "arbitrary feelings" symbolized by yin metal. Feelings are considered arbitrary insofar as they are conditioned by subjective emotions.

In the center of these four sets is a set of five and ten dots, standing for yang earth and yin earth. Yang earth symbolizes "original energy," described as nontemperamental energy, also associated with what is called true will or true attention, the capacity of deliberate control on the focus of the totality of feeling, awareness, and thought. Yin earth symbolizes random or wandering attention, the disorderly, distracted will or attention, unsettled by the influence of physical conditions and psychological impacts.

These five elements are further aligned with five virtues, conceived as functions of the specific qualities of the five elements. The quality of original vitality (water) is clarity, its function is wisdom. The quality of original spirit (fire) is pervasive awareness, its function is courtesy. The quality of original essence (wood) is gentleness, its function is kindness. The quality of original sense (metal) is firm strength, its function is justice. The quality of original energy (earth) is purity, its function is faithfulness.

For the purpose of the educational processes developed by the schools that integrated Taoism, Confucianism, and Buddhism, this inner design is considered primal, inherent in human beings. It is therefore taken as a model for humanity "before the fall," that is, before human potential is commandeered by mundane influences.

Turning to the lower dimensions, the acquired or temporal reflections of the five elements, these are also defined in terms of specific natures and functions. The nature of the fickle turbid vitality (water) is folly, and in action it produces sadness. The nature of the intellectual spirit (fire) is greed, and in action it produces pleasure. Temperament (wood) is called the "roaming higher soul," benevolent by nature, producing joy when moved. Arbitrary feelings (metal) are called the "ghostly lower soul," malevolent by nature, producing anger when disturbed. Arbitrary attention (earth) is hyperactive, disorderly by nature, producing craving.

The purpose of this traditional analysis is not, of course, to define these as separate domains but to bring certain propensities into relief. Even the primal and temporal, or higher and lower, reflections of the five elements are considered originally one; in the idealized pristine state of humanity that practitioners aim to recover, the negative potentials are controlled by the positive potentials.

Thus the five virtues can be further defined in temporal terms. To be unconfused by what one sees and hears is considered wisdom, the visible edge of the original vitality (water). A mood of harmony and peace is considered courtesy, the visible edge of the original spirit (fire). The innocence of the infant, without prejudice, is considered the epitome of kindness, the visible edge of the original essence (wood). Forgetting discrimination against others in favor of oneself is considered justice, the visible edge of the original sense (metal). Complete sincerity is considered truthfulness, or faithfulness, the visible edge of the original energy (earth).

The practical implications of this design revolve around the distinction between calm and agitation, which reflect the dominance of the positive or negative potentials. This is not taken to mean the same thing as the distinction between inactivity and activity, in that the control of the primal, or higher, faculties is not necessarily hindered by the activity of the temporal, or lower, faculties. In the state of calm, according to Liu I-ming, "In both action and stillness it is the primal that does the work. From time to time there may be traces of joy, anger, sadness, and pleasure, but all of them come out unminding—one may be joyful without dwelling on it, angry without transferring it to others, sad without suffering from it, happy without indulging in it."

In standard traditional technical terms, the means to accomplish this balance is called "centered harmony." The "center" refers to the stage before emotions emerge, while "harmony" refers to emotions emerging in appropriate measure. Centered harmony is said to be characterized by freedom from cravings, which allows the five elements to function in balance, under the direction of the primal, or higher, faculties.

The so-called uncontrived Tao, or Tao of nondoing, that the River Diagram is said to represent is a matter of preserving the primal to remain immune to coercion by the influence of the temporal. This is done by keeping the "heart"—another name for the center, also called "sincerity" in a technical sense. In Taoist terms, this is referred to as the "opening of the mysterious female," described as an indefinable experience beyond the reach of the elements, an experience of complete openness and awareness, free from partiality and subjective bias. In Confucian terms this is called the "universal limit," "the absolute," or "the infinite"; in Buddhist terms it is called the "original face before birth."

THE LO WRITING

The Lo Writing (Lo Shu) is another of the most ancient artifacts of Chinese civilization. Whereas the River Diagram is traditionally considered to be of prehistoric origin and associated with the primal Tao, the Lo Writing is attributed to historical times and associated with the temporal Tao.

Like the River Diagram, the Lo Writing is said to have been found in the pattern on the back of a supernatural creature, this time an uncanny turtle that emerged from the Lo River at the time of a great flood in the late third millennium B.C.E. The River Diagram is associated with the time of the prehistorical culture hero Fu Hsi, whose work is thought of as creative, while the Lo Writing is associated with the time of the later king Yu, a quasi-historical culture hero whose work is thought of in terms of rescue and salvation.

To illustrate the idea, Liu I-ming says of the Lo Writing, "Nature has the quality of love for life, so it used an uncanny turtle to divulge the Tao of restoration and return, to guide people to return home and recognize their origin, to set their feet on the fundamental basis of essence and life."

The design of the Lo Writing is very simple, consisting of nine sets of dots—one set in each of the cardinal and intermediate directions and one set in the center—that stand for the yin and yang five elements. In these terms, the "fall" of humankind is described as follows: turbid vitality overcomes the original spirit, the intellectual spirit overcomes the original sense, arbitrary emotions overcome the original essence, temperamental nature overcomes the original energy, and wandering attention overcomes the original vitality.

Liu I-ming summarizes this "fall" in these terms: "The real gets buried and the false runs wild. People have all sorts of emotions, feelings, and desires, developing complex and involuted psychologies. A hundred worries disturb their minds, then the thousand things tax their bodies. They think what is miserable is enjoyable, they think what is false is real. They have entirely lost the original state."

The remedy for this is again said to be in the center, which represents will, attention, sincerity, or truthfulness. According to Liu, the set in the center of the Lo Diagram signifies that kindness, justice, courtesy, and wisdom are all rooted in truthfulness, while the surrounding sets represent using truthfulness to operate kindness, justice, courtesy, and wisdom.

Truthfulness, Liu continues, has the meaning of true belief: "Truly believe in kindness, and you can be kind. Truly believe in justice, and you can be just. Truly believe in courtesy, and you can be courteous. Truly believe in wisdom, and you can be wise. Truthfulness alone can be kindness, justice, courtesy, and wisdom, all according to the changes that take place in the mind."

Pursuing the definition of truthfulness to a deeper level, Liu calls it the means to restore the primal and equates the experience of the return of the primal with truth. For a practical expression of truthfulness as a means, Liu turns to a section of the Taoist classic *Tao-te Ching* traditionally used as a meditation guide: "In a flash of enlightenment, something is there. In the utter darkness, vitality is there. That vitality is very real, at its center is a truth." This truth, Liu says, is the experience of the return of the primal, attained through profound abstraction.

Liu also uses the scheme of the five virtues to elaborate on the outgrowth of this return to truth, or restoration of the primal. When wisdom is based on truthfulness, he says, knowledge is not used randomly; you are free from greed and ambition, your mind is peaceful and its energy is harmonious. Then you are pleased with reality and produce courtesy from within wisdom. When courtesy is based on wisdom, you can harmonize with those unlike yourself and you do not do anything discourteous; impatience sublimates, so that you no longer become angry but instead become just.

When justice is based on courtesy, Liu continues, you are just without bias, able to adapt to changes while following guidelines in your actions. Then you delight in good and develop kindness. When kindness is based on justice, you are kind without being weak, as good as possible, without evil, sincerely whole-hearted, without duplicity. Then you are free from selfish desires and are therefore truthful.

When truthfulness is based on kindness, forming the final link in the circle, you are steadfast and unwavering; true will appears, and wandering attention quiets down. Celestial and mundane intentions combine, so that you can be joyful, angry, sad, or pleased, all without selfish desire.

This state is called the subordination of the temporal to the primal; Liu says, "Merged with the design of nature, not conceiving human desires, you return to the origin of life, so that you realize your original self." In Taoist terms, this is called the formation of the spiritual embryo, or the crystallization of the gold pill. In Confucian terms, it is called clarifying the good and returning to the origin. In Buddhist terms, it is called great wisdom reaching the ultimate aim.

COMBINATION OF THE RIVER DIAGRAM AND LO WRITING

The River Diagram and Lo Writing are further abstracted into a circle and a square, respectively. The roundness of the circle symbolizes heaven, representing the effortless natural Way; the squareness of the square symbolizes earth, representing the Way of deliberate transformation. The circle stands for mastery of essence, or spirit, while the square stands for mastery of life, or energy.

In complete Taoist practice, the effortless Way, technically termed "nondoing," is practiced primarily by people in whom the primal energy is still intact and who therefore do not need restorative work. The Way of deliberate transformation, on the other hand, is practiced primarily by people who have lost their innocence, and who are inhibited by personality and constitution, burdened by accumulated habits. Without deliberate effort, there is no way for such people to restore what has been lost.

Commentary on the *Earth* hexagram of the *I Ching* says, "Use seriousness to straighten the inside, justice to square the outside." This passage, favored as a guide to self-cultivation in the neo-Confucian school of Inner Design, is understood in neo-Taoism to represent the two modes of practice, the effortless and the deliberate, technically known as "nondoing" and "doing."

According to Liu I-ming, seriousness means being careful and contained, to straighten means to be balanced and upright, without bias. Using seriousness to straighten the inside is the Way of going along with essence, the effortless, natural Tao represented by the River Diagram. Justice means change and adjustment, to square means to be immovable and unwavering, following guidelines in practice. Using justice to square the outside is education in practicing the Tao, the deliberate transformative Tao represented by the Lo Writing.

Nondoing is used to cultivate the inward, Liu continues, while doing is used to cultivate the outward. Cultivation of the inward refers to essence, cultivation of the outward refers to life. In the case of those in whom the primal is still intact, when they cultivate essence, life is simultaneously established, so they understand through sincerity. Those who have already lost their innocence, on the other hand, need to cultivate life before cultivating essence, so they become sincere through understanding.

Understanding and sincerity are part of the essence of people in whom the primal is intact, Liu goes on, but require education in those who have lost the primal. The purpose of the combination of the abstract River Diagram and Lo Writing is thus to illustrate how people of superior qualities cultivate the inside to regulate the outside, "first round and then square," while those of lesser qualities cultivate the outside to pacify the inside, "first square and then round."

Liu I-ming emphasizes the importance of avoiding two common mis-understandings about Taoist practice. The natural, effortless Way of non-doing does not mean quietism or inaction; it involves a subtle kind of "work" to preserve the primal immune to temporal influences. The deliberate, transformative Way, on the other hand, does not mean cutting off social relations and entering into some sort of cult; it involves practicing the principles of the Way based on phenomena in the world.

These points have been thoroughly confused by both devotional and academic cultists, as reflected in the distinction made between so-called "philosophical" and "religious" Taoism. It is popularly believed, for example, that the *Tao-te Ching* speaks only of nondoing, and this biased view has skewed countless interpretations of this text and its terminology. In complete schools, imbalance in practice is commonly defined in terms of attachment to either essence or life, resulting in characteristic exaggerations like quietism or slavery to forms.

Historically, over the last thousand years in China, Zen Buddhists have commonly fallen into attachment to essence, while Taoists and Confucians have commonly fallen into attachment to life. There are, of course, any number of complex off-balance combinations of varying degrees of these attachments, but the general concepts have provided a powerful tool for analysis of once practical teachings gone awry and frozen into cults and sects.

THE PRIMAL HORIZONTAL DIAGRAM

The primal horizontal diagram illustrates the generation of the eight trigrams and sixty-four hexagrams of the *I Ching:* one absolute divides into two modes, two modes divide into four images, four images divide into eight trigrams, eight trigrams permute into sixty-four hexagrams (illustration 6).

The one absolute is the original true mind, "empty, clear, and free, perfectly open and selfless." It contains what is known as the living potential, the primal true unified energy, the root of essence and life, the source of creative evolution, the basis of birth and death. According to Liu I-ming, "This energy is contained in open selflessness, neither existent nor nonexistent, neither material nor void, lively and active. It is also called true emptiness. True emptiness is not empty but open, open without being empty."

The two modes are yin and yang, here understood as stillness and movement. Liu says, "Since there is a point of living energy within open selflessness, this is the absolute containing unified energy, the One making its appearance from within nothingness. Once the one energy has appeared, it cannot but have movement and stillness. Movement is yang, stillness is yin."

The four images are essence, sense, vitality, and spirit. Since each of these in turn have two modes, this produces eight trigrams representing stillness and activity of the four modes. According to Liu I-ming's recasting of the abstract horizontal diagram into what he calls a diagram of producing being from nonbeing, the associations of the trigrams are as follows: *Heaven* stands for movement of sense, *Lake* stands for stillness of sense, *Fire* stands for movement of spirit, *Thunder* stands for movement of nature, *Wind* stands for stillness of nature, *Water* stands for movement of vitality, *Mountain* stands for stillness of vitality, and *Earth* stands for stillness of spirit (see page 361).

In ordinary terms, movement of sense means emotion, stillness of sense means intuition. Movement of spirit means thought, stillness of spirit means silent awareness. Movement of vitality means passion, stillness of vitality means desirelessness. Movement of nature means mood, stillness of nature means clarity.

This scheme of correspondences can be used to formulate a special program for calling up hexagrams to consult the *I Ching*. This usage corresponds to the outward, deliberate, "square" study of life. The inward, spontaneous, "round" study of essence, on the other hand, focuses on the discovery and preservation of the "absolute," the open, selfless, unified energy from which all these elements derive.

Liu I-ming says, "If you lose the open, selfless, unified energy, then movement and stillness will not be timely, the four images will not be in harmony, the eight trigrams will be in confusion, and good and bad luck will divide from here." Thus the crux of the matter is brought back to the origin:

> Heaven and earth can enslave whatever has form, but cannot enslave the formless. Heaven and earth can enslave the emotional but cannot enslave the unemotional. Heaven and earth can enslave those with desire but cannot enslave those without desire. If you can find out the root source, rest your mind in open selflessness and nurture your mind in one energy, then you will find the two modes, four images, eight trigrams, and sixty-four hexagrams are all operating there at the root of open selflessness. None of them has ever left it. Myriad forms are all empty—there is just an open sphere. Let us ask, how can good or bad luck affect this open selfless energy?

By keeping contact with the source energy, Liu suggests, it is possible to avoid confusion by its transformations. Thus it is possible to integrate the primal and temporal: "If people can find out the fundamental source where the signless produces signs, they will suddenly see their original selves and will then know about this open selfless energy, how it is nothing at all yet includes everything, how it is completely empty yet completely full, how it is formless but can metamorphose, so its metamorphoses are endless."

THE CENTER

As illustrated not only in the arcana associated with the River Diagram and Lo Writing but also in the interpretation of the lines of the *I Ching*, the focal sense of the center is of critical importance in the practical lore of Chinese developmental systems. To illustrate the pragmatic ideal, Confucianism uses the term "centered equilibrium," Taoism uses the term "centered harmony," and Buddhism uses the term "central path." Liu I-ming says, "Confucianism speaks of holding to the center, Taoism speaks of keeping to the center, Buddhism speaks of opening the center: the center is the psychological principle of all the sages of all three teachings, the way to cultivate essence and life so as to attain the great Way. All that the thousands of scriptures and classics explain is this one word 'center.'"

The mandala known as the Diagram of the Center is primarily to be found in medieval Taoist lore such as the famous *Book of Balance and Harmony*, where the unity of Taoism, Confucianism, and Buddhism is strongly emphasized. Like many Taoist mandalas, it is based on ancient Chinese writing. In ancient writing, the word "center" was written as a circle with a vertical line bisecting it (illustration 11). Liu explains, "The circle stands for what is innate in humans, completely good, something round and bright. This is what is called the primal real unified energy. The vertical line means that in the total pattern of nature, one energy ascends and descends, circulating ceaselessly."

Liu further analyzes the Center Diagram in Buddhistic terms, by reference to a saying by a Taoist mystic that is often quoted in Zen Buddhist literature: "The Taoist master Tao-kuang said, 'There is something before heaven and earth; it has no name, it is originally silent. The master of myriad forms, it does not wither with the seasons.' The silence is the circle, the master of myriad forms is the line. Ultimately nonexistent yet containing ultimate existence, ultimately empty yet containing ultimate fulfillment, it is therefore called the center."

This sense of balance between being and nonbeing is a pragmatic expression of the Buddhist central path, or middle way. Liu continues, "This center does not lean to one side; it has no front or back, no head or tail. It is not existent, not nonexistent. It is not material, not void. It is open yet complete, unfathomable. It has no form yet can be master of all forms. It is shapeless yet can fashion shapes."

In some Taoist yoga, the "center" is also interpreted in a literal sense as the center of the torso, used as a focal point of attention in exercise to open the lateral energy channels. In some Taoist yoga, the meaning of "inside" is also applied, in the context of the exercise of "inner gazing." Liu I-ming, however, was among those Taoists who emphasized the harm in obsession with these provisional techniques and stressed purely metaphysical understanding and experience of the center: "In human beings it is not the center of the body, nor is it the center as opposed to the outside. It has no location, no fixed position. Look for it and you cannot see it, listen for it and you cannot hear it, try to grasp it and you cannot find it."

In medieval Taoist lore—as in Zen Buddhism, known for its elaborate and colorful symbolism—there are many names given to the center, most of them illustrative of the sense of balance and potential. The crossroads, the main square, the main intersection, the gate of celestial and mundane will, the gate of the mysterious female, the opening of the mysterious pass, the house of life giving and death dealing, the gate of punishment and reward, the pass of life and death, the door of yin and yang, the opening of essence and life, the root of heaven and earth, the pass of humanity and animality, the hanging womb cauldron, the furnace of creation, the gate of all wonders—these are all names for this "center."

Asserting that all the ideas or experiences represented by these terms are summed up in the word "center," Liu I-ming goes on to extol the critical importance of the center: "The center is the great root of the world. All the sages, immortals, and buddhas of all times are born from this center. It is so vast that there is nothing outside it, yet so minute that it has no inside. In expansion, it fills the universe; in concentration, it retreats into storage in secrecy. Those who awaken to this immediately ascend to the ranks of sages, while those who miss this are sunk for eons."

Using the familiar Taoist terms "essence" and "life," referring to mastery and unification of spirit and energy, Liu stresses that the center is not just an abstract idea but must be experienced in actual practice: "This center is the root of essence and life. It is the center as long as primal essence and life are as one; in the temporal, it divides into essence and life. In reality, when you restore the primal in the midst of the temporal, so that essence is realized and life is solidified, essence and life return to the root, and are, as before, one center."

Liu also focuses on the terms "valley spirit" and "mysterious female" from the famous Taoist classic *Tao-te Ching*, traditionally used in Complete Reality Taoism as key expressions of practical issues. First Liu quotes the *Tao-te Ching*, "The valley spirit does not die; this is called the mysterious female. The gate of the mysterious female is called the root of heaven and earth." Then Liu quotes *Understanding Reality*, the premier text of the Complete Reality school, indicating the pragmatic significance of this classic passage: "If you want the immortality of the valley spirit, you must set up the basis from the mysterious female."

Taking up these traditional terms to explain the center, Liu says, "The valley spirit is the center. The mysterious female is yin-yang, essence and life. The immortality of the valley spirit is the center containing essence and life. Setting up the foundation on the mysterious female is essence and life constituting the center. Those who keep to this center are sages, those who lose this center are ordinary mortals. The division between sages and ordinary people is right in between finding and losing the center."

Liu then goes on to elaborate what it means to lose the center: "Ordinary mortals are controlled by their temperament and influenced by accumulated habits. Their essence and life separate, and there is damage to the center. As the damage increases day by day, essence becomes deranged and life is shaken; the spirit dims and energy becomes polluted. Eventually they lose the original center completely. Once the center is lost, essence and life are rootless, so even though the physical body is still moving, the spirit is already dead."

Turning to practicalities, Liu makes a point of the extreme subtlety of the process of finding the center: "It is not easy for people to see this center and not easy for them to know it. It cannot be consciously sought, it cannot be mindlessly kept. If you seek it consciously, you fall into forms; if you keep it mindlessly, you enter into empty silence. Neither of these is the central Way. The true center is not being or nonbeing yet is at once being and nonbeing. It is neither formed nor open yet both formed and open. Without falling into partiality for the empty circle, seek it in ecstasy, look for it in darkness, and you may get near it."

Again, Liu stresses the dangers associated with concentration on physical locations, referring to the various spots associated with the center in various grades of Taoist yoga: "Students everywhere are ignorant of just what this center is—some say it is the center of the body, some say it is the center of the top of the head, some say it is the region of the heart, some say it is the center of the forehead, some say it is the throat, some say it is in the middle of the space between the kidneys and the genitals. Vainly hoping for eternal life, they cling to points in this ephemeral body and call that keeping to the center and embracing the one. Not only will they not live eternally, they will even hasten death."

Finally Liu returns to key phrases from Confucian, Taoist, and Buddhist traditions to reiterate centering directions. According to Confucian teaching, "When emotions are inactive, this is called the center"; again, "Not being biased is called the center." In the Taoist language of alchemy, "After the first half-moon, before the second half-moon, the flavor of the elixir is even, the formation of the energy is complete"; again, "The matching of yin and yang is due to their mutual sensitivity; in equivalent measure they are spontaneously intimate." Traditional Buddhist teachings say, "I have something that supports the heavens above and the earth below; it has no head or tail, no back or front"; again, "Form is not different from emptiness, emptiness is not different from form; form is emptiness, emptiness is form."

"These sayings," Liu concludes, "all speak of the real locus of the center. If people can focus their minds on these points, going as deeply as possible into them and finding out their subtleties, and then go to real teachers to have their understanding corrected, so that they can find the true center, then they can reach the aim without wasting any effort. From there they can proceed directly along the great road, walking at an unhurried pace, eventually to arrive at home. It is not for nothing that classics says, 'Get the one, and myriad tasks are done.'"

THE GOLD PILL

The gold pill is the alchemical elixir of immortality. Gold symbolizes stability and incorruptibility, the pill symbolizes roundness, completeness. Liu I-ming, following Complete Reality Taoist tradition, calls it "open, selfless, unified energy," and refers to it in these terms: "This pill is completely nonexistent, yet it contains ultimate being; it is completely empty, yet contains ultimate fulfillment. It is shapeless and formless. Its substance is established primordially, its function is activated temporally. It cannot be known by knowledge, it cannot be perceived by perception. Try to describe it and you lose it; whatever you say about it is not it. Ancients drew it as a circle and gave it the names 'Tao,' 'open selflessness,' 'primal unified energy,' 'the infinite,' 'the great ultimate'" (illustration 12).

It will be noticed that Liu speaks of the gold pill in much the same terms as the center, except that in the case of the gold pill there is somewhat more emphasis on the aspect of energy: "The pill is the original, primal, real, unified energy. This energy, when passed through fire to refine it, becomes permanently indestructible, so it is called the gold pill." He also says, "The open, selfless, one energy is the root of heaven and earth, the source of yin and yang, the progenitor of myriad beings."

As in his treatment of the center, Liu also devotes considerable attention to addressing popular misconceptions of the gold pill and potentially harmful exercises based on these ideas:

> People of the world do not know what the gold pill is—they imagine it in defined locations in the body, or they think it is made from minerals, or they think it is crystalized from the energy and blood of male and female, or they think it is solidified by interaction of the energies of the heart and genitals, or they think it exists through a clustering of vitality and spirit, or they think it is in the elixir field or ocean of energy in the lower abdomen, or they think it is in the center of the torso or the top of the head, or they think it is in the center of the forehead or the back of the brain, or they think it is between the kidneys and genitals. It is impossible to mention all comparable varieties of notions about the gold pill, so many are they. All of them take what is artificial to be real. That is

why those who study the Tao are as numerous as ox hairs, while
those who accomplish the Tao are as rare as unicorn horns.

Liu emphasizes the idea of formulation of the gold pill as restorative, the
process of recovering lost potential: "It is just because of their being con-
stricted by inherited temperament and influenced by accumulated habit that
people follow acquired mundanity and lose the original source, going along
without control, forgetting how to turn back, not knowing how to stop.
Sages since ancient times have set up the science of formulating the gold pill
as an act of compassion to liberate people by awakening them. They just
wanted everyone to go back to the root and return to life, to restore the
original being."

Here again, however, there is a distinction made between those who have
already lost their original being and those who are still innocent; while the
former are in need of restoration, the latter are in need of preservation. Restoration is called "doing," while preservation is called "nondoing." Liu explains, "People of higher wisdom practice the path of nondoing to incubate
the open circle. Middling and lesser people practice the path of doing, preserving being by way of nonbeing, to return to the open circle. In reality,
when they reach this return, they wind up at nondoing. When nondoing is
consummate, you are complete, illumined, clear, naked, free, stable, securely settled, forever incorruptible."

One of the main blunders frequently committed by those who attempt to
carry out the practice represented by the alchemy of the gold pill is to
plunge into it without adequate understanding of the process. There are
countless examples past and present of people who have been spiritually
maimed by malpractice, particularly in Zennist cults, where intensive exercises are regularly carried out without understanding of principles, and Taoist yoga cults, where energetics are pursued without corresponding spiritual
development.

Liu I-ming constantly reiterates this point: "The great Tao of sages, the
science of investigating the inner design of reality and making use of the
entirety of the essence of the mind to arrive at the true destiny of life, involves procedures in order. There is passive practice and active practice, a
time to hurry and a time to relax; there are preliminaries and advanced procedures, there is a time to stop at sufficiency. The slightest deviation produces
an enormous loss, so if you want to practice, you must know how."

THE CAULDRON, FURNACE, MEDICINES, AND FIRING PROCESS

As explained in the discussion on the so-called gold pill, the elixir of spiritual alchemy by which the temporal mind is transformed and the primal

mind restored, it is considered necessary to understand the principles and processes of this science in order to put it effectively into practice. Although there are a number of models used to represent these principles and practices, the most complete model is the text of the *I Ching* itself. Using the vocabulary of alchemy, the sixty-four hexagrams of the *I Ching* are thus referred to as the cauldron, furnace, medicines, and firing process by which the gold pill is manufactured.

According to this scheme, the first and second hexagrams, *Heaven* (*The Creative*) and *Earth* (*The Receptive*), known as the parent hexagrams, are called the cauldron and furnace; the twenty-ninth and thirtieth hexagrams, *Water* and *Fire*, also referred to as the sun and moon, are called the medicines. These being the equipment and ingredients, the other sixty hexagrams represent the process (illustration 2).

Liu I-ming explains:

> The Tao of the deliberate manufacture of the gold pill is the Tao of transformation of the temporal. The Tao of transformation has *Heaven* and *Earth* for its substance, *Water* and *Fire* for its function; the other sixty hexagrams, beginning with *Difficulty* and *Darkness*, are the energy phases, going through their cycle and then beginning again, the circulation of one energy.
>
> The science of the gold pill has *Heaven* and *Earth* for its cauldron and furnace, *Water* and *Fire* for its medicinal ingredients; the other sixty hexagrams, beginning with *Difficulty* and *Darkness*, are the firing process, yin to yang, yang to yin, yin and yang operating alternately, also the circulation of one energy. The science of the gold pill is not outside the Tao of transformation, the Tao of transformation is not outside the Tao of evolution of yin and yang of heaven and earth, sun and moon.

Liu then goes on to explain the pragmatic associations of the four key hexagrams. Firmness is the cauldron of *Heaven*, flexibility is the furnace of *Earth*; openness of the temporal mind is the medicine of *Fire*, fullness of the primal mind is the medicine of *Water*:

> If people can make firm strength the cauldron and flexible accord the furnace, then heaven and earth are set up as the cauldron and furnace. If people can empty the human mind, the essence of awareness will not be obscured; if they can activate the mind of Tao, then sane energy will always be present. Then the medicinal substances of sun and moon have been obtained.
>
> When the cauldron and furnace have been set up and the medicinal substances have been obtained, you follow the pattern of heaven and earth, imitating sun and moon. When it is appropriate to be firm and strong, be firm and strong; then firm strength will wind up balanced and correct. When it is appropriate to flexibly

accord, accord flexibly; then flexible accord will wind up balanced
and correct.

The main outlines thus established in the framework of the four key hexagrams, the timing of strength and flexibility, and their corresponding qualities and capacities, are indicated by the lines of the other sixty hexagrams:
Liu continues, "Be both kind and just, active yet calm, diligent by day and
wary by night, working without defect, in accord with the time, adapting to
the situation—the principles of the *I Ching* are in our hearts, so it is certainly
possible for us to realize the Great Way and master our essential life."

As so often in his works, Liu I-ming turns to the Taoist classic of spiritual
alchemy, *Understanding Reality*, to summarize the essential principles of *I
Ching* practice. Liu quotes the first of the sixty-four verses of the second section of the classic, which is modeled on the sixty-four hexagrams of the *I
Ching*: "First take heaven and earth for the cauldron, then cook the medicines of the sun and moon. Having chased the two things into the center,
you can produce the gold pill." According to Liu's explanation, heaven and
earth are firmness and flexibility, innate knowledge and innate capacity;
sun and moon are the conscious knowledge of the human mind and the
real knowledge of the mind of Tao. The purpose of the practice is to balance
and unify these elements.

In his commentary on *Understanding Reality*, Liu I-ming expands upon
these themes to provide an overall picture of the principles of practice through
which balance and unification are achieved:

> The mind of Tao is that which is unconfused in all situations; not
> being confused is real knowledge. The human mind is capable
> only of conscious knowledge, not of real knowledge; its nature is
> weak, so it is called yin. Since the mind of Tao has real knowledge,
> it is also capable of conscious knowledge; its energy is strong, so it
> is called yang.
>
> Even sages have the human mind, and even ordinary people
> have the mind of Tao. Sages have the human mind in that they
> cannot annihilate perception; ordinary people have the mind of
> Tao in that they have moments of lucidity. The reason sages are
> different from ordinary people is simply that in them reality and
> consciousness are unified, they have knowledge and perception,
> and they are capable of permanent lucidity. The reason ordinary
> people are different from sages is that for them reality and con-
> sciousness are separated, and though they have knowledge and
> perception they are incapable of permanent lucidity.
>
> The human mind has discriminatory awareness in it, which uses
> consciousness to create illusions. Seeing objects, it gives rise to
> feelings, reverberating with whatever influences it. So conscious-
> ness takes refuge in the false, and the human mind is insecure.
> With the human mind insecure, perverse energies are rampant

and sane energy weakens; the mind of Tao does not come to the fore, and becomes faint.

Practice of Tao refines the firmness of the real knowledge of the mind of Tao, restoring it to proper balance, and refines the flexibility of the conscious knowledge of the human mind, restoring it to proper balance. This is the joining of firmness and flexibility, the matching of strength and obedience. Precisely unified, one maintains true balance; innate knowledge and innate capacity are merged in the design of nature, and unified energy flows."

The process symbolized by the sixty hexagrams circulating within the framework of the four key hexagrams is divided into two main aspects called the yang fire and yin convergence, meaning the exercise of firm strength and flexible accord. In terms of the hexagrams, it begins with *Darkness* and *Difficulty* and ends with *Settled* and *Unsettled*. Liu I-ming explains, "*Difficulty* is when the yang energy stirs within yin energy, *Darkness* is when yang energy falls into the midst of yin. *Settled* is when yin and yang have joined, *Unsettled* is when yin and yang do not interact."

As explained in *The Taoist I Ching*, in the arrangement of the hexagrams of the text of the *I Ching* the "yang fire" and "yin convergence" intertwine, with the odd-numbered hexagrams representing the yang fire and the even-numbered hexagrams representing the yin convergence. In his explanation of the *I Ching* mandalas, Liu I-ming assigns these to day and night, following the symbolic associations of light and dark, in accordance with the standard watchword of Taoist practice, "*Darkness* in the morning, *Difficulty* at night."

Liu explains, "To foster yang when the yang energy first stirs, in order to promote the yang fire, is the work of the daytime. To nurture yang when the yang energy has fallen, in order to operate the yin convergence, is the work of the nighttime." In Liu's terminology, "day" and "night" are used symbolically for psychological time, but for introductory study of the text of the *I Ching* this paradigm can be projected on the traditional practice of reading one hexagram in the morning and one at night, so that each day the reader learns one hexagram from the yang series and one from the yin series.

Turning to the hexagrams *Settled* and *Unsettled* at the end of the intertwined yang and yin series, Liu explains, "When settled, yin and yang have joined, and one should preserve settlement at all times. Preserving settlement means using yin to complete yang. When unsettled, yin and yang not interacting, one should await the appropriate time to seek settlement. Seeking settlement is using yang to help yin."

Summing up the yang fire and yin convergence, Liu continues, "Using yang to help yin is promoting the yang fire. This is represented by thirty hexagrams from *Difficulty* to *Settled*. This is the way to effect settlement. Using yin to complete yang is operating the yin convergence. This is represented by thirty hexagrams from *Darkness* to *Unsettled*. This is the way to avoid becoming unsettled."

When the thirty-hexagram series representing the yang fire is taken as a whole and the thirty-hexagram series representing the yin convergence is also taken as a whole, the traditional model of the yin convergence following the yang fire can also be projected on a textual study program to produce a format in which the odd-numbered hexagrams are read in series first, followed by the even-numbered hexagrams. This results in an impression of the book that is quite distinct from that produced by daily readings of one hexagram from the yang series and one from the yin series.

Ultimately, of course, it is to be understood that these fixed programs are only for the purpose of developing familiarity with the text and that the fluctuations in energy represented by the movements of yin and yang, the psychological states represented by the "times" of the hexagrams, do not take place mechanically according to standardized measurements of terrestrial time. The systematic approaches to external familiarity with the total system of the *I Ching* are there to provide balanced approaches to the whole range of relations it represents, in order to sensitize the reader to changes as they actually take place.

Liu I-ming sums up this point in his conclusion on the overall purpose and consummation of *I Ching* practice: "Beginning with *Difficulty* and *Darkness*, ending with *Settled* and *Unsettled*, the sixty hexagrams are all part of the yin convergence or yang fire; the other fifty-six hexagrams can be figured out by analogy with these. The subtle function, however, is all in the ultimate return of water and fire, yin and yang, strength and accord, to correct alignment in the center. When strength and accord are centered correctly, then from *Difficulty* and *Darkness* in the beginning to *Settled* and *Unsettled* in the end, the process happens thus spontaneously, without any room for forced effort."

THE SIX YANGS AND SIX YINS OF THE YANG FIRE AND YIN CONVERGENCE

The yang fire, "restoring yang in the midst of yin, fostering its qualities of firm strength so as to restore the primal," is ordinarily conceived of as the first half of the cycle of work involved in the spiritual practice of the *I Ching*, while the yin convergence, "using yin in the midst of yang, exercising its qualities of flexible accord, to nurture the primal," is thought of as the second half of the cycle. Elaborated in the sixty-four hexagrams of the *I Ching*, the yang and yin phases are also traditionally summed up in a set of twelve hexagrams used as guides to the others.

These twelve hexagrams (see pages 363–364) represent the full cycle of yang and yin, within which the other fifty-two hexagrams are latent. Taken in order, the six yang hexagrams are as follows.

1. *Return* (24): one yang, five yin
2. *Overseeing* (19): two yang, four yin
3. *Tranquillity* (11): three yang, three yin
4. *Great Power* (34): four yang, two yin
5. *Parting* (43): five yang, one yin
6. *Heaven* (1): all yang

The six yin hexagrams are

1. *Meeting* (44): one yin, five yang
2. *Withdrawal* (33): two yin, four yang
3. *Obstruction* (12): three yin, three yang
4. *Observing* (20): four yin, two yang
5. *Stripping Away* (23): five yin, one yang
6. *Earth* (2): all yin

Liu I-ming explains, "Even though there are sixty-four hexagrams, they are all summed up in these twelve hexagrams. When the first yang of *Return* advances, all the hexagrams with yang in the first place are therein. When the second yang of *Overseeing* advances, all the hexagrams with yang in the second place are therein. So it is with the third yang, the fourth yang, and the fifth yang. So it is also with the operation of yin."

In terms of the developmental work that these hexagrams are taken to represent, Liu says

> When the practices of the yang fire and yin convergence are both perfected, firmness and flexibility match, strength and accord are both complete. There is yin within yang, there is yang within yin: yin and yang are one energy, wholly integrated with the natural design; round and bright, clean and naked, bare and free, the spiritual embryo is complete, a tiny precious pearl hanging in cosmic space.
>
> Serene and imperturbable yet sensitive and effective, sensitive and effective while serene and imperturbable, always responsive yet always calm, always calm while always responsive, the face of original, innate knowledge and innate capacity becomes fully manifest. This is what is referred to by the saying, "Swallow a grain of the gold pill, and then you'll realize your fate does not depend on heaven."
>
> Now go on to do advanced work to refine the spirit back into space, then break through space to liberate the real body that never decays. This is what is referred to by the saying, "What is sacred and cannot be known is called spiritual." You progress to the realm of physical and mental sublimation and union with the Tao in reality.

Index

Printed in the United States
by Baker & Taylor Publisher Services